Focus on African Films

Focus on African Films

EDITED BY
FRANÇOISE PFAFF

INDIANA UNIVERSITY PRESS

Bloomington and Indianapolis

This book is a publication of

Indiana University Press
601 North Morton Street
Bloomington, IN 47404-3797 USA

http://iupress.indiana.edu

Telephone orders 800-842-6796
Fax orders 812-855-7931
Orders by e-mail iuporder@indiana.edu

© 2004 by Indiana University Press

Library of Congress Cataloging-in-Publication Data
Focus on African films / edited by Françoise Pfaff.
    p. cm.
Includes bibliographical references and index.
   ISBN 0-253-34388-7 (cloth : alk. paper) — ISBN 0-253-21668-0 (pbk. : alk. paper)
  1. Motion pictures—Africa. I. Pfaff, Françoise.
   PN1993.5.A35F63 2004
   791.43′096—dc22
2003021199

1 2 3 4 5 09 08 07 06 05 04

To my mother and grandmother,

whose spirit and strength have nurtured me over the years.

To my daughter, Marie-Hélène Pfaff,

whose love and *joie de vivre* helped me carry

this book to completion.

Contents

Acknowledgments

My thanks to the contributors, who did their utmost to meet deadlines and responded cordially to editorial requests. I wish to express my gratitude to María Roof for her careful review of the manuscript; to James H. Kennedy for his critical reading of several chapters; to Jeanick Le Naour for greatly facilitating my viewing of films at the Cinémathèque Afrique (ADPF, Paris); to Ruth Rhone for transcribing most of my recent interview with Haile Gerima; to Laverne Page, African and Middle Eastern Division, for assisting my research at the Library of Congress (Washington, D.C.); to Cornelius Moore for his enthusiastic collaboration; to Michael Lundell at Indiana University Press for his interest and guidance; and to Howard University for its support of my research and scholarship.

Focus on African Films

Introduction
Françoise Pfaff

Cinema is one of Africa's newest and least known art forms. Although the tradition of cinema in northern and southern Africa goes back almost a century,[1] the use of film as a means of expression and communication by Subsaharan Black Africans is a more recent phenomenon. The formal independence of a number of African nations in the late 1950s and early 1960s facilitated access to the medium of film, as did the later end of apartheid. African eyes began to offer new perspectives on the continent that contrasted sharply with views popularized by Western jungle melodramas, where Africa was a mere backdrop —with stereotypically uncivilized, childish, or cruel natives—for triumphant acts by great White hunters and treasure seekers. Motion pictures implicitly championing such colonial and/or racist ideologies include, for example, *King Solomon's Mines* (1937 and the 1950 remake), films like the 1961 *Hatari* (the 1986 *Out of Africa* did not fare much better!), and the countless *Tarzan* films.

The pioneer Senegalese director Ousmane Sembene[2] makes this comment: "Before we started to make films, Europeans had shot films about the African continent. Most of the Africans we saw in those films were unable to set one foot in front of another by themselves. African landscapes were used as settings. Those films were based on European stories" (qtd. in Pfaff 1984, 3). Ethiopian filmmaker Haile Gerima described such productions thus:

> Africa is generally a very good place for films and they undermine our misery by putting us in the background, which is where we are in Western history. Africans are betrayed on the screen but this is also true of Asians, Arabs, Indians and Mexicans. Usually Third World people are backgrounds for Tarzan, John Wayne and other Western heroes. They are part of the landscape and they are used for a function—like to bring an orange juice to the master—and they walk out of the scene. We are never human beings. We are underdeveloped characters. Our sex life, our feelings of love and hatred are not explored because they don't see us as part of a society." (qtd. in Pfaff 1977, 28)

In order to challenge hegemonic Western iconography and assert their African identity, committed Black directors set out to emphasize Africa's cultural wealth and diversity—historical, political, economic, social, ethnic, cultural, ideological, and geographical. They did so with enduring faith, limited funds, and poor production/distribution infrastructures—traits that still largely characterize African cinema today. Director Gaston Kaboré (Burkina Faso) declares:

The ability to picture oneself is a vital need. In fact, if a man were to live without the capacity of forging a picture of himself, he would have no aspirations, no desires, no dreams of his own.

The same applies to a community, a society and a people. A society daily subjected to foreign images eventually loses its identity and its capacity to forge its own destiny.

The development of Africa implies among other things the production of its own images. (1995, 23)

The 1975 Algiers Charter on African Cinema, drafted by a international group of progressive filmmakers, stipulated the "vital" role African film should play as "a means of education, information and consciousness-raising"[3] addressed primarily to African viewers but also to non-Africans. Often serious and didactic rather than escapist although not lacking in humor and irony, the early films by these directors, who have often compared themselves to the griots (bards/chroniclers) of traditional African cultures, depict an evolving continent at precolonial, colonial, and postcolonial stages. In Sembene's terms:

> We had to see, feel, and understand ourselves through the mirror of film. For us, African filmmakers, it was then necessary to become political, to become involved in a struggle against all the ills of man's cupidity, envy, individualism, the nouveau-riche mentality, and all the things we have inherited from the colonial and neo-colonial systems. (qtd. in Pfaff 1984, 11)

Several scholars have developed critical approaches that provide panoramic views of Subsaharan movie production. In his insightful 1987 thematic categorizing of African films, Tunisian filmmaker and critic Férid Boughedir stresses a frequent focus on conflicts between indigenous traditions and European mores, and identifies several "tendencies," among them:

1. A political or sociopolitical trend that purports to "awaken" African viewers to react against oppressive institutional or governmental forces and class-based exploitation of the masses. He cites as examples Med Hondo's *Soleil O* (O Sun, Mauritania, 1970); Ousmane Sembene's *Xala* (Senegal, 1974); Cheick Oumar Sissoko's *Nyamanton* (Mali, 1986); and others.[4]

2. Moralist or moralizing films that emphasize the need for change in individuals rather than institutions, such as Sanou Kollo's *Paweogo* (Burkina Faso, 1982) and Désiré Ecaré's *Visages de femmes* (*Faces of Women*, Ivory Coast, 1985).

3. A cultural trend whose aim is to provoke debates about cultural practices rather than political or moral issues, represented, among others, by Ababacar Samb's *Kodou* (Senegal, 1971); Jean-Pierre Dikongue-Pipa's *Muna Moto* (Cameroon, 1974); Oumarou Ganda's *L'exilé* (The Exiled, Niger, 1980); and Nangoyama Ngoge's *Mariamu's Wedding* (Tanzania, 1983).

4. Cinematic narratives with "self-absorbed," generally autobiographical plots, which explore identity and philosophical dilemmas of Westernized Africans, for example, in Pierre-Marie Dong and Charles Mensah's films *Identité* (Identity, Gabon, 1975) and *Obali* (Gabon, 1977).

5. Commercial productions like Daniel Kamwa's *Pousse-Pousse* (Tricycle Man,

Cameroon, 1975); Sanya Dosunmu's *Dinner with the Devil* (Nigeria, 1975); Eddie Ugbomah's *The Mask* (Nigeria, 1979); and Arthur Si Bita's *Les coopérants* (The Cooperants, Cameroon, 1983). (See Boughedir 1987, 39–48)

Boughedir describes an aesthetically innovative film, Djibril Diop Mambety's *Touki-Bouki* (Senegal, 1973), which he considers more stylistically than politically revolutionary, and movies that offer a "happy synthesis" of sociopolitical concerns and the valorization of African cultures like Sembene's *Ceddo* (1976) and films by the Malian director Souleymane Cissé: *Baara* (Work, 1978); *Finyé* (The Wind, 1982); and *Yeelen* (Light, 1987).

Malian film critic and historian Manthia Diawara, in his important 1992 book *African Cinema, Politics and Culture*,[5] categorizes Subsaharan African film output into various groupings:

1. "Social realist narratives," which thematize "current sociocultural issues" (141) such as Mahama Johnson Traoré's *Njangaan* (Senegal, 1974); Ngangura Mweze's *La vie est belle* (Life Is Rosy, Democratic Republic of the Congo, 1987); and Sissoko's *Finzan* (Mali, 1989).

2. "Films of historical confrontation that put into conflict Africans and their European colonizers" (152): Sembene's *Ceddo* and *Camp de Thiaroye* (1988); Hondo's *Sarraounia* (Mauritania, 1987); Kwah Ansah's *Heritage Africa* (Ghana, 1988); and others based on history.

3. "Return to the source" movies, which stress "the existence of a dynamic African history and culture before the European colonization" (160): Gaston Kaboré's *Wend Kuuni* (Burkina Faso, 1982) and Idrissa Ouedraogo's *Tilai* (Burkina Faso, 1990), among others.

These attempts at film taxonomy are largely valid today and offer general guidelines for interpreting aspects of the corpus of African films. For instance, two recent films, Moussa Sene Absa's *Ainsi meurent les anges* (And So Angels Die, Senegal, 2001) and Alain Gomis's *L'Afrance* (Senegal-France, 2001) exhibit thematic similarities, in their exploration of migration and identity issues, to such early films as Ababacar Samb's *Et la neige n'était plus* (There Was No Longer Snow, Senegal, 1965); Désiré Ecaré's *Concerto pour un exil* (Concerto for an Exile, Ivory Coast, 1968); and Hondo's *Soleil O.* However, a glance at fifty years of film practice in Subsaharan Africa reveals that changes have taken place within an undeniable continuity. Many nuances and new directions have emerged.

Historical films, for example, have evolved, no longer offering dichotomous representations of idyllic precolonial life corrupted and destroyed by European colonizers. Sissoko's *Guimba* (Mali, 1995) critically explores traditional systems of government that led to abuses of power. And Gnoan M'Bala's *Adanggaman* (Ivory Coast, 2000) forcefully investigates the responsibilities of Africans in the establishment of the transatlantic slave trade. Describing a much more recent past, Flora Gomes's *Mortu Nega* (The One Whom Death Refused, Guinea-Bissau, 1988) and Issa Serge Coelo's *Daresalam* (Let There Be Peace, Chad, 2000) question the uncertain and sometimes disheartening aftermath of independence and civil wars. In addition, recent African films have broken with prior "puri-

Wend Kuuni (1982) by Gaston Kaboré (Burkina Faso).
Photo courtesy of California Newsreel.

Guimba (1995) by Cheick Oumar Sissoko (Mali).
Photo courtesy of California Newsreel

4 *Françoise Pfaff*

Daresalam (Let There Be Peace, 2000) by Issa Serge Coelo (Chad).
Photo courtesy of California Newsreel.

Dakan (1997) by Mohamed Camara (Guinea).
Photo courtesy of California Newsreel

Karmen Gei (2001) by Joseph Gai Ramaka (Senegal).
Photo courtesy of California Newsreel.

tanical" modes[6] and unabashedly include explicit, intimate heterosexual scenes, as in Ouedraogo's *Le cri du Coeur* (*Cry of the Heart,* Burkina Faso, 1994) and Joseph Gai Ramaka's *So Be It* (Senegal, 1997), as well as images of homosexuality in Mohamed Camara's *Dakan* (Guinea, 1997) and Ramaka's *Karmen Gei* (2001). The latter film is a musically vibrant drama, freely adapted from the work of nineteenth-century French author Prosper Mérimée. In this sense it continues a trend that links African and European creativity in new ways, as did Mambety's 1992 *Hyenas,* which showed that Western writers such as Durrenmatt could be successfully "Senegalized" and adapted to the screen.

Less prevalent today than in early postindependence films are the serious, didactic, political, social realist, and naturalistic tendencies (where physical and metaphysical worlds are often interrelated, however), cogently delineated by Boughedir and Diawara. Although Mambety's *La petite vendeuse de soleil* (*The Little Girl Who Sold the Sun,* Senegal, 1999) continues this tradition, increasingly, Subsaharan filmmakers have turned to more commercially attractive film products, perhaps in response to the tremendous success of Nigerian video melodramas and to African moviegoers' passion for Western detective stories and comedies, Indian musicals and melodramas, and kung fu movies. Finances may also have played a role in this shift, since, for example, the elimination of the French Ministry of Cooperation, which had subsidized many African films, meant directors had to seek funding elsewhere—from private production companies, the European Community, and other sources. African films with com-

La petite vendeuse de Soleil (The Little Girl Who Sold the Sun, 1999) by Djibril Diop
Mambety (Senegal).
Photo courtesy of California Newsreel.

mercial value might provide more substantial profits, a degree of self-sufficiency,
and the possibility of continuous productivity for directors.

To continue in the profession, a number of African filmmakers might have
to rethink the nature of their craft and endeavors—the dedication of vital en-
ergies to obtaining foreign funds, then laboriously producing only one film
every five to ten years, as sometimes happens, or the creative dispersion of
filmmakers who are simultaneously scriptwriters, producers, directors, and even
distributors of their motion pictures! Some have switched from a purely auteur-
ist status to the realm of entrepreneurship, as Kwah Ansah (Ghana), Haile
Gerima (Ethiopia/USA), and some Nigerian directors have done, including Ola
Balogun, video producers, and others. Such newly found financial independence
might give birth to styles close to indigenous, popular dramatic arts. The late
French film critic Pierre Haffner predicted this in terms of the possible influence of the Malian Koteba theater on Malian motion pictures.[7] A similar transfer can be observed in the realm of Nigerian films and video productions, some
of which use plots and structures directly influenced by Yoruba theater.

Taking a cue from prior commercially successful films like Kamwa's *Pousse-
Pousse*, Henri Duparc's *Bal Poussière* (Dancing in the Dust, Ivory Coast, 1988)
and Mweze's *La vie est belle*, recent works such as Mweze's *Pièces d'identités*
(Identity Papers, 1998); Imungu Ivanga's *Dôlé* (Money, Gabon, 2001)—and

even, to a certain extent, Sembene's *Faat Kiné* (2000)—point in the direction of more popular, less didactic, Subsaharan films, which certainly reach out to African masses, ironically fulfilling the "popular" and "democratic" goals of African cinema as inscribed in the early 1975 Algiers Charter.[8]

African films, even within the current commercial veins, should be as diverse as the registers and deliveries of griots, with amplitude for a broad range of views—from the stylistically innovative documentaries of Jean-Marie Teno (Cameroon) and Abderrahmane Sissako (Mauritania/Mali), and the "documentary fiction" of Mahamat-Saleh Haroun (Chad), to the vibrant art films of a Jean-Pierre Bekolo (Cameroon) and the new films from South Africa. There is also room for mythic and metaphorical renditions such as *Mossane* (1996) by Safi Faye (Senegal), *Sia, le rêve du python* (Sia: The Dream of the Python, 2001) by Dani Kouyaté (Burkina Faso), or *Ndeysaan, le prix du pardon* (Ndeysaan, The Price of Forgiveness, 2001) by Mansour Sora Wade (Senegal). The aspirations and issues presented in African films, their significance in world culture, and their contribution to our intercultural heritage lie at the core of this collection of essays.

This book, *Focus on African Films,* provides unique and pluralistic perspectives on filmmaking from varied areas of Africa—Ethiopia, Nigeria, Senegal, and South Africa, among others—rather than a reductive assessment of the cinematic output of the continent.[9] Previous books on African cinemas concentrated on historical accounts of the development of filmmaking on the continent or in specific geographical or even linguistic areas. This volume, in contrast, provides an innovative, kaleidoscopic analysis of African films released since the 1950s. These films reflect quite distinct thematic, stylistic, and socioeconomic characteristics, as detailed in the studies.

The first section of *Focus on African Films* explores how a number of postcolonial motion pictures challenge "official history" in order to express African sociopolitical and historical viewpoints. Robert Cancel studies documentaries and feature films made in South Africa and elsewhere that brought to American audiences and others greater awareness of the evils and oppressive nature of the apartheid system. Samba Gadjigo shows that Ousmane Sembene's conceptualization of art and films on history runs counter to the dominant paradigms of Hollywood commercial historical drama and historical romance. Mbye Cham presents a survey and critical discussion of recent African film productions that revision and rewrite the African past from African subject positions and render that past relevant and productive for the present and the future. Josef Gugler explores the relationship between fiction and historical record in three films set in Africa and claims the need for criticism to address the historical record that is explicitly or implicitly invoked by films.

The second section engages in the deconstruction of contextual spaces. Françoise Pfaff demonstrates how African filmmakers use urban colonial architecture and landmarks as well as urban topographic disparities to reflect power relations between Africa's exploitative elite and the impoverished masses.

Madeleine Cottenet-Hage investigates how Francophone African films, whether Africa-based or France-based, position France in their didactic discourse and view it as geographical and social space, colonial memory, institutional traces, and El Dorado. Using postmodern and postcolonial critical tools, Kenneth Harrow scrutinizes El Hadj, the protagonist of Sembene's film *Xala*, and, contrary to prior perceptions of him as the reformed capitalist, the restored militant, or the revitalized symbol of an emasculated Senegal, views him as the quintessential failed trickster. Brenda Berrian's essay, which focuses on Sembene's *Ceddo*, uses a new approach to reconnect music and other sounds to the progression of images. In so doing, she analyzes the interaction between Manu Dibango's "soundscape" for *Ceddo* and the film's narrative.

Devoted to new cinematic practices, the third section of this work includes N. Frank Ukadike's examination of recent African documentaries and the strategies used in the construction of the cinematic "reality" of Africa. In doing this, he redefines the relationship between the dominant (Western) and oppositional (Pan-Africanist) cinematic representations of Africa. Françoise Balogun provides a uniquely well-informed personal and sociological account of Nigeria's recent video boom.

The book's fourth section projects beyond Africa's borders to incorporate resonances between Africa and other areas of the world. It examines the works of expatriate filmmakers who reside in non-African settings but produce Africa-related films. Beti Ellerson provides a retrospective of the career of the Paris-based Senegalese pioneer woman filmmaker Safi Faye as well as interviews and discussions with her. Françoise Pfaff presents excerpts from interviews she has conducted over a quarter of a century with the Washington-based Ethiopian director Haile Gerima and a recent conversation with him.

African filmmakers did not forge their trade in a vacuum. Many of them acquired their film training abroad and were early participants in the cross-cultural fertilization of the global age. In the fifth section of our study, new attention is given to connections grounded in their study, work, and other experiences abroad. Josephine Woll analyzes the relationship between the Soviet cinematic tradition and the work of Ousmane Sembene, Souleymane Cissé (Mali) and Abderrahmane Sissako (Mauritania/Mali). María Roof documents and gives a critical assessment of cinematic connections between Latin America and Africa, two areas that exhibit similar economic conditions and sociopolitical concerns. In a final section, Valerie Wheat facilitates the task of researchers and others in her annotated compilation of sources where African films can be located in Africa, Europe, the United States, and Canada.

Focus on African Films is a collection of essays by African, American, and European scholars, many of whom have significant publications in film studies. Their different origins, geographic and institutional locations, and fields of expertise further enrich the volume's pluralistic nature. Their essays offer an innovative and in-depth look at crucial topics. Most of the contributions included here are original and were specifically written for this book. It is my hope that this volume supplies useful information to the general public, scholars, students, and other readers interested in film and African studies, in French and Francophone studies, and in Third World cinemas and foreign cultures in general.

Notes

1. In his book *Le cinéma africain*, the Benin-born filmmaker and film historian Paulin Soumanou Vieyra cites *Ain el Ghezal* (Daughter of Carthage, 1924) by Tunisian filmmaker Chemama Chikly as the first film produced and directed by an African (1975, 15). Motion pictures were produced in South Africa at the very beginning of the twentieth century. In his *In Darkest Hollywood*, Peter Davis names *The Great Kimberly Diamond Robbery* (1910), also called *The Star of the South*, produced by Springbok Film Company, as the first fiction film made in South Africa (1996, 13).

2. In other publications, this director is called "Sembene Ousmane," with or without an accent on "Sembène." Personal names of African directors often vary in order and have different spellings. Sometimes for political or cultural reasons the first and last names are reversed, or the "colonized" French first name is dropped. We use the form generally accepted by film critics and historians and have attempted to be consistent throughout the text.

3. The 1975 Algiers Charter on African Cinema is included in Bakari and Cham, eds. (1996, 25–26).

4. A note on film titles: Titles are given in italics in the original language, followed by the title in English unless the original is a proper noun. An English title in italics indicates the title by which the film is distributed in Anglophone countries. An English title not in italics is simply a translation of the title. Subsequent references to a film's title use the one that is likely to be most familiar to moviegoers and film historians.

5. See especially Diawara's chapter 10, "African Cinema Today" (1992, 140–66).

6. For comments on this subject, see Pfaff's "Eroticism and Subsaharan African Films," in Bakari and Cham, eds. (1996, 252–61).

7. Haffner (1978, 61–65). Elements of the Koteba theater are present in *Finzan*.

8. Sembene, one should recall, repeatedly advocated didactic African films, comparing them to a "night school."

9. I use the term "African films" rather than "African cinema" in the book's title in deference to Med Hondo's statements to me in a number of conversations in which he maintained that there is no true African cinema in the sense of a homogeneous body of works or a structured industry but "only African filmmakers struggling hard to make films."

Works Cited

Bakari, Imruh, and Mbye Cham, eds. 1996. *African Experiences of Cinema*. London: British Film Institute.

Boughedir, Férid. 1987. *Le cinéma africain de A à Z*. Brussels: OCIC. *African Cinema from A to Z*. Trans. Dalice A. Woodford. Brussels: OCIC, 1992.

Davis, Peter. 1996. *In Darkest Hollywood: Exploring the Jungles of Cinema's South Africa*. Randburg: Ravan; Athens: Ohio University Press.

Diawara, Manthia. 1992. *African Cinema, Politics and Culture*. Bloomington: Indiana University Press.

Haffner, Pierre. 1978. *Essai sur les fondements du cinéma africain*. Abidjan: Les Nouvelles Editions Africaines.

Kaboré, Gaston. 1995. "L'image de soi, un besoin vital/The Ability to Picture Oneself: A Vital Need." Fédération Panafricaine des Cinéastes. *L'Afrique et le Centenaire du Cinéma/Africa and the Centenary of Cinema*. Paris: Présence Africaine.

Pfaff, Françoise. 1977. "Toward a New Era in Cinema: Harvest, 3000 Years." *New Directions: The Howard University Magazine* 4.3: 28–30.

———. 1984. *The Cinema of Ousmane Sembene, A Pioneer of African Film*. Westport, Conn.: Greenwood.

———. 1996. "Eroticism and Subsaharan African Films." In *African Experiences of Cinema*, ed. Bakari and Cham, 252–61. London: British Film Institute.

Vieyra, Paulin Soumanou. 1975. *Le cinéma africain*. Paris: Présence Africaine.

Part One: Reexamining
                        "Official History"

1   "Come Back South Africa": Cinematic Representations of Apartheid over Three Eras of Resistance

Robert Cancel

He was grave and silent, and then he said somberly, "I have one great fear in my heart, that one day when they are turned to loving, they will find that we are turned to hating."

—Reverend Msimangu (Paton, *Cry the Beloved Country*)

"One settler, one bullet." "Boers, they are dogs."

—Anti-White slogan and an old Xhosa song lyric
(Magona, *Mother to Mother*)

Overview

For nearly thirty years, the South African Information Service kept American schools and even public movie theaters supplied with films about South Africa. These were offered at low or no cost, had high production values, and invariably sought to explain South Africa's apartheid system in positive terms. During most of these years, it was unusual for U.S. audiences to view documentaries or feature films depicting the other side of the apartheid equation—South Africa's non-White populations. In the realm of feature films, only the early 1950s production of Alan Paton's best-selling novel *Cry the Beloved Country* (1951) was easily accessible to American filmgoers; its successful musical theater version, *Lost in the Stars,* was produced by Maxwell Anderson and Kurt Weill in the early 1950s and made into a film in 1974.[1] The 1959 production of *Come Back Africa* by Lionel Rogosin did not make much of an impact at the box office and remained hard to rent or buy for a long time.

By the early 1970s, a series of documentaries depicting the monstrous nature of apartheid began to trickle down to American university campuses, activist community groups, and a handful of public theaters and television stations. *Last Grave at Dimbaza* (1974), secretly filmed in South Africa by Nana Mahomo, and *Six Days in Soweto* (1979), a BBC documentary on the 1976 student uprising, were among the best known of these films. Educators, particularly at the university level, had to look far and wide to find such films, and even then there were virtually no feature films available that took the side of the South Africans who had been disenfranchised by apartheid. This situation stood in contrast to what was a relatively prolific internal South African film industry, catering most particularly to White audiences in that country.[2] One of the interesting, somewhat ironic results of these localized films was the unprecedented international success of Jamie Uys's *The Gods Must Be Crazy*, Parts I (1980) and II (1989). Less known, but running counter to most mainstream South African films, was a series produced for television, adapting six Nadine Gordimer short stories, and a feature film version of Athol Fugard's *Boesman and Lena* (1973).

During the last and most militant years of the anti-apartheid struggle, Schmitz and Mogotlane secretly produced, within South Africa, the dynamic and powerful anti-apartheid film *Mapantsula* (1988). At around the same time, several Western-made feature films were released that, on varying levels, addressed the issue of apartheid in serious, if somewhat simplistic, ways. Today, more than ten years after apartheid's demise, we have an opportunity, in retrospect, to see how these productions constructed competing visions of South Africa and how these visions reflected, over some forty odd years, the sociopolitical contexts of their times.

I want to focus on a few specific films that depicted the effects of apartheid over periods of those years. Properly contextualized, with literary and historical references, the films reveal a great deal about the gulf between Black and White existence during those times. I want to historically divide that time span into three eras, marking the context, strategies, and intensity of anti-apartheid struggles.

The decade of the 1950s was the period of the initial internal efforts to thwart the growth of apartheid policies that came into effect with the 1948 election victory of the National Party. Politically, this includes the time of the Defiance Campaigns, the Freedom Charter, the beginning of the treason trials, and the Sharpeville massacre.[3] Culturally, we must consider the dynamic lives and writing of the so-called *Drum* generation of writers: Modisane, Nakasa, Themba, and others.[4]

The post-Sharpeville era can be framed between 1960 and 1976, which saw the emergence of the Black Consciousness Movement out of the initial brutal repression and exile of anti-apartheid activists. Externally, the anti-apartheid struggle would take many forms, including the successful international sports boycott against South Africa and, later, the cultural boycott. Culturally, this was the time of the rise of the exile writing of Mphahlele, LaGuma, and Nkosi and the focus, later in the period, on Black Consciousness in the poems and stories of Serote, Kgositsile, and Mzamane.[5] It was also the period of the activism of Steve Biko and the South African Students' Movement.

A third period entails the era after the 1976 Soweto uprising[6] through to the 1990 freeing of Nelson Mandela.[7] This era saw the growing success of the international campaigns of economic disinvestment and boycotts, the internal growth in the power of unionism, the politically motivated violence of Black townships, the coming to office of J. W. de Klerk, and the beginning of negotiations that would result in the 1994 elections. Cultural production inside South Africa included not only more militant writing but also the supplanting of written literature by the rejuvenation of oral literature and drama. Dramatists such as Mda and Mtwa[8] produced plays and musicals depicting the harsh yet vibrant township lives in post-Soweto, activist South Africa. Moreover, as government repression of cultural expression grew, people took to singing vernacular oral poetry in the streets and performing scriptless plays in factories to avoid incriminating documents while playing on the dynamic qualities of living performance and improvisation.[9] Films from each of these eras reveal sociocultural dynamics within and outside of South Africa that allow us to understand the various ways apartheid was thematized for international consumption.

The 1950s

[. . .] looking at himself in the mirror behind the bar and saying in his mind to the young, tan-colored, dark-eyed face with the new stubble and the cigarette dangling from the lips, Okay, trouble-shooter. You're a mighty tough hombre. Fastest man in Tuscon.... (LaGuma, "A Walk in the Night")

In 1958 American documentary filmmaker Lionel Rogosin traveled to Johannesburg to find out about the lives of Black South Africans and develop a screenplay that would reflect their realities. Rogosin, a White engineering graduate of Yale University, had earlier produced a powerful documentary, *On the Bowery,* depicting the harsh lives of the homeless denizens of what was often referred to as "Skid Row" in New York City. His reputation as an activist cineast, obviously not well understood by the South African government that allowed him into the country to film what was thought to be some kind of industrial documentary, gave Rogosin access to an unusual core of Black urban residents. The resulting production, *Come Back Africa,* remains one of the more interesting films to emerge from South Africa—perhaps out of all of Africa, in fact—in that period. The film tells the story of a man named Zacharia, who comes to Johannesburg from a rural area to seek employment. He begins by working in the mines but finds the job hazardous and inadequately compensated. He then hires on as a domestic and is constantly berated and insulted by his employers until he is fired for drinking the homeowner's liquor. Another job at a garage is short-lived when he and a coworker are caught driving a customer's car. And a job as a waiter is terminated when he accidentally sees a naked White woman in a hotel room. After Zacharia's wife joins him, they argue over whether or not she should try to find work, and eventually a hoodlum who had had a run-in with Zacharia murders her in revenge. Zacharia ends the film violently, wrecking his small home in a fit of grief, despair, and anger.

On the one hand, *Come Back Africa* can be seen as a standard variation of the "Jim Comes to Jo'burg" theme that predominated much of both Black and

White writing as well as some early South African films about the relationship between urban life and rural African migrants. The same theme is at least partly invoked in Paton's novel *Cry the Beloved Country*, in which the city is seen as the site of evil and debauchery, and the rural areas as the true and natural home of Black Africans, the land representing the source of life and continuity. On the other hand, the film is more complex than that. This is partly due to a set of secondary characters played mostly by a group of young men who at the time were best known as writers for *Drum* magazine and its Johannesburg publication, the *Golden City Post*. They had, in fact, taken Rogosin under wing, so to speak, and showed him the vibrant urban life of Sophiatown—that storied Black suburb of Johannesburg which was soon to be razed by the government—while also providing firsthand evidence of the harsh conditions under which most working class Africans lived. In his autobiography *Blame Me on History*, Bloke Modisane provides some interesting details about this interaction. In fact, it seems clear that several scenes in the film were built around the attitudes of these extraordinary young men. Gatherings at *shebeens*, or illegal drinking clubs, are depicted, wherein conversations range over many topics, but especially the situation in the country and the ambiguous relationships of these sophisticated, sardonic city-dwellers with well-intentioned White liberals. Many of the points are echoed in the writings of Lewis Nkosi and Modisane, particularly how liberals somehow needed to portray Africans as innocent, rural, and passive. In a later piece touching on Paton's novel, Nkosi decries the idealized images of rural Africans and the seemingly supplicating cleric, Stephen Kumalo:

> If we rejected Stephen Kumalo, Paton's hero, it was partly because we, the young, suspected that the priest was a cunning expression of white liberal sentiment. Paton's generosity of spirit, his courageous plea for racial justice, and all the qualities which have earned him the undying respect of many Africans, were not of course in question. What was in question was Paton's method, his fictional control of African character which produced an ultimate absurdity like Stephen Kumalo: an embodiment of all the pieties, trepidations and humilities we the young had begun to despise with such a consuming passion. (1983, 4)

These conversations in the film both inform the audience of this other urban class of Africans and, as Modisane puts it, portray the "alienation of the rural African, the confusion of being in the midst of black intellectuals" (1986, 283). The urban characters in these scenes are played by Modisane and Nkosi themselves as well as Can Themba and Morris Hugh Letsoalo, all in one way or another known for their efforts as writers and cultural figures in Sophiatown. In addition, Miriam Makeba, soon thereafter to leave South Africa and become a recording star of international renown, makes several appearances to sing some of her songs.

Overall, the film captures several vital qualities of the period. Rogosin, Modisane, and Nkosi scripted the production, which often allowed characters to improvise and speak their own words. The actor playing Zacharia was actually a working-class man who was basically, as Modisane says, "being asked to live again his life before the camera" (1986, 282). This transparency between real life and cinema was particularly striking to Modisane in the final scene where the raging Zacharia smashes his home. "The crack-up of the character, and the man, were so closely linked that we were horrified to be in the presence of the destruction of a man. It was a nightmare which we could not control or stop or turn our faces from" (282).

The other dimension of the movie reveals that urban side of Black South African life that was so consistently ignored or even criticized by social commentary of the time. Instead of victimized, decontextualized rural peasants, we are shown a group of sophisticated, politically knowledgeable Africans who have few real ties to the countryside and who unabashedly prefer the fast, albeit at times dangerous, life of the city. These discussions in the film reveal a tough young intellectual class exhibiting a high level of self-knowledge and a broader feel not only for their country but for the wider world and its history and politics as well. The social tragedy of apartheid and the sense of cultural loss to both the working class and the talented urban writers and artists emerge from this seminal production. Moreover, it becomes clear just how distant from each other the urban African intelligentsia and migrant laborers had become. The film depicts the poignant mix of exuberance, resistance, hope, and despair that characterized the lives of Sophiatown's residents and the wider Black population of South Africa in that period.

Post-Sharpeville: 1960–1976

We also used the same laboratory—originally designed as just another classroom—for Biology, Physics and Chemistry. Now instead of providing what was needed most, here were the authorities wasting valuable resources and forcing us to study woodwork and domestic science—the terms "carpentry" and "home economics" just never caught on. (A student view of some of the tenets of "Bantu Education" in Mzamane, *The Children of Soweto*)

After Sharpeville, political resistance was officially outlawed, creating an ever-escalating repression by the government and a streaming of anti-apartheid writers and activists into exile. If the beginning of the 1960s was characterized by desperate flights out of the country—and harassment, imprisonment, torture, or worse for those who remained to oppose the system—the end of the decade saw the rise of the Student and Black Consciousness movements. As activists outside the country fought to isolate South Africa from world sport and eventually from cultural exchange, internally, a growing number of young Black students, artists, and trade unionists developed an inward-looking, community-oriented philosophy of self-help and education. Where the government would not supply proper schooling under the Bantu Education Act, community schools began to emphasize pride and self-reliance, moving away from even White liberal structures of assistance (see Mzamane 1982, particularly "My School Days"). U.S. audiences were more and more often exposed to striking documentaries, often illegally filmed in South Africa, portraying the stark and violent nature of the apartheid system. South African audiences saw virtually nothing along these lines. Even television would not become a viable medium in South Africa until 1976, nearly four decades since the technology was demonstrated in that nation in 1939.

Images of South Africa as carried by the activist cinema practiced by documentarians such as Nana Mahomo in *Last Grave at Dimbaza* (1974) would expose many people outside South Africa to alternative views from those that the official information services were distributing to Western audiences. For example, I recall clearly the impact Mahomo's film had on both the scholarly community and wider public when it was shown on American television, on educational stations, and in institutional film screenings at schools, universities, and churches. Powerful images remain in one's memory: Black sanitation workers running to empty heavy trash cans into a slow-moving, never-stopping truck; an African woman domestic worker feeding a White toddler spoonfuls of nutritious food while the narrator tells us her own child died of malnutrition; the heart-wrenching scenes at the Dimbaza *Bantustan*,[10] where freshly dug graves wait in anticipation for the bodies of children dying daily and regularly of malnutrition and preventable diseases; and, near the end, close-ups of the simple grave markers with names and dates of birth and death, decorated with small remembrances of the children: a baby bottle, a pacifier, a small doll. These images were interspersed with a clinical narration and written texts providing statistics about the relative wealth or incomes of Whites and Blacks in South Africa, educational statistics, health statistics, and numbers of people "relocated" from their urban homes to rural *Bantustans* or suburban townships. The images often employed great contrasts, juxtaposing White urban or suburban homes with Black migrant workers' quarters or township and squatter housing. White South Africa is portrayed as well-armed, supported by Western governments, and determined to maintain the status quo. Apparently filmed clandestinely, and utilizing grainy images and long shots of off-limits official buildings and activities, the film struck a shocking chord of horror and revelation concerning a place and issues that had been long ignored or suppressed by U.S. audiences.

One reaction by the South African government to such films was to produce counter-documentaries that questioned their assertions. Perhaps the most concerted effort to cast doubt onto a series of anti-apartheid films was the production *To Act a Lie* (1980), put out by the Information Service (see Tomaselli et al. 1986). While this is an excellent example of trying to establish a counterdiscourse by reinterpreting data and more or less parsing the specific claims of films like *Last Grave at Dimbaza*, it is even more revealing to look at a production that was in common distribution much earlier, *Land of Promise* (ca. 1975). This was the kind of short shown before regular feature films in American cinemas. It was intended for audiences with only the vaguest understanding of South African history and the apartheid era. I might add that its logic would appeal to a viewership that was receptive to the paternalistic beliefs that underlie, even unconsciously, both the apartheid system and the subtly lingering racism wrought by the "Jim Crow" era in the United States. The production values are attractive, featuring clear color images, smooth—or, more accurately, "slick" —editing, and an evocative musical soundtrack. The pace moves quickly over many diverse, even diverging images. The film begins with wildlife scenes, the images most familiar to American audiences when thinking of Africa in general. There is an interesting visual evocation of Darwinian social evolution when animals give way to San people walking on the *veld* (bush/plains) and White people flying helicopters over the wildlife and, by implication, the San. Image juxtaposition throughout *Land of Promise*, as in *Last Grave at Dimbaza*, though for different purposes, is crucial in transmitting the official ideological message about South Africa's complex diversity and its apparently inescapable remedy: apartheid.

An interesting discourse is maintained in the film that suggests a schizophrenic view of "separate development." On the one hand, the country is finding ways to handle the complexity of containing "several nations within our borders." Population breakdowns similarly suggest that there are "fifteen million [people comprising] . . . eight different black nations," as well as "the white nation of more than four million." Dividing the fifteen million by eight suggests that the "white nation" of four million is somehow numerically parallel. The narrator addresses the film's viewers in a manner that confides the answer to this situation:

> But you want to know, don't you, what about apartheid? Well, before it's anything else, our apartheid policy is a vast program for the multinational development of our peoples. It's designed to create several independent countries inside the boundaries of South Africa, where people with different customs and languages can live in a society where their identity will be preserved. Where our black people can control their own destinies.

Much is made, as the production unfolds, about the coming political autonomy of the African "homelands"—the term *Bantustans* seems at this point to have lost its euphemistic cachet—including their own parliaments.

At the same time that this picture of impending "independence" is drawn, the gist of the film seems focused on how much money and attention are being lavished on Black education and housing. This includes scenes of pulling down township housing and building new and improved homes—an example of the kind of relocation that broke down longstanding communities and became, along with the passbook, one of the most hated manifestations of apartheid laws. One question that came to mind was why, if Blacks were soon to have their own nations, there was such an emphasis on Black township development around major cities. Another question had to do with statistical claims, such as that 83 percent of "our blacks" between the ages of eight and twenty-one are literate. There are similar claims for the high quality of housing and employment opportunities for Blacks. Which "blacks" is the film referring to? The ones living in the homelands? The ones living in urban townships? The ones employed in thriving business sectors at the lowest levels? If the care and feeding of "our blacks" is of paramount concern, then what is the purpose of the independent homelands?

Finally, the film combines a fascinating confluence of double-speak and outright lies, which pass so quickly that, like the quick-edit images, they are hard to pin down. The opening claim of the narration revolves around a comparison of South Africa to European nations and how, though South Africa's social problems are much more complex, there is much in common: "We are five times the size of Britain. We are governed by a parliamentary democracy, with an independent court system and a free press." This is a fairly simple statement to unpack. Undoubtedly, South Africa, even not counting the "independent homelands" (roughly 13 percent of the nation's land), probably is five times larger than Britain. The parliamentary democracy is definitely in place, if only for the White population, the only group with the vote. The independent court system is free to enforce the laws of the land, since they are based on the overarching principles of apartheid. And a free press is a fairly blatant lie, since censorship of the media was a well-known practice of the government and its court system. One way to "read" the film's discourse is to try to identify the many times it changes its frames of reference, from descriptions of realities that only apply to Whites to claims about benefits provided to the Black population without specifying how many and which of the Black "nations" or subgroups were included in these benefits. The terms "relocation," "passbooks," "influx control," "Bantu Education," and "Immorality Act," and the myriad of notorious laws and practices meant to keep down the majority of Blacks are never alluded to in *Land of Promise*.

After the Soweto Rising: 1976–Early 1980s

When the fires finally died down several months later, there were four hundred black corpses, or five hundred, or seven hundred, and the police were firmly back in control. Newspapers proclaimed that the situation had returned to normal, but there was no longer any such thing. South Africa's psychic landscape had been transformed. Blacks saw that they had shaken the white power structure to its very foundations, and they suddenly had hope. The tide of history had turned. (Malan, *My Traitor's Heart*)

Amandla! Ngawethu! (Xhosa-language slogan, "Power! It is ours!")

When, around the time of *Land of Promise*'s release, the government mandated Afrikaans[11] as the medium of Bantu Education and the school children rose in Soweto, the stakes of Black Consciousness and the commitment to militant resistance rose higher than the ruling forces could have expected. If, during the late 1960s and early 70s, the dominant film genre portraying South Africa to the world, both by pro- and anti-apartheid producers, was the documentary, the post-Soweto years saw an even more defined upsurge in such documentaries. In particular, anti-apartheid cinema focused on the growth of resistance movements and the violent government reaction to these movements (e.g., *Six Days in Soweto,* 1979; *Crossroads South Africa,* 1979; *You Have Struck a Rock,* 1978). While much could be said about these remarkable films, I will discuss feature and television films in the early 1980s that are based on literary works by White South Africans.

In 1982–83 a series of six short films was released based on short stories by Nadine Gordimer. The series was screened on many public television stations in the United States around that time and was made available on video for schools and universities. Most of the stories were originally written years—in one or two cases more than a decade—earlier. The exception was "Oral History," which was set in the later stages of Zimbabwe's war for independence. It is revealing to compare the short stories with their film versions to see how they were altered and contextualized for the period of their production.

The film *Six Feet of the Country,* directed by Lynton Stephenson in 1977, was the original half-hour adaptation that acted as a "pilot" for the five other hour-long productions. Both film and text are set mostly in a rural area outside Johannesburg. The film and story have a male narrator who provides a context or point of view for both works. In the film version, the plot depicts the lives and conflicts of a White couple trying to find some kind of peace and fulfillment in running a small farm while the husband continues his Johannesburg office job—it would seem, according to the film, at a travel agency. As the wife becomes close to the farm workers, the husband is surprised to see how much she enjoys the agrarian life. The central conflict arises when the workers reveal that they have been harboring a visitor, who has taken ill and died. This throws the household into an uproar because such Black visitors are not legally permitted, particularly since this one had come from Rhodesia—soon to be Zimbabwe. Police must be called in, a brief investigation takes place, and the body is taken away for an autopsy and not seen again. One worker comes to the couple to request that the body be returned for proper burial. It takes the husband a good deal of moving through a maze of official channels until the body is released to the family. During the burial ceremony, it is discovered that the authorities have provided the wrong body. Again, efforts by the husband to sort out this gruesome error force him into a complex series of bureaucratic interactions, but this time the dead man cannot be found. The film ends with the husband and wife arguing over his failure to pursue the matter of the body and confronting the apparent failure of their own relationship.

This bare plot summary does not entirely reflect the film's import. Certainly, a political statement is being made about a system that not only prohibits relatives from visiting one another across borders but also treats Black Africans in such an indifferent manner, unknowingly and/or callously substituting one dead Black man for another. However, the production spends as much time, if not more, on dissecting the marital relationship. It is clear that the couple have deep differences between them. One way these are revealed is in their interactions with, and attitudes toward, their farm workers. The husband keeps them at a distance—a respectful distance, but a distance nonetheless. This is made very clear when, on having a worker come to them in the middle of the night to request help for the "sick" man, the husband is agitated and insists his wife take a gun with her to the laborers' quarters. She adamantly refuses. When the funeral and burial procession takes place, the wife uses the farm pickup truck to carry the coffin. The husband observes it all from a distance as he practices his golf shots, wondering abstractly if he should pause or play through as the group passes by. He is not enthusiastic about helping to recover the dead man's body for his relatives, bemoaning the fact that "Africans" would rather spend money they don't even have on funerals when they have so many needs for the living. The wife, on the other hand, not only supports these efforts but contributes money to the cause. In the last scenes of the film, it is clear that the couple have pretty much split apart, despite the husband's conciliatory stance. Inside their home, he looks at his wife, who is framed by his gaze and the camera's lens in front of a window behind which stands a group of workers. This final association with the Black Africans highlights the distance that has grown between the couple.

On one level, the film preserves Gordimer's original ironic, cool framing of what seems to be a domestic story around a politicized event. That is, the couple's story seems in many ways to overshadow, at least from the point of view of the husband, the plight of the farm workers. As with much of Gordimer's fiction, the theme is a combination of small-scale concerns of individual lives with deeper political insights percolating under the surface. If anything, the film can be seen by censors as a the tale of the unfortunate Black family as unwitting victims of common bureaucratic indifference or inefficiency—something akin to getting the runaround at the Department of Motor Vehicles. This adaptation is actually more obviously political than the original story, since the husband is clearly more conservative and fearful of his Black laborers than was the case in the text, where he portrayed himself as liberally protective of his workers: "We have no burglar bars, no guns... we've always rather prided ourselves that the poor devils have nothing much to fear, being with us" (Gordimer 1986, 8). The film, in fact, adds a degree of women's political and personal assertion to the couple's interactions. Their quarrels are portrayed as rancorous, with the wife accusing the husband of trying to stifle her and contaminate her with the death that emanates from his "world" of guns and violence and official repression.

It was the political updating of at least one of these Gordimer stories that spurred South African censors to single out the production A Chip of Glass Ruby (1983)—which also contained dialogue and events that were more politically pointed and reflective of the period of the early 1980s than the original text. Keyan Tomaselli notes that the Censor Appeal Board stated of certain productions, "The more popular the material, the more likely it is to be undesirable." In that particular case, Tomaselli says, "the reading of Nadine Gordimer's [story] by a literate elite is considered less of a threat to the security of the state than if it is seen in film form by millions of people on television or in the cinema" (1988, 24). We might also conclude that the updating of these texts to more closely resonate with the times was a factor in their being targeted for closer scrutiny as films.

Late 1980s

[. . .] though you may not know politics much, but you know where the money comes from. Like most of the people tell you that, "Hey, look. If you want to get money, go to the white man—he has money. Go to town and steal in town. (Thomas Mogotlane, qtd. in Davis, *In Darkest Hollywood*)

By the late 1980s, South Africa was irrevocably moving to a direct confrontation between government and anti-apartheid forces. The battle lines were drawn across many sites of resistance, from militant trade unionism; increasingly violent school and university and township demonstrations; a set of movements outside the country to disinvest and boycott economic and cultural links; the rising rate of bombings and military operations carried out by *Umkhonto we Sizwe*, the militant arm of the ANC; and the growing realization that South Africa was, indeed, finding itself alone on the continent and in the world.

Two important books by White South African writers engaged the interest of Western filmmakers and resulted in *A Dry White Season* (1989) and *Cry Freedom* (1987). Both films were moderate successes with American audiences and served, at least in some respects, to raise their consciousness, even if that awareness is of a certain familiar and simplistic liberal bent. Actually, *A Dry White Season*, directed by Martinican Euzhan Palcy, packs a more powerful ideological punch than *Cry Freedom*, due in great part to her desire to create a story from a more African point of view.[12]

Perhaps not surprisingly, one of the most potent anti-apartheid films took the documentary format that had proven so effective in the 1970s, combined it with the energy of popular music, and aimed at the broad audience of young people in the United States and other parts of the world—the MTV generation. *Sun City* begins with the music video production "Sun City" by Artists United Against Apartheid, then documents the making of that video by interviewing the many musicians and artists involved. The production was part of a wider response to the cultural boycott, supported by the United Nations, which prohibited signatories from intellectual and cultural exchanges of all types with South Africa.[13] The original music video brought together, for the first time, many seemingly disparate genres of popular music: rap, rock, jazz, salsa, R&B, funk, punk, reggae, new wave, and alternative.[14] The message of the song and the ensuing documentary put all artists, especially musicians, on notice that if they chose to play a venue like Sun City, the resort in the Bophuthatswana,[15] they would be guilty of breaking the boycott and would be labeled by their colleagues as supporters of the apartheid regime. The song and music video are part of a longer, musically innovative album of songs created by some of the many performers on the video and in the documentary. As a strong political statement counterbalancing the Reagan administration's refusal to entertain economic sanctions and persistence in the useless policy of "constructive engagement," the music video and documentary reached an audience of millions in the United States and abroad.

The music video is an excellent example of the postmodern techniques of pastiche, both musically and visually. The production begins with a drum track accompanying images of violent confrontations in urban areas between police and Black demonstrators in South Africa: police swinging clubs against unarmed demonstrators, firing tear gas into large crowds, and firing bullets into crowds; armored cars ("hippos") cruising into groups of people; and even rifle-toting security forces shooting into townships from hundreds of yards away. Some of the scenes are actually recognizable as taken from the Soweto uprising, with a young man being repeatedly shot in the side as he tries to throw a stone. These disturbing images then give way to images of the musicians singing the song that keeps reiterating the haunting refrain, "I ain't gonna play Sun City." Little Steven Van Zandt; rappers Melle Mel, Afrikaa Baambata, and Kurtis Blow; rockers Bruce Springsteen, Bono, and Ringo Starr; soul artists David Ruffin, Eddie Kendricks, and Darlene Love; avant-gardist Lou Reed; punker Joey Ramone; reggae's Jimmy Cliff; jazz's Miles Davis and Herbie Hancock; salsa's Ruben Blades and Ray Barreto; country/blues's Bonnie Raitt; folk/rock's Bob Dylan; and funk's George Clinton are only some of the many famous artists who lent their talents to the video and song. This merging of musical genres, the coming together of several races, and the unifying images of a final scene in Washington Square Park are exemplary of the message of the film—to unify against apartheid.

Visually, the video is extremely sophisticated and innovative. Documentary footage of events in South Africa are interspersed and at times visually merged with images of the violence of the Civil Rights struggle in the United States. Dogs and club-swinging police are shown attacking demonstrators in both urban South Africa and the urban southern United States. Scenes of Mandela are interspersed with clips of Martin Luther King Jr. giving his "I have a dream" speech. Marchers in South Africa seem to march alongside the thousands on the National Mall in Washington, D.C. in 1964. The production also uses computer-generated animation to overlay images of stylized clenched fists over the activist footage. At times the fist becomes a hand and tears away part of one image on the screen to reveal another imbedded image. Stylized images of barbed wire frequently link, and at the same time divide, images on the same screen. The throbbing beat of the music and the dancing of the musicians culminate in a march at the video's conclusion that nearly seamlessly combines the footage of the artists with images of South African demonstrators "toyi-toyi-ing"[16] at a rally. Finally, the martial music's beat fades into the somber and soulful strains of "Nkosi Sikelel' iAfrika," the ANC anthem, sung over the still images of young Black South Africans behind barbed wire, raising clenched fists in determined defiance.

The documentary then proceeds to interview many of the principal artists in the video as well as the production people. Little Steven Van Zandt is in some

Mapantsula (1988) by
Oliver Schmitz and
Thomas Mogotlane (South
Africa).
Photo courtesy of
California Newsreel.

ways the focal point of the film, being the originator of the project and coproducer of the music. But the documentary builds in a manner similar to the
video, as more and more interviews are interspersed with pieces of the music
video. There is a clear line, in the eyes of many of the African American performers, between racism in South Africa and in the United States. Even Peter
Gabriel, the British musician, makes the point that his participation is in part
stirred by his sense of debt to the music of Black artists and how the issue of
apartheid is part of a larger tapestry of historical oppression. Jamaica's Jimmy
Cliff and Nigeria's Sonny Okosun project a clear understanding of the long-
term anti-apartheid struggle, while Miles Davis says thinking of South Africa
makes him sick: "I can't even play." A representative from the Africa Fund, a
Black South African named Khumalo, attempts to explain the situation in his
country while statistics are exhibited on the screen. There is even a scene from
the "Donahue Show," in which Little Steven confronts Sol Herzer, of Sun Hotels,
over the legitimate status of Bophuthatswana as an "independent homeland"
and the economic exploitation of Black labor carried out in the Sun City resort
and, by extension, in South Africa. Overall, the documentary, though in some
ways simplifying the complex history of South Africa and the realities of the
apartheid struggle, was responsible for bringing the situation into national and
international prominence for its youthful audience.

At the same time, however, South African filmmakers Oliver Schmitz and Thomas Mogotlane produced *Mapantsula* (1988), filmed around Johannesburg and passed off to the authorities as an apolitical gangster movie. The film has an immediacy that is born of its subject matter but more visually tied to the actual militant demonstrations that seemed to engulf many urban townships at the time. The main character of the film is a *tsotsi*[17] whose *nom de guerre* is Panic. He pursues what can be seen as somewhere between an immoral and amoral lifestyle. One of the film's earliest and most powerful scenes depicts Panic picking the pocket of a White man in a business suit in downtown Johannesburg, then languidly brandishing a very large blade when the victim has the temerity to confront him, sending the man scurrying away. The evolution of the plot sees Panic serially move through relationships with his partner in crime, his live-in girlfriend, his landlady and her son, a local neighborhood political activist, cell-mates in a Johannesburg jail, and, finally, members of the Special Branch of the police force. Although this movement is complexly depicted in a series of alternating present-time and flashback scenes, for the most part Panic remains indifferent to his own negative behavior and the nascent activist feelings of his girlfriend Pat and his landlady's son. Only at the end of the film does the audience see the culmination of all these interactions as an almost surprising resolve by Panic not to inform on the activists with whom he has come in contact.

There are many sides of this rich film that reveal the tenor of the times. Filming in the streets is an obvious technique that evokes a documentary quality within the fictional plot. Panic's power as a criminal is in part explained as the reaction to the impotence he has felt working menial jobs for racist White bosses. His posturing and violent assertion of territorial claims over criminal and sexual turf also depict a kind of power that is ambiguous in its elevation of a Black man's agency while suggesting its regressive basis in selfishness and counterrevolutionary indifference. Underscored by a marvelous township music sound track, the film vibrates with the immediacy of Black African assertion in a time of growing violent protest and brutal government reaction. In the end, Panic makes the difficult, perhaps fatal choice of supporting the activists at the cost of his own freedom and well-being.

Images set in the jail reveal the cohesion and resolve of anti-apartheid activists. Picked up in the broad net of a police sweep of demonstrators, Panic soon feels himself isolated in the same cell from the other prisoners, who spend their time exchanging encouraging words and slogans and singing liberation songs. This kind of music is paired with the "toyi-toyi" of demonstrators in the township, who militantly brandish fists in defiance of the armed police who observe their protests. In turn, this kind of activist performance is contrasted to the nightclub music and dancing that leads people to forget their troubles and that often frames violent confrontations over money and women. Panic, in essence, moves from one kind of cultural expression to another more progressive one. In the end, despite his past as a police informant, Panic emerges as a hero of the struggle. It is this attitude of sacrifice and fearlessness in the face of death that characterizes the radicalization of the Soweto generation, the eventual dramatic release of Nelson Mandela, and the official demise of the nationalist government and its apartheid apparatus.

Thus, films that we now have available to us can reflect and highlight elements of South African sociocultural history of the apartheid era. Close viewing of these films as well as comparison, where appropriate, of related literary texts, combined with solid contextualization of those periods, can reveal the links between art and society during this unique and alternately shameful and inspiring chapter in African history.

Notes

1. Alan Paton, a White South African from the Natal region, published his highly acclaimed novel in 1948. He was at that time a successful principal at the Diepkloof Reformatory for boys. He introduced progressive ideas of training and an honor system that were conducive to skill development and eventual self-reliance for the boys in the institution. His novel of a devout African cleric from the rural Zulu area of Natal who goes to Johannesburg to find his wayward sister and son was an international bestseller. It depicted the harsh conditions under which people of color lived in South Africa, conditions that became even harsher at the time of the book's publication, which saw the victory of the National Party and the advent of apartheid policies. Paton would go on to be a founder of the nation's Liberal Party and was that party's leader for many years. Because of his and his party's opposition to apartheid, he was harassed by the government and at times banned. For many years, from the 1950s through the 1980s, *Cry the Beloved Country* was dismissed and disparaged by activist Black South Africans as overly accommodationist in its tenor and outlook. In the 1990s, somewhat ironically, the film's tone of reconciliation and forgiveness seemed to strike a vital chord in the "New South Africa" of Nelson Mandela. A 1996 remake of the film was warmly welcomed and endorsed by the post-apartheid government.

2. The workings of the South African film industry were rather complex, almost arcane, as regarded financing, content, and distribution. There was a censorship board to assess all finished films, and there were many government rules concerning the kinds of films to be financed by official or even external funds (see Tomaselli 1988).

3. These many efforts to stall or repeal apartheid policies were most often orchestrated by the African National Congress and, later in the decade, the Pan-African Congress. Most of the activities focused on the injustice of the passbook all non-Whites, but especially Black Africans, were forced to carry, the forced resettlement of Black urban communities into rural areas or government mandated townships, and the enforcement of separate education syllabi and facilities for the nation's races. During one of the growing number of anti-apartheid demonstrations, on 21 March 1960, in the Johannesburg township of Sharpeville, police fired on a large crowd of loud but unarmed demonstrators, killing 69 and wounding 108. This event would shock the world and mark the point at which the South African government outlawed most opposition parties, sending many activists to jail, into hiding, or into exile.

4. Bloke Modisane, Nat Nakasa, Can Themba, Ezekiel Mphahlele, and Lewis Nkosi all worked for *Drum Magazine* at around the same time in the 1950s. Though White-run, the magazine was popular all over English-speaking Africa. Its related newspaper, the *Golden City Post*, was popular among Black readers in South Africa, often mixing tabloid style stories with crisp, sometimes sardonic reporting on the hardships wrought on or-

dinary people by the proliferating apartheid laws. Mphahlele (*Down Second Avenue,* 1959) and Nkosi (*Home and Exile,* 1965), in particular, became well known for their critical and literary works after they left South Africa. Alex LaGuma, a "coloured" writer, was a political activist in South Africa, a member of the Communist Party who was forced to flee into exile, where he became perhaps the most accomplished of this generation of writers (*A Walk in the Night,* 1962; *Time of the Butcherbird,* 1974).

5. These writers were influenced by the events and political developments of the anti-apartheid movement in the decades immediately following the Sharpeville Massacre. Of particular influence on their work were the tenets of Black Consciousness, as espoused by Steve Biko. A partial outgrowth of what in the United States was called the "Black Power Movement," Black Consciousness stressed independence and empowerment of South African Blacks based on their own history and culture and not relying on unsatisfactory dependence on government or even White liberal ties. Some of the works produced by these authors include: Mongane Wally Serote, *No Baby Must Weep* (poems), 1975; Keorapetse Kgositsile, *The Present Is a Dangerous Place to Live* (poems), 1974; and Mbulelo Mzamane, *The Children of Soweto: A Trilogy* (prose), 1987. Steve Biko, who died in police detention in 1977 after the Soweto uprising, had a volume of his essays published posthumously, *Black Consciousness in South Africa,* 1979.

6. A sprawling city on the outskirts of Johannesburg originally identified as the "Southwest Township," Soweto was the site of a seminal revolt against government authority on 16 June 1976. School children, in great part inspired by Biko's Black Consciousness ideas and the related South African Students Movement, were angered over the new government decree that the language of education would henceforth be Afrikaans instead of English and attempted a mass demonstration of defiance. This gathering was met with deadly force and resulted in the death, wounding, and maiming of, eventually, several thousand school children; some of them as young as five or six years old. Like Sharpeville before it, the events in Soweto would shock the world and lead to a new stage in the anti-apartheid struggle. Many young people were irrevocably radicalized by what happened there. These same students would refuse to return to schools that espoused the inferior syllabus of "Bantu Education"; they would demand that their parents obey rent strikes, boycotts of discredited shops and chain stores, and labor stoppages. Many would leave the country and join Umkhonto we Sizwe (Spear of the Nation), the militant arm of the ANC, training in other countries to return as insurgents.

7. One of the ANC's most dynamic young leaders of the 1950s, Nelson Mandela was imprisoned in 1964 for his activities meant to bring down the apartheid government. Over time he became the most prominent detainee in the world, a symbol of both the treachery of apartheid and the unquenchable spirit that prevailed in those dedicated to the struggle. Originally sentenced to "life plus five years," Mandela emerged from prison in 1990, after twenty-six years, to lead his country to its first truly free elections. He headed the first majority-elected ANC government.

8. Zakes Mda produced a series of plays in the 1980s based in the urban milieu of township South Africa, some of which are collected in *The Plays of Zakes Mda.* Percy Mtwa similarly set his plays around the same time and places. At least two of them won international acclaim when performed abroad: *Bopha!* (published 1995) and *Woza Albert* (with Mbongeni Ngema and Barney Simon, published 1983).

9. Often this emerged in the form of guerrilla-style oratory and theatre performed in union halls and the work place. *Staffrider* magazine, coming out of Johannesburg by Ravan Press, published a fascinating issue on "Worker Culture" in 1989 (vol. 8, nos. 3 and 4).

10. *Bantustan* is an Afrikaans word. In a shifting game of semantics regarding what to call the rural areas set aside for "permanent" Black occupation, this particular term came between the older "Native Reserves" and the later "Black Homelands."

11. Afrikaans is the language of the Afrikaners, the Dutch-descended White population that originally settled in what would be called Cape Town in the 1650s. The Afrikaners dominated, in fact instituted, the politics and government of apartheid. For more than 150 years, they have comprised 60 percent of the White population of South Africa, the other 40 percent being of English-speaking descent. Many Black South African students considered Afrikaans an oppressor's language, spoken only in South Africa and meant to isolate them from other ideas and freedom struggles in other parts of the world. That they reacted so strongly to its installation as the language of education was not surprising.

12. See Rob Nixon's "Cry White Season," in *Homelands*, pp. 77–97.

13. See Rob Nixon's essay "Sunset on Sun City: The Dilemmas of the Cultural Boycott," in *Homelands*, pp. 155–72.

14. A few years earlier, following on the example of recording artists in Britain, an eclectic group of American musical artists calling themselves "USA for Africa" put out the song and video "We Are the World," addressing the issue of the devastating famine that at the time was plaguing parts of the Sahel and the Horn of Africa. The production was extremely successful, raising millions for famine relief.

15. Bophuthatswana was a so-called independent homeland, where Blacks from South Africa were supposed to have their own countries based on their ethnicity: Zulu, Xhosa, and, in this case, Tswana. Sun City was a resort, on the lines of a Las Vegas resort/casino, that allowed White South Africans to cross the "border" and do things that were outlawed in puritanical South Africa: gambling, viewing uncensored films, buying pornography, engaging prostitutes. Virtually no country in the world recognized the "independent" nature of these homelands, and the owners of Sun City were willing to pay extravagant fees to well-known international recording artists to come and entertain their clientele.

16. "Toyi-toyi" is the name of the militant "dance" done by demonstrators, often with fists upraised and simulating bouncing, or running in place. It is often accompanied by singing or chanting slogans. In some respects it recalls very old military dances performed before and after combat by Zulu *impis* (regiments) or similar steps by other southern African warrior legions. The dance is also linked to more contemporary revolutionary protest movements as they took to the streets in Moscow, Paris, Tehran, Montgomery, and other sites of twentieth-century radical social change.

17. *Tsotsi* is a local township term that became a generic label of young men who often ran in gangs and who were associated with criminal acts such as robbery, assault, and murder; they were something like "gangsters" or "juvenile delinquents." The word itself is probably directly derived from the style of pants popular among South African urban youth in the early 1940s, resembling the American "zoot suits." For more on this storied subculture, see Glaser.

Works Cited

Come Back Africa. 1959. Directed and produced by Lionel Rogosin.
Davis, Peter. 1996. *In Darkest Hollywood: Exploring the Jungles of Cinema's South Africa.* Randburg: Ravan; Athens: Ohio University Press.

Glaser, Clive. 2000. *Bo-Tsotsi: The Youth Gangs of Soweto, 1935–1976*. Portsmouth, N.H.: Heinemann.

Gordimer, Nadine. 1986. *Six Feet of the Country (Short Stories)*. New York: Viking Penguin.

LaGuma, Alex. 1967. *A Walk in the Night and Other Stories*. Evanston: Northwestern University Press.

Land of Promise. ca. 1975. South African Information Service.

Last Grave at Dimbaza. 1974. Directed by Nana Mahomo.

Magona, Sindiwe. 1998. *Mother to Mother*. Cape Town, South Africa: David Philip.

Malan, Rian. 1991. *My Traitor's Heart*. New York: Vintage International.

Mapantsula. 1988. Directed and produced by Oliver Schmitz and Thomas Mogotlane.

Mda, Zakes. 1991. *The Plays of Zakes Mda*. Randburg: Ravan.

Modisane, Bloke. 1986. *Blame Me on History*. New York: Simon/Touchstone.

Mphahlele, Ezekiel. 1959. *Down Second Avenue*. London: Faber.

Mzamane, Mbulelo Vizikhungo. 1982. *The Children of Soweto: A Trilogy*. Essex, U.K.: Longman.

Nixon, Rob. 1994. *Homelands, Harlem and Hollywood: South African Culture and the World Beyond*. New York: Routledge.

Nkosi, Lewis. 1983. *Home and Exile and Other Selections*. London: Longman.

Paton, Alan. 1948. *Cry the Beloved Country*. New York: Scribner's.

Six Feet of the Country. 1977. Directed by Lynton Stephenson.

Sun City. 1985. Directed and produced by Hart Perry and Stephen Reed, with Jonathan Demme.

Tomaselli, Keyan. 1988. *The Cinema of Apartheid: Race and Class in South African Film*. New York: Smyrna/Lake View.

Tomaselli, Keyan, Alan Williams, Lynette Steenveld, and Ruth Tomaselli. 1986. *Myth, Race and Power: South African Images on Film and TV.* Bellville, South Africa: Anthropos.

2 Ousmane Sembene and History on the Screen: A Look Back to the Future
Samba Gadjigo

Any history is a constructed story in which the characters are as constructed as the events.

—Paul Ricoeur, "Histoire et mémoire" (my translation)

The 1971 release of *Emitai*, Ousmane Sembene's first historical feature film, introduced a new strategy in African cinema, the appropriation of African history, and served as a catalyst for other new stories about the African past. Among the most noted of the early historical films were Med Hondo's *West Indies* (1979), based on a book by Daniel Boukman (Martinique), and *Sarraounia* (1986), the adaptation of a novel by Abdoulaye Mamani (Niger); *Mortu Nega* (The One Whom Death Refused, 1988) by Flora Gomes; *Testament* (1988) by John Akomfrah; and *Heritage Africa* (1988) by Kwaw Ansah.[1] More recent historical films are: *Sankofa* (1993) by Haile Gerima; *La Genèse* (Genesis, 1999) by Cheick O. Sissoko; and *Adanggaman* (2000) by Roger Gnoan M'Bala.

History became one of the dominant concerns in Sembene's filmography. Six years after *Emitai*, he wrote and directed *Ceddo* (1977), and he codirected *Camp de Thiaroye* in 1987 with Thierno Faty Sow. Though Sembene has not released another historical film since the end of the 1980s, he did complete a three-volume, 2014-page script for his most ambitious project to date, *L'Almamy Samori Touré*, not yet produced for lack of funding. Indeed, this historical project about nineteenth-century resistance to French colonial imperialism in West Africa is so important to Sembene that he once declared: "If I die without finishing Samori, you may write that I have failed in my career" (qtd. by Diop, personal interview).[2]

This chapter will summarize Hollywood's treatment of the past and show that Sembene's idea of art in general, and of films about the past in particular, runs counter to the dominant paradigms of Hollywood commercial historical drama and historical romance. Then, by examining *Emitai*, *Ceddo*, and *Camp de Thiaroye*, we will show how Sembene used the medium of film to "hijack" the hegemonic narratives of Senegalese "official" historiography with a twofold

Ousmane Sembene.
Photo by Françoise Pfaff.

purpose: to expound divergent Senegalese identities, and to deflect the field of historical knowledge from the sanctioned view of "the past as a fatality"— Ricoeur's history as the science of the men of the past—into a practice of cinematic history as the "present of past unfulfilled dreams" (1998, 27).

Hollywood's History

Historian Robert A. Rosenstone raised questions relevant to our analysis when he collaborated on the screen adaptation of two of his historical works: *Reds* (1982), about the last five years in the life of American artist, journalist, and activist John Reed, and *The Good Fight* (1984), a chronicle of the Abraham Lincoln Brigade during the Spanish Civil War. The transmutation required to film these two works recalled, for Rosenstone, Plato's assertion that "when the mode of the music changes, the walls of the city shake." Rosenstone then suggests that our time has a vital question to ponder: "If the mode of representation changes, what then may begin to shake?" (1988, 1185).

Cinema, introduced to Africa around 1900, and television have become important mirrors in which a large majority of urban, and even some rural, Africans see the world around them and, occasionally, themselves. Visual imagery is a dominant form of representation in the cultural evolution of the "postliterate" societies of Europe and the United States. On September 11, 2001, the entire Western world viewed the attacks on the World Trade Center in New York and the Pentagon in Washington, D.C., and shared a tragedy "in the making."

However, the power of the moving image is not limited to the way it mirrors our present; we also receive our ideas about the past from motion pictures and television in feature films, docudramas, miniseries, and network documentaries. Indeed, not only has Hollywood gone "historian" (Rollins 1998, 6), but Oliver Stone has even dubbed himself a cinematic historian. Hollywood's myths and symbols have become the major vectors of America's historical consciousness, according to Rosenstone: "Today, the chief source of historical knowledge for the majority of the population—outside of the most despised textbook—must surely be the visual media, a set of institutions that lie almost wholly outside the control of those of us who devote our lives to history" (1988, 3). Hence, as Robert Brent Toplin suggests, the first question that needs to be answered is: "What happens to history when Hollywood filmmakers put their hands on it?" (1996, 9).

This question raises the issue of the production of history: What determines the choice of historical topics by Hollywood producers, directors, and writers? In a capitalist economy and value-laden world, any form of activity, including artistic activity, must, above all, bow to profit-making and to the totalitarianism of market forces: the laws of supply and demand, mass production, and mass consumption. Although a feature like *Reds* (with a production budget of $50 million) or Oliver Stone's *JFK* (1991; production budget, $80 million) may have tangentially exposed viewers to the revolutionary ideals of John Reed or to the unsolved mystery of Kennedy's assassination, the ultimate barometer of the films' success or failure in Hollywood terms was undoubtedly box-office revenues.

Under such pressure, as *JFK* shows, producers will finance historical films only if they have the potential to appeal to the moviegoing public with its tastes and preconceived ideas about the past. As Serge Halimi forcefully demonstrated, the very success of Stone's megaproduction (with a gross of $200 million) rests, not on the claim that it sheds new light on the Kennedy assassination, but, rather paradoxically, on a blatant falsification of historical records and the erasure of all elements that contradict the director's conspiracy theory. For instance, Oliver Stone mentions a memorandum signed by President Johnson "a few days after" the assassination that supposedly reversed Kennedy's Vietnam disengagement policies. In reality, Halimi emphasizes, "that memo confirmed Kennedy's engagement policies in Vietnam for the simple reason that it was Kennedy himself, and not Johnson, who signed the document just before he left for Texas." This falsification of the truth, Halimi contends, is what attracted the American audience. Why? "Because it conformed to and confirmed the national belief which links all America's problems to the disappearance of a providential man (Kennedy)" (1995).

By maintaining and reinforcing the public's "taught" memory and hence its false historical consciousness, films like *JFK* hinder any interrogation of, and critical engagement with, the past. One would expect this "reopening" of an important chapter of American history to lead Oliver Stone to shake up ingrained certainties about the past. However, in the case of Hollywood as an "entertainment" industry, this appears to be mission impossible. Moviegoers are consumers who pay to experience a two-hour induced dream; they want to be "diverted" from present reality, a present that, in Ricoeur's formulation, "is more than a break on an imaginary line; it is 'a live present,' pregnant with the past and the impending future" (1998, 21). Hollywood's ideological twist is that to please its consumers, when it reopens the past, it must at the same time provide a sense of "closure," a finality that has the social function of reinforcing the public's quest for reassuring images that in no way interfere with the hedonistic search for entertainment and distraction from problems raised by the present. Paradoxically, Hollywood's appeal to the past has the effect of muting its dialogue with the present and of concealing its bearing on the future. As the case of *JFK* suggests, Hollywood's historical features project the past, not as a "problem," but rather as a setting for action and romance. Even when it purports to interrogate and challenge official versions of past events, the quest of Hollywood directors for public appeal and profit determines their way of telling the past, a way aimed, not at challenging, but rather at repeating the public's myths and false memories.

In order to achieve such a level of de-historicization of the past, Hollywood, very aware of its consumers' psychology, uses common, tested strategies of "packaging." The most obvious of these is the use of well-known professional actors with genuine public appeal. For example, part of public enthusiasm for Spike Lee's *Malcolm X* (1992) rests on the broad shoulders of Denzel Washington.

As a corollary to the financial pressure, most Hollywood historical films are also more driven by action (historical drama) or by romance (historical romance) than by historical truth. As Rosenstone summarizes:

> Here costumes, "authentic" set and locations, and well-known actors take precedence over any attempt at historical accuracy. . . . [The Hollywood historical film] locks both filmmaker and audience into a series of conventions whose demands— for love interest, physical action, personal confrontation, movement toward a climax and denouement—are almost guaranteed to leave the historian of the period crying foul. (1988, 1178)

When history is more than a mere setting, Hollywood tends to attribute change to the actions of dynamic individuals rather than to impersonal collective forces.[3]

Sembene's History

As the multiplication of African films on history suggests, it is fair to say that Ouagadougou, like Hollywood, has "gone historian."[4] This engagement with the African past also implies that African filmmakers have followed Ousmane Sembene's lead and awakened to the role historical films can play in the construction and representation of African identities. In Africa perhaps more than anywhere else on the globe today, textbooks cannot be the main channel for the dissemination of knowledge. Across almost the entire continent, the level of illiteracy in the European and Arabic languages of textbooks is such that direct oral communication still remains the dominant form of expression and social exchange. It is easy to see what fertile ground this context can offer to cinema and television. No matter how long the detour may be, it is the cinema that brings many Africans closer to their cultural reality. Thus, thanks to its wide reach in many segments of African societies, cinema has become the best forum to disseminate ideas, be they about the present, the past, and/or the future. The growth in the number of African "histories" on the screen also indicates that in our globalizing era of borderless images and electronic media, the screen is becoming a major "alternative" source of historical knowledge. Thus, in the endeavor to project African history on the screen, Sembene can be considered more than a pioneer, since he also defined a new strategy to combat the established dominant Hollywood tradition of historical representation, which was well known to African film audiences.

To shed more light on Sembene's departure from Hollywood's conception and practice of historical films, let us briefly recount his early development, historical and political trajectories and their potential influence on his work, and how, in the early 1970s, his camera hijacked the grand narratives of African institutional history. Only then can we explore the way he came to embody, within the field of African historiography, a singular voice that was consistently at odds with both the official and the popular memory of the African past.

By all conventional accounts, Sembene came to writing and later to film from the margins. A middle-school dropout at age thirteen, he was familiar with the hard life of the working class, since he often manned the oars on his fisherman father's boat on the Casamance River. In 1938, two years after leaving school, he went to Dakar and became a bricklayer and a mechanic. There he lived in a ghetto in the very heart of the Plateau, surrounded by a growing number of French residential, commercial, and administrative buildings. By day, he earned a living at colonial construction sites; by night, he dreamed before the screens of segregated movie theaters. In 1944 Sembene joined the French colonial infantry, was stationed in Niger for eighteen months, and returned to Senegal in 1946. The war had ended, and a new chapter was opening in the history of French colonial empire. As a construction worker, Sembene participated in the first comprehensive trade union strike that shook the foundations of the French colonial empire in Africa.

In 1947 Sembene sailed to Marseille and became a dockworker and active member of the Confédération Générale du Travail (CGT), then the most radical and powerful French workers' union. In 1950 he became a card-carrying member of the French Communist Party (PCF) and an active participant in many leftwing organizations, such as the Mouvement contre le racisme, l'antisémitisme et la paix (MRAP), a former wartime Jewish resistance organization. While a longshoreman, Sembene wrote his first semiautobiographical novel, *Le docker noir* (*Black Docker*, 1956). "I had read all that was written about Africa by both Europeans and Africans; and nowhere did I find my Africa: the Africa of the workers, the farmers, the women; the Africa that suffers but also struggles," he recorded in "Archives sonores" (n.d.).

Sembene became the first Soviet-trained African filmmaker and the first writer-director and producer to bring images of the African past to the screen. Beyond the thematic issues treated in films, however, the reality of cinema as an industry has loomed large for him. The caption on a poster of Lenin in Sembene's home office reads: "An artist must make money in order to live and work..." As the most expensive art form, historical films must be "massively" consumed for Sembene to generate revenues and make other films. However, he also uncompromisingly adheres to the second term of the poster caption: "...but he should not live and work just to make money."[5] Ousmane Sembene's cinema is unique in that, throughout his film career, he has not adapted or directed any work of which he is not the writer, director, producer, and/or coproducer. In relative control over the financing and content of his films, Sembene manages to minimize the tyranny of market forces. He once commented on this industrial aspect of cinema and on how he and other African filmmakers have thus far managed to avoid the total commodification of their work:

> The cinema is too hard because its existence rests on money. . . . The producers don't want to lose money; so they don't allow certain improvisations. They really want something tidy, so they can count on returns. In the case of Africa, we have an advantage in that we can do pretty much what we want, since most African directors up to now [the 1970s] have been their own scriptwriters. . . . [I]t's the director alone who is in fact the owner of the film. (Dembrow and Troller 1975, 8–9)

As a director, Sembene sees himself first of all as a committed artist and activist for social change, and, as Sheila Petty rightly perceived, his films are intended as a "call to action."[6] He began to write at a time when African writers and Marxist intellectuals mingled in France and when many advocated resistance to European colonialism in various regions of the world. In this context and given his own background, it can be easily understood why, for Sembene, the significant historical subject was popular resistance movements, starting with those that led to independence in Africa, and not the intellectual or emotional life of the African elite. He always dissociated himself from discussions and theorizations about Blackness epitomized by the Negritude movement. His major concern was the struggle of Senegalese people. In a continent where the only and uncontested vision and version of the past came from academics and public officials, both in "borrowed" languages, the African filmmaker had an essential advantage, a tool that "can speak across the divisions created by illiteracy and language, . . . can produce a culture in which the Wolof language can play a major role; it can bring the Wolof culture into the modernity of the post-colonial" (Mulvey 1991, 36). Some Senegalese academic historians admit that today "more than the other arts and the humanities, cinema is more effective in configuring the competing modernities, be they religious, ethical, political or economic, and whatever their setting: the city, suburbia or the countryside" (Diouf 1996, 17). With the magic of cinema, African filmmakers at last had a medium to disseminate alternative, counterhegemonic histories or to reconfigure existing ones differently.

Emitai

In Sembene's historical films, conceived primarily as educational tools, the past is not evoked in order to set the stage for personal drama, nostalgia, or dreams meant to truncate or interrupt our relationship to reality. Commenting on *Emitai*, Sembene voiced his philosophical view of history and historical cinema: "Each generation should *create* its own history and tell it with its own means. The role of the artist is to teach everyone about history. Who could talk about people's resistance without having lived it? Historical cinema should play that role" (Dembrow and Troller 1975, 9). Unequivocally, for Sembene history is not a given waiting to be found; it is created by artists who intensely live and witness the struggle of the people.

In order to educate through realistic images rather than merely entertain or provide escapist distraction, Sembene seldom uses professional actors, since "they are only good to play gangsters and dead kings" (Flatley 1969). On the contrary, he insists on using nonprofessionals with whom the public can identify without being distracted from the didactic purpose of the film. Although *Ceddo* stars Makhouroudia Gueye, already well known from other motion pictures, the most meaningful segments of the film, and its thematic thrust, rest mainly on group actions and not on the exceptional deeds of individual heroes.

Thus, for Sembene, film in general, and historical film in particular, constitutes a pedagogical medium ("une école du soir"—night school, as he has said) for political action. Unlike Hollywood historians, Sembene holds that although historical films cannot escape the general laws of supply and demand, their main purpose is to recapture a particular vision of the past in order to engage viewers in a constant interrogation on their present and future.

However, as the banning in France of *Emitai* and *Camp de Thiaroye*, the decade-long argument between Sembene and Senghor over *Ceddo*, and the "stifling" of Samori also imply,[7] the field of African history itself has become a site of competing and contentious imaginations. The various attempts by both the French and Senegalese governments to muffle Sembene's historical films are evidence of an effort to silence an imagination and a voice that create turmoil in the calm sea of official historiography. They also show that Sembene's iconoclasm represents a direct threat to established versions of history.

In 1979, after the lifting of the eight-year ban on *Emitai* in France, Sembene made these enlightening comments:

This movie . . . tells *a true story* that took place in southern Senegal, in the Casamance. It was the first time we dealt with the contemporary history of colonization in a movie. We go from Pétain [the collaborationist marshal] to de Gaulle. We know what de Gaulle represents for Africa [the image of de Gaulle popularized by politicians and academic historians]: he is the father, people cry on his grave, he is revered, streets and avenues are named after him; one cannot compare de Gaulle with Pétain. It is said that he is the father of decolonization (let's leave the responsibility for such a statement to the historians), but if we want to be objective, there is no difference between Pétain and de Gaulle. Maybe that's what explains the difficulties the film encountered in France. In 1971, at a showing of the film at the Moscow festival, the French ambassador left the screening room. This had repercussions at the Quai d'Orsay, and the film was banned. . . . The film talked about de Gaulle in a historical way that was not favorable to him. (Dembrow and Troller 1975, 4–5)

Emitai and *Camp de Thiaroye* are both filmic representations of colonial resistance and colonial massacres that took place in Senegal. Released in 1971, *Emitai* was shot on location in the village of Effok in Casamance, some of whose inhabitants were killed by the French colonial army in 1942. To summarize the *mise en scène:* WWII is raging; France is under Nazi domination; the army needs recruits to fight the war and the colonial economy to sustain both the war-ravaged metropolis and the fighting troops. As Abbe Diamancoun Senghor stated to me in an interview:[8] "Basse Casamance and Balantacounda were subjected to multiple forms of taxation: tax in "human cattle" (soldiers), forced conscription of soldiers to fight the war, tax in cash, in honey, and mostly in rice, not to mention that for us the imposition of [the cultivation of] peanuts [as a cash crop] meant the destruction of the forest, which is very sacred for us."

The film focuses on Diola resistance to conscription and the requisitioning of their rice by the colonial administration. Sembene's goal was to celebrate the unsung heroes of that resistance:

> While the film was being shot, some extras came from Guinea Bissau, and the fighters and the resistance people of the time [from Guinea Bissau's PAIGC, which fought Portuguese occupation in the 1970s under Amilcar Cabral] helped us a lot. Cabral came to see the film with some fighters. . . . I say this, because when certain intellectuals in Europe think about the liberation of Africa, they ignore internal resistance. For the struggle against neo-colonialism, it is possible to reactualize all these scattered and little-known battles. (Ghali 1987, 41–42)

The story in *Emitai* was inspired by the heroic but little-known actions of a young Diola woman named Aline Sitoe Diatta of the village of Cabrousse in southwestern Casamance. Born in 1920, Aline Sitoe is said to have been a maid, first in Ziguinchor and then in Dakar, where, as the story goes, she began to hear voices calling her on a mission: to fight for the liberation of Casamance. She answered that call in 1940 by going back to her village and other neighboring towns, where she started preaching rebellion against French authority. Soon the entire region and the French heard about Aline. The news of her preaching, spread by Tété Diatta, a mail deliveryman on a bicycle, soon attracted crowds; and the French arrested her on January 28, 1942, and exiled her, first to Saint-Louis and then to Timbuktu. Until 1971, when Sembene released *Emitai,* she remained relatively unknown, because before independence, the colonial authority omitted her from textbooks, and after independence, Senghor's government continued the strategy of silence. But then, as Abbe Diamancoun Senghor recalls, "There was a policy of recuperation. At the time, Senghor asked a historian, Iba Der Thiam to conduct research on Aline. Since then, stadiums [municipal stadium Aline Sitoe Diatta in Ziguinchor], schools, and public buildings [University Cheikh Anta Diop women's residence] bear her name." Likewise, *Emitai,* shot in the Diola language, contributed to the restoration of Aline Sitoe's memory and to a sense of pride among the people of Casamance as Sembene held public screenings in various villages and conducted discussions afterwards.

Moreover, as the above quote illustrates, *Emitai* was meant as a counter-memory, a questioning of the popular memory regarding de Gaulle, "manufac-tured" by *les historiens:* de Gaulle the liberator, the healer of the wounds caused by the pro-Nazi Maréchal Pétain, and the father of African independence. By telling a different story of the Casamance rebellion and thus challenging the popular image of de Gaulle (in a scene in *Emitai,* Sembene, playing himself, comments on pictures of Pétain and de Gaulle), Sembene manages to introduce important new variations in the colonial and postcolonial history of Casamance. On the one hand, such variations fill an important critical function in that they contradict the prejudices of popular and official memory. On the other, they show that, as Ricoeur put it: "Recollection presents itself as the result of a work, of a laborious reconstruction. It is not a given. It does not present itself as an involuntary flow, as Proust suggested; it is the result of a conquest" (1998, 26).

Additionally, a critical function of *Emitai* lies in its timing, which clearly demonstrates Sembene's goal to foster a different understanding of the bloody battle that continues today between the Mouvement des Forces Democratiques de Casamance and the governments of Senghor and, later, Abdou Diouf, a battle that started with the creation of the separatist movement on March 4, 1947, in Sédhiou. As Sembene has said: "When intellectuals in Europe think about the liberation of Africa, they ignore internal forces." After the release of *Emitai,* not only did Senegalese politicians try to claim Aline Sitoe, but writers such as Boubacar Boris Diop and Marouba Fall also memorialized her in novels and plays, thus joining Sembene in the grand project of repudiating the falsified co-lonial and neocolonial versions of the Casamance independence movement. Mamadou Diouf sums it up: "The plurality of historical interpretation is at the very heart of Sembene's message, demanding that the viewer bring an end to all images authorized or configured by an authority. . . . The inversion has a double function, as the radical reading of a rupture and as a technique of sub-version of the established order" (1996, 27). By inverting the source of memory and calling for a plurality of historical interpretations, *Emitai* stands against other discourses regularly deployed in political, legal, ritualistic and religious practices. It was the first African film to do so.

Camp de Thiaroye

With *Camp de Thiaroye,* Sembene hijacked another grand narrative of African history, the participation of African soldiers in World War II and the continuing debate not only over the relations between France and its former overseas colonies but also over African and French histories. Like *Emitai, Camp de Thiaroye* is a story about the massacre of a contingent of the *tirailleurs* who fought in Europe during World War II and were detained in German camps as prisoners of war.[9]

The plot of *Camp de Thiaroye* is rather simple. On November 14, 1944, a regiment of *tirailleurs sénégalais* embarks in France for return home. Passing through Casablanca, they get new uniforms from the American commander. They arrive in Dakar on November 25, 1944, to the chant of "Vive de Gaulle! Vive la France!" and the Governor General orders them to be housed in the Thiaroye transit camp outside Dakar. Before departing from France, however, these former prisoners of war were supposed to be paid some entitlements, including their military pension. Already frustrated by the French authorities, who had compensated all the White French soldiers, they faced discrimination, racism, and injustice upon their arrival in Thiaroye. On November 26, when their French currency was to be changed into CFA francs used in West Africa, they were told they would only receive 50 percent of the exchange rate. "It's too much money for a nigger," comments one of the French officers. For these soldiers who had fought in Europe, however, an important psychological change had happened: they witnessed the fall of France under the power of German forces; the myth of France fed to them by the colonial propaganda machine was stripped naked. It was a mental fracture: "Up until now we have fought for France, now we are fighting for Africa," says Chief Sergeant Diatta.

The rebellion of these soldiers at the Thiaroye camp was not an isolated case in the French colonial empire. On September 1, 1940, 200 soldiers from the war had also protested in the Degedou camp, Ivory Coast; on February 13, 1941, soldiers rebelled in Aboiso, Ivory Coast; in April and May 1944, the 17th regiment of *tirailleurs sénégalais* had rebelled in Fort Lyautey, Morocco.

These protests by African soldiers who had fought for French freedom could not have happened at a worse time for France. Indeed, at the start of 1944, in opening a conference in Brazzaville, de Gaulle clearly indicated that keeping its colonies was a *sine qua non* if France were to regain the status as world power that it had lost with its defeat in 1940: "The goals of the civilizing work accomplished by France in the colonies rule out all idea of autonomy, all possibility of evolution outside the French empire. The eventual constitution, even in a far future, of self-government in the colonies is to be excluded" (qtd. in Gueye 1995, 4). In other words, the new demands by the *tirailleurs,* cast as a right, constituted a long-term threat to de Gaulle's grand vision for France. In that context, any concession made to the *tirailleurs* was seen by the colonial authority as the beginning of the demise of the empire. Thus, on December 1, 1944, as a measure that could be considered "political therapy," an order was given to massacre the returning soldiers.

In 1995, trying to shed light on these 1944 events, Senegalese historian Mbaye Gueye voiced his frustration: "We would have liked to go further than the archives on these collective disobediences. But the archives have kept a disturbing silence on this issue. . . . The criminal kills twice, the second time in trying to bury his victims in the pits of amnesia" (8). Not only did the archives keep silent about this massacre, but even Radio AOF maintained a total blackout on the event at Thiaroye, and the Senegalese public did not hear about it until months later. This silence of the press and the archives is also undoubtedly what motivated Sembene to make *Camp de Thiaroye*.

In December 1944, Senghor, also a World War II veteran and a former prisoner of war, had already written a poem on the Thiaroye massacre (later published in his 1948 collection, *Hosties noires*) in which he wondered: "Black prisoners, I mean French prisoners, is it true that France is no longer France?" But it is with Sembene's work that many Africans and Europeans became aware of Thiaroye. For the record, it should be noted that before finding its way to Sembene's hands, the project of a film on Thiaroye was initiated by Ben Diogaye Bèye and Boris Diop, whose script *Thiaroye 44* was financed by the SNPC but not filmed.

Whereas in *Emitai* the purpose was to counter a falsification of history that results in the creation of false historical consciousness, in *Camp de Thiaroye* Sembene's main goal was to lift the veil on a well-kept secret, a secret detrimental to France's historical self-image:

> When Europeans talk about WWII they only talk about European soldiers. Likewise, Americans also only talk about their own soldiers; that is not true: Africa also participated in that war, and I think it is our duty to talk about it, without hate, but to show our contribution to world history. Every year, in Senegal, we honor the graves of these soldiers killed in Thiaroye. We do not have the right to forget; we have to keep the memory. ("Interview with Ousmane Sembene," 1996)

Memory and amnesia are no doubt at the very heart of *Camp de Thiaroye*. After the massacre, Sembene's camera surveys the destroyed camp littered with the bodies of fallen soldiers, and as day breaks, we can see the broken sign at the camp gate with only "CAMP DE . . . " and missing "THIAROYE," buried under the rubble. It is no surprise that Algeria joined in the coproduction of the film because it also suggests the 1954 Sétif massacre that sparked the Algerian war of liberation, which French officials would prefer to erase from archives and history books. Against this silence, Sembene's *Camp de Thiaroye* constitutes the rebuttal of a victim and a witness who refuses to be an accomplice.

Ceddo

Between *Emitai* and *Camp de Thiaroye*, which can be considered Sembene's war diaries, there is *Ceddo*, the most controversial of his historical movies. *Ceddo* was released in 1977 at the pinnacle of Senghor's presidency. As already mentioned, Sembene started his career as a novelist and, as his 1960 *Les bouts de bois de Dieu* (*God's Bits of Wood*) shows, he did not wait for cinema to deal with issues related to the African past. With other African fiction writers, he anticipated the exploration of the African past by professional historians in the seventies.[10] Moreover, *God's Bits of Wood* clearly indicates that the study of history has a prospective function and aims at identifying in the past the foundations for the future. Thus, only a month into the West African railroad workers' strike in the novel, Sembene notes: "Something new was being born in them, as if the past and the present were reaching for each other to give birth to a new type of men" (127).

With *Ceddo*, Sembene's main desire is to root Senegalese collective identity, not in present factors alone—national heroes, commemorations and ritualization, and other national symbols—but also in a symbolic evocation of the past, a past itself posed as a question. Unlike *Emitai* and *Camp de Thiaroye*, which deal with a recent past (WWII), *Ceddo* deals with a more distant period, the sixteenth, seventeenth, and eighteenth centuries. At the opening of the film, the local king Thioub and all the dignitaries of his regime have converted to Islam, putting in jeopardy their traditional religion, social structure, and cultural values. In a second move, the Imam tries to extend his religion to the mass of the Ceddo. In protest, a Ceddo kidnaps Princess Dior Yacine, the king's daughter. Despite the Ceddo's protest, however, Islam gains ground and imposes patriarchy while eroding the traditional social and political systems, religion, and way of life. The only alternatives for the rebels are conversion, exile, or slavery. At the same time, a White merchant in the village trades in European goods and slaves, and a Catholic priest tries in vain to attract new disciples (and has only one convert in the film). Using violence and murder, the Imam seizes power, conducts a mass conversion, assigns new Muslim names to the former Ceddo, and has the kidnaper killed to free the princess he plans to marry in order to give more legitimacy to his power. In the final shot, however, the princess kills the Imam.

Even without further details from this well-known film, it is clear why Sembene ran into trouble from both the Senegalese politicians, led by Senghor, and the Muslim brotherhoods. In a country with over 85 percent Muslim population and where oftentimes the religious leadership has played an important role in political elections, he imagined and posited an alternative past for Islam in Senegalese identity.

Sembene's project in *Ceddo* is better understood when viewed in light of the epigraph to the first volume of his *L'Almamy Samori Touré*, entitled "Faamaya Sila" (The Road to Power):

> The goal is not to make up a history that would be more beautiful than others' in order to anesthetize the people during the struggle for national independence. Instead, the goal is to start from the evident premise that each people has its history. . . . It has become indispensable for Africans to interrogate their own history and their civilization, and to study them, in order to know themselves better.[11]

More than in *Emitai* and *Camp de Thiaroye*, in *Ceddo*, Sembene "creates" history counter to official knowledge invented by politicians and intellectuals and aimed at "doping" the people for the purpose of nation-building. Moreover, as Mamadou Diouf has pointed out: "The film is constructed on the ruins of nationalist history and of political trajectories centered around a patronage tightly controlled by the group in power, its imperialist patrons and its allies, the peanut-producing heads of Islamic brotherhoods and other trustees of ethnic and historical legitimacy" (1996, 25). In sum, like his other historical films, Sembene's *Ceddo* invites its viewers not only to rethink critically the place of Islam in Senegalese society but also to reflect on its social, political, and religious order.

Conclusion

Ousmane Sembene's questioning and filmic reconfiguration of early and contemporary African pasts and his challenge to French and Senegalese governments that seek to silence his vision and version of history indicate that both the filmmaker-turned-historian and the "official" trustees of Senegalese history have come to understand that to write history is also to make history. What Sembene did was not just to cast a nostalgic gaze at a fossilized past. Through all his artistic works, when he turns to the past, it is in order to interrogate it. He questions the stories being told and offers counterstories by telling them differently. Additionally, through the medium of film, Sembene humanizes the past. By bringing the viewer into the present of characters who belong to the past, the filmmaker reminds us that those men and women had an open future and that they left behind unfulfilled dreams. Or, as Paul Ricoeur has pointed out: "By awakening and bringing back to life the unkept promises of the past, we strengthen our own future with the buried future of those who came before us" (1998, 27).

For Ousmane Sembene, historical films should be neither mere entertainment nor a nostalgic imagining of the past as something closed that cannot be reopened and changed. Quite the contrary. For Sembene, a look at history is a look back at the future.

Notes

1. This list of early historical films of the 1970s and the 1980s was compiled by Mbye Cham (1993).

2. My translations throughout, except where noted.

3. For a more detailed examination of Hollywood historical fiction films, see Grindon 1994.

4. Ouagadougou is the capital of Burkina Faso (formerly Upper Volta) and the site, since 1969, of the biennial African Film Festival, FESPACO (The Ouagadougou Pan-African Film Festival).

5. This statement is attributed to Karl Marx.

6. Here I borrow the title of Sheila Petty's (1996) edited collection of essays on the work of Sembene.

7. Although the script of Samori was completed decades ago, no European public or private institution would finance the film because of its obvious anticolonial stance and its questioning of African official colonial history.

8. At the time of the interview with me in 1996, Abbe Diamancoun Senghor was

under house arrest at his Ziguinchor residence. Until June 2001 he was the leader of the MFDC (Mouvement des Forces Democratiques de Casamance), fighting a guerrilla war against the Senegalese armed forces.

9. Codirected with Thierno Faty Sow, this megaproduction, costing 350 million CFA francs (colossal by African standards—about US $500,000) was coproduced by Senegal's Société Nouvelle de Promotion Cinématographique (SNPC); Algeria's Entreprise Nationale de Production Cinématographique; Tunisia's SATPECE; Ousmane Sembene's own production company, Filmii Domireew; and a Thiès-based production company, Film Kayor.

10. For the exploration of the past in the African fiction writing, see studies by Hazoumé (1938), Niane (1960), and Boni (1962).

11. Cheikh Anta Diop, *Nations Nègres et Cultures* (1954), cited by Sembene as an epigraph to the first volume of the unpublished script "L'Almamy Samori Touré."

Works Cited

Boni, Nazi. 1962. *Le crépuscule des temps anciens.* Paris: Présence Africaine.

Cham, Mbye. 1993. "Official History, Popular Memory: Reconfiguration of the African Past in the Films of Ousmane Sembene." In *Ousmane Sembène: Dialogues with Critics and Writers,* ed. Samba Gadjigo, et al., 22–28. Amherst: University of Massachusetts Press.

Dembrow, Michael, and Klaus Troller. 1975. "Interview with Ousmane Sembene." Transcription, Kiki Dembrow. Trans. Michael Dembrow. Bloomington: Indiana University Press.

Diop, Boubacar Boris. Personal interview. Dakar. July 1996.

———. 1990. *Les Tambours de la mémoire.* Paris: L'Harmattan.

Diouf, Mamadou. 1996. "Histoires et actualités dans *Ceddo* d'Ousmane Sembène et *Hyènes* de Djibril Diop Mambéti." In *Littérature et cinéma en Afrique francophone: Ousmane Sembène et Assia Djebar,* ed. Sada Niang, 15–34. Paris: L'Harmattan.

Fall, Marouba. 1988. *Aliin Sitooye Jaata ou la Dame de Kabrus, suivi de Adja la militante de G.R.A.S.* Dakar: Nouvelles Editions Africaines.

Flatley, Guy. 1969. "Senegal Is Senegal, Not Harlem." *New York Times,* 2 November, D17.

Ghali, Noureddine. 1987. "An Interview with Ousmane Sembene." In *Film and Politics in the Third World,* ed. John D. H. Downing, 41–54. New York: Autonomedia.

Grindon, Leger. 1994. *Shadows of the Past: Studies in the Historical Fiction Film.* Philadelphia: Temple University Press.

Gueye, Mbaye. 1995. "Le 1 Décembre 1944 à Thiaroye ou le massacre de tirailleurs sénégalais anciens prisonniers de guerre." *Revue Sénégalaise d'Histoire* ns 1: 3–23.

Halimi, Serge. 1995. "Le film *JFK* d'Oliver Stone, De l'histoire ou du cinéma." *Manière de voir* 26:50.

Hazoumé, Paul. 1938. *Doguicimi.* Paris: Larose.

"Interview with Ousmane Sembene after the screening of *Camp de Thiaroye* at Rice University." 1996. Houston Public Television, 16 February.

Mulvey, Laura. 1991. "*Xala,* Ousmane Sembene 1976: The Carapace that Failed." *Third Text* 16–17: 19–37.

Niane, Djibril Tamsir. 1960. *Soundjata ou l'épopée mandingue.* Paris: Présence Africaine.

Petty, Sheila, ed. 1996. *A Call to Action: The Films of Ousmane Sembene.* Westport: Praeger.

Ricoeur, Paul. 1998. "Histoire et mémoire." In *De l'histoire au cinéma: Histoire du temps présent,* ed. Antoine de Baecque and Christian Delage, 17–28. Paris: Editions Complexes.

Rollins, Peter C., ed. 1998. *Hollywood as Historian: American Film in a Cultural Context,* rev. ed. Lexington: University Press of Kentucky.

Rosenstone, Robert A. 1988. "History in Images/History in Words: Reflections on the Possibility of Really Putting History onto Film." *American Historical Review* 93.5: 1173–85.

Sembene, Ousmane. n.d. "Archives sonores de la littérature noire." Paris: Radio France Internationale.

———. 1960. *Les bouts de bois de Dieu.* Paris: Amiot Dupont. *God's Bits of Wood.* Trans. Francis Price. Garden City, N.Y.: Doubleday, 1962; London: Heinemann, 1970.

———. 1987. *Le docker noir.* Paris: Nouvelles Editions Debresse, 1956. *Black Docker.* Trans. Ros Schwarz. London: Heinemann, 1987.

Senghor, Abbe Augustin Diamancoun. Personal interview. Ziguinchor, 1996.

Senghor, Léopold S. 1948. "Tyaroye." In *Hosties noires.* Paris: Editions du Seuil.

Toplin, Robert Brent. 1996. *History by Hollywood: The Use and Abuse of the American Past.* Urbana: University of Illinois Press.

3 Film and History in Africa: A Critical Survey of Current Trends and Tendencies
Mbye Cham

Like other forms of creative expression by Africans, filmmaking constitutes a form of discourse and practice that is not just artistic and cultural, but also intellectual and political. It is a way of defining, describing, and interpreting African experiences with those forces that have shaped their past and that continue to shape and influence the present. It is a product of the historical experiences of Africans, and it has direct bearing and relevance to the challenges that face African societies and people of African descent around the world both in the present moment and in the future. Thus, in looking at filmmaking in particular, and the other creative arts in general, one is looking at particular insights into ways of thinking and acting on individual as well as collective realities, experiences, challenges, and desires over time. African thinking and acting on their individual and collective realities are diverse and complex; and cinema provides one of the most productive sites for experiencing, understanding, and appreciating such diversity and complexity.

A significant portion of what constitutes African cultural, symbolic, and intellectual thought and practices—be they oral, written, dramatic, visual, or filmic—can be characterized as responses to, and interventions in, the factors and forces that have shaped Africa over time. Generally conceived as triple, these factors and forces have been described by Kwame Nkrumah (1964) and, more recently, by Ali Mazrui (1986) as: (1) indigenous, (2) Arab-Islamic, and (3) Euro-Christian. The patterns of interaction and cross-fertilization and the tensions and conflicts between and among these forces over many centuries on African soil have produced a wide range of complex dynamics and transformations that have resulted in the shape of Africa at the present moment. They have also spawned diverse patterns of thought and practice in many domains of life in Africa, particularly that of filmmaking.

African cinema functions as a mode of entertainment. At the same time, it assigns itself a pivotal role in definitions, enactment, and performance of African notions and ideologies of individual as well as community and humanity. In this respect it is like its counterparts, the indigenous oral narrative traditions and written literature in both African and European languages. African filmmaking co-exists and interacts with these other forms of creative practice on the level of subject matter, theme, form, and style, and of conceptions of art and artist and their role in, and relationship to, society.

African participation in cinema as producers and transmitters of their own images is a relatively recent phenomenon, however, dating back only to the 1960s. The initial position of Africa in this civilization of cinema was that of a receiver/consumer of film products made primarily in and by the West. Many of these films also used and continue to use Africa and Africans as resources to invent and disseminate images and discourses of Africa and Africans radically at odds with the actual histories and realities of Africa and Africans. In spite of its youth and the variety of overwhelming odds against which it is struggling, cinema by Africans has grown steadily over this short period of time to become a significant part of a global cinema civilization to which it brings many significant contributions.

More specifically, African cinema is part of a worldwide film movement aimed at constructing and promoting an alternative popular cinema, one that corrects the distortions and stereotypes propagated by dominant Western cinemas and that is more in sync with the realities, experiences, priorities, and desires of their respective societies. As such, a significant portion of the films that constitute African cinema share a few elements in common with radical film practices from other parts of the Third World. These include Third Cinema, as articulated by Fernando Solanas and Octavio Getino; Imperfect Cinema, as developed by Julio García Espinosa; and Cinema Novo, as articulated by Glauber Rocha and others. They also exhibit similarities to the work of independent African American and Black British filmmakers and of Indian filmmakers such as Satyajit Ray and Mirnal Sen. These parallels are manifested not only at the level of form and theme but also in their production, distribution, and exhibition practices and challenges.

A significant development in African film culture in the last two decades especially, is the turn toward the subject of history. Since its inception in the 1960s and 70s, a significant portion of African cinema has focused and continues to focus on issues of racism, colonial exploitation and injustice, tradition and modernity, hopes, betrayals and disaffections of independence, immigration, and many other social justice issues. Historicizing these issues, as well as creating narratives based primarily on events, figures, and subjects of history, has emerged in recent years as a prominent trait of African film culture, as a cursory glance at African film production in the past two decades will demonstrate.

The subject of African history has commanded the attention of a steadily growing number of films by Africans in recent years. Many of these films are devoted primarily or in part to a critical engagement with, and interrogation of, the African past for the purpose of contesting, visioning, and revisioning—to invoke Rosenstone's categories—aspects of that past from African points of view. These films also take up history as a way of reflecting on, and coming to terms with, the many crises and challenges confronting contemporary African societies as well as the future.

Stories of the African past, it is generally established by now, have been rendered predominantly from the perspective of Europeans who colonized and dominated much of Africa. These dominant European versions focus predominantly on the story of Europeans in Africa and present these as authentic histories of Africa. In these versions, Europe is presented as the bringer of history and civilization to an ahistorical Africa. History is thus pressed into service to rationalize and justify the project of imperial and colonial expansion as well as of a civilizing mission that is portrayed as benevolent, benign, and sanctioned by God. As such, these versions of history erase and exclude stories of Africa before the advent of Europeans and Arabs.

Like the works of many African oral artists, creative writers, and historians, a good number of recent African films present versions of the African past from African perspectives that contest and subvert official as well as popular European accounts and that present more complex and balanced histories, especially the histories of slavery, imperialism, colonialism, and postcolonialism. Their subject matter and time spans are broad, covering individual figures as well as collective movements and events in the precolonial, colonial, and postcolonial periods of African history. The approaches and styles encountered in these films are also diverse, ranging from linear realist approaches to ones that are nonlinear, symbolic, and, sometimes, experimental. While their interrogation and reconstruction of history draw partially and in critically transgressive ways from sources such as official documents and narratives as well as from traditional Eurocentric scholarly accounts, their foundation is the African heritage of oral traditions and memory. Whether documentary or fiction, these films are less interested in a history that merely celebrates a glorious past for European consumption, what Mazrui (1996) calls "romantic gloriana," than in a critical and purposeful reflection on, and interrogation of, the ways history—in its varied constructions and uses—is inextricably implicated in systems of domination, subjugation, and liberation of Africans and is, as well, inscribed in the African present and future.

The genesis of this current African cinematic preoccupation with history and its implications for the present and the future can be traced to the early works of the man popularly referred to as the "father of African cinema," Ousmane Sembene. Sembene's entire oeuvre, literary as well as cinematic, deals with history, even when the more immediate subject matter may be betrayals and challenges of the postcolonial present. His style of reconfiguring African historical experiences draws significantly on his own biography and experience as a veteran of the French colonial military and a trade union activist in order to tell the stories of Africans under French colonial domination, their struggles of resistance and efforts to reclaim their own histories and cultures and to build a different future.

Sembene's films also effectively deconstruct French founding principles of *"liberté, égalité, fraternité."* His 1971 film *Emitai* is a narrative about the responses of the Diola people of the Casamance region of Senegal to French military pillage and massacres during World War II. In *Camp de Thiaroye* (1988), he returns to the subject of Africans in the French colonial military, retelling this time the repressed story of the December 1944 massacre by the French military of a group of demobilized African soldiers just returned from fighting for France in Europe. Sembene's 1977 feature *Ceddo* demonstrates the depth of Sembene's historical vision, for in this film he goes beyond the dominant model of Europe and Christianity as the sole external colonizing force in Africa to include Islam and Arabism as the flip side of the same colonial coin. *Ceddo* recasts the history of Islam, Christianity, and slaving activities in the Senegambia region.

Revisioning the Algerian war of independence from France is also central in numerous films such as Mohamed Lakhdar-Hamina's 1975 epic, *Chronique des années de braise* (*Chronicle of the Years of Embers*); Slim Riad's *Al-Tariq* (*The Way*, 1968); and, more recently, Mohamed Chouick's *Youcef ou la légende du septième dormant* (Youcef, or the Legend of Seventh Sleep, 1993). Rachida Krim's *Sous le pied des femmes* (*Where Women Tread*, 1997) foregrounds the participation and experiences of Algerian women in the armed struggle, experiences that are confined mostly to the background in numerous male-directed films on this subject. In a somewhat different vein, but with memory as its motor force, Moufida Tlatli's brilliant *Les silences du palais* (*Silences of the Palace*, 1994) revisions and rewrites a certain moment of Tunisian history, the period of the "beys," the last rulers of Tunisia. She does this from a female perspective and in refreshingly imaginative ways that privilege and highlight individual lives and desires. These films present more complex and balanced accounts of the nature and implications of the participation of women in these struggles for liberation. More significantly, they indict the regressive tendencies of their male compatriots who in many cases retrogress by insisting on pushing women back and restricting them to domestic spheres once the armed phase of the struggle is over—hence, the imperative of a second liberation struggle for women in these narratives.

The armed struggles of Africans against various European colonial powers have provided rich narrative material for a number of African filmmakers who preserve this glory moment of their history on film and also use it to speak about the pressures and challenges of postliberation. Portuguese colonialism in Angola, Guinea-Bissau, and Mozambique and the armed resistance to it is the subject of a number of films. A most significant figure in this sense is pioneer female filmmaker Sarah Maldoror of Guadeloupe, who has, perhaps more than any other African director, documented and worked on other documentations of the liberation struggles of Africans against colonialism. After working as assistant to Gillo Pontecorvo on his epic *Battle of Algiers* (1966), Maldoror went on to make *Monangambee* (1970), a parody on colonial ignorance shot in Algeria. It was based on a short story by Angolan writer Luandino Vieira, who at the time was imprisoned by the Portuguese colonial authorities in a labor camp in Tarrafal in the Cape Verde Islands. Maldoror's next film on the armed resistance in Guinea-Bissau was *Des Fusils pour Banta* (Guns for Banta, 1971), a film shot on the guerrilla battlefields in Guinea-Bissau. Her first feature film, *Sambizanga* (1972), shot in Congo-Brazzaville, remains to this day the most imaginative and moving portrait of the initial phase of the Angolan liberation struggle against Portuguese colonial domination. A most important feature in Maldoror's rewriting is the way she restores and highlights the role of women in the struggle, something that was somewhat muffled in Vieira's novel *The True Life of Domingos Xavier,* from which the film is adapted.

Like Maldoror, Flora Gomes of Guinea-Bissau also undertakes the task of preserving and moving beyond the experience of armed struggle in Guinea-Bissau in his critically acclaimed first feature, *Mortu Nega* (The One Whom Death Refused), made in 1989, some fifteen years after independence from Portugal. Triumphalist as well as skeptical, *Mortu Nega* celebrates the heroism of the freedom fighters, especially that of the female comrades, and at the same time questions and indicts the betrayal of the ideals for which people were mobilized and motivated to fight. Liberation and independence brought negligible changes in the life circumstances of the majority rank and file, but the few elite who replaced the ousted colonialists profited from their positions. Gomes's other well-received film, *Udju azul di Yonta* (*The Blue Eyes of Yonta,* 1991), as well as his most recent feature film, *Nha Fala (My Voice,* 2002), take up this issue again to some extent and extend it to explore the meaning of the liberation struggle for the younger generation who did not witness it. "A luta continua" (the struggle continues), these films seem to be saying.

Mozambicans and their numerous supporters from different parts of the world have also produced a significant number of films that document as well as revision their experiences with Portuguese colonialism and its legacies. These films provide perspectives on the oppression, exploitation, and resistance of Mozambicans that stand in stark contrast to the manipulative dominant narratives of Afrocommunism and anticommunism propagated by the Portuguese as well as by the apartheid South African state. They range from support and mobilization documentaries such as African American Robert Van Lierop's classic *A Luta Continua* (*The Struggle Continues,* 1970), to the first feature by Ruy Guerra, *Mueda: Memoria e Massacre* (*Mueda: Memory and Massacre,* 1979) based on the 1960 massacre of six hundred people by the Portuguese in the village of Mueda, and to the more recent reflections on the aftermath of the post-liberation debacle with apartheid-South African supported RENAMO.

Because the interval between the events and their documentation on film was in many cases very brief, some of these films, as well as the many others that deal with the South African resistance to apartheid, can also be seen as instances of what Michael Green, in reference to similar moves by novelists in South Africa, labels "the present as history." Here filmmakers, like novelists in similar contexts, "charted the events of the day with an immediacy born of the almost instant recognition of their 'historical' significance" (Green 1997, 16).

South African cinema in the postapartheid moment has yet to probe more profoundly the rich and troubled history, both distant and more recent, of this part of the continent. To be sure, there are many films that allude to aspects of the past; however, the history film as a genre, particularly films from the points of view of the historically oppressed majority, is yet to emerge in South African film culture. Hollywood and Hollywood clones such as John Badenhorst's *Slavery of Love* (1998) have thus far usurped the task. Perhaps the few projects currently in process that I am aware of, as well as the South African National Film Foundation identification of history and stories of liberation as subjects for priority funding, will begin to effect a significant turn in this direction in the years to come.

In the meantime, one has to look to a few short films as well as to a number of series commissioned by various bodies and organizations for such narratives of memory and exorcising of the past. A number of these were inspired by the proceedings and revelations of the Truth and Reconciliation Commission under the chairmanship of Bishop Desmond Tutu. Examples would include Sechaba Morojele's *Ubuntu's Wounds* (2001), a film that probes the issue of memory, revenge, and forgiveness. Sechaba's film resonates interestingly with Raoul Peck's 1988 film *Haitian Corner* as well as with the novel *Bitter Fruit* by fellow South African Achmat Dangor. Khalo Matabane's *The Young Lions* (1991), the story of three friends and anti-apartheid activists who endured and survived prison and torture, also deals with the recent past. One of the comrades is suspected by the other two of snitching and betraying them, and the film shows their encounter years later to talk about the experience and to reconcile.

Also of interest here are a number of films, mostly made-for-TV dramas, that have emerged recently in South Africa, revisiting certain moments and figures of the distant and more immediate past. The 1999 courtroom drama series *Saints, Sinners and Settlers* readily comes to mind. Five films make up this series: *The Real Estate Man: The Trial of Dingane* by Micky Madoda Dube; *The Good Doctor: The Trial of Dr. H. F. Verwoerd* by Robbie Thompson; *Days of the Two Suns: The Trial of Xhosa Prophetess Nongqawuse* and *The Reluctant Settler: The Trial of Jan van Riebeeck*, both by John Matshikiza; and *To the Bitter End: The Trial of Lord Kitchener* by Minky Schlesinger. Three other films of great significance and masterful artistry but steering clearly away from the sometimes troubling comic overtones of some films in the above series are Zola Maseko's *The Life and Times of Sara Baartman: The Hottentot Venus* (1998); *A Drink in the Passage* (2002), adapted from Alan Paton's short story of the same title; and Lindy Wilson's *The Guguletu Seven* (2000).

The SACOD-produced four-part series *Landscape of Memory*[1] also offers critical perspectives on many aspects of the struggles for liberation and reconciliation in Namibia, South Africa, Zimbabwe, and Mozambique. Of particular interest is the film by Richard Pakleppa, *Nda Mona* (*I Have Seen,* 1999), which takes a critical look at the internal dynamics of the SWAPO-led liberation struggle against apartheid South African colonialism. Those labeled as collaborators and traitors and who survived the punitive actions of the guerilla movement remember their experiences and narrate them on film. These voices stand in opposition to the official postliberation arguments to forget, reconcile, and move forward. Juxtaposing these opposing voices, the film dramatizes a clash of memories and throws up a different dimension to the question as to what happens when local/individual memory and state discourse come into conflict in what Richard Werber terms "the making of political subjectivity" (1998, 9).

Nda Mona foregrounds the other side, so to speak, of the SWAPO-led liberation struggle: the actions against its own adversaries—or those tagged as such—in much the same ways as the postapartheid South African Truth and Reconciliation Commission insisted on laying bare the actions of the ANC and other anti-apartheid groups and individuals that some labeled as "crimes." Are these instances of blaming the victims? Are such interrogations of actions taken in the heat of struggle ideological and premature, especially in light of the fact that the story or stories of the struggle from the point of view of the combatants have yet to be told? These are some of the questions raised in relation to films such as *Nda Mona* and others that are seen to place in the background the narratives and actions of the colonial state that the liberation movements were fighting against. In Zimbabwe, *Flame* (1996) by British-born and Zimbabwe-naturalized Ingrid Sinclair has occasioned similar debates.

Further north, memory work in a number of films by Ethiopian filmmakers tends toward a radical break with a feudal past that is projected as fetishized nostalgia and a more recent bloody experiment in socialist transformation. The thread that runs through Haile Gerima's *Harvest: 3000 Years* (1976) and *Imperfect Journey* (1994), Salem Mekuria's *Yewonz Maibel* (*Deluge*, 1995), and Yemane Demissie's *Girgir* (*Tumult*, 1996) is a project to revision the foundational narrative of a 3000-year Solomonic Ethiopia in light of the experience with feudalism and a failed revolution and their legacies.

Harvest: 3000 Years casts a critical glance at the ways the feudal state under Haile Selassie, especially, manipulated legend and myth to perpetuate allegiance to a glorious past that was able to keep the vast majority of Ethiopian peasantry under feudal control. Made at a moment of transition between the end of the feudal regime and dawn of the revolutionary regime of Mengistu Haile Mariam, *Harvest* contests and subverts the reigning feudal narratives and also anticipates, somewhat prophetically, the still-unfinished struggle against similar forces of subjugation in the postfeudal era. *Tumult*, for its part, revisits the failed attempts by 1960s students, in alliance with segments of the military, to topple Haile Selassie's regime. Deploying a class analysis, Demissie chronicles the psychological fallout of this moment for individuals, and the competing narratives of history that the film eloquently presents provide a solid foundation for better understandings of the continuing struggles in contemporary Ethiopia. Salem Mekuria also accomplishes this in *Deluge*, which revisits, from a more personal point of view, the 1970s and 1980s—Ethiopia under the "Dergue," the regime of Mengistu Haile Mariam.

Mekuria's second major work, *Yewonz Maibel*, is a moving personal journey back to the post-Haile Selassie Ethiopia and the 1978–79 bloody period of the Red Terror campaign of Colonel Mengistu Haile Mariam against his opposition. The human toll of the conflict that pitted relatives, families, and close friends against each other, as well as the difficult but necessary process of healing and reconciliation in the 1990s when the film was shot in Ethiopia, are highlighted. Using her first-person voice as the narrative vehicle, Mekuria reconstructs events with the aid of personal correspondence with, and memories of, her brother and her best friend, using photographs, archival footage, paintings, and music. Mekuria's brother, Solomon, and her best friend, Nigist Adane, grew up together and started out as comrades in a common struggle to bring down the feudal monarchy, but they ended up on different sides in the new revolutionary order under the dictatorship of the military. Solomon was executed by Nigist's party, allied to the Dergue, but Nigist ended up losing her life at the hands of the same Dergue, all on ideological grounds. Through this personal and self-reflexive narrative, the recent history of a whole nation and region is laid bare and reinterpreted, and its implications for the future of the region are made explicit.

Not all Ethiopian filmic revisioning of history posits total rupture with the past. Many films embrace and celebrate those aspects of the past deemed heroic and usable in the present. The proud history of resistance to foreign domination, particularly the fact that Ethiopia is one of two African countries that were never formally colonized, is a central theme in Ethiopian historiography, one that has imposed itself in different ways in most Ethiopian films. Theo Eshetu's *Il Sangue Non E Acqua Fresca* (*Blood Is Not Fresh Water*, 1998) uses the filmmaker's grandfather, Tekle Tsadik Mekouria, a historian in his own right, as the principal narrative vehicle for retelling the story of Ethiopia across broad time spans, events, and achievements. An impressive mosaic of images, archival footage, personal testimonies, and humor is mobilized with great skill and imagination to speak about Ethiopia of Solomonic origins; its ancient and proud heritage of culture, religion, and art; and the experiences of invasion in 1936 by fascist Italy, seemingly to avenge its defeat a half-century earlier in 1896 at the Battle of Adwa. This is the same glory moment in Ethiopian history that Haile Gerima retells and claims, not just for Ethiopia, but for the whole of Africa in his recent film, *Adwa: An African Victory* (1999).

The kind of critical embrace and celebration of such glory moments of African history and their projection into the present and the future that is evident in Gerima's *Adwa: An African Victory* as well as in many other films, such as Cameroonian Jean-Marie Teno's *Afrique, Je te plumerai* (Africa, I Will Fleece You, 1991), informs *Lumumba* (2000), the recent masterpiece of Haitian director Raoul Peck. The heroic figure of Patrice Lumumba, the first prime minister of the Congo and great Pan-Africanist, looms so large in the consciousness and memory of Peck that he devotes two different films to the life and times of this exceptional revolutionary hero. Peck first made a documentary in 1991 based on stories about Lumumba that his mother told him while he was a child in the Congo at the time of Lumumba. Almost ten years later, he developed a feature film on the same figure that has, among many other things, reignited a long-repressed debate in Belgium regarding Belgian colonial terror in the Congo and its complicity in the brutal murder of Lumumba. Peck's *Lumumba* is the latest in a series of well-crafted and highly acclaimed films that rewrite African history from African points of view.

Pièces d'identités (Identity Papers, 1996) by Ngangura Mweze (Democratic Republic of the Congo). Photo courtesy of California Newsreel.

Another equally great work is the 1998 film *Pièces d'identités* (Identity Papers, 1996) by Congolese filmmaker Ngangura Mweze. The distinction, charm, and effectiveness of this film derive from the focus and precision of a captivating story, its mastery of film language, the sophistication and elegance of the visual style, and the complexity and sharpness of its critical evocation and analysis of the past and the present, as well as the imaginative blending of tradition and modernity. The journey from Congo to Belgium and back by Mani Kongo in search of his daughter opens up the different and diverse world of African immigrant communities in present-day Brussels. At the same time, it opens up for memory, scrutiny, and reinterpretation the Belgian colonial past and its legacies. Like Peck's *Lumumba*, Mweze's film is simultaneously entertainment, sociology, anthropology, history, politics, and art. In it we encounter old and new Africa, old and new Belgium, and the new products of the myriad encounters between all of these over the years. Hybrid identities and the ways they give shape to notions of globalization are evoked in many ways in the film.

Another important film on history in the Congo is Monique Phoba's *Un rêve d'indépendance* (Dream of Independence, 1998) on the subject of Congolese medical assistants during the period of Belgian colonization. Phoba uses the case history of her own grandfather and family to critically portray and reflect on Belgian colonial practices and thirty-seven years of independence in the Democratic Republic of the Congo.

If Peck's *Lumumba* reiterates Patrice Lumumba as a heroic figure of African history, the Cameroonian Bassek Ba Kobhio's *Le Grand Blanc de Lambaréné* (The Great White Man of Lambaréné, 1995) reiterates the figure of Albert Schweitzer as nonheroic. Universally acclaimed for his sense of philanthropy and concern for the welfare of the African wretched of the earth, Schweitzer is celebrated in dominant European accounts of his life and work as a missionary figure who gave up bourgeois comforts and privileges for a life of struggle to save and bring civilization to "natives in the heart of darkness," in Gabon, deep in the "jungles" of central Africa. Ba Kobhio's film offers a radically different account of this philanthropist-missionary as he takes a subversive look at Schweitzer's motivations, methods, styles, work, and relationships with, and attitudes toward, his adopted environment from the point of view of the "natives."

Seen from the perspective of Kumba, the young boy who grew up to fulfill his aspiration of becoming a doctor, an aspiration considered unrealistic and unachievable for a native by Schweitzer, the film presents Schweitzer as racist, condescending, patronizing, arrogant, dictatorial, and completely detached from and insensitive to the desires, aspirations, and culture of the local people he has come to save. Kumba fittingly rebukes Schweitzer: "The independence of the people has never been your concern. You only wanted to share their hell in the hope of reaching your heaven." In short, the film rewrites the relations between Schweitzer and the host population as colonial. Significantly, *Le Grand Blanc de Lambaréné* also tells the story of postcolonial disillusionment by chronicling the path taken by the protagonist/narrator Kumba, from a young man aspiring to become a physician to actually becoming one, and then becoming a leader in the struggle to end colonial rule and also a leader in the postcolonial government. It is as much about the hopes and betrayals of independence in late-twentieth-century Africa as it is about Schweitzer in early-twentieth-century Gabon.

The style of history film that would respond to Ali Mazrui's label of "romantic gloriana," a proximate of the traditional Hollywood costume drama, is practically absent in African cinema, except, perhaps, for the epics of Egyptian filmmaker Youssef Chahine and two historical epics by Nigerian filmmaker Adamu Halilu. Halilu's 1976 film *Shehu Umar* is a vast chronicle of the life and times of the eponymous turn-of-the-century figure whose life story he traces in this narrative about Islam in West Africa. The film is an adaptation of the novel *Shaihu Umar,* written in 1955 in Hausa by Alhagy Sir Abubakar Tafawa-Balewa, the first prime minister of Nigeria. Halilu followed this film in 1979 with another 165-minute epic, *Kanta of Kebi,* the story of a Hausa hero who fought against the invasion of the town of Kebbi by the Songhai in the fourteenth century.

Such narratives of heroism in ancient Africa coincide with similar moves in African historiography of the 1970s that tended to focus on the grandeur of

Keita, l'héritage du griot (*Keita: The Heritage of the Griot*, 1994) by Dani Kouyaté
(Burkina Faso).
Photo courtesy of California Newsreel.

precolonial empires and grand figures. African filmmakers still look back at
such moments of the past but with different formal strategies and ideological
goals. For example, in *Keita, l'héritage du griot* (*Keita: The Heritage of the Griot*,
1994), Burkina Faso filmmaker Dani Kouyaté reenacts the Mande "master" narrative, the epic of Sundiata Keita, the thirteenth-century founding figure of the
Mali Empire. However, Kouyaté is interested less in retelling the entire epic—he
limits the narrative to the point where Sundiata leaves for exile—than in using
it as a springboard to reflect on the imperative of producing more imaginative
and productive uses of heritages of the past for the present as well as the future.

A pronounced absence in African films about history is a sustained focus on
issues of slavery. African filmmakers have, in the main, shied away from this
aspect of African world history, with the exception of a few recent works with
slavery as primary narrative focus: *Addangaman* (1999) by Roger Gnoan Mbala
(Ivory Coast); *Slavery of Love, Sankofa, Asientos,* and *West Indies: Les Nègres
marrons de la liberté* (West Indies: Black Maroons of Freedom, 1979) by Med
Hondo (Mauritania); *A deusa negra* (*Black Goddess*, 1978) by Ola Balogun (Nigeria); and *Reou Takh* (1972) by Mahama Johnson-Traoré (Senegal). Many have
referenced this aspect of the African historical experience in films with other
narrative and thematic focus, for example, Med Hondo's classic *Soleil O* (O Sun,
1970), but only a handful have taken up the issue as a central subject. One has
to look to the work of Diaspora Africans in the United States, the Caribbean,
and Latin America, as well as Hollywood, for a more significant corpus on this

question.[2] However, there are signs of change, judging by some of the products of the last decade, especially.

Reou Takh, Black Goddess, and *Asientos* (1995) by François Woukoache (Cameroon) are related by their overarching concern with slavery and its legacies for Africans as well as for people of African descent in the Diaspora. However, the representational codes deployed by Woukoache stand in radical contrast to those used by his predecessors, notwithstanding the imaginary flashback to slavery times in *Reou Takh* and in *Black Goddess.* All three films privilege a search motif. To the extent to which it has an African American return to a now-independent Senegal in search of his roots, *Reou Takh* anticipates the much-heralded *Roots* TV series of the late 1970s in the United States. *Black Goddess* is a kind of "*Roots*-in-Reverse." The temporal location of the film is the present, and it tells the story of a Nigerian who goes back to contemporary Bahia in Brazil in search of descendants of his family captured and taken away during the slave trade. To help his search, he carries with him the piece of a pair of twin carvings that are heirlooms of his family that remained in Nigeria. The other piece was carried away to Brazil by a member of the family who was captured and enslaved. Armed with this carving, he succeeds in reconnecting with family in Bahia when the other piece is produced and identified.

In *Reou Takh,* an African American returns to Gorée Island in Senegal. Standing at the "Door of No Return" in the Slave House and ambling around other places on the island, the African American protagonist of the film engages in a series of imaginary flashbacks to the times when the island was active as a slave fort, the last point of contact with Africa for the millions of captured Africans on their way across the Middle Passage to the New World of plantation slavery in the Americas. His encounters with contemporary Senegal, especially in the capital city of Dakar, also reveal the cruel legacies of colonialism, a proximate cousin of slavery, in the social inequities, conflicts, and injustices rampant in the society. *Reou Takh* reconstructs the African past and speaks to its present in the same breath.

Asientos repeats this feat, but with signal differences. It retraces the institutions and practices of slavery and inserts them within prevailing discourses of race and capitalism, all from the point of view of a young African attempting to come to grips with this repressed chapter of history. The film visually revises the image of Gorée Island and thereby extends its significance for the present. Like *Reou Takh,* its most apparent concern is slavery, and as far as the latter is emblematic of human suffering, the film posits possible parallels with contemporary abuses of human beings in Africa in general, with visual references to recent events and tragedies in Ethiopia and Rwanda. It ruminates on the past while linking it to the present, and it poses questions about the future.

Unlike the linear realist narrative mode of *Reou Takh, Asientos* undertakes the task of re-memory, reconstruction, and reconnection by means of a skillful and highly imaginative blend of collage (of disparate images, sounds, and silence), of documentary and invention, juxtapositions, contrapuntal montage, poetry, direct address, and rhetorical questions. Its visual style and rhythm endow the film with formal elements that mark it as different, if not "new," relatively speaking. However, despite its novelty *Asientos* bears certain formal and stylistic marks of Djibril Diop Mambety's 1972 classic *Touki-Bouki* as well as Med Hondo's *Soleil O* and Haile Gerima's *Sankofa*.

The film that has thus far been hailed as the most imaginative and compelling revisioning of the story of slavery and resistance from an African point of view is no doubt Haile Gerima's *Sankofa*, which foregrounds race and gender in a Pan-African renarration of the experience of slavery. At the beginning of *Sankofa*, an off-screen poetic voice combines with Kofi Ghanaba's "atumpan" drums along with a montage of diverse images and sounds to invoke and exhort the spirits of the dead, the maimed, the damaged, the raped, and the brutalized to rise up and tell their story. Embodied in this verbal and nonverbal call, addressed primarily to the present heirs of a brutalized past, is Gerima's belief and faith in the ability—indeed, the imperative—of the Black wretched of the earth to assume positions of primary agency in the construction of a different present and future order by interrogating and learning from the past. What the past can do for the present and the future is, indeed, what *Sankofa* is mostly about, and as the Akan proverb states, "*Se wo were fi na wo sankofa a yenkyi*" (It is not a taboo to go back and fetch it if you forget). We are permitted to return and retrieve. *Sankofa* starts in the present (a present that articulates and resonates with the past), then flashes back into history (a history momentarily interrupted to call forth the present), and "ends" in the present (a present projected into the future). Thus, *Sankofa* is as much about the past as it is about the present and the future of Black people all over the world.

Sankofa resonates with Gerima's other films, which all foreground African and Black subject positions to tell stories of oppression and, more importantly, of active resistance, self-affirmation, and liberation: *Child of Resistance* (1972); *Bush Mama* (1976); *Wilmington 10, USA 10,000* (1976); *Harvest: 3000 Years* (1976); *Ashes and Embers* (1981); and *Adwa: An African Victory* (1999). In all these films, Gerima not only privileges African and Black points of view, but equally significant is his imaginative deployment of Black *habitus*, the use of a broad range of the artistic resources of African and Black traditions of narrative, music, and movement to construct filmic narratives that are at once complex, multilayered, multitextured, multilingual, and extremely compelling. In Gerima's work, form—or more generally, representation—is of paramount importance, aesthetically and politically, for it is the *ways* in which he avails himself of the full range of the artistic heritage of a broader Pan-African world to construct his narratives that constitute much of the force and originality of his oeuvre. This is certainly the case with *Sankofa*.

In *Sankofa*, Gerima, an Ethiopian, appropriates an indigenous Akan (West African) metaphor of past, present, and future to retell the story of slavery from Pan-African subject positions. The result is a refreshingly innovative and extremely engaging and complex filmic version of this moment in Black history, a version that is radically different from dominant Hollywood and academic narratives of slavery. *Sankofa* details the brutality and inhumanity of slavery from the point of view of a Black woman, Shola (played by Oyafunmike Ogun-lano, an African American), who seamlessly interweaves her own personal narrative with that of the other subjugated Blacks on the Lafayette slave planta-tion. Gerima approaches the brutality and inhumanity of the slave system in ways that position the spectator to transcend it in order to focus more on the characteristics of creativity, strength, resilience, and will and on the liberatory struggles and actions of those subjected to its regime of oppression and dehu-manization. More significantly, it posits these characteristics as potent cultural armor, the most enduring legacy of the past, still useful and enabling for the present as well as the future.

Gerima's *Sankofa* offers a complex perspective in contrast to dominant nar-ratives on slavery, which tend to be apologetic and patronizing and which pro-ject a generally homogenized, historyless, passive Black victim-object who re-signs him- or herself to the condition of slavery—usually masked as benign and a form of salvation from African barbarity—and who may occasionally make demands, through some mild actions, for better treatment by "massa." *Sankofa* problematizes, subverts, and ultimately negates slavery's claims of absolute con-trol of the minds and bodies of those it subjugates—a perspective that perme-ates most dominant narratives. It constructs the subjugated as complex subjects with histories, desires, and differences; and it represents them as individuals with a clear sense of self and other, actively resisting and contesting and, at times, collaborating with an inhumane system, but more often actively articu-lating freedom and struggling for liberation.

Subjugation in *Sankofa* is a temporary condition. The narrative thrust is to-ward struggle, change, and liberation; and spectators are put on alert from the very beginning to orient themselves to this direction. Whereas dominant nar-ratives adopt a linear mode to freeze slavery in the past, fix it predominantly in America, and thus posit a radical rupture between Africa and the Diaspora that slavery created in part, *Sankofa* critically deploys the Akan metaphor of unbro-ken spiral—"sankofa"—in order to connect the past to the present and to erase geocultural boundaries between Africa and the Diaspora. Hence, Gerima's sus-tained focus on the internal dynamics of the subjugated Black community in the narrative. The amount of screen time occupied by White slave masters and their essentialist discourses is limited, as is their staying power. They appear only to eventually fade away, be eliminated, and give way to Black subjugated voices in all their diversity and complexity—for *Sankofa* is, indeed, their story.

The narrative strategies adopted by Gerima in *Sankofa* enhance the pro-foundness and complexity of the story. Nonlinearity; constant temporal and spatial shifts; use of mythic elements such as the buzzard to enable such shifts; contrapuntal montage; repetition; multiple layering of sound, music, and voices; shifts in narrative points of view even while privileging that of a female captive, Shola; stories within stories; flashbacks; memory—all these are skill-fully conflated to invent a film language that most effectively and appropriately captures and conveys the heartbeat of this story of struggle, of change, and of liberation. It is in the area of narrative technique and form that *Sankofa* distinguishes itself, and Gerima's skill and bold inventiveness with film language enable him to make spectators see and discursively experience slavery in new ways.

Nunu (Alexandra Duah of Ghana), Shango (Mutabaruka of Jamaica), the numerous courageous field hands, and the Maroons constitute the principal agents of this movement. Their stories are filtered through the voice of Shola, a central figure who, along with Nunu, incarnates the metaphor of the past present future. Mona, the contemporary model who has "forgotten" her Africanness, or Blackness—she protests that she is an American—is able to construct a different sense of her identity only after she returns mentally to the past, inhabits the body and soul of Shola, her soul sister of slavery times, and learns from the struggles of Shola and the people around her, such as Nunu and Shango. In Mona, reincarnated as Shola, the present and the past come together. Mona physically returns to Africa as a model/tourist, to Cape Coast Castle in Ghana, the site of operations of slavery, and descends into the dungeons of the castle like the other White tourists to hear the guide narrate aspects of the castle's story. But unlike these other tourists, she receives a different lesson in history. She is confronted with and captured by the spirits of captive Africans of history and is obliged to make a mental journey back into this history across the Atlantic Ocean. When she emerges from the depths of the dungeon from her communion with Shola, she has undergone an epiphany—one that enables her to see, experience, and read the meaning and significance of the castle for herself, in particular, in new ways. Similarly, Joe (Nick Medley), who also experiences a severe identity crisis, arrives at a different sense of self only after embracing the heritage of his mother, Nunu, of whom he was ashamed and whom he tragically murdered along with Father Raphael, after negating the teachings of the latter.

These are two examples of the nature of the discourse of subjugation and change that *Sankofa* engages. It is a process that anchors itself in history and in African cultures, and it is a complex sense of history and culture that Gerima represents in complex and aesthetically challenging ways. The call of the poetic voice over, the call of Kofi Ghanaba's "atumpan" drums, the call of history, has been heard by many in the Diaspora, and some of these are the ones seated on the cliffs of Cape Coast Castle facing the waters of the Atlantic awaiting others like Mona, the most recent *arrivant*.

Significantly, Gerima's wife, Shirikiana Aina, in her 1998 film *Through the Door of No Return,* profiles these Diaspora Africans who responded to the call of Kwame Nkrumah, the first president of Ghana, in 1957 for African Americans to consider Ghana a home to which they can return. Aina's film not only explores the personal histories, vision, and motivation of these returnees but also, most importantly, asks the Ghanaian hosts if they "remember us": those who were taken across the ocean centuries earlier.

In contrast to *Sankofa* and a few other films that indict Europe and its agents as major culprits in the tragedy of slavery and the slave trade, the most recent film by Roger Gnoan Mbala, *Adanggaman,* focuses exclusively on the part played by Africans in this tragedy. *Adanggaman* positions itself as a radical departure from its few predecessors in that its subject matter and target of criti-

West Indies: Les Nègres marrons de la liberté (West Indies: Black Maroons of Freedom, 1979) by Med Hondo (Mauritania).
Françoise Pfaff collection.

cism and indictment is the indigenous African ruling elite, which deployed military and coercive powers to wage war on and subjugate rival populations, some of whom were then sold into slavery. Mbala tells the story of one such despot somewhere in Africa in the seventeenth century, highlighting the role played by the legendary female military regiments, the Amazons. Using a love story to anchor his revisioning of this aspect of African history, Mbala also dramatizes the resistance by individuals and communities to these indigenous despots.

Another recent film that also brings to the fore and interrogates the African role in the slave trade, albeit in a different register, is the docufiction *Middle Passage* (1999) by Guy Deslauriers (Martinique). *Middle Passage* revisions the experience of slavery from the point of view of the captives holed up in the slave ships as they make their way across the ocean to the New World. Deslauriers is also the director of *L'Exil de Behanzin* (Exile of Behanzin), a 1994 feature about the Dahomean monarch, King Ahydjère Behanzin, who, after many years of resisting the French, was subdued and forced into exile to Martinique in 1890 by the French.

The films of Med Hondo, *Soleil O, West Indies,* and *Sarraounia,* inscribe themselves within a different current of revisioning history on film. Hondo is generally regarded as one of the most talented, vocal, and rather uncompromising advocates for a genuinely revolutionary African and Black cinema, in terms of both subject matter and technique. The ensemble of his cinematic oeuvre constitutes a significant segment of the African and Third World cinema "movement" whose project is to redefine and reorient the use of cinema in the context of the historical as well as contemporary experiences and challenges of these societies.

Hondo's work also registers a certain shift away from much of mainstream African cinema, particularly in matters of thematic focus, approach, tone, and temperament. The dominant preoccupation in films ranging from his first feature *Soleil O* (1970) to *Les Bicots-Nègres vos voisins* (Arabs and Niggers, Your Neighbors, 1973) to *West Indies* (1979), for example, is the conditions and struggles of immigrant workers and populations in France, whose experiences with French nationals and institutions are figured as a metaphor for slavery, colonialism, and their legacies in Africa and the Caribbean. This focus on the Black experience in France, seen from the perspective of history, and Hondo's transgressive deployment of a broad range of cinematic, linguistic, and musical codes combine to confer on his work a kind of enduring relevance and poignancy well beyond the temporal setting of the narratives. To be convinced of the staying power and prophetic dimension of Hondo's early and mid-1970s narratives, one has only to cast a quick glance at the present climate in France, with the ascendancy of Jean-Marie "the-Holocaust-was-a-detail-of-history" LePen and his far-right neo-Nazi primitive nationalist program and the insidious nod and complicity of the Gaullist right and segments of the liberal center-left.

Sarraounia is the fourth feature length film by Med Hondo. The result of seven years of constant struggle with insufficient financial resources and extremely difficult conditions of production, *Sarraounia* has been hailed as one of the first truly African cinematic epics. Neither historical nostalgia nor a romance of past glory, *Sarraounia* is a song in praise of dignity, determination, difference, and devotion to ideals of freedom, justice, tolerance, understanding, and love. It is also a study on the mentality of terror as well as a lament about closed minds and their dehumanizing consequences.

An adaptation of a novel by Abdoulaye Mamani of Niger, who culled the material for his narrative from oral traditions as well as written documents, *Sarraounia* reconstructs and reinterprets an important and tragic period in the history of West Africa and its encounters with European colonialism. The narrative is based on actual events that transpired in Niger and the surrounding Sahel subregion at the end of the nineteenth century, the high moment of terrorism, pillage, dispossession, and subjugation directed at Africa and Africans in the name of progress, reason, God, country, and civilization. The dawn of the age of empire and colony, this was also the moment of the British ransacking of Benin.

In the wake of the Berlin Conference of 1884–85, at which European countries arbitrarily carved up the African continent into colonies and spheres of influence, France and England, in particular, embarked on a vigorous campaign to effectively occupy, establish, and expand those spaces allotted to them. As part of this program of effective occupation and colonial expansion, the French dispatched a military column under the command of Captains Paul Voulet and Charles Chanoine from the French Sudan (present-day Mali) in 1898 to undertake the conquest of Chad in the east and to put a halt to the advance of Rabah, an Arab adventurer whose project was to set up a kingdom in the heart of Africa. The scorched-earth methods and wanton terrorist cruelty of France's expeditionary force, composed of 8 French officers, 180 regular foot soldiers, 70 nonuniformed auxiliaries, 390 war captives and porters, 260 concubines and female cooks, and their materiel, laid waste to kingdom after kingdom in its path and instilled widespread panic, fear, and destruction among peaceful villages, many of which actually welcomed them with open arms in hope of being spared.

While some kingdoms readily collaborated with the invaders in the hope of finally subduing their feared and independent rival, Sarraounia, and others capitulated without a fight, Sarraounia, queen and military leader of the Aznas, mobilized her people and resources, military as well as magical, to confront the French force that launched a fierce attack on her fortress capital of Lougou. Overwhelmed by the superior firepower of the French, Sarraounia and her fighters retreated tactically from the fortress and engaged the attackers in a protracted guerrilla battle that eventually forced the French to abandon their project of subduing her.

News of the savage atrocities of the Voulet-Chanoine expedition prompted the French military command headquarters to dispatch a seasoned "colonial hand," Colonel Klobb, to go after Voulet and terminate his command. Rather than submit, Voulet killed Klobb, renounced France, and resolved to push on, independent of any French authority. However, before he was able to embark on this lone adventurism, some African foot soldiers revolted and shot him to death.

Having successfully resisted the French, Sarraounia abandoned her former palace and stronghold and set up a new settlement composed of the surviving Azna as well as resisters and refugees from the other neighboring kingdoms that were decimated by French military terror.

Med Hondo follows these events of African and French colonial history to produce a counternarrative that, in its scope, structure, style, tone, and language, accomplishes the compound tasks of recovery, retelling, and reinterpretation in a manner that makes the past speak in new and different ways in the accent of a renovated sense of life and humanity.

Paradoxically, if the film *Sarraounia* un-silenced and unburied an aspect of the African and French colonial past, contemporary French distribution and exhibition circuits worked to silence it again by withdrawing the film from all but one minor theater in Paris three weeks after its opening, while the normally loud and loquacious French television and newspaper film reviewers and critics remained silent. A conspiracy to shield the average French person from engaging a not-so-glorious moment of the land of *liberté, égalité, fraternité*? This is a debatable question, but one that mobilized more than a hundred critics, filmmakers, artists, academics, politicians, and lawyers in France to petition in protest. Perhaps Jean Suret-Canale captures it best when he expresses his anxiety: "Je crains moins pour lui l'attaque directe . . . que l'étouffement insidieux, la consigne du silence" (More than the direct attack, I fear for him . . . the insidious stifling, the order to silence). A similar fate was also meted out to Ousmane Sembene's *Camp de Thiaroye* (1988) when, it is reported, instructions were given to all French Cultural Centers in Africa not to screen the film in their facilities.

Sarraounia relates parallel narratives of struggle, sacrifice, determination, and vision—one historical and the other contemporary. The conflation of the past and the present in the story of the legendary Queen Sarraounia and in the story of the production, distribution, and exhibition of the finished film itself is a revealing and instructive aspect of African creativity and resilience.

Like other Africans engaged in memory work and history, such as traditional oral artists, griots, creative writers, visual artists, and scholars, African filmmakers have increasingly undertaken the task of retelling the African past and of looking at the present in the past from their own diverse subject positions. Such tasks take on the aura and weight of a cultural duty and obligation, for as Frantz Fanon correctly observed: "Colonialisation is not satisfied merely with holding a people in its grip and emptying the native's brain of all form and content. By a kind of perverted logic, it turns to the past of the oppressed people, and distorts, disfigures and destroys it" (1963, 170).

The histories of Africans as well as former colonies—written, authorized, and validated by non-Africans—have been characterized by "exclusions, erasures, silences, distortions, and arbitrary fictions"; and because of this, filmmakers and others have taken on the task of "purging their histories of imposed remembrances" and privileging the voices of hitherto suppressed subjects in order to construct different histories of Africa and Africans (Francia 1983). Filmmakers engaged in such projects inscribe themselves within a tradition of radical counterhistoriography and discourse exemplified in the work of Cheikh Anta Diop, John Hendrik Clark, Walter Rodney, Basil Davidson, and many others.

As I have indicated elsewhere (Cham 1993), a few common features run through these different film versions of history, as the preceding descriptions and analyses have, I trust, identified. These films recover and rearticulate aspects of African popular memory and subaltern voices to preserve as well as reconfigure past events. They seem to take to heart the perceptive observation by Malian sage Amadou Hampaté Ba that in Africa, "when an old person dies, it's like a library burning down." In their radical reconstruction of Euro-Christian as well as Arab-Islamic histories and how these are implicated in African history, these films also conflate Euro-Christianity and Arab-Islam as two sides of the same colonial coin, as cognate systems of cultural domination.

The national as well as the Pan-African nature and dimension of these histories, as well as the recovery and reconstitution of African women's histories (mostly from male viewpoints because of the predominance of male filmmakers), are also highlighted in many of these films. Moreover, these films deconstruct European ideologies of self and other, and construct and privilege more diverse and complex African subject positions with particular attention to categories of race, ethnicity, religion, and gender. Most importantly, all of these films affirm African agency and subjectivity, grounding their versions of history, as Stuart Hall observes in another context (1992, 222), not on archeology and simple recovery, but on imaginative, purposeful production and retelling, anchored in a fusion of individual vision with a shared collective memory to put in place what the late South African novelist Bessie Head calls a "sense of historical community."

Notes

Part of the research for this essay was made possible by the generous support of the Howard University-Sponsored Faculty Research Program in the Social Sciences, Humanities and Education, and the National Endowment for the Humanities.

An earlier version of the text was presented at the First International Conference on Film and History, University of Cape Town, Cape Town, South Africa, July 6-8, 2002.

1. SACOD stands for Southern African Communications for Development. The four films in the *Landscape of Memory* series are: *Nda Mona* (*I Have Seen,* 1999) by Richard Pakleppa, Namibia; *From the Ashes* (1998) by Karen Boswall, Mozambique; *Soul in Torment* (1998) by Prudence Uriri, Zimbabwe; and *The Unfolding Sky* (1998) by Antjie Krog and Ronelle Roots, South Africa.

2. Some of the significant works here include: *Night John* by Charles Burnett, United States; *Rosewood* by John Singleton, United States; *Daughters of the Dust* by Julie Dash, United States; the courtroom dramas of Christian Lara of Guadeloupe: *Vivre libre ou mourir* (Live Free or Die, 1980) and *Sucre amer* (Bitter Sugar, 1997); and Raoul Peck's revisionings of Haitian history in *Haitian Corner* (1987), *L'Homme sur les quais* (Man By the Shore, 1993), *Chère Catherine* (Dear Catherine, 1992), and *Haiti: Le silence des chiens* (Haiti: The Silence of Dogs, 1994). There is also an interesting body of work on the subject of slavery and resistance from Cuba and Brazil.

Works Cited

Cham, Mbye. 1993. "Official History, Popular Memory: Reconfiguration of the African Past in the Films of Ousmane Sembène." In *Ousmane Sembène: Dialogues with Critics and Writers,* ed. Samba Gadjigo et al., 22–28. Amherst: University of Massachusetts Press. Reprinted in *The Historical Film: History and Memory in Media,* ed. Marcia Landy, 261–66. New Brunswick, N.J.: Rutgers University Press, 2001.

Fanon, Frantz. 1963. *The Wretched of the Earth.* Trans. Constance Farrington. New York: Grove.

Francia, Luis. 1983. "The Other Cinema." *Village Voice,* 17 May, 63.

Green, Michael. 1997. *Novel Histories: Past, Present and Future in South African Fiction.* Johannesburg: Witwatersrand University Press.

Hall, Stuart. 1992. "Cultural Identity and Cinematic Representation." In *EX-ILES: Essays on Caribbean Cinema,* ed. Mbye Cham, 220–36. Trenton, N.J.: Africa World Press.

Mazrui, Ali A. 1986. *The Africans: A Triple Heritage.* PBS/BBC Documentary Series.
Nkrumah, Kwame. 1964. *Consciencism.* London: Heinemann.
Rosenstone, Robert A., ed. 1995. Introduction. In *Revisioning History: Film and the Construction of a New Past,* 8–13. Princeton, N.J.: Princeton University Press.
Suret-Canale, Jean. 1986. "*Sarraounia,* un film de Med Hondo." *L'Afrique Aujourd'hui* 33.
Werber, Richard, ed. 1998. *Memory and the Postcolony: African Anthropology and the Critique of Power.* London: Zed.

4 Fiction, Fact, and the Critic's Responsibility: *Camp de Thiaroye, Yaaba,* and *The Gods Must Be Crazy*
Josef Gugler

> Any "historical" film, like any work of written, graphic, or oral history, enters a body of preexisting knowledge and debate. To be considered "historical," rather than just a costume drama that uses the past as an exotic setting for romance and adventure, a film must engage, directly or obliquely, the issues, ideas, data, and arguments of the ongoing discourse of history. Like the book, the historical film cannot exist in a state of historical innocence, cannot indulge in capricious invention, cannot ignore the findings and assertions and arguments of what we already know from other sources. Like any work of history, a film must be judged in terms of the knowledge of the past that we already possess. Like any work of history, it must situate itself within a body of other works, the ongoing (multimedia) debate over the importance of events and the meaning of the past.
>
> —Robert A. Rosenstone, *Visions of the Past*

Film is a powerful medium. The profound emotional experience it can provide may be matched by prose fiction, but visual images convey unfamiliar settings more effectively than writing, and they make abstract concepts come alive. Cinema draws together and embodies in individual characters aspects of politics, society, and culture that tend to be separated in scientific accounts. Films can play a unique role in familiarizing Westerners with Africa, in understanding the continent and its people, and in becoming engaged with African experiences. For these very reasons, the veracity of feature films introducing viewers to Africa is a matter of concern.

Scholars are prone to dismiss such concerns by emphasizing the fictional character of feature films. And indeed, directors of feature films, like writers of fiction, have every license to rewrite the past as well as the present. They may argue that what matters is not factual accuracy but the significance of events, and they may claim artistic license to influence the audience more effectively: to make us empathize with their heroes, reject their villains, or experience ambiguity. Still, the "this is just fiction" response fails to acknowledge the power of fiction in shaping ideas and influencing action. This matters all the more because feature films, as a rule, reach a much wider audience than documentaries, the supposed vehicles to convey "the facts," and are more likely to have viewers identify with their characters. Fiction is particularly powerful when audiences have little factual information and tend to assume that fiction and fact coincide. Such is the case for many viewers, especially non-African viewers, of African films. The naïve assumptions of many such viewers that they are being introduced to African "reality" are fostered by the realistic presentation that most African films adopt.

Many scholars reinforce the "this is just fiction" stance by observing that there is no such thing as "fact" anyhow—history is selective and subject to alternative interpretations; all history can be considered fiction. Thus, when we introduce the historical record to contextualize fiction, we constantly confront the challenge: Whose record? In many cases, however, there can be little argument that fiction diverges in important ways from the history it claims to portray. In this chapter, three feature films, each significant in its own right in terms of the status of its director, critical acclaim, and/or popular success, will illustrate how directors omit key elements in the historical record, add new elements, or significantly alter historical events.

The creators of fiction are free to take liberties with the historical record. It is incumbent on the critic, however, to alert audiences to significant divergences between the historical record and fiction. Where critics endorse fictional recreations, if only by failing to problematize the accuracy of depiction, they are instrumental in rewriting history. Moreover, they miss the opportunity to enrich our understanding of fiction, because gaps between historical record and fiction reveal the historical perspectives and political agendas of directors as well as their aesthetic and dramatic strategies.

Camp de Thiaroye

Our culture and our past have been denied for a long time. History has been buried, and our dead have refused to die a second death. We have to recover the everyday dimension, the relations we had with our colonizers.

—"Sembene Ousmane parle" (my translation)

Camp de Thiaroye, the accomplished film by Ousmane Sembene, Africa's most prominent director, and Thierno Faty Sow, relates a specific historical event in 1944, the revolt of African soldiers who were mistreated as they awaited discharge from the French army in Senegal and the infamous massacre that ensued. The event remained deeply embedded in the memory of African veterans. Many, not only in Senegal but in distant former French colonies, were able to recall it thirty years later. For a younger generation of Francophone Africans today, *Camp de Thiaroye* presents a fitting monument to the abuses of colonial rule (Echenberg 1991, 169–70).[1] However, while personalizing the story and dramatizing the action, the film took major liberties with the historical record.

The camp at Thiaroye, just outside Dakar, held some 1,280 Africans about to

Poster of *Camp de Thiaroye*. Published as *Nuovi Graffiti d'Africa* #36 by the Centro Orientamento Educativo, Milan, Italy.

be demobilized and repatriated. Early in World War II they had become prisoners of war when French resistance to Germany collapsed in 1940. Held in prisoner of war camps in occupied France, they were liberated when the Allies invaded France in 1944.[2] Later that year they were the first contingent to be shipped back to Africa. They had fought fascism alongside troops from metropolitan France, suffered imprisonment together with the French, and gained a measure of recognition and respect in France, but now they encountered French colonial officials intent on returning them to the position of colonial subjects. Resentment for such treatment was exacerbated by conflicts over back pay and the conversion of their French francs into CFA francs, the currency in French West Africa. They briefly held a general hostage, and their subsequent mutiny was brutally repressed (Echenberg 2002).

Camp de Thiaroye is a Pan-African production with funding and resources from Senegal, Tunisia, and Algeria and no financial or technical support from Europe.[3] The subject matter may also be the reason that this film, codirected by Africa's foremost filmmaker after a hiatus of twelve years, was not invited to the Cannes Film Festival and received no distribution in France (Armes 1996). At the Venice Film Festival, *Camp de Thiaroye* received the Special Jury Prize for its technical quality. The film was enthusiastically acclaimed by established specialist critics such as Manthia Diawara (1992, 156–58), John Downing (1996, 193, 196–204), and Nwachukwu Frank Ukadike (1994, 292–97).

Kenneth Harrow (1995) has raised the lone dissenting voice problematizing the historical perspective in *Camp de Thiaroye*. He shows that Sembene elaborated a ready-made truth that relied on binarism, eliding the complexity of history. The film omits any suggestion of conflict among soldiers recruited across Africa from different ethnic groups and with different religious beliefs. It presents an easy understanding between an African sergeant and an African-American soldier. And it never shows the soldiers carrying out the massacre—fellow Africans.[4] While such simplifications are common in a medium that tends to present less differentiated stories than does written fiction, their impact on unaware viewers is problematic. Even more problematic is that *Camp de Thiaroye* altogether misrepresents the events leading to the massacre.

In *Camp de Thiaroye,* the release of the hostaged general is followed by the film's harrowing climax as tanks arrive in the middle of the night and proceed to shell the sleeping soldiers' barracks—the film poster features a tank lit up by a search light. The massacre actually took place under very different circumstances. Myron Echenberg, the foremost authority on the *tirailleurs sénégalais,* provides a detailed account and analysis of events at Thiaroye on the basis of archival research and interviews with veterans, including one sentenced to prison for his involvement. Echenberg describes the events leading up to the mutiny and its suppression:

> Hostility on money matters and especially toward the manner in which French colonial officials were treating them nearly spilled over into violence on November 26 as the French began to convert the soldiers' money into French West African currency. The conversion took place amid loud protests from the soldiers that they were being cheated out of their money. Some soldiers were said to have remarked, "Thieves! We earned our money; we won't leave this camp until we have killed these French pigs!" Only with difficulty were the French able to restore order. So uneasy had the situation become that the military command decided two days later to dispatch some 500 men toward Bamako [Mali], and the Commanding General of Dakar and region, General Dagnan, made a personal visit to assure this

departure in a calm manner. So angry had the men become that they went as far as to capture General Dagnan and hold him prisoner for a few hours. On his promise that the men would receive their money within three days, he was released.

The French had no intention of letting events deteriorate further. Upon learning of the mutinous state of the ex-POWs, the Commanding General for West Africa, General de Boisboissel, ordered reinforcements of troops and police sent down from Saint Louis [Senegal]; these additional forces surrounded the camp of Thiaroye on November 30, the day the French had now decided upon for dispatching the 500 men to Bamako. For some reason, the dispatching was postponed once again, this time to the next day, December 1, 1944. The French effort to ship out these men that morning was the signal for the mutiny to begin. The soldiers began jostling their officers, most of whom were reservists from metropolitan rather than colonial units, that is, officers with little experience or rapport with their men. After the call to order failed, a first salvo was fired in the air. The men ran to the barracks to get their weapons. Now the order was given to shoot to kill with the result that 35 men fell immediately and the same number lay seriously wounded.

Order was quickly restored. Some 34 men were arrested and marched through the streets of Dakar under machine gun escort, a decision deliberately taken in order to intimidate the local population. (Echenberg 2002, 116)

As for the tanks, the French had none in West Africa in 1944 (Echenberg, personal communication).

Within days of the repression, the Governor General of French West Africa wrote to the Minister of Colonies that the use of force "could not be permitted to be repeated, under any pretext whatsoever" (Echenberg 2002, 120). Still, the arrested men were all found guilty and sentenced to prison terms ranging from one to ten years. Political pressure from African members of the French National Assembly, Léopold Sédar Senghor prominent among them, and veterans' associations led to a general amnesty proclaimed in November 1946 for the convicted men and those still in prison to be released in June 1947. The massacre gave impetus to the establishment of veterans' associations all across French West Africa and had major repercussions for the nascent independence movement (Echenberg 2002). As the generation of veterans was dying, *Camp de Thiaroye* created a new public awareness of the massacre. December 1 became National Veterans' Day in Senegal in 1993, just ahead of the fiftieth anniversary the following year.

Camp de Thiaroye created dramatic impact by proceeding from the release of the hostage to the impressive sequence of tank cannon and machinegun flashing in the dark of the night and the camp going up in flames.[5] According to Thierno Faty Sow, he and Sembene had "drawn on the national archives, Sembène's personal documentation, books on the history of the *tirailleurs*, newspaper clippings, and above all, accounts of survivors of the drama of Thiaroye" (Gharbi 1988, 17, my translation). But failing to acknowledge that the massacre was a direct response to mutinous soldiers about to fetch their weapons also profoundly distorts the record.[6] There are plenty of colonial abuses that remain unexposed, but distortion of the historical record served little purpose a generation after independence.[7] Indeed, it may be argued that demonizing the colonial Other hinders an understanding of colonialism and its aftermath.[8] Such understanding requires, to return to the point made by Kenneth Harrow, moving beyond Manichaean constructs and accepting that Africans were active participants in colonial rule and neocolonial manipulation.[9]

Almost all critical comment on *Camp de Thiaroye* appears eager to endorse Sembene's representation of French colonialism. None of the critics bothered to query the film's version of events.[10] Such is the case even for those familiar with Echenberg's work, who endorsed fiction without regard for fact.[11]

Yaaba

> *Yaaba* is based on tales of my childhood and on that kind of bedtime storytelling we hear just before falling asleep. (Idrissa Ouedraogo)

Idrissa Ouedraogo's *Yaaba*, set in Burkina Faso, is one of the finest African films and has become a classic. A beautifully filmed morality tale, it touchingly conveys the humanity of its characters and offers a message of tolerance.[12] In 1989 *Yaaba* won the International Critics' Prize at the Cannes Film Festival, the Special Prize of the FESPACO Jury, and the Sakura Gold Prize at the Tokyo International Film Festival. And it is one of the few African films to have achieved substantial commercial distribution.

Yaaba introduces viewers to life in an African village. We see simple dwellings and begin to comprehend complex relationships. We witness cooperation and conflict in a family and come to see that it extends beyond the nuclear family. We get a sense of a village community as its members unite to assist a family that has lost its food supplies, dance together to celebrate a wedding, and mourn a dying child. And we come to appreciate what it means to be cast out by such a community, as is an old woman in the film, or to be marginalized, as is a drunkard. The film conveys a slow peasant mode: Ouedraogo uses long shots as the camera leisurely pans the wide open landscape, as it follows the slow progress of characters dwarfed by the vast expanse. All speech in *Yaaba* is in Moré, the language of the Mossi villagers portrayed. Indeed, if viewers are so inclined, they can learn some Moré, as they count with children playing games, pick up a greeting phrase, and perhaps hear a couple of insults. Ouedraogo shot the film in Tougouzagué, a village a few miles from his birthplace. He recruited villagers and relatives as actors and managed to get them to act naturally. Ouedraogo succeeded at presenting an exemplary account of village life.[13]

Ouedraogo based *Yaaba* on tales of his childhood, and the film portrays a village outside of history. Nothing takes the viewer to precolonial times, nor is there any indication of a colonial presence. Ouedraogo himself put the village squarely in the present: "This village lives as I show it in the film; there is no reconstitution; everything was shot in natural settings" (Gavron 1989). But he also acknowledged that "the reality of Africa today is not as untouched as in my film" (Bernard 1989, my translation). While the setting is contemporary, the isolation of the village belongs to a distant past. All traces of government, taxes,

ARCADIA FILMS PARIS, LES FILMS DE L'AVENIR OUAGADOUGOU, THELMA FILM A.G. ZURICH PRESENTENT

UN FILM DE IDRISSA OUEDRAOGO

YAABA

AVEC SANGA FATIMATA / NOUFOU OUEDRAOGO / ROUKIETOU BARRY / RASMANE OUEDRAOGO

Poster of *Yaaba*. Published as *Nuovi Graffiti d'Africa* #50 by the Centro Orientamento Educativo, Milan, Italy.

schools, or clinics have been eliminated. Market relations do not reach beyond a big tree within walking distance where a few people gather with local products. About ten percent of the population of Burkina Faso does temporary work in foreign countries at any one time, yet there is no indication that any migrant ever returned to this village; no trace of anything he might have sent, or brought, or be using now; no transistor radio, not even a single T-shirt. The film poster emphasizes this isolation by showing the three principal characters against a barren landscape. A village such as this would be hard to find in Africa today— or anywhere else for that matter.[14]

As Manthia Diawara has pointed out, the isolation of the village in *Yaaba* ignores complex social, political, and historical issues (1992, 162). Instead, the plot turns on animistic beliefs and human foibles and becomes a plea for tolerance. Western viewers are unlikely to connect an old woman's outcast position to her history as an orphan who lacked family support. Rather, they are encouraged, once again, to assign "superstition" to the Other while taking their own supposed rationality for granted. The constancy of two friendships—between a boy and the old woman and between two children—assures us that we are witnessing a society in harmony but for "superstition" and personal failings.

Presenting the village as isolated from time immemorial makes *Yaaba* particularly attractive to Western audiences that are interested in such a different culture but would rather not be reminded of the West's role in slavery and colonialism, its continued dominance in the contemporary world, and the manifold problems plaguing contemporary Africa. Western viewers may appreciate their good luck at not living in village poverty, but in *Yaaba* that poverty is taken for granted; its causes are not at issue. We see the empty landscape of the Sahel, but people have food reserves to share when a family's granary burns down. The old woman is destitute because she has been outcast, not because of a general state of poverty. She and the two children are beautifully drawn, but the film's focus on them raises a further issue. Their very status, two children and an old destitute woman, invite the patronizing Western gaze: Western viewers are encouraged to strike, once again, a posture of benevolence vis-à-vis Africans. Françoise Pfaff (1993) was prompted to raise the troubling question of whether *Yaaba* had been conceived in terms of its European cosponsors.[15]

Yaaba introduces Western viewers to African peasants and their village context. But it is incumbent on the critic to alert viewers to the fact that the film cannot be taken as the depiction of a contemporary African village. Furthermore, many viewers need reminding that very different kinds of villages are to be found across the continent (Gugler 2002).

The Gods Must Be Crazy: The World According to Apartheid

> I asked him through an interpreter if he would like to work for us, but they have no word for "work" so he didn't understand. Then I just asked if he would like to come with us, and he immediately said O.K. (Jamie Uys, speaking of N!xau, in a 1984 interview with Janet Maslin)

The Gods Must Be Crazy was produced, written, directed, filmed, and edited by Jamie Uys, a well-established South African filmmaker. It is a very funny movie about an African Garden of Eden. Voice over of !Kung[16] and Tswana dialogue and a dubbed English version of the Afrikaans original make

Poster of *The Gods Must Be Crazy*.
Courtesy of Ace Films Corporation.

it more easily accessible than most African films. It has been a huge success. On its release in South Africa, *The Gods Must Be Crazy* shattered every box office record. The film had its greatest success in Japan, where it was the highest grossing movie in 1982. In France, it won the Grand Prize at the Chamrousse Festival dedicated to film comedies in 1982 and became the top box office success in 1983. In the United States, after a false start in 1982, it was released afresh in

1984, moved from art houses to commercial theaters, and became the biggest foreign box office hit in movie history. A major television network continues to show it, and most video stores carry it. The film's triumph inspired a sequel, *The Gods Must Be Crazy II*, as well as three Hong Kong productions featuring the movie's African protagonist, N!Xau.

Slapstick and broad humor are so persuasive that many Western viewers fail to perceive the underlying ideology. *The Gods Must Be Crazy* pokes fun at the tyranny of the clock over "civilized man," and Andrew Steyn, the bumbling Afrikaner scientist, is good for many laughs. But as we encounter Africans, we are initiated into the worldview of apartheid. The film introduces us to four kinds of Africans: traditional Africans who are happy and content until modern society intrudes; good Africans who are grateful for the help of White people; incompetent Africans who run governments; and bad Africans who have been led astray by evil foreigners.

!Xi, the "traditional" African, is the film's chief protagonist. He is not an individualized character, but rather the representative of the "bushmen," to use the derogatory term employed in the film. The film starts out as a documentary about the "bushmen." We are told that they live in the Kalahari Desert, which "is devoid of people, except the little people. Pretty, dainty, small, graceful, the bushmen... They must be the most contented people in the world... No crime, no punishment, no violence, no laws, no police, no judges, no rulers or bosses." It takes a Coca Cola bottle, dropped from an airplane—the ultimate symbol of Western superiority, to shatter the happy life of people who do not know money and are not used to walls. And we listen to their voices, which go "click," "click," "click." !Kung does use click sounds, but the film overlaid some of the dialogue with extra clicks, thus enhancing its exoticism for the benefit of Western viewers (Volkman 1988). The !Kung, however, do not get much of a voice. Most of the time the narrator speaks for !Xi and his family. Only in a few instances are !Xi's thoughts or words translated.

The !Kung, or San, have seen their land encroached upon by European settlers for centuries. And they happen to have been the subject of a great deal of anthropological research as well as a series of documentaries produced by John Marshall between 1951 and 1978. Marshall drew on his documentaries and the work of a leading researcher, Marjorie Shostak (1983), to produce *N!ai, the Story of a !Kung Woman.* Unlike Uys's tale, he shows traditional !Kung life as characterized by severe hardships. The hunt was difficult: it might take four men five days to track down a giraffe. Early marriage—!Nai was married at age eight to a thirteen-year-old boy—was traumatic for girls who wanted to stay with their mothers. Sexual conflicts and jealousies were rampant. Childbirth was extremely dangerous, the death of children common, and the men who tried to help and cure went into life-threatening trances. By the time Uys made his film, the !Kung had experienced profound changes.

Uys claimed reality for his fictional portrayal of the !Kung by fictionalizing the production of the film. The stories he told reviewers varied. According to one account, he spent three months crisscrossing the Kalahari Desert look-ing for the right man to play !Xi. He took photographs of all likely faces, then "marked the longitude and latitude, so that we could find them again." In Bot-swana he finally found N!Xau, who had seen in his whole life only one other White man, a missionary. When Uys asked him, through his interpreter, if he would come and work with him, N!Xau "didn't understand, because they have no word for work." Every three or four weeks, N!Xau would be flown back to his home in the bush "so he wouldn't suffer culture shock," said Uys. N!Xau had no use for money. Uys found that the money given him "had blown away"—just as in the movie (Klemesrud 1985, 15).

Marshall's documentary, *N!ai, the Story of a !Kung Woman,* reveals the fic-tional character of Uys's account. It shows the filming of *The Gods Must Be Crazy* with N!ai playing !Xi's wife in the hut. We are at the Tshumkwi camp that the South African authorities have established in the northeastern corner of what was still South West Africa. The !Kung live on food handouts, and tuber-culosis is rampant. N!ai's first child and only son died as an adult at Tshumkwi. The South African Defence Force offers a way out of the miserable camp life: it is recruiting !Kung for its war against the SWAPO guerrilla forces fighting for the independence of what was to become Namibia in 1990. As for N!Xau, he had never been the hunter the film depicts. He grew up as a herd boy on a Herero farm in Botswana. In 1976 he moved to Namibia to work as a cook in the Tshumkwi school where Uys found him. N!Xau knew the uses of money very well, but he was paid a mere pittance, 2,000 Rand, then about US$1,700, for *The Gods Must Be Crazy*—which made a fortune: the film cost US$5 million and earned US$90 million in its first four years. Even after these record earnings and after N!Xau had become a national hero in Japan, he had to settle for 5,000 Rand and a monthly retainer of 200 Rand for the lead role in the sequel *The Gods Must Be Crazy II* (Tomaselli 1992; Klemesrud 1985).

In the film, the arrival of Kate Thompson, a South African of British descent, provides a glimpse of the good Africans found in Botswana.[17] She has come to teach Africans—just a few years after hundreds of students had died in South Africa protesting the inferior education imposed on them—and lo and behold, the entire village rises to chant the praises of the good lady! Also in Botswana, a border guard and police officers appear with the forces of good in several scenes. Trouble is, they are invariably surpassed by events. It takes a White man to subdue the forces of evil.

Incompetent Africans run Harare. Here and elsewhere, *The Gods Must Be Crazy* mixes up the geography of southern Africa. But for those who know that Harare is the capital of Zimbabwe, the reference to that country is obvious. We see a cabinet meeting devoted to spending money. The irruption of guerrillas serves to suggest the instability of African government, and the comic vagaries of the army's pursuit of the guerrillas demonstrate that African armies are not to be taken seriously. This way of characterizing neighboring Zimbabwe was particularly pertinent to the concerns of White South Africans. Zimbabwe became independent in 1980, the very year *The Gods Must Be Crazy* was released, and South Africa lost the buffer of a fellow minority regime. As a matter of fact, the newly independent country was subject to subversion instigated by the South African regime and incursions by the South African army.

Guerrillas, of course, are bad Africans. The White minority regime in Zimbabwe had to accept majority rule after a protracted guerrilla war, but *The Gods Must Be Crazy* offers reassurance to the holdouts in the South African White laager. Its guerrillas are dangerous and destructive all right, but they are also indolent and inept. In the end, even Kate Thompson gets to disarm one of them. Their leader, Sam Boga, articulates what the film is showing us about African guerrillas: "Why do I have to work with amateurs?" He, in turn, serves to confirm the apartheid credo that Africans would be happy with the White dispensation were it not for foreigners fomenting discontent and making trouble. While his first name recalls Sam Nujoma, the leader of SWAPO, his Latin looks and his beard à la Fidel Castro reminded South African viewers of the Cuban troops that had come to Angola in response to South Africa's invasion when Portuguese colonial rule came to an end.[18]

The Gods Must Be Crazy introduces viewers to one more distinction. Mpudi, a mechanic from Botswana, would be considered "coloured" in South Africa. As he banters with Steyn, we begin to wonder about his status. Indeed, even if Mpudi feels for the San people, he is just as patronizing as the narrator: "They are the sweetest little buggers." But then we are reminded of the great difference that separates "civilized" Whites from all the other "races": Mpudi, it turns out, has seven wives. Eventually we learn that Mpudi had to flee into the Kalahari Desert and nearly died because he slapped a British colonial officer who had insulted his father. Uys readily condemns colonialism—while perpetuating the myths of apartheid: an ordered world with Whites on top, a world where Africans are content but for the interference of outsiders.

Key elements in the discourse and promotion of *The Gods Must Be Crazy* are reproduced in the South African poster for the film. It features a Cola bottle about to impact like a missile. In the foreground is !Xi in a pose of anguish, behind him four signifying photos: Uys at the camera, in his outfit as the reverend he plays in the film, trades on recognition of the director in South Africa; Steyn carrying Thompson across the stream conveys the love interest; Boga holding a gun to Thompson's head promises suspense; and !Xi and the monkey are presented as part of nature. The text also draws on the director's reputation: "Jamie Uys . . . delighted you with 'Beautiful People,' convulsed you with 'Funny People,' now you'll go crackers with 'The Gods must be Crazy.'" Outside of South Africa, posters obfuscated the racist message, usually by presenting the film as slapstick comedy.

Overseas, *The Gods Must Be Crazy* was released as a "Botswana" production. Still, it sparked vigorous protests, especially in Europe, less so in the United States, which did not hinder the film's smashing success. Japanese and Western audiences were drawn to the story of an African Eden. A condescending and patronizing attitude toward Africans and outright ridicule, such as were no longer acceptable vis-à-vis African Americans, did not impede entertainment at the expense of Africans, whether "traditional," "good," "incompetent," or "bad." The apartheid regime, for its part, fully appreciated that *The Gods Must Be Crazy* was the most successful promotion ever of its ideology. After three decades of producing films, Uys received the highest South African civil decoration in 1983. The citation read in part: "And most especially for having given the example . . . of faith in the future of our country and our people" (Tomaselli 1986, 26; my translation from the French).

Some critics pointed out the film's distortions and racist slant, but most critics readily endorsed Uys's claim of reality for his fiction and argued that any distortions were acceptable because "this is just fun."[19] After all, didn't he ridicule time obsession among his fellow South Africans? Wasn't an Afrikaner the recurrent butt of jokes? However, I am inclined to rejoin: Did the ironic take on Western "civilization" and a Western scientist serve to camouflage the apartheid ideology that the film subtly conveys to its viewers? If that ideology came naturally to the director, why were so many Western critics not sensitive to it several years after the Soweto uprising?

The "this is just fun" argument fails to acknowledge the differential impact of the various elements of the film. Western viewers are competent to reevaluate Western culture and people, no matter how the film misrepresents them. They are familiar with time constraints and, for the most part, don't see them as characteristic of a funny society. And they know the figure of the bumbling scientist from many a comedy and don't generalize to scientists. When it comes to Africa and Africans, however, most Western viewers take film more or less at face value and generalize from its representation of cultures and individuals.

Conclusion

Posters for the three films convey the fictions that are central to the films they promote: in the middle of the night, French tanks kill African men who have fought for France; African villagers live in primordial isolation; the San live in a world apart. Viewers may feel outrage about colonialist perfidy, they may assume that they are introduced to African village life, and they may long for a Garden of Eden. But it is the responsibility of the critic to alert them that what they are seeing is fiction and that it departs in important ways from the reality of Africa and its people.

I began with a quote from Robert Rosenstone, an eminent historian who has engaged film to a greater extent than perhaps any other social scientist. He sets a standard: the critic who accepts a film as "historical" has to judge it in the context of historical knowledge. I would extend that standard to films we view as portrayals of Africa, whether past or present, and that are shown to audiences to introduce them to Africa. We have to judge such portrayals against knowledge of Africa that is already available to us.

Notes

I am grateful to Rachel Gugler, Eileen Julien, Françoise Pfaff, and María Roof for comments that greatly improved this essay, and to Myron Echenberg, who readily responded to my queries. The discussion of *Yaaba* and *The Gods Must Be Crazy* draws on my book *African Film: Re-Imagining a Continent*.

1. In 1985 Ben Diogaye Bèye prepared a film script on the same events, *Thiaroye 44*, but the project did not proceed beyond his text. Boubacar Boris Diop's play *Thiaroye terre rouge* presents the *tirailleurs* preparing an armed uprising against colonial rule.

2. The film resituates some of the men as members of the Free French Forces that were recruited after the 1940 armistice in the French colonies that gave allegiance to Charles de Gaulle and that participated in the liberation of France in 1944.

3. *Camp de Thiaroye* was also Pan-African in the sense that the so-called *tirailleurs sénégalais* were recruited from across the French colonies. Sembene recruited his actors from several former French colonies as well ("Sembene Ousmane parle," 25).

4. Ousmane Sembene's earlier film, *Emitai*, does show African soldiers on the side of colonial oppression.

5. A title in the film indicates that the massacre took place on December 1 at 3 A.M. The date is correct; the time is wrong. An earlier title has the general being taken hostage on November 30 at 10 A.M. The date appears to be wrong, but the time is plausible.

6. Another film classic of military mutiny, *The Battleship Potemkin*, similarly misrepresents events, but the need to sustain the young and embattled Soviet revolution may have been considered urgent.

7. At independence, Sembene published his chef d'œuvre, *God's Bits of Wood*. Like *Camp de Thiaroye*, it recreated a major historical event, the five-month strike of railway workers in French West Africa in 1947–48. The novel exaggerates the violence of French repression. In particular, Sembene created two incidents not found in the records: shootings on the first day of the strike that killed eight people, and a march by women that ended with some of them shot and killed. As Jones (2000) points out in his discussion of the novel, such incidents were unlikely to remain unreported in the colonial records. The historical juncture at which *God's Bits of Wood* was published presents an altogether different issue: Sembene exalted the proletariat at a time when its position was privileged vis-à-vis the peasant masses (Gugler 1994).

8. Michael Atkinson (1993) contrasts the outrage in *Camp de Thiaroye* with the gray-shaded dualities that make Sembene's other films so rich.

9. *Xala*, perhaps Sembene's finest film, presents a trenchant denunciation of neo-colonialism at a time, little more than a decade after independence, when the French presence in its former African colonies was powerful. It depicts the new African elite as *compradores*. For a detailed discussion of the film and the eponymous novel, see Gugler, *African Film*.

10. Instead of focusing on the central theme of the film, the circumstances surrounding the massacre, several critics cited historically inaccurate minor details, which were surprisingly many, as it turns out. Most strikingly, the film identifies some of the *tirailleurs* as former prisoners at Buchenwald concentration camp in Germany, but that camp was not liberated by the Allies until spring 1945. Captain Charles N'Tchorérè was summarily executed by one of his German captors at Airaines, in northern France rather than at Buchenwald, as the film would have it (Echenberg 1991, 166–68).

11. For a recent example of Sembene's fiction becoming historical fact, see Edwards 2002.

12. For an enthusiastic account of the cinematic qualities of *Yaaba*, see Cardullo 1991.

13. For a discussion of *Yaaba* and other African films as anthropological sources, see Pfaff 1990.

14. The portrayal of village life in *Yaaba* bears comparison to that in the most widely read African novel, Chinua Achebe's *Things Fall Apart*. In response to Western accounts that diminish and stereotype Africans, both stories depict differentiated individuals in their full humanity and avoid the temptation to romanticize the African past that characterized earlier attempts to present an African perspective. The key difference between *Yaaba* and *Things Fall Apart* lies in Achebe's situating his novel explicitly at a specific historical juncture. This was a time when the village's relations with the outside world took on new dimensions with the intrusion of Christian missions, the introduction of Western education, greatly expanding trading opportunities, and imposition of colonial rule.

15. The contrast between the critical and popular success of *Yaaba* and the lack of response to Ouedraogo's most recent film, his fine *Kini and Adams,* is striking. Neither critics nor the general public appear ready to forsake village tales for the small dramas of contemporary rural life (see Gugler 2003).

16. "!" serves to indicate the click sound that distinguishes some languages in southern Africa.

17. Botswana's relationship with South Africa was uneasy. On one hand, Botswana, unlike Zimbabwe, was not seen as a threat to the apartheid regime. On the other, South Africa repeatedly attacked South African refugees, supposedly guerrillas, in Botswana.

18. In *The Gods Must Be Crazy II,* a Cuban soldier is just as incompetent as his African adversary. Both soldiers are taken prisoners by a White woman, a corporate lawyer from New York, no less. The film was released in 1989, one year after Angolan government troops and their Cuban allies halted an attack of the South African Defence Force on Cuito Cuanavale that had inflicted heavy losses. The defeat presaged South Africa's retreat from Angola as well as from today's Namibia.

19. For a comprehensive critique, see Davis (1996, 81–94). Tomaselli (1992) reviews the critics' arguments.

Works Cited

Achebe, Chinua. 1958. *Things Fall Apart.* London: Heinemann.

Armes, Roy. 1996. "The Context of the African Filmmaker." In *A Call to Action: The Films of Ousmane Sembene,* ed. Sheila Petty, 11–26. Westport, Conn.: Greenwood.

Atkinson, Michael. 1993. "Ousmane Sembène: 'We Are No Longer in the Era of Prophets.'" *Film Comment* 29.4: 63–67, 69.

Battleship Potemkin / Bronenosets Potemkin. 1925. Film directed by Grigori Alexandro and Sergei Eisenstein, written by Nina Agadzhanova and Sergei Eisenstein. 71 minutes.

Bernard, Jean-Jacques. 1989. "Un plongeon en Afrique." *Première* 149 (August): 29.

Camp de Thiaroye. 1988. Film written and directed by Ousmane Sembène and Thierno Faty Sow. Produced by Société Nouvelle de Promotion Cinématographique (Senegal), ENAPROC (Algeria), and SATPEC (Tunisia). Distributed in the U.S. by New Yorker Films. 152 minutes.

Cardullo, Bert. 1991. "Rites of Passage." *Hudson Review* 44: 96–104.

Davis, Peter. 1996. *In Darkest Hollywood: Exploring the Jungles of Cinema's South Africa*. Randburg: Ravan; Athens: Ohio University Press.

Diawara, Manthia. 1992. *African Cinema: Politics & Culture*. Bloomington: Indiana University Press.

Diogaye Bèye, Ben. Film script of *Thiaroye 44*. Unpublished typescript.

Diop, Boubacar Boris. 1981. *Le Temps de Tamango; Thiaroye terre rouge*. Paris: L'Harmattan.

Downing, John D. H. 1996. "Toward a Richer Vision." In *Cinema, Colonialism, Postcolonialism: Perspectives from the French and Francophone World*, ed. Dina Sherzer, 188–228. Austin: University of Texas Press.

Echenberg, Myron J. 1991. *Colonial Conscripts: The* Tirailleurs Sénégalais *in French West Africa, 1857–1960*. Social History of Africa. Portsmouth, N.H.: Heinemann.

———. 2002. "Tragedy at Thiaroye: The Senegalese Soldiers' Uprising of 1944." In *African Labor History*, ed. Peter C. W. Gutkind, Robin Cohen, and Jean Copans, 109–28. Sage Series on African Modernization and Development 2. Beverly Hills: Sage.

Edwards, Brent Hayes. 2002. "Evidence." *Transition* 90: 42–67.

Emitai. 1971. Film written and directed by Ousmane Sembène. Produced by Myriam Smadja (Senegal) and Filmi Doomireew (Senegal). Distributed in the U.S. by New Yorker Films. 101 minutes.

Gavron, Laurence. 1989. "Ouedraogo et sa 'grand-mère' d'Afrique." *Libération*, 12 May, 35.

Gharbi, Neïla. 1988. "Le réalisateur sénégalais Thierno Faty Sow: *Camp de Thiaroye* un bel example de coopération Sud-Sud." *7e Art* 65: 17–18.

The Gods Must Be Crazy. 1980. Film written and directed by Jamie Uys. Produced by New Realm, Mimosa, and C.A.T. Film (South Africa). 108 minutes.

The Gods Must Be Crazy II. 1989. Film written and directed by Jamie Uys. Produced by Boet Troskie (South Africa). 90 minutes.

Gugler, Josef. 1994. "African Literature and the Uses of Theory." In *Literary Theory and African Literature. Théorie littéraire et littérature africaine*, ed. Josef Gugler, Hans-Jürgen Lüsebrink, and Jürgen Martini, 1–15. Beiträge zur Afrikaforschung 3. Münster: LIT Verlag.

———. 2002. "Images of Villages in Four Recent African Films." In *African Writers and Their Readers: Essays in Honor of Bernth Lindfors*, Vol. 2, ed. Toyin Falola and Barbara Harlow, 501–25. Trenton, N.J.: Africa World Press.

———. 2003. *African Film: Re-Imagining a Continent*. Bloomington: Indiana University Press; Cape Town: David Philip; Oxford: James Currey.

Harrow, Kenneth. 1995. "*Camp de Thiaroye*: Who's That Hiding in Those Tanks, and How Come We Can't See Their Faces?" *iris* 18: 147–52.

Jones, James A. 2000. "Fact and Fiction in *God's Bits of Wood*." *Research in African Literatures* 31.2: 117–31.

Kini and Adams. 1997. Film directed by Idrissa Ouedraogo, written by Idrissa Ouedraogo, Olivier Lorelle, and Santiago Amigorena. Produced by Noé Productions (France), Les Films de la Plaine (France), Polar Productions (Britain), and Framework International (Zimbabwe). Distributed in Southern Africa by DSR2, in France by PolyGram. 93 minutes.

Klemesrud, Judy. 1985. "'The Gods Must Be Crazy'—A Truly International Hit." *New York Times*, 28 April, section 2: 15, 18.

Maslin, Janet. 1984. "A Bushman and the Clash of Cultures." *New York Times*, 6 July, section 3: 8.

N!ai, the Story of a !Kung Woman. 1979. Documentary directed by John Marshall. Distributed in the U.S. by Documentary Educational Resources. 59 minutes.

Ouedraogo, Idrissa. 1989. "Synopsis." Press kit for *Yaaba.*

Pfaff, Françoise. 1990. "Africa from Within: The Films of Gaston Kaboré and Idrissa Ouedraogo as Anthropological Sources." *Society for Visual Anthropology Review* 6.2: 50–59.

———. 1993. "Impact de la co-production sur les composantes socioculturelles du cinéma d'Afrique francophone." In *Cinémas et liberté: Contributions au thème du FESPACO 93,* 43–48. Paris: Présence Africaine.

Rosenstone, Robert A. 1995. *Visions of the Past: The Challenge of Film to Our Idea of History.* Cambridge, Mass.: Harvard University Press.

Sembene, Ousmane. 1960. *Les bouts de bois de Dieu: Banty mam yall.* Paris: Le Livre Contemporain. *God's Bits of Wood.* Trans. Francis Price. Garden City, N.Y.: Doubleday, 1962.

———. 1988. "Sembene Ousmane parle du *Camp de Thiaroye.*" *Jeune Cinéma* 191: 24–25.

Shostak, Marjorie. 1983. *Nisa: The Life and Words of a !Kung Woman.* New York: Vintage.

Tomaselli, Keyan. 1986. "Le rôle de la Jamie Uys Film dans la culture afrikaner." *Ciném-Action* 39: 24–33.

———. 1992. "The Cinema of Jamie Uys: From Bushveld to 'Bushmen.'" In *Movies-Moguls-Mavericks: South African Cinema 1979–1991,* ed. Johan Blignaut and Martin Botha, 191–231. Cape Town: Showdata.

Ukadike, Nwachukwu Frank. 1994. *Black African Cinema.* Berkeley: University of California Press.

Volkman, Toby Alice. 1988. "Out of South Africa: *The Gods Must Be Crazy.*" In *Image Ethics: The Moral Rights of Subjects in Photographs, Film, and Television,* ed. Larry Gross et al., 236–47. New York: Oxford University Press.

Xala. 1974. Film written and directed by Ousmane Sembène. Produced by Société Nationale de Cinématographie (Senegal) and Filmi Doomireew (Senegal). Distributed in the U.S. by New Yorker Films. 123 minutes.

Yaaba. 1989. Film written and directed by Idrissa Ouedraogo. Produced by Arcadia Films (France), Les Films de l'Avenir (Burkina Faso), and Thelma Film (Switzerland). Distributed in the U.S. by New Yorker Films. 90 minutes.

Part Two: *Deconstructing Contextual Spaces*

5   African Cities as Cinematic Texts
Françoise Pfaff

Francophone African filmmakers, who are often city residents, use African urban settings for several reasons: familiarity—the city is the environment they know best; convenience—filming in African cities is logistically much easier than in remote areas; and inspiration—the African city, with rapid changes and demographic explosion resulting from rural-urban migration, is an extraordinary source of interesting stories. As sociologist Josef Gugler observes: "Africa South of the Sahara continues to be one of the least urbanized regions in the world, but over the last three decades Africa has been transformed by urban growth faster than in any other region" (1996, 221). The African city thus contains a wealth of human experiences captured by politically committed African cinematic creators as a microcosm of the dynamic historical and social forces that affect their nations as a whole. Nowhere but in contemporary African cities is the clash between tradition and modernity better expressed. And it is precisely the dramatic rendition of this theme that lies at the core of the greatest number of African films, especially those set in urban contexts.

An Overview of African Cities Most Represented in Francophone African Films[1]

Malian filmmakers have primarily set their present-day urban plots in Bamako, the capital, despite the photographic possibilities of historical cities such as Timbuktu and other Malian towns along the River Niger. The majority of Senegalese filmmakers have elected Dakar as the location for their city-related stories, though with a few prominent exceptions, such as *Karim* (1971) by Momar Thiam, which partly takes place in Saint-Louis, the first part of *Xew xew...la fête commence* (Xew, xew...Celebration Begins, 1982) by Cheikh Ngaido Ba, which unfolds in Rufisque, and Sembene's *Guelwaar* (1992), shot in Thiès. The same pattern characterizes the work of directors from the Ivory Coast, Burkina Faso, Niger, Cameroon, Chad, and the Democratic Republic of the Congo. Francophone African films are rarely situated in small towns: they either take place in villages or in big cities, mostly capitals. Significantly, Francophone African filmmakers have often used the iconography of large cities, most of which are colonial creations, as the basis of their political discourse denouncing neocolonial facets of their independent nations.

Major West African cities in former French and Belgian colonies that became sovereign states in the early 1960s have geographic differences and unmistakable individual characteristics, but because of their history they also have many common traits. Most Francophone Subsaharan capitals and significant urban economic centers were founded or greatly expanded at the end of the nineteenth century and the first quarter of the twentieth century after the 1885 Berlin Conference divided Africa amongst European powers. The intention was to serve the economic interests of European colonialism—that is, to funnel trade between African colonies and Europe—and not necessarily the interests of the native populations. Not surprisingly, the capitals and commercial centers are strategically located on the coast (Abidjan, Conakry, Dakar, Douala, Libreville), on important rivers (Bamako, N'Djamena, Niamey, Kinshasa) or at geographic crossroads, the intersection of former trade routes, in landlocked areas (Ouagadougou).

To comprehend how and why Francophone African filmmakers have opted to represent major African cities (with populations ranging from N'Djamena's 250,000 inhabitants to Kinshasa's 5,000,000) and their neocolonial architecture and topography, it is of primary importance to survey the cities' history as well as their urbanization patterns. For instance, the site of Abidjan, the seaport capital of the Ivory Coast, was chosen by the French in 1903 to establish a railhead on a line linking the coast with the interior of the country. The decision led to Abidjan's growth into an important economic and administrative city. Conakry, the capital of Guinea, lies at the tip of the Kalum Peninsula on the West Coast of Africa. An old African town that was part of the empire of Mali (thirteenth to fifteenth centuries), Conakry became, at the turn of the twentieth century, the administrative center of the French colony of Guinea. Dakar is similarly situated at the tip of the Cape Verde peninsula. Growing from a mere fishing village in 1857, it is now Senegal's capital, having been the capital (from 1902 to 1960) of France's West African colonial empire, which in turn led to great improvements in port facilities and the building of a railroad from the Atlantic coast to the Niger River (the Dakar-Bamako line).

Unlike Abidjan, Conakry, Dakar, and Libreville, Douala is not a capital city but is Cameroon's major seaport and economic center, accounting for 80 percent of the country's modern industrial production. A significant stop along the slave trade route, Douala had Portuguese, Dutch, English, and French influences in the eighteenth and nineteenth centuries. From Douala, German colonialism forcibly penetrated into the interior until the close of World War I, when this part of Cameroon reverted to France. Douala's most significant expansion started after World War II, and the city is linked to Yaoundé (founded in 1888 under German colonialism), the capital, by extensive rail and road systems. Yaoundé, situated inland, has a small industrial sector, functioning primarily as a political and administrative center. In an effort to modernize the capital, a number of preindependence historical buildings have been destroyed, thus lessening the colonial architectural legacy of the city and its symbolic potential use for films.

Far from the coast, Bamako, N'Djamena, Niamey, and Kinshasa owe their importance to their location on rivers, which also facilitated colonial conquest, trade, and settlement. Like Timbuktu, Bamako, on the left bank of the Niger River, was a medieval Islamic center (founded in the fifteenth century), but its significance had decreased over the centuries, and it was a small fishing village when conquered by the French. Bamako served as a military garrison during the French colonial wars, and the foundations of modern Bamako were laid in the late nineteenth century. It became the administrative capital of French Sudan (now Mali) in 1908 and later the administrative and commercial capital of independent Mali, linked by rail with Dakar.

Located at the convergence of the Logone and Chari rivers, Chad's capital, N'Djamena, was founded in 1900 by the French as Fort-Lamy after the French major who died in battle against an indigenous chief. Because of its location in the center of Africa, it is an important air junction and also a major station on the East-West pilgrim route to Mecca, and it has grown mainly since the country's independence.

Like Bamako, Niamey, the capital of Niger, is on the left bank of the Niger River. It was a fishing settlement until the French established a military post there at the beginning of the twentieth century. In 1926 it became the capital of the French colony of Niger and remains the country's nerve center. It is located at the crossroads between North and Subsaharan Africa and connected by roadways to Mali, Burkina Faso, and Chad. The city greatly expanded in the 1970s due to the extraction of uranium bought mainly by France for its nuclear program.

Developed under Belgian colonialism, Kinshasa (preindependence Leopoldville), is the capital of the Democratic Republic of the Congo (formerly Zaire). A fishing village when it was claimed by the explorer Stanley for Belgium's King Leopold II in the 1880s, Kinshasa has become a megalopolis. Both a political and economic center, Kinshasa houses one third of the country's industry. As a port on the Zaire River, the city benefits from water, rail, and roadway connections for the shipment of goods into the interior as well as the export of minerals from inland areas.

Ouagadougou, Burkina Faso's capital, is atypical of the Francophone West African urban centers already mentioned in that it is neither a sea nor a river port, nor is it a major industrial or commercial city. It has, however, a significant precolonial history due to its location at the intersection of ancient trade routes. Founded about 1050, Ouagadougou became the capital of the area ruled by the Mogho Naaba, the traditional leader of the Mossi ethnic group. The French captured the city in 1896.

Monuments as Metaphors

As part of their didactic anticolonial discourse, Francophone African filmmakers have often punctuated their urban narratives with buildings and monuments that are concrete icons of former European colonial rule. This is a significant contrast to the different use by early Soviet filmmakers such as Eisenstein and Pudovkin of statues and monuments of the czarist era, whose on-

Le Franc (1994) by Djibril Diop Mambety (Senegal). Photo courtesy of California Newsreel.

screen toppling or destruction symbolized the coming of a new political order. The very fact that Francophone African directors incorporate into their films the buildings and monuments of the old colonial order is in itself an accusation that the new governments, supposedly representing a new order, still metaphorically and concretely dwell within the neocolonial influence of the former rulers.

As headquarters of the government of French West Africa, Dakar had more colonial structures than other major African urban centers. Senegalese directors have thus meaningfully punctuated their films with this evidence of Dakar's colonial legacy, whether to situate their story via familiar landmarks (as a French filmmaker might shoot the Eiffel Tower to signal Paris), or to indicate France's political, economic, and cultural interference in their independent states. In *Contras' City* (1969), the Senegalese director Djibril Diop Mambety focuses on vestiges of Dakar's colonial times: the president's palace (former residence of the French governor, built in 1907), the neo-Greek style Chamber of Commerce, the Catholic cathedral, the City Hall (constructed in 1914), and the train station (decorated with Moorish style mosaic—an instance of local aesthetics inspiring colonial architecture). In *Badou Boy* (1970), *Touki-Bouki* (1973), and *Le Franc* (1994), Mambety records strolls through the city with an ironic look at such colonial sites standing strong (physically as well as symbolically!) in independent Senegal.

Ousmane Sembene also portrays Senegal's confused dynamics as an independent nation that still defines its identity through icons created by the French during the colonial period. In *Borom Sarret* (1963), he uses low-angle shots to film imposing government buildings and European dwellings erected during the French colonial era; while in *La Noire de...* (*Black Girl*, 1966), he shoots at length Dakar's center, the Place de l'Indépendance (Independence Square), formerly the Place Protêt, a square created by the French on the site of an old French fort erected in 1857 during the colonial conquest of Senegal. In the latter film, he ironically focuses on a World War II memorial on Independence Square with its inscription "For Our Dead, A Grateful Nation," tying political independence to the sacrifice of the Senegalese who died fighting for France. The war memorial was built by the French, and the "grateful nation" is France. This wording has remained unchanged just as, by implication, France's voice and inscriptions endure in today's Senegal. Sembene's editing emphasizes the irony: he includes newsreel clips of Senegalese dignitaries who place wreaths at the foot of the monument to the sound of French military drumming, while Senegalese war veterans hoist the flags of the French regiments in which they served.

The protagonist in *La Noire de...*, a maid named Diouana, playfully skips on the World War II memorial, which looks like a mere wall to those who are illiterate and remain unaware of its symbolic value. There she joyfully announces to her boyfriend her plans to go to France with her employers, but her ignorance of Dakar's colonial monuments triggers the boyfriend's outrage, and he shouts: "Come down! It's a sacrilege! Will you come down! Don't stay up there! You hear me! Run!" They flee, probably in fear of police. This scene stresses distinct sociocultural positions in postcolonial Senegal of the 1960s. Diouana's boyfriend was educated in French colonial schools, seems to be a professional, and, well aware of Senegal's past, respects the symbolic value of the monument. Therefore, it is implied, he can adequately function in Senegal's postcolonial society, which still bears France's topographic and historical imprint. Diouana is not able to do so. She could be penalized, in independent Senegal, for being unaware of the codes and spaces created by the colonial order.

The action in Sembene's *Emitai* (1971) takes place in 1942 in Casamance in Southern Senegal, but he ironically includes a brief cameo of a Dakar statue located on Tasher Square and dedicated "To the Founders of French West Africa and the Glory of the Black Army." Filmed laterally and frontally against the sky, which stresses heroic stature and unflinching will, the statue represents a French and an African soldier (Dupont and Demba) from World War I. The Frenchman holds the African rifleman (a *tirailleur sénégalais*) by the shoulder with one hand, and with the other, shows him the way to glory, holding what appear to be the laurels of victory. Both carry rifles and look upward and forward with a common determination. The African military role appears less important, however, because the French soldier wears a helmet as appropriate for combat, while the African wears the distinctive noncombat cloth fez worn by *tirailleurs*. This paternalistic statue, which suggests a friendly relationship between African and French soldiers, sharply contrasts with the film's opening scenes in which young Senegalese villagers are literally kidnapped in the bush and forcibly conscripted into the French colonial army. In *Emitai*, the statue ironically concretizes the falsely romanticized French presentation of war and camaraderie illustrated in the previous scene, where the French recruiting officer encourages newly enlisted soldiers to be as valiant as their fathers in World War I, promising them glory and recognition, with no allusions to war dangers, the loss of lives, and the casualties they may incur on African and European battlefronts.

Public Spaces and Their Symbolic Meaning

Sembene's *Xala* (1974), which portrays the economic and sexual impotence of a middle-aged Senegalese businessman, prominently features the 1930 neo-Greek Dakar Chamber of Commerce. Built by the French, the Chamber building symbolizes two periods of imperialism, Greek and French. It appears at the very beginning of the film, and the screen time devoted to the slow revelation of its name carved into the stone of the frontispiece, through a left-to-right panoramic shot of the façade, emphasizes the solidity of French economic power, which proves to be a reality as the film unfolds. *Xala*'s first sequences, meant to satirize Senegal's shift from colonial rule to formal independence, show the ostentatious and theatrical ejection from the Chamber of French representatives and their icons, including two busts of Marianne, the female symbol of the French Republic. This event takes place amidst festive drumming and traditional dancing. Filming through low-angle shots to stress its crucial significance, Sembene uses the architecture of the building (which Mambety ironically compares to a theater in *Contras' City*) to establish a physical and hierarchical distance between the African elite, the new leaders of Senegal parading in traditional attire at the top of the front step as if on stage, and the masses who remain below in the street. However, these scenes are soon followed by the return of the French to a meeting, coming literally through the back door to buy off the new leaders. Sembene suggests that independence is but pretense, since France exerts strong, if behind-the-scenes control over the economy and thus over the politics of postcolonial Senegal.

Dakar's cathedral, with its Byzantine dome and Sudanese-style minarets resembling towers, consecrated by French Cardinal Verdier in 1929, is also part of Sembene's urban iconographic discourse. Sembene shows details of the ceiling in the ironic flash forward of his 1976 *Ceddo*, otherwise set in seventeenth-century Senegal. Here the missionary chaplain of the French settlement, who seems quite aloof and unconcerned by its slave trade, has converted only one African man, who serves as altar boy. The missionary celebrates mass before empty wooden benches in a rudimentary thatched hut used as a chapel. During mass one day, he notices Madior, the king's nephew, squatting in front of the chapel observing his ritualistic gestures. Perhaps under the impression that he may win an important new convert, he ceremoniously descends from the altar to greet Madior with outstretched arms. As he pauses on the threshold of the chapel, the emaciated priest lifts his eyes to the sky and has a visionary, almost mystical experience, accented initially by organ music: he suddenly sees, through the eye of a spinning camera, the ceiling of the cathedral's dome painted with Black characters ascending to heaven, symbolizing the glorious apotheosis of the Catholic Church in Africa. This segment is followed by scenes of a modern outdoor mass in the town of Popenguine, located some fifty miles from Dakar, where a huge gathering of African and European devotees annually commemorates the appearance there of the Virgin Mary (Rémy 1976, 164). Interspersed with excerpts from the mass are scenes where the film's main characters—the Ceddo, king, court griot, princess, imam, and so forth, Muslims and animists alike—receive communion from Black hands. These sequences are accompanied by the singing of "Alléluya Afrik," a syncretism of Christian hymns and African rhythms.

Madior appears as a cardinal officiating at the missionary's funeral. The body lies intact in the heat, unaltered by putrefaction, a sign of sainthood. This sequence cuts abruptly to the simple wooden cross atop the chapel, followed by a downward tilting of the camera, which reveals the missionary, eyes upward, in the same position as before the flash forward. He approaches Madior, who stands up and walks away. The camera zooms in to the priest, who looks at his literally and metaphorically empty hands and returns to his empty church.

For the priest, his vision of the Dakar Cathedral dome painting signals the heavenly triumph of his work, since the outdoor mass shows his ultimate dream of canonization as reward for his martyrdom. Sembene's incorporation of Black figures from the Dakar Cathedral and the open-air mass attended by a racially mixed public, along with the Madior ascription to high status in the Catholic hierarchy, are counterpoints to the priest's failure in proselytizing his faith and suggest that Catholicism can no longer remain a Western (and neocolonial) institution confined within the walls of a colonial building; it has to Africanize itself if it is to successfully survive in a country whose population is 90 percent Muslim. Here again, Sembene implicitly criticizes the inadequacies of France's religious presence in Senegal since the beginnings of colonial times.

Like churches, hospitals form part of France's institutional architectural legacy in large Francophone African cities. Directors frequently portray hospitals as places where people die for lack of proper medicine and health services. With exceptions such as *Djeli* (1981) by Kramo-Lanciné Fadika (Ivory Coast), *Saaraba* (1988) by Amadou Saalum Seck (Senegal), and *Dakan* (1997) by Mohamed Camara (Guinea), hospital buildings from the colonial era are commonly shown as antiquated, dark, and ill-maintained—perfect breeding grounds for epidemics. Patients must purchase medicine elsewhere in order to be treated, and the delay in getting it, for lack of money, often proves fatal. The Dakar psychiatric ward depicted in Ababacar Samb's *Kodou* (1971), appears barely adequate. N'Djamena's Central Hospital is shown as overcrowded and dirty in *Un taxi pour Aouzou* (A Taxi to Aouzou, 1994) by Issa Serge Coelo (Chad). The protagonist's wife is forced out of the hospital immediately after giving birth because of a shortage of beds.

Hospitals come to represent not health but death. In *Le Certificat d'indigence* (Certificate of Destitution, 1981), Moussa Bathily (Senegal) depicts the plight of a poor woman whose sick child is denied hospital care because she lacks the necessary "certificate of destitution" for obtaining free services. Her treatment by the staff of the unnamed Dakar hospital reveals an intricate, inefficient bureaucracy, corruption, and gross professional negligence. After many delays, the child is finally admitted to the emergency room and promptly dies. Bathily shot the film—based on actual facts—in a real hospital, recording its filth with documentary accuracy. According to critic Derrick Knight, "the film—shown widely in Senegal—helped to change the law relative to free healthcare" (1983, 43). In *Saaraba* (1988), Amadou Saalum Seck uses a filthy Dakar hospital to denounce disparities between services rendered to the poor and the rich. In *Nyamanton* (1986) by Cheick Oumar Sissoko (Mali), the hospital sojourn of a poor pregnant woman in Bamako ends fatally when her baby survives but she dies while her husband is borrowing money to fill the doctor's prescription. Clarence Delgado (Senegal) used a short story by Ousmane Sembene in his 1991 *Niiwam* to craft a similar portrayal: a fisherman and his wife travel with their gravely ill infant daughter to a Dakar hospital where a nurse informs them: "This hospital is a hospital in name only. The patients buy their medicine. Here one doesn't always die of sickness, but often for lack of drugs." The child dies while the father is seeking the medicine. The hospital portrayed is the actual Le Dantec Hospital, formerly Hopital Central Indigène, built during the colonial era and already shown in a lesser state of dilapidation in *Njangaan* (1975) by Mahama Johnson Traoré (Senegal). These kinds of depictions are corroborated by Sembene, who in an interview sarcastically stated: "We know that in a lot of our inadequate hospitals, people frequently die from illnesses that could easily have been cured, which explains why, when they are sick, our leaders go to Paris, London or Portugal."

Prisons, too, appear as urban spaces signifying repression, filth, and corruption. Only the façade of the Bamako prison is shown by José Laplaine (Democratic Republic of the Congo) in the opening scenes of his 1996 *Macadam Tribu* (Asphalt Tribe), a comedy that does not seriously treat sociopolitical issues. The threatening and ominous nature of such penitentiary structures is accented by a slow traveling shot of the bare, high prison wall on which passersby are individually profiled, and by a low-angle shot of the huge prison sign "MAISON CENTRALE D'ARRET BAMAKO" above the building's main gate. In their 1987 *Histoire d'Orokia* (The Story of Orokia), based on real events in the 1960s, Jacques Oppenheim and Jacob Sou (Burkina Faso) go behind prison walls in Ouagadougou to examine the case of a young village woman sentenced to five years for unintentionally killing her brother-in-law and attempting to poison her husband, a rich old polygamist to whom she was forcibly married. A guard rapes and impregnates her. She is eventually freed, but the degradation she endured as a female inmate will mark her forever.

With few exceptions, most Francophone African films reflect distrust of legal and penal processes and institutions. The frequent representation of inadequate prisons and courthouses erected under France's colonial rule also stand for ill-adapted and unfair justice systems inherited from the French. Yet the administrative buildings used cinematographically to signal the many paradoxes and failures of their nations do not all date from the colonial era. New government structures are also associated with the dishonest practices of the new elite that replaced colonial rulers. The Dakar National Assembly, briefly shown in *La Noire de...*, serves as the background to a conversation among elected officials discussing their self-serving and corrupt initiatives. The same edifice appears briefly, along with allusions to political corruption, as a character in Sembene's 1970 *Taw* ponders the dishonesty of Senegal's *députés* (congressmen).

Some public buildings in African capitals, even if they predate independence, connote the possibility of a better future for individuals, nations, and the continent. The University of Dakar, founded in 1957, is associated with self-searching and truth-seeking people in *Touki-Bouki* and *Xala*, as well as in *Saaraba*, where the Western-educated protagonist goes to read books on Africa in order to acquire knowledge about his cultural roots and identity. *Sango Malo* (1991) by Bassek ba Kobhio (Cameroon) contains brief shots of Yaoundé's Advanced Teachers College, an institution attached to the University of Yaoundé (opened in 1962), which the hero considers as the fertile ground of pragmatic educational training that is essential to the country's progress. In *Waati*, made in 1995 by Souleymane Cissé (Mali), the South African protagonist develops her pan-African ideals at the University of Abidjan, built after the independence of the Ivory Coast. However, urban state-run elementary schools, whether built during or after the colonial era, are generally shown as ill-equipped, overcrowded, and often inaccessible to the urban poor, for example, in *L'autre école* (The Other School, 1985) by Nissi Joanny Traoré (Burkina Faso); *Dunia* (1987) by Pierre Yameogo (Burkina Faso), whose setting is Ouagadougou; and *Nyaman-ton*.

With the exception of bars and movie theaters, Francophone African cinema has not included many performative spaces in its representation of major urban areas. This may stem from the decision by a number of African filmmakers to produce serious, didactic social issue films rather than works for pure entertainment. It may also reflect a desire to show images of Africans divested of certain Western stereotypes—Africans as born entertainers and gifted athletes. The griot of *Borom Sarret* uses a Dakar sidewalk as a stage to sing the praises of the cart driver in an impromptu fashion; a griot at the Bamako market in Cissé's *Baara* (1978) suddenly glorifies the past of a factory manager. Other instances of spontaneous performances by artists and street peddlers, often at outdoor markets, occur in *Pousse-Pousse* (1975) by Daniel Kamwa (Cameroon) and *Wariko, le gros lot* (1995) by Kramo-Lanciné Fadika, set, respectively, in Douala and Abidjan. Some elaborate spectacles take place in the yards of private homes on special occasions, such as happens in *Pousse-Pousse* and in *Keita—L'héritage du griot* (*Keita—The Heritage of the Griot*), made in 1995 by Dani Kouyaté

(Burkina Faso), where a traditional dance group comes to entertain wedding guests in Ouagadougou. In *Ta Dona* (1991) by Adama Drabo (Mali), professional dancers and musicians animate a party hosted by a high government official at his luxurious Bamako residence in honor of his daughter.

One memorable depiction of an officially delineated performative urban space is presented in *Touki-Bouki,* where scenes of a real traditional Senegalese wrestling match at the Dakar arena are mixed with the young protagonists' attempt to steal money they need to realize their dream of going to France. The scheme involves stealing the gate money at the contest, but they discover that the coffer contains nothing but a skull and an amulet—one of the contestants' fetishes!

A former actor of the Daniel Sorano Theater in Dakar, Djibril Diop Mambety builds and then animates with appropriate sound the stage-like setting of his scenes, which he then incorporates into a broader sociohistorical and political scope through an off-screen voice. A medium shot shows protagonists Mory and Anta resting on empty arena seats as they plan the robbery. This scene ends with the off-screen sound of drums and cuts to a medium close-up of drums diagonally crossing the screen. Here, the drumming sound starts at the end of the previous Mory-Anta scene and precedes the visual image that matches it, indicating a passage of time from the quiet moment shared by the main characters to the loud animated sequence of the wrestling match, which occurs on a different day. The subsequent shots, accompanied by continuous drumming, are of empty seats, followed by shots of the drummers. The device of overlapping sound serves as a carryover to shots of wrestlers preparing for combat and long shots of the audience, including older men with war medals pinned to their boubous, cheering enthusiastically at the graceful *capoeira*-like gestures of the wrestlers. Mory and Anta leave the crowd to commit their intended larceny. As these images are seen on the screen, a commentator exclaims: "This is a great day for Senegal. Longstanding ties bind France and Senegal. Our greatest champions today risk their titles with the noble aim of helping us make our contribution toward the construction of the Charles de Gaulle Memorial." The pronouncement accents the link already established visually between the wrestling champions and the war veterans in the crowd whose medals distinguish them as heroes—champions of another sort. Although in different arenas, both are or were engaged in combat.

In *Touki-Bouki,* as in his earlier *Contras' City,* Mambety uses an off-screen voice to make sarcastic statements and to denounce France's neocolonial presence and influence in Senegal. Ironically, the money made in a traditionally Senegalese space will be dedicated to building the memorial to a French figure who is part of the colonial and postcolonial legacy, since he proclaimed the independence of French colonies in Africa. De Gaulle's association with Senegalese war veterans is significant because he encouraged them to fight for the liberation of France as a patriotic duty, a call to which many responded and sacrificed their lives in World War II.[2]

Mambety's arena sequence suggests the same incongruous elements highlighted by Sembene in his representation of French colonial military memorials as icons of independent Senegal. The arena is not simply the environment where entertainment occurs, but rather an intrinsic element in the visual construction of an ideological, political, or sociological statement. In representations of public and institutional spaces such as Chamber of Commerce buildings, cathedrals, hospitals, prisons, courthouses, schools, and entertainment areas, Francophone African filmmakers generally either cast a sarcastic glance at the incongruity of France's neocolonial presence in independent African nations, or denounce the socioeconomic oppression continuously exerted on disenfranchised masses by new African elites, which are often linked to, if not directly put in place by, the former colonizers, as Sembene suggests in *Xala*.

Dual Urban Landscapes and Their Cinematic Representations

"One bright fall morning we left our room near the center of Nairobi and walked to the edge of the city. We passed through many worlds: A modern city with tall buildings, international shops, and large imported cars. A shanty town of open markets for petty trade and squatter houses made of locally available materials" (Hanna and Hanna 1981, 1). This observation by a sociologist and an anthropologist coincides with the portrayal by filmmakers of major cities in Francophone Africa. Often their motion pictures are tales of two cities in one, opening with traveling or panoramic shots of areas that show the disparities between two drastically different worlds: the business district and the villas of affluent neighborhoods, and the modest or poor quarters. Peter C. W. Gutkind explains this heritage:

> Although urbanism existed in western Africa as early as the ninth century, contemporary urbanization developed during the colonial period (1880s–1960s, particularly after 1945). . . . [T]he colonial city was dominated by colonial administrators and foreign-controlled commerce. The often-large indigenous population made the city an 'entrepôt between colonizer and colonized.' . . . [C]olonial urbanization created European enclaves that encouraged a segregated spatial system, forcing Africans to establish their own neighborhoods well beyond European residential areas. (1997, 328)

The narrow streets characteristic of African sections of old cities were generally demolished and redesigned in the European image. While the British were keen on building golf courses and cricket fields, the French liked parks and open-air cafés: "French urban planning imitated Baron Haussmann's Paris plan (grand avenues, boulevards, parks, monuments), notably in Dakar and Abidjan, but Africans were confined to . . . the Medina in Dakar, or in *centres extracoutumiers* in the Belgian Congo (Zaire), all invariably starved of basic services" (Gutkind 1997, 328–29). Robert Stock confirms this division of colonial cities along racial lines:

Urbanization during the colonial era reflected a concerted attempt to control the form, size and function of cities and to achieve orderly development through the application of European town-planning principles. The grid pattern of streets, the central business district, and the architecture of public buildings were all reminiscent of Europe. Other attributes of colonial cities reflected the particular concerns of Europeans living in Africa. Cities were deliberately and rigidly segregated on racial grounds. European, Asian and African living and working spaces were placed in separate parts of the city. (1995, 198)

Since the independence of most African nations in the early 1960s, a shift in population, rather than true population redistribution, has occurred in major African cities:

Formal racial segregation, one of the fundamental principles of colonial urban design, has been superseded by informal divisions reflecting the class structure of society. African elites have moved into higher-class districts where only whites had formerly lived. Class-based segregation also extends to the middle and lower classes, who tend to occupy separate neighborhoods. (Stock 1995, 205)

Such urban dichotomy is at the core of Cameroonian director Jean-Marie Teno's works:

All the films I have made take place in the city, probably because I grew up there. During my childhood, saying "I am going to town" in Yaoundé meant that you were going in the direction of the administrative areas or the large market place, in other words, the old European city. In contrast, the "quartier" represented the outlying zones of the old African city, where ordinary local people lived . . . [which] is not organized for living. These areas are managing, surviving, and are abandoned by official infrastructures that, for me, reflect the social injustice of the country. (Teno 1998–1999)

Even though modern international styles of architectures have been added to buildings of the colonial era, the old European part of the city typically forms its downtown and upper-class residential areas, whereas former "native" sections are mainly inhabited by low-income Africans. New areas where government subsidized housing was established have been allocated to mid- or low-level civil servants, although they often were originally built for low-income and poor people who proved unable to pay for them or did not have the necessary connections to get them. This socioeconomic and architectural contrast in the spatial organization of major African cities is stressed by many Francophone African filmmakers, who explore the interaction between characters and their urban environment. By preferring location shooting to indoor or studio sets—a choice often linked also to limited budget and filming convenience—these directors provide documentary-like depictions of recognizable spaces that they repeatedly include in their works as the primary landmarks of their dialectical argumentation. Teno explains his use of cities:

I try to make realistic films, with an aesthetic close to what life is really like. When I arrive in the street with my camera, I don't like to intrude on real life. I show people living their everyday lives, I let them carry on talking. I try to capture these moments of life and recreate them, bringing in my opinion, my thoughts, which can be accurate or not and which evolve with the years, but always reflect who I am at that moment. (Teno 1998–1999)

The Guinean director Mama Keita provides another perspective:

I need a dense city, streets that sweat, where you can feel the tension mount. I do wild filming. Movie camera carried, hidden, cameramen behind a motorbike. . . . Without the money to recreate reality, I film live. I do not portray the city, I take what it has to offer life. I throw my characters into the street like in a bowling alley. I am a kleptomaniac. (Keita 1998–1999)

Directors often open their films with shots that visually establish the contrasts of urban spaces. From an airplane we catch the first sights of Douala in Kamwa's *Pousse-Pousse:* well-designed parks and streets, tall administrative buildings, green areas and swimming pools, followed by more densely populated areas of low houses with corrugated metal roofs, narrow streets filled with women carrying large loads on their heads, vendors and transporters, including a man pushing a cart, the film's eponymous character. Even films less interested in highlighting the gap between haves and the have-nots present views of cities from an elevated point: in *L'Etoile noire* (1975) by Djingareye Maiga (Niger), for instance, an introductory aerial view of Niamey and its highways precedes shots of the modest but decent housing built in rectangular blocks for government employees after Niger's independence. The rest of the film will show us a whole society undergoing change rather than clashes between opposite social strata. The credits of *Niiwam* roll against Dakar's modern skyline; Delgado slowly pans left and then right on the tall business and apartment buildings of the downtown area. He then abruptly focuses on the city's Sandaga Market, the harbor, and the shantytown districts, interspersing brief shots of the Chamber of Commerce and Independence Square, the combination visually suggesting Senegal's postindependence socioeconomic failures. Similar connotations are cued in *Le Franc,* where the tall building of the BCEAO—Banque Centrale des Etats d'Afrique de l'Ouest (West African States Central Bank)—serves as backdrop; in this instance, the bank's acronym metaphorically extends Senegal's deficiencies to other West African countries. Shots that document incomplete modernization by framing piles of garbage against modern high rises also appear in films such as Teno's *La tête dans les nuages* (*Head in the Clouds,* 1994), set in Yaoundé, and in the very first sequence of *TGV* (1998) by the Senegalese Moussa Touré, which takes place partly in Dakar.

Unlike the distant scenes of contrasting physical aspects of the city in *Pousse-Pousse* and *Niiwam,* Sembene's camera follows the protagonists' steps in *Borom Sarret, La Noire de...,* and *Taw* as they traverse the disparate rich and poor Dakar sections with varying degrees of ease or discomfort, depending on their familiarity with the area. In *Borom Sarret,* different film techniques underscore the protagonist's relationship to physical spaces. In the Medina, the camera remains closer to the character; whereas longer shots illustrate the cart driver's alienation in downtown Dakar, where his cart is eventually confiscated by a policeman because carts are forbidden downtown. The camera reduces the on-screen size and thus the stature of the cartman, emphasizing his social unimportance in the modern Plateau area (Dakar's administrative and commercial sector) and his vulnerability to outside forces, in contrast to his larger image in the neighborhood where a griot sang his praises and stressed his noble lineage. Moreover, the cartman's journey through distinct sociocultural worlds is accentuated by a radical change in the film's soundtrack, which segues from a Wolof guitar to an orchestra playing Mozart. This makes an ironic comment on the power shift between the former colonizers and the Westernized urban élites in postcolonial Africa and constitutes a good example of sound used as a narrative device. After being crushed and overwhelmed by the height of modern buildings, the busy streets, and the blinking traffic lights, the cartman finds relief as he returns to the comforting space of his neighborhood, even though he is coming home penniless from a fruitless workday. Walking alongside his horse, he reflects: "This is my neighborhood, my village. Here I feel better. It is not like back there. Here there are no cops, nobody. We are among ourselves."

Diouana in *La Noire de...* confidently crosses her own neighborhood but encounters hostility and unknown rules outside of it. Her boyfriend yells at her in the war memorial sequence in the Plateau, a European woman in the apartment building where she looks for work loudly rebukes her, and she has to run away from the barking dogs of rich villas. *Taw*'s protagonist strolls nonchalantly near his home in the Medina but is fright-stricken in the administrative district, where the mere sound of a police siren makes him jump up from a bench where he was lying, for fear of being arrested as a vagrant.

Other filmmakers use a moving camera and traveling shots to convey a dynamic view of the city and make us share the character's experience. In several films, Dakar is seen through the eyes of the film's main character as he is driving or riding a vehicle, and in either case, the kind of vehicle used literally determines the person's social condition and point of view. In *Borom Sarret*, the main character's cart, moving on uneven ground, is used as a dolly for jolting shots. The same effect is sought in *Le Franc*, where the leading character lies atop a small local bus passing under treetop arches (although here Mambety's artistry transforms a shaded thoroughfare into the hero's own triumphant royal road!).

In a less poetic and more realistic fashion, jerking shots of Dakar's streets are presented through the windows of colorful local buses in *TGV* and also in *Yalla Yaana*, made in 1994 by Moussa Sene Absa (Senegal). In *La vie est belle* (Life Is Rosy, 1987) by Ngangura Mweze (Democratic Republic of the Congo), when the protagonist Kourou enters Kinshasa's business section riding on the back of a truck, the low-angle shot of the camera mounted on a parallel moving vehicle shows us tall buildings. This matches Kourou's upward vertical movement of head and eyes and his surprise at the urban architecture so drastically different from his home village. In *Saaraba*, Tamsir's point of view is revealed through shots from his uncle's Mercedes as he rides through a variety of poor neighborhoods en route from Dakar's airport to his relatives' comfortable villa. An iden-

La vie est belle (Life Is Rosy, 1987) by Ngangura Mweze (Democratic Republic of the Congo).
Photo courtesy of California Newsreel.

tical device shows Abidjan in Henri Duparc's 1992 *Joli-Coeur* and 1993 *Rue Princesse* (Princess Street) and in Sidiki Bakaba's 1994 *Tanowe des lagunes* (Tanowe of the Lagoons). In *Rue Princesse,* Jean drives his jeep across Abidjan's shaded residential sections to go to Rue Princesse, in a much less affluent popular prostitution area. This neighborhood is shown as poor but not miserable; if it were, the film's comic and carefree mood would certainly be hampered.

These shots reflect the social and spatial urban dualism of African cities. Jean-Marie Gibbal notes that "the contrast between central downtown sections with tall buildings, and the peripheral neighborhoods with low, horizontal dwellings; the contrast between very comfortable neighborhoods and those deprived of modern services, which constitutes precisely the exclusive characteristics of the urban milieu in Africa: running water and electricity, for instance" (1974, 13; my translation).

The same urban disparity has been noted in Francophone African literature set during and after the colonial era in which "the European section of town asserts its domination through its verticality, the height of its buildings, often erected on a hill, in opposition to the low shacks of the African neighborhood" (Chemain 1981, 89; my translation). The dominant/domineering verticality of the European sections symbolizes power, in contrast to the horizontality in low-income or poor sections, whose inhabitants often feel a sense of powerlessness. This is brilliantly demonstrated by Sembene in his 1966 novel *Le mandat* (*The Money Order*), later adapted to the screen as *Mandabi* (1968), in which an illiterate Medina dweller, coming from a neighborhood of low wooden houses with tin roofs, is lost in the bureaucratic meanders of Dakar's imposing government buildings. What words describe in novels, camera movements emphasize in film. Comparing the sociopolitical mood of Sembene's *Taw* to the earlier *Borom Sarret*, Michael Sevastakis observes: "This time the tracking shots of the modern city of Dakar, as the three unemployed friends run down its avenues in search of work on the docks, is even more ominous. The rich modernism of the city contrasts greatly with the hovels of the poor, appearing as disastrous signs of the gulf between great wealth and poverty" (1973, 40).

Un taxi pour Aouzou by Issa Serge Coelo ends with a slow panoramic shot that reveals a seemingly never-ending landscape of flat tin roofs in one of N'Djamena's poor neighborhoods, while the protagonist, a taxi driver, states in voice over: "If you look for me, that's easy. I'm in N'Djamena somewhere between the rich and the poor. That's my address." The taxi driver's simple words candidly acknowledge the social dichotomy of his city. Similarly, the poster (and videocassette cover) for *Wariko* visualizes this dichotomy: it shows the film's lottery winner emerging from an area of low houses, his body below the waist hidden by the houses, his raised arm, waving his policeman cap, ascending to the skyline of Abidjan's high rises. In *Paweogo* (1982) by Sanou Kollo (Burkina Faso), the verticality of Abidjan's skyscrapers also becomes synonymous with great expectations and happiness, urban icons to which many people are attracted in their socioeconomic aspirations. Bila, who escorts Borobi from village to town to meet her future husband, tells her: "Your husband works where there are very tall houses, houses which are as high as mountains. You'll see how happy you'll be there." However, and in spite of a happy ending, the rest of *Paweogo*'s plot at times denies the dreamlike visions of city life by emphasizing its harshness, corruption, and countless traps.

Urban environments are often represented as sites of frustration and disillusionment, except for a few films such as *La vie est belle* or *Mariage précoce* (Precocious Marriage, 1995) by Amadou Thior (Senegal), which shows Dakar as a city where the victim of a forced marriage finds freedom. This dual representation of the city can also be found in African literature, as discussed in Chemain (1981) and Kurtz (1998). Similar urban characteristics are present in the recent phenomenon of Nigerian video films as well, as described in Haynes (2000) and Oha (2001).

Conclusion

Over the forty years of independent Francophone African cinema, the dichotomies of African cities invariably articulate relations of power. It has become a cinematic topology, a paradigm of the exploitative power of Africa's new elite, often associated with Western capitalistic interests, over the lower classes confined to horizontal dwellings and unable to access vertical buildings that are seats of power—banks, administrative offices, headquarters of international firms and organizations, apartment buildings, luxurious hotels—except as menial maintenance workers. Nowhere is this better represented than in the filmic texts of Ousmane Sembene from his early *Borom Sarret* to his most recent *Faat Kine* (2000), about which film critic Samba Gadjigo writes:

> Sembene's beautifully directed and photographed takes (panoramic views of the urban space and haunting close-ups of its architectural and human diversity) mesmerize the viewer with shocking images of the most contradictory nature, compelling images that tell the story of the internal contradictions within the Senegalese postcolonial urban world. In the same space of opening frames, women carrying water buckets, with babies tied on their backs, walk across paved avenues saturated with the noise and smell of antiquated public mini-buses hiccuping alongside dazzling European and Japanese "reconditioned" luxury cars. Arrogant high-rises erected by a globalizing venture capitalism coldly tower over a decaying urban landscape, symptomatic of failed postcolonial economic, social, and cultural programs. . . . In *Faat Kine* as in other Sembene films, the urban setting provides a locus in which the viewer must come to terms with scorching visual images of failure, of life without ideals in a decaying physical and moral environment. (2001, 124)

In view of the continuously contrasted representation of alienating archetypical urban contexts that highlight an unmistakable relationship between spatial and sociopolitical/economic spheres, one could very well postulate that Francophone African filmmakers have created an aesthetics of spatial dualism (verticality vs. horizontality), which reflects Africa's social disparities between the oppressed masses and the oppressive elites, not only in urban surroundings but at the national level as well. In addition to the denunciatory symbolic meaning of such rich/poor urban dualism, the ironic and accusatory view of post-independence urban architectural contexts, replete with long-lived icons of the former colonial order, may be seen as constant reminders of the failures and even betrayals of many of Africa's new leaders, who abide by the dictates and interests of Western or transnational powers to achieve their individualistic wealth, neglecting the welfare of increasingly impoverished masses.

Notes

1. The following information is based on studies by Bobb (1988), Clark and Phillips (1994), Collelo (1990), Decalo (1977), Delancey and Mokeba (1990), Imperato (1986), Mainet (1985), Middleton (1997), and Mundt (1987).
2. For more information on African soldiers in World War II, see Echenberg 1991.

Works Cited

Bobb, F. Scott. 1988. *Historical Dictionary of Zaire*. Metuchen: Scarecrow.
Chemain, Roger. 1981. *La ville dans le roman africain*. Paris: L'Harmattan & ACCT.

Clark, Andrew F., and Colvin Phillips. 1994. *Historical Dictionary of Senegal*. Metuchen: Scarecrow.

Collelo, Thomas, ed. 1990. *Chad, A Country Study*. Washington D.C.: Library of Congress, Federal Research Division.

Decalo, Samuel. 1977. *Historical Dictionary of Chad*. Metuchen: Scarecrow.

———. 1997. *Historical Dictionary of Niger*. Metuchen: Scarecrow.

Delancey, Mark W., and H. Mbella Mokeba. 1990. *Historical Dictionary of the Republic of Cameroon*. Metuchen: Scarecrow.

Echenberg, Myron. 1991. *Colonial Conscripts: The Tirailleurs Sénégalais in French West Africa, 1857 1960*. Portsmouth: Heinemann; London: James Currey.

Gadjigo, Samba. 2001. "*Faat Kine*, Ousmane Sembene." *African Studies Review* 44.1: 123–26.

Gibbal, Jean-Marie. 1974. *Citadins et paysans dans la ville africaine; l'exemple d'Abidjan*. Grenoble: Presses Universitaires de Grenoble.

Gugler, Josef. 1996. "Urbanization in Africa South of the Sahara: New Identities in Conflict." In *The Urban Transformation of the Developing World*, ed. Josef Gugler, 211–51. New York: Oxford University Press.

Gutkind, Peter C. W. 1997. "Colonial Era." In *Encyclopedia of Africa South of the Sahara*, Vol. 4, ed. John Middleton, 328–31. New York: Scribner.

Hanna, William John, and Judith Lynne Hanna. 1981. *Urban Dynamics in Black Africa: An Interdisciplinary Approach*, 2nd ed. New York: Aldine.

Haynes, Jonathan, ed. 2000. *Nigerian Video Films*. Athens: Ohio University Center for International Studies.

Imperato, Pascal James. 1986. *Historical Dictionary of Mali*. Metuchen: Scarecrow.

Keita, Mama. 1998–99. "From Paris to Dakar, Passing Through the World." Interview with Isabelle Boni-Claverie. Trans. Davina Eisenberg. *Africa Urbis* 31: 88.

Knight, Derrick. 1983. "African Films Turn on the Heat." *New African* (April): 42–43.

Kurtz, J. Roger. 1998. *Urban Obsessions, Urban Fears: The Postcolonial Kenyan Novel*. Trenton, N.J.: Africa World Press.

Mainet, Guy. 1985. *Douala, croissance et servitudes*. Paris: L'Harmattan.

Middleton, John, ed. 1997. *Encyclopedia of Africa South of the Sahara*, Vol. 4. New York: Scribner.

Mundt, Robert J. 1987. *Historical Dictionary of the Ivory Coast*. Metuchen: Scarecrow.

Oha, Obododimma. 2001. "The Visual Rhetoric of the Ambivalent City in Nigerian Video Films." In *Cinema and the City*, ed. Mark Shiel and Tony Fitzmaurice, 195–205. Oxford: Blackwell.

Rémy, Mylène. 1976. *Senegal Today*. Paris: Jeune Afrique.

Sembene, Ousmane. Personal interview. July 1978.

Sevastakis, Michael. 1973. "Ousmane Sembene's Five Fatalistic Films—Neither Gangsters Nor Dead Kings." *Film Library Quarterly* 6.3: 13–23, 40–48.

Stock, Robert. 1995. *Africa South of the Sahara: A Geographical Interpretation*. New York: Guilford.

Teno, Jean-Marie. 1998–99. "Cities of Sorrow." Interview with Isabelle Boni-Claverie. Trans. Davina Eisenberg. *Africa Urbis* 31: 87.

6 Images of France in Francophone African Films (1978–1998)

Madeleine Cottenet-Hage

More than forty years have passed since the former French colonies in Africa achieved their independence. It is arguably easier to reject the political domination of a colonizer than to erase the concrete traces imprinted on colonized space and landscape, the surviving institutional structures, and, perhaps more importantly, the mental images in the minds of formerly colonized subjects. In the decade following independence, one expected African cinema to engage and confront such images. But as time passed, these images from a postcolonial heritage would gradually fade, and filmmakers would be free to turn to specifically African realities and concerns. Or so we predicted.

To a certain extent, the centrality of themes such as polygamy, the status of women, and the confrontation of tradition and change in today's African cinema did and do support these predictions. Yet history has a way of burrowing into the present, and economic policies, in particular, have a way of ensuring the survival of ties. And so it is: postcolonial Francophone Africa has remained tied to France by threads with varying degrees of visibility: economic assistance,[1] often coupled with economic exploitation; linguistic dominance in the context of pluralistic ethnic languages; and, of course, employment possibility, with France providing opportunities for immigrant workers willing to accept low-paying jobs.

So, not surprisingly, Francophone African cinema has continued to struggle with images of France and the French, even as it has turned inward. In the two decades following independence, France was repeatedly depicted in African cinema as an inhospitable, racist society, for instance, in *La Noire de...* (*Black Girl*, 1966) by Ousmane Sembene (Senegal); *Soleil O* (O Sun, 1970) and *Les Bicots-Nègres vos voisins* (Arabs and Niggers, Your Neighbors, 1973) by Med Hondo; and *Nationalité immigré* (Nationality: Immigrant, 1975) by Sydney Sokhona (Mauritania). But in 1978, *Safrana ou le droit à la parole* (Safrana, or The Right to Speak) by Sokhona seemed to signal a change. Labeled as fiction, though moving along more like a documentary,[2] the film took a fresh, hard look at the possibilities of Franco-African intercultural cooperation and learning. Its subject and tone announced a turning point in African cinema, a movement away from romantic musing about the future and nostalgic representations of Africa, or, at the opposite end, from militant denunciation of colonial and postcolonial exploitation.[3] Sokhona's film marked the beginning of what I will call "the second generation" of Francophone African films, which is the focus of this chapter.

Among the productions screened for this discussion, twenty-three films offered images of France in various interesting guises. The filmmakers came (in decreasing numbers) from Senegal, the Ivory Coast, Burkina Faso, Cameroon, Mauritania, Guinea, the Democratic Republic of the Congo (formerly Zaire), and Burundi.[4]

Some film critics express concerns that Francophone African filmmakers in more recent decades have turned "their backs on politics and a serious questioning of the oppression of women and the marginalized" (Diawara 1992, 140). One could argue, on the other hand, that they have become more aware of nuances, more attentive to the varieties of situations, issues, and individuals in our societies. Audiences, too, have developed more complex cognitive styles and are better educated and more able to position themselves differently relative to cinematic realities. For these reasons, the days of militant cinema may be behind us unless it too proposes more complicated and complicating pictures of the world than was the case earlier. A film like Med Hondo's *Lumière noire* (Black Light, 1994) shows that it is possible to remain true to a certain political vision while offering the viewer a layered narrative in which "France"—as a nation and as a society of individuals—figures as villain, hero, and victim.

This chapter examines how Francophone African films, whether Africa-based or France-based, view France as geographical and social space, as colonial memory, as institutional traces, and finally, as El Dorado.

France as Geographical and Social Space

Relatively few films among more recent productions are set in France, and all of these are set in or around Paris, with the notable exception of *Le cri du Coeur* (*Cry of the Heart*, 1994) by Idrissa Ouedraogo (Burkina Faso), which is set in Lyon. These films, I suggest, are emblematic of a new African cinema that paints a relatively more nuanced picture of urban France. African migrants portrayed have secured work; families are reunited or are in the process of being reunited; and settlement in France seems permanent—at least no visible dark clouds obscure the future when the screen goes black.

Ouedraogo's protagonist in *Le cri du Coeur*, Ibrahim Sow, has become the manager of a garage less than five years after migrating to France and is in a position to send for his wife and young son, Moktar. The two leave their African village and a dying grandfather for France, where they face the difficulties of acculturation. Moktar's fantasies about the presence of a prowling hyena—the nightmarish translation of his anguish at separation from both his grandfather (whose totem is the hyena) and his native village—are dispelled only when he is befriended by Paulo, a middle-aged "hippie" of sorts, who helps him overcome his feeling of separation and exile. In Ouedraogo's film, France is seen as a location where economic success is attainable, where a few "good" people are ready to help, and where, as a result, cultural alienation may be overcome. The filmmaker shows that he is aware of the racism to which his characters are exposed, but on the whole, the film presents a more optimistic image of France than its predecessors.

Similarly, in *Bouzié* (1996) by Jacques Trabi (Ivory Coast), an African who has found work in France sends for his mother, Bouzié, and hopes to be able to provide for her. But tensions run high between the mother and her daughter-in-law, and Bouzié is diagnosed with AIDS, putting an end to dreams of reconstituting, outside Africa, an enlarged family unit.

Like the two previous films, *Une couleur café* (Coffee Color, 1997) by Henri Duparc (Ivory Coast), also set in Paris, provides opportunities for the camera to move intermittently to Africa. Here an immigrant from the Ivory Coast, working as a suburban hospital aide and therefore jokingly nicknamed "Docteur," returns to Africa to find a second wife to take back to France. But he runs afoul of the French Embassy, which does not recognize polygamy, and takes the young woman to France as his daughter, where she becomes pregnant by another man. Subsequent developments are easy to imagine. Once again, the scene is set for a clash of cultures, which Duparc, who believes that laughter is the best weapon to reach an audience, treats in a lighthearted, comical fashion.[5]

Une couleur café's protagonist makes an illuminating comment about social spaces when he forcefully asserts: "France stops at my doorstep" (my translation). If we overlook that he has no doorstep, no *maison*, but rather cramped space in a residence for immigrants, he actually is correct and also clairvoyant in that he speaks for the immigrants in this and other films (and so often in real life, too!). Immigrant communities cope with exile by claiming a place, no matter how small, where they can reinvent or import, so to speak, pieces of their native lands.[6] This translates on the screen into a sociorealist, bipolar organization of space, where the insiders' space, occupied by the "legitimate" owners of the soil, is immediately identifiable as different from the outsiders' space, that of the exiles living mostly on the margin. Such spatial division is played out both visually and aurally. Fabrics, sculptures, cooking utensils, posters, articles of clothing, musical instruments and scores, and of course languages, intonations, and accents recreate Africa within a French setting. African wares being sold at an outdoor market transform a French suburb into "Montreuil-sous-Bamako" (a humorous coinage linking a Paris suburb to the capital of Mali).

These markers of space, of course, have intentional aesthetic and ideological consequences: the visual contrast between linear, cold, unwelcoming French buildings and tarred thoroughfares, where drably attired humans go their separate ways, and animated, chaotic, and colorful "minority spaces" weaves a subtext of exile and loss that resonates on the viewer at an emotional level. The opening sequences of *Toubab bi* (1991) by Moussa Touré (Senegal) play on this contrast most eloquently. The film opens with noisy, crowded scenes—one in particular of an outdoor Dakar marketplace where secondhand clothing is being sold. The colors are vivid; the protagonist, who has been looking for warm clothes because he is leaving for France, is dressed in a blue and red African toga. Then the scene shifts to a French airport. Not only is it cold (we see him and the young boy with him shivering as they exit through a glass door), but the environment is chilling: the cold lines of modernity with its glass, metal, and whites and grays everywhere are in stark contrast to the African environment they left a few hours before.

Such contrasts are often heightened by the cutting in of African scenes in which rich, luxuriant nature provides a natural foil for artificial French spaces where greenery is rare, tamed, or stunted. In African scenes even deserts are shot with soft colors and bathed in seductive light. Such images underscore the in-hospitality of the other side of the Mediterranean, and a nostalgic aura hovers over the film.[7]

An exception to this representational interplay of the "picturesque familiar" and the "unwelcoming Other" is Med Hondo's *Lumière noire*. Although Hondo seems to have given up political cinema for more mainstream action films, this 1994 production proves that he can still bare his very acerbic teeth. In it, he deliberately eschews the temptation of local color and romanticization and con-demns France's territorial policies and police practices by using the expulsion of Malian workers as part of the plot. A driver has been killed by police at a roadblock near the Roissy airport, and his passenger, Yves Guyot, who witnessed the killing, contests the police report based on the testimony of two "witnesses" spending the night at a nearby hotel. Guyot sets out to find these two witnesses and in the process discovers that 101 Malians were held at the same hotel before deportation. He learns that one of them saw the killing. Guyot's search for the truth will take him first to the Malian community in Paris, then to Bamako, where he will find Boudjougou, one of the witnesses.

Here Hondo inverts the usual "itinerary" of Africans moving from Africa to France by having a sympathetic French man travel to Africa in search of truth. But *Lumière noire* does not play one country against another, one landscape against another. The truth he finds is as dark on the African continent as it is in France. The Paris suburbs are bleak because they are the scenes of the crimes—both real, with the killing of Gérard Blanc, the driver, and symbolic, with the killing of human hope: the deportation of the poor. The suburbs are appro-priately dark and appear usually in night scenes (the title's double entendre is evident).[8] The African scenes are devoid of picturesque effects: here is under-development, unemployment, hopelessness. And the "return" (of the camera) to Africa is no cause for celebration.

But again, Hondo's film remains an exception, and the temptation to offer a dichotomous representation that equates France with cold, harsh, urban, arti-ficial settings and Africa with untamed natural settings is detectable even in films that are set in Africa. In this respect, African cinema remains constrained by old clichéd visions. The same uneasy "cohabitation" of two forms of spatial arrangement opposes villages and cities—villages that are poor but where com-munity life embraces the individual, and urban settings where existence is anomic and individuals are frequently heartless. Emblematic is *Zan Boko* (1988) by Gaston Kaboré (Burkina Faso), a film that tells of the encroachment of Oua-gadougou on Tinga's small village in Mossi country. Its sympathetic representation of African village life is set in sharp contrast to life in the luxurious villas (with their pools and gated gardens) where the vain, corrupt, inhumane African bourgeoisie lives. The stark white office buildings and the modern residences of urban Africa serve as filmic metonymies for modernity's encroachment into the African continent, a clear reminder of the French colonial era, the loss of tradition, and the harsh realities that await Africans if they cross the seas. The "subterranean" presence of France on African soil is thus affirmed in these images even as African films are increasingly turning to the African continent for location and subject[9] and distancing themselves from direct cinematic representation of French urban centers.

In France-based movies, low-paid immigrant workers (with or without their families) and unemployed males in search of jobs continue to be presented, just as unequal economic development continues to create the conditions for immigrant labor and exploitation. Yet there are signs of a more stable insertion of African males into French society (the case of women needs to be made separately, and I will return to it), as African filmmakers use a wider cast of characters in their stories, as illustrated in *Le cri du Coeur* and *Une couleur café*. We also encounter more *educated* protagonists (in what may be semiautobiographical narratives), as in *Toubab bi*. The film tells the story of Soriba, who leaves for France to study filmmaking, entrusted with two missions: taking the young Iddi to his father in France, who has not seen the boy for years, and finding a former friend, Issa. Culture clashes and racism, played out thematically in multiple variations in this thoughtful film, belong to the quest narrative genre in African cinema. Significantly, however, in this film the nature of the quest has changed: the search is not for economic but for emotional and existential survival. Soriba is presented as a man with a strong, assured sense of self, grounded in his African culture, who can respond to racist outbursts by White people with wonderful quirkiness, appropriate anger, or feigned ignorance of the subtle sneer. He is also a good and gentle man in need of companionship: we see him in the attentive role of a surrogate father to Iddi, telling him stories before he goes to sleep. A relationship with a young White female drifter whom he meets by chance develops into tender feelings and perhaps love. But Soriba has a wife and child in Senegal, about whom the film conveniently forgets, as the story of Issa moves to the forefront and brings the film to conclusion.

Issa's story involves a most dramatic loss of identity in France. Issa has responded to prejudice and harsh factory working conditions by becoming a pimp. When Soriba finally tracks him down, he is clad in leather, with studded boots, a new nickname ("Prince"), new accent, and a successful business in pornography, women, and drugs. He rejects Soriba's entreaties to return to Africa most categorically, claiming that he now enjoys power and recognition and is seemingly slipping into the (admittedly shady) French scene. When Soriba visits Issa's home, he discovers that African objects and African wives dressed in African clothing have transformed a French suburban villa into a surreal Africa and bespeak Issa's divided identity.[10] In the final scene, Issa is being deported. Is it because of some criminal action hinted earlier, or because rites performed by his African family have worked magic in order to bring him back home? Touré's ending invites viewers to draw their own conclusions—magic realism or plain realism.

In yet a further overturn of expectations, a minor role is played in the story by a Black man whose part-time job is to take care of a nutty old lady, a task that he handles with laudable attention and quick-witted comments. Not only is his French impeccable, but his body language and demeanor also cue the viewer that he is probably a second-generation African who has settled comfortably in France, notwithstanding a relationship to "Prince" that is never clarified. At the same time, his job as "nanny" for an old woman jolts our notions of gender roles. No African male in Africa or French male in France would perform this function without raising eyebrows. It is therefore unclear whether we are witnessing merely a gender shift, where color is not the issue but cultural norms are, or another instance of casting a Black man in a subservient domestic position. However, the old White woman's outrageous and imperious demands, her age, and, even more, her state of mind place her in a state of dependency, while they give her "caretaker" full control. Thus, the film plays with our usual responses to characterization and role relationships: we feel pity for her, albeit tinged with amusement; and we respect his ability to perform with self-assurance and to humor his "patient."

In *Taxcarte,* a 1997 short by Joseph Kumbela (Democratic Republic of the Congo), we see two African filmmakers in Paris for a festival. One of them, Touré, a garrulous Don Juan, has borrowed a telephone card from a White girlfriend to call his wife back home as she is delivering a baby. Meanwhile, another White girlfriend joins the two. A minor jealousy scene ensues. Touré's fickleness, shameless lies, and exploitation of his "victims"—by the time he has finished palavering, the phone card has run out of money—are treated humorously. It is hard to decide whether this vignette is intended as satire or as an indulgent laugh at the stereotype of the "oversexed" African male. It does make us appreciate the more stylistically innovative satire *Les Princes noirs de Saint-Germain-des-Prés* (The Black Princes of Saint-Germain-des-Prés, 1975) in which Ben Diogaye Bèye (Senegal) portrays penniless but foppishly dressed young Africans who would seduce young European women by claiming princely ancestry in faraway African kingdoms. It also brings to mind, at the other end of the generic spectrum, the scene in Med Hondo's *Soleil O* in which a French blonde decides to test the "legendary" sexual powers of the African male. It is hard to recall a more bitter and definitive denunciation of the myth than this scene.

While the depiction of African males in French settings does point to increased complexity, the story is different when we turn to women characters in films set in France. Women characters continue to be broadly classified as fulfilling three roles: African wives and/or mothers, Black prostitutes, and White mistresses and girlfriends. At the same time, even within these three categories, some changes, albeit limited, are taking place.

The wives, almost always taking a back seat to male protagonists, have greater difficulty negotiating adaptation than their spouses. Unlike the men, who as workers or job seekers must confront the "outside," the wives stay at home in a space still ruled by African traditions. Their interaction with the outside is restricted to episodic contact with their children's schools and with shopkeepers, social workers, and so forth. Their more sustained interchanges are with their African "sisters," other African women in exile. Yet at the same time, some show remarkable adaptive capacities in the home sphere. On the whole, these are the women who suffer most from the perpetuation of African cultural practices, such as responsibility for extended family members and polygamy.

When transported into a French context, polygamy, a very frequent subject in Africa-based cinema today, provides a privileged social situation for highlighting critical cultural conflicts. Though confined to their home environment, African wives in France constantly observe a monogamous society, if only from afar, and what was tolerated in the home country becomes more difficult to tolerate away from it. "La France te-dévergonde" (France is leading you astray), complains the husband in *Une couleur café*. This film builds upon the topic of polygamy in two interesting ways. On the one hand, it shows the unraveling of a polygamous situation: the young woman taken to France by the *Docteur* has become educated both formally and informally and now holds a job—a relatively rare show of independence on the part of African women characters (if we except the cohort of Black hospital workers who can often be seen in the background). She falls in love with a young North African man and leaves, dashing the would-be polygamist's hopes for an extended wifery! On the other hand, the film playfully opens up polygamous possibilities across racial lines when *Docteur* brings home a White coworker with whom he is having an affair. As expected, the situation unravels when she discovers that she has rivals, and the man may in the end have to be content with one and only one obedient wife.

If we abandon the dutiful wife to her segregated close quarters, we find that France continues to be the arena where transracial sexual fantasies are played out either in the privacy of the bedroom or, more frequently, in the more public sphere of the prostitution ring. In Kumbela's *Perle noire* (Black Pearl, 1994), Blandine, a young African woman, lured by the promise of a European paradise, marries Roland, thrice-divorced and a total failure, whom she meets through the personals. In order to pay his debts and satisfy his taste for luxury, Roland dreams up the perfect solution: he arranges for his wife to work in a popular French brothel. At first she complies, as a dutiful African wife "should." But when she decides to demand her share of the gains, she meets with refusal and violence. At this point Kumbela, suggesting that female solidarity is stronger than racial and cultural differences, introduces an old White prostitute who helps Blandine on her way to freedom. A not-too-dissimilar scenario unfolds in *Mousso* (1996), a short feature by Cheikh Ndiaye (Senegal). Rama, a young Senegalese woman who has received a traditional education in Dakar, falls in love with Ass, a handsome but, as she will discover, sleazy manipulator. She follows him to Paris only to find herself enmeshed in a "high-class" prostitution ring. Unable to face the situation, she rebels and kills one of her clients.

Prostitution scenes enable filmmakers to offer samples of male fantasies that the specifically Black female body supposedly arouses. Nothing is new in the role money plays in the objectification and exploitation of the Black immigrant female. What African filmmakers end up saying, however, is that in this willingness to exploit sex, race does not matter: the White man and the Black man find themselves "in bed together," as it were!

The commodification of the Black body and the fantasies that it elicits are not restricted to women, however. As mentioned earlier, the theme of the "oversexed" Black male is common in France-based African narratives. In a very vivid reiteration of this theme, *Safrana ou le Droit à la parole* shows a White couple "recruiting" a Black man and driving him back to their home, where he is expected to have sex with the woman while the husband watches. But the Black man refuses and flees.

Although statistics show that the number of interracial marriages is on the rise, we look in vain for filmic love narratives in Francophone African films featuring a White male and a Black woman. It would be interesting to speculate on the reasons why this is so. If filmmakers show less reticence in exploring a Black male/White female relationship, such relationships tend to be transient, often reduced to fleeting images of a transracial couple on a motorbike or a couple walking down a Paris street. White girlfriends are not given roles to play in the narratives. As *Taxcarte* tells it, they serve to enhance the Black male's image of self (and public image). This is why films like *Toubab bi* and *Gito L'Ingrat* (*Gito the Ungrateful*, 1992) by Léonce Ngabo (Burundi), which explore the possibility of positive interracial relations, are interesting signs of a shift. In *Gito L'Ingrat*, the young Parisian Christine is in love with a law student from Bujumbura (at least if we believe the dialogue rather than the not-very-convincing images). She follows him to Africa after he returns to Burundi, only to find that she has an unsuspected Black rival by the name of Flora. Both women, feeling betrayed, end up becoming allies and seek revenge on faithless Gito, after which Christine has no choice but to return to France. However, Ngabo provides a positive counterpoint to this narrative of failure by introducing another interracial couple in Bujumbura that has achieved a durable relationship. As a result, the French wife provides support and encouragement to Christine until the very end.

Christine is an interesting character who defies the norms of representation in narratives in which a White, educated woman finds herself in poor African surroundings. Not only is she presented as a very likable character, but she is genuinely interested in Africa, its people, and its ways of life. In a scene rare in African cinema, she is shown visiting Gito's farming family in the countryside, working in the fields and endearing herself to the parents, while the son treats them with conspicuous disdain. Though the farcical treatment of African males returning to their country with a degree in hand and high pretensions is relatively common, the fact that Ngabo's satirical camera is trained solely on him, while the women characters are treated—with few exceptions—seriously and with sympathy, challenges our expectations.

In summary, French scenes are urban, with one exception, *Safrana ou le droit à la parole.* Spatial representations and arrangements conform to stereotypes, but the cast of characters, particularly male characters, accounts for a fuller, more diverse reality. The clash of cultures is explored in narratives that enable the protagonists to learn from each other; good and evil are no longer as neatly divided along color lines; and African filmmakers feel freer to use a greater range of genres to explore serious issues, including comedy and film noir.

France as Colonial Memory

While many Francophone African filmmakers have turned to contemporary issues in realistic films that, in various ways, address the tensions between modern and traditional norms, developed and developing societies, change and resistance to change in today's African societies, some have sought their material in the African colonial past, necessarily implicating the role France played in it. Their films, often referred to as "heritage films," respond to the need and desire to retrieve and re-present glorious, often little-known events or the dark colonial (or precolonial) days and by so doing constitute a filmic "memory" of African history.[11] Two important films belong to this category: Med Hondo's epic, *Sarraounia* (1986), and Ousmane Sembene's *Camp de Thiaroye* (1988).

Hondo's *Sarraounia,* a visually grandiose reconstruction, relates the armed resistance of Sarraounia, queen of the Aznas, against a terrorizing French military expedition in 1899. *Camp de Thiaroye,* a much less spectacular enterprise, tells the tragic story of a company of Senegalese soldiers coming to the transit camp at Thiaroye in 1944, fresh from fighting the Nazis on the battlegrounds of Europe. They are proud and expect that France will recognize their services both monetarily and socially. But the racist French military establishment is quick to forget the sacrifices of these men for whom they have nothing but contempt. In retaliation for being humiliated and denied the money they had been promised, the Senegalese seize a general. They, in turn, are tricked, and tanks are sent to put an end to the rebellion.[12] Similar scenes of the humiliation of African soldiers, replete with haughty and disdainful French officers, form a backdrop in *Blanc d'ébène* (Ebony White, 1991) by Cheik Doukouré (Guinea), set in French West Africa in 1943.

The unrecognized and unrewarded service of African soldiers in French wars is frequently featured in short incidental vignettes in a number of films set in Africa. In *Toubab bi,* for example, an ex-soldier, still wearing the kepi and khaki uniform of World War II, all the worse for wear, appears in two short scenes in which his boastful accounts of his time in the French army and the respect he and his peers received draw taunting comments from a group of villagers eager to remind him of France's ungrateful treatment of its African "subjects."

Le Grand Blanc de Lambaréné (The Great White Man of Lambaréné, 1995) by Bassek ba Kobhio (Cameroon) makes use of a very different past and in a different way. This piece of historical fiction is centered on twenty years (1944–65) in the life of a controversial figure of French colonial times, Doctor Albert

Le Grand Blanc de Lambaréné (The Great White Man of Lambaréné, 1995) by Bassek ba Kobhio (Cameroon).
Photo courtesy of California Newsreel.

Schweitzer, who set up and ran the well-known Lambaréné Hospital in the Gabonese back country. Based on real events and people, it introduces the character of a young boy raised in the hospital whose story enables the filmmaker to expose the white doctor's failures. The film shatters the myth of missionary zeal that enveloped this iconic figure of colonial "selflessness" and with it, the myth of a benevolent colonial France. At the same time, the picture gets complicated when some of the Gabonese from Lambaréné return from fighting in the French army in World War II. Their eyes have been opened, and they can no longer accept Schweitzer's authoritarian ways in running the hospital. They also understand that education will bring them power, and they encourage Koumba to leave for France and study medicine. After independence, Koumba, now a doctor, is elected representative and is pitted against the very man he revered as a child. In Kobhio's film, France exists, therefore, both as an undesirable colonial presence to be overturned and as a space of learning, the source of positive experience.

Le Grand Blanc de Lambaréné is arguably the one film in this category that challenges the re-presentation of history in novel ways. By now, the abhorrent behavior of the French colonial military establishment is no longer a secret, and exposing it is more in line with films of the preceding era. On the other hand, exposing a popular, admired figure like Doctor Schweitzer implies a new form of revisiting the past, raising questions about unexamined notions of "assistance" and "benevolence."

France as Institutional Traces

Of all the colonial institutions that outlived France's direct hegemony in Africa, the school system may be the one most deeply imprinted onto African societies and, consequently, the one most often exposed in Francophone African cinema. In *Sango Malo* (1991) by Bassek ba Kobhio, we encounter a school headmaster modeled after the authoritarian, inflexible French educator type that ruled French schools well into the twentieth century and whose methods were exported to African training colleges. Rote learning, dictations, the use of French canonical texts—in this case a seventeenth-century fable by La Fontaine—the use of France as referent,[13] and the use of punishment identify the old system inherited from colonial times. But here enters a new teacher, trained in new methods in the city. We hear the children singing a song about freedom, "Nous avons la liberté," and we see them being taught how to farm the land, hoeing and digging, to the dismay of the elders in the village for whom education is learning the traditional subjects in the old ways. When the new teacher quits for lack of support and because his message, republican and universalist (whereby we can verify that the French intellectual imprint endures in less damaging ways than we have seen up to now), is misunderstood, a woman teacher is sent to the village. She too has been trained to make her teaching relevant to African realities. Striking a happy (?) medium between the open classroom of her young predecessor and the authoritarian irrelevance of the *directeur,* she tests the children's spelling with a dictation on the equatorial forest.

Similarly, the 1991 film by Cheik Doukouré, *Blanc d'ébène,* features a young African who has just finished his training and goes to a small Guinean village to head the school. At one point the film offers a succinct indictment of the old French-based teaching method. As a teacher observes, France has alienated "Negro culture." Under the baton of a White schoolmistress, the students intone one of French children's best known songs, "Il pleut, il pleut, bergère," about a shepherdess of olden times being advised to gather her white sheep into the fold because of rain. The scene, of course, mocks not only the geographical but also the historical irrelevance of what is being taught in an African context.

Few other institutions attest as visibly as schools to the continued, subtle presence of the French colonial infrastructure, but we also get glimpses of government, police, and military institutions that Francophone viewers easily identify with colonial times. Officials and bureaucrats of all types generally speak French, wear European clothes, and treat their subordinates with the same haughtiness and disrespect that we are used to seeing in older films. This is part of the more general pattern of "cultural mimicry" that characterizes the African bourgeoisie in Africa-based, usually satirical cinema. Discarding African dress and languages are markers of class mobility and assimilation. The "purer," that is, the more accent-free the French, the higher the speakers' social status. Thus, shifts by characters from local languages to French clearly signal shifts in interpersonal relationships and social politics. In *Keita, L'héritage du griot* (*Keita, The*

Heritage of the Griot, 1994) by Dani Kouyaté (Burkina Faso), for instance, the young protagonist's parents, a bourgeois couple, speak French, while the griot speaks Bambara to him. Kaboré's *Zan Boko* (1988) and Sembene's *Guelwaar* (1992) are rich with similar language shifts throughout. But the risks of not mastering the "master's" language exist. In *Ablakon* (1984) by Gnoan Mbala (Ivory Coast), a teacher unaware of the notion of language register teaches the village children slang words, with comical effects.

But cultural mimicry extends beyond language to mores and tastes. *Ablakon* is a comedy about an urban villain who returns to his village hoping to dazzle the inhabitants and embezzle money, and the story satirizes the ways urban bourgeois have adopted French practices. Town women learn to dance the cha-cha-cha and French kiss, and they begin to spurn "uncouth" local men in favor of slick urban types. In the slightly earlier film *Notre fille* (Our Daughter, 1980), Daniel Kamwa (Cameroon) created a dinner table conversation to mock the ways and tastes of an upstart village woman: fruits from France are better than local products, she claims, unless the latter have been canned in Europe. French cooking is superior, and *ratatouille* has no equal among African dishes.[14] Later we meet the son of a villager back from studying law. In his suit of thick man-made material, he too is the image of inauthenticity—neither a Frenchman nor a Cameroonian.

Thus, the filmic exposure of miscarriages of education, satirical treatment of urban African types and mores, and examination of traditional norms and their clashes with modernity—synonymous with French, or more generally Western, civilization—can be interpreted as attempts by filmmakers to uncover and retrieve authentically African cultural practices. The rejection of a postcolonial legacy in recent Francophone African cinema is less openly inspired by political ideology than was the case in the years following independence. But Duparc is right: after anger, laughter may well be "the best weapon to correct mistakes" and to educate audiences (in Hennebelle and Ruelle 1978, 58).

France as El Dorado

Cultural mimicry brings us back to notions of geographical and social space because adhering to exogenous models implies seeking legitimacy for one's own values and practices beyond one's own territory. Such "looking beyond" takes on an additional significance for Africans, since that space beyond the Mediterranean is invested with hopes for material success. In *Cinéastes d'Afrique noire*, director Djibril Diop Mambéty (Senegal), speaking about his film *Touki-Bouki* (1973), chastised those Africans who, like himself, "are pining for Europe ["malades de l'Europe"], Africans who consider that Europe is the door to Africa and that one must have gone there in order to come back home and gain respect. In some sense it is about going to Europe for a training program in civilization" (in Hennebelle and Ruelle 1978, 44; my translation).

So for many, the dream leads to a difficult confrontation with reality. In *Une couleur café*, a young African woman is lured away from home by *Docteur*'s praises of life in "the White man's country." In that same film, when a White woman friend asks why he came to Paris, *Docteur* replies, "Paris is beautiful."[15] Such declarations—of which we find many restatements in Francophone African cinema in the form of songs, slogans, and catchphrases—belong to a mythical construct about France and Europe that Africans have absorbed through schooling, radio programs, films, television, and, especially, the stories that immigrant "returnees" tell because failure is so difficult to admit.

Much of Francophone African cinema set in France, consequently, is replete with stories that belie the lie, showing audiences how it *really* is. Again in *Une couleur café,* the two women in *Docteur*'s household complain about the lack of comfort and the absence of a television. *Docteur* himself amends his own "Paris is beautiful" by adding, "But Paris is dirty." The duality of his sentiment toward his country of exile is echoed later in the film, when a guest at an African wedding in a Paris suburb declares, "Paris is a hell that is sweet." It is sweet because for most needy Africans, exile is not a matter of personal choice but of economic necessity. And though living conditions are shown to be harsh, the more recent cinema indicates that many have found some measure of well-being.

Une femme pour Souleymane (*A Girl for Souleymane,* 2000) by Dyana Gaye (Senegal) brings a needed corrective to a view that is in danger of being overly positive, while at the same time making the issue more complex. At first it seems to restate what earlier films, and some of the most powerful, like *Soleil O* and *La Noire de...*, portrayed. The film depicts the loneliness and poverty of a Senegalese immigrant worker in postcolonial Paris who writes home about an imaginary life of success. Back home, his sister still awaits the money he promised to send her so she can join him and go to school. Back home too, they are preparing to meet the bride about whom Souleymane writes, though she exists only in his dreams. Paris, however, has changed since the 1970s. Africans have slowly been gaining acceptance, and second-generation Blacks have become part of the French social landscape. But Souleymane rejects companionship and offers of help. Early in the film, he is befriended by a lovely and vivacious African adolescent girl, whose attention he rejects (although we understand that he has paid the late rent for her and her father). Later, he walks into a small Black-owned *café-restaurant,* not an unfriendly place, where three Africans sitting at a table invite him to join them. Souleymane does not. He walks out into the Paris gloom. Incidentally, in this film, as well as in *Toubab bi,* urban scenes seem reminiscent of French poetic-realist films of the 1930s, with their lonely characters victimized by Fate and cast against dreary Paris backdrops—particularly Métro entrances and the "colonnades" below the elevated trains (see, for instance, the 1946 *Les Portes de la nuit* [*Gates of the Night*] by the French filmmaker Marcel Carné).

Finally, Souleymane receives news that his brother is about to visit him. Unable to bear the thought that his failure to live up to the dream—the dream of a successful migration—will be unmasked, he disappears. Has he killed himself? Has he left for another city, another country? It is tempting to read the film, not so much as an indictment of the social exploitation of Blacks or of Fate hanging over a duped immigrant, as the depiction of a personal, psychological tragedy, the failure of a lonely man to establish connections with reality. This is a universal subject, and while in this case color adds poignancy to the narrative, it does not explain it away. It does illustrate, however, the force of the dream of success that lures Africans across the Mediterranean and the "degrees of separation" between their expectations and reality.[16]

In some ways, *Le ballon d'or* (The Golden Ball, 1993) by Cheik Doukouré constitutes a counterexample to filmic attempts to deflate the myth. It is the story of a dream come true in which France does figure as the El Dorado, with a White woman cast as the fairy godmother. Bandian, a twelve-year-old African boy from the village of Makono, has always dreamed of becoming a soccer star. With the help of a kindhearted White woman from the organization Doctors without Borders who gives him his first leather ball, he gradually overcomes all the obstacles to stardom. His dream is fulfilled when he is sent to play for the French champion soccer team in Saint-Etienne. On his glorious ascension from Africa to France, he will meet several characters: some White; some Black; some uncooperative, like his own father, from whose house he flees to town; some exploitative; and some kind, like the destitute, homeless dwarf. But the scenario conveniently stops where the story might have begun. What will happen to this twelve-year-old who has been shipped to the other side of the Mediterranean? And, judging from our outside knowledge, what are the chances of his being totally destroyed? In fact, the film was inspired by the success story of the Malian soccer player Salif Keita, but the film's open-endedness allows one to contemplate a different outcome. An answer may be found in *Toubab bi*, in which the story of Issa could serve as a sequel to Bandian's story, since Issa, who presumably left for France full of hopes, is destroyed. Moussa Touré's 1991 film however, is a more complex narrative than one of failure. It rests upon the interconnections between two inverse trajectories: one of loss, the other of gain, both located in the same Paris landscapes.

Finally, we return to the 1978 film *Safrana ou le droit à la parole*, which is not about myths but about the construction of reality, and therefore a refreshing film that introduces a different cast of characters: independent-minded Africans in search of the *means* to bring about change. The film opens with a quote from Mao Zedong, ending with these words: "If we study what is positive abroad, it is not to copy but to create and rely on our own strengths" (my translation). There follows a series of vignettes touching on various issues relevant to the condition of African immigrants and racism, frequently showing both the Right *and* the Left, and both Whites *and* Blacks as at least unresponsive, if not actively responsible, for their condition.

To some extent, this is a road movie, in that the unifying pretext for these vignettes is a trip by a group of African men to the French countryside, where they wish to visit an experimental farm. On the way, they witness scenes of abuse, neglect, and injustice involving their African brothers. Black garbage pickers are juxtaposed to a White chauffeur; Black construction workers complain about racist politics among the unions and not receiving raises; Africans sacrifice their gains for the benefit of the griot and marabout; French lessons are equally ineffectual whether taught by a French social worker who denounces the Left or by a Leftist who ignores the needs of women to be educated. Finally, the group arrives at the farm, a rare scene in an African film. After a discussion on the distribution of food surpluses, a young farmer shows the Africans how he uses a wind pump to water his crops, a simple technology that could easily be exported to their own countries. The film ends with shots of a young French man playing music on what the Africans identify as a *balafon*—the West African version of the xylophone. All share in the unifying pleasure of listening to and making music. *Safrana ou le droit à la parole* has evolved from a denunciatory journey to one of acceptance and reconciliation: what the Africans discover in rural France is the possibility of integrating their customs, their dreams, and their education with the knowledge they have gained from their visit.

But let us return to the idea that the existence of the French "space" remains, at least for the time being, intricately bound to African cinema, if not always as "real" space, at least as "phantasmic" space—the location of hopes, dreams, references, disappointments, uncertainties, divided loyalties. To what extent, one must wonder, is this a reflection of, or the inscription of, the filmmakers' own ambivalence toward France? They have frequently been trained in France, have received French funding for their films, and depend on distribution in France and Francophone countries to promote their work.[17] Perhaps resentment and recognition are subtly intertwined in the representation of a country that, like an unwanted parental presence, continues to be felt.

Conclusion

So, what conclusions can we draw from this sample of films? If we think in terms of two "generations" of films, those made between 1960 and 1978 and those since, one may argue that the second generation, even when restating what the first one had said, has found a new, mellower tone and, more importantly, has moved away from docufiction to work with fictional scenarios in which France, when present, no longer is represented as the land of exile and dereliction. It is not clear that a new Désiré Ecaré (Ivory Coast) would still title a film *A nous deux, France* (France, Here We Go, 1969) in the twenty-first century. But of course, France is no land of asylum either, as Med Hondo and Moussa Touré remind us.

Is "mellow" simply a euphemism for an African cinema that has lost some of its bite and is more concerned with entertaining than providing food for thought? Is it now a cinema that, in its search for scenarios that will please and thus be economically viable and saleable, has lost its desire to present powerful, disturbing images of a postcolonial Europe where the rights and the woes of Black people, of African nations, continue to be slighted? Or is it simply that times having changed, that the world is no longer ready to hear the messages of some of the most explicit, eye-opening filmmakers of the first two decades? Or again, is it that with France having changed in complex ways, more complex realities do not lend themselves to being read through the lens of ideologies or theories but tend to resist unified visions?

One area in which France has changed is in the existence on its soil of a second-generation Black population that considers it home, a population that is increasingly part of the French scene and therefore of French cinema, as the audiences of Mathieu Kassovitz's *La Haine* (Hate) or Claire Denis's *No Fear No Die* will remember. The Black man in *Une couleur café* who was born in Nantes and has visited Africa only once may serve as a fitting sign of the inevitable and irretrievable intertwining of both African and European notions of identity, citizenship, and culture. It is indeed a new France that African cinema must confront, as Blackness and the Black experience can no longer be appropriated by it but belongs to a much wider filmic domain. What does it mean? That Black faces on the screen no longer belong to one continental cinema but gesture toward the universalization, or if one prefers, the globalization of cultures and human experiences? In this opening, images of France are bound to change.

Notes

1. Resentment against France's "perverse" economic assistance is voiced by the main protagonist in Moussa Touré's *Toubab bi.*

2. *Nationalité immigré* (Nationality: Immigrant, 1975), Sokhona's earlier film denouncing the harsh conditions of immigrant workers in France was called a "docufiction."

3. There were films like *Afrique-sur-Seine* (Africa on the Seine, 1955) by Mamadou Sarr (Senegal) and Paulin Vieyra (Benin/Senegal) that contemplated a future of peaceful coexistence of the races and *métissage* as well as economic well-being. And films such as *Et la neige n'était plus* (There Was No Longer Snow, 1965) by Ababacar Samb-Makharam (Senegal) showed Africans returning to an Africa of traditions to find personal stability and meaning for their lives, oblivious to the existing problems that followed independence. At the other end of the spectrum were filmmakers like Ousmane Sembene and Med Hondo, for whom cinema was a means of political action and who used the medium to denounce the ills of colonialism and postcolonialism, both in Africa and in France.

4. I wish to thank the staff at the ADPF Cinémathèque 6, rue Ferrus, Paris, who made many of these films available to me for screening.

5. See interview with Henri Duparc (Guinea/Ivory Coast) in Hennebelle and Ruelle (1978, 57–59) on Duparc's opting out of "un cinéma de réflexion"—cinema with a message—after *Mouna ou le Rêve d'un artiste* (Mouna or An Artist's Dream, 1969), and turning to popular cinema and "une grammaire cinématographique facile"—an easy filmic language.

6. In Duparc's film this is confirmed when the action moves temporarily to an Arab family.

7. Even in Djibril Diop Mambety's *Touki-Bouki* (1973), a sort of African *Bonnie and Clyde* but with a biting, sarcastic tone, the contrasts between urban and rural landscapes do not completely eschew a certain romantic nostalgia. Mory's days as a cow herdsman hover over the film, and the ending suggests that he might go back to his former existence.

8. So is the choice of Blanc for a name: the White man and the Black man alike

are subjected to violence. Med Hondo's film is based on a murder mystery by Didier Daeninckx, who is also credited as a coscriptwriter. Some of the bleakness of *Lumière noire* thus belongs to the murder mystery genre, but it takes on added symbolic significance in Hondo's film. Evidently, the film narrative is also borrowed from Daeninckx.

9. Nor do they commonly explore other geographical places, which makes the more recent African cinema a very "continental cinema," as if in the last two decades it has felt the need for a *repli*, a withdrawing upon itself to explore the tensions that development had brought to a head some twenty years after independence. Among the notable exceptions are *Clando* (1966) by Jean-Marie Teno, which takes place partly in Cologne, Germany; *Octobre* (1992) by Abderrahmane Sissako (Mali/Mauritania), which shows the tribulations of an African student in Moscow; *L'Etranger venu d'Afrique* (The Foreigner Who Came from Africa, 1998) by Joseph Kumbela (Democratic Republic of the Congo), the story of an African man and a Chinese woman in Beijing; and *Pièces d'identités* (Identity Papers, 1996) by Ngangura Mweze (Democratic Republic of the Congo), which takes an African king to Brussels in search of his estranged daughter.

10. The theme of divided loyalties is explored with increased frequency in films, in part as a reflection of the existence of second-generation blacks whose ties with Africa are looser—or even nonexistent.

11. French newsreel images of *tirailleurs sénégalais* proudly marching down the Champs Elysées on Bastille Day must be some of the most enduring images left of the post–World War II period.

12. Some critics have pointed out that Sembene took liberty with historical facts in the film.

13. The *directeur* gives a dictation about the port of Marseilles, a doubly irrelevant text since the class has no knowledge either of what a port is, since they live away from the sea, or of life in a port.

14. The reference is particularly amusing because vegetable stews such as *ratatouille* are a staple of West African cuisine.

15. This comment may be in reference to Inoussa Ousseini's 1974 film, *Paris c'est joli* (Paris is Beautiful), obviously a very ironic title. Also, in *Touki-Bouki* we hear parts of a well-known song sung by Josephine Baker about the "beauty of Paris."

16. Mweze's film *Pièces d'identités*, set mostly in Belgium, explores similar issues.

17. Doukouré studied in France; Duparc, at l'IDHEC, an institute for cinematic study in Paris now known as FEMIS; and Sokhona, at the University of Vincennes, near Paris. Hondo lives in France. On the "dependency" of Francophone African film directors, see Diawara 1992, 21–34.

Works Cited

Diawara, Manthia. 1992. *African Cinema: Politics and Culture*. Bloomington: Indiana University Press.

Hennebelle, Guy, and Catherine Ruelle, eds. 1978. *Cinéastes d'Afrique noire*. Special issue of *CinémAction-III / L'Afrique litteraire et artistique* 49: 1–192.

Le Festival Panafricain du Cinéma et de la Télévision de Ouagadougou and L'Association des Trois Mondes. 2000. *Les cinémas d'Afrique: Dictionnaire*. Paris: Karthala/ATM.

Pfaff, Françoise. 1988. *Twenty-five Black African Filmmakers*. Westport, Conn.: Greenwood.

7   The Failed Trickster
Kenneth W. Harrow

Robert Pelton begins his authoritative study of the West African trickster with these words: "Loutish, lustful, puffed up with boasts and lies, ravenous for foolery and food, yet managing always to draw order from ordure, the trickster appears in the myths and folktales of nearly every traditional society" (1980, 1). In a sense, this description would seem to fit El Hadj Abdou Kader Beye, the unfortunately afflicted businessman of Ousmane Sembene's *Xala* (1974),[1] especially if we interpret the ending, as Sembene would seem to be suggesting, as the moment of a passage from capitalist, neocolonial degradation to the assumption of authentic African manhood. On the other hand, we might reverse the terms and view El Hadj's final ordeal as a descent into the ordure of the abject, the liminal space occupied of necessity by the trickster, from which he would not be able to emerge. We might term the first the classical Sembenist interpretation, or more simply, the trickster's comeuppance. The second represents a deconstructionist's view in which the trickster's control over the process is only apparent as the foundation for the final transcendental transformation is called into question.

Pelton's opposition of ordure and order is built on a more fundamental Levi-Straussian concept, the "raw" and the "cooked," that is, nature and culture. In his interpretation of the trickster's role, Pelton emphasizes the ways in which the trickster negotiates society's need for disruption in order to ensure its ultimate health; the trickster enables society to deal with ordure so as to establish order. The trickster becomes an instrument of inoculation, the one who will save Africa from AIDS by transfiguring its infected penis into a magic wand of fertility. This trickster figure is Sembene, the putative griot,[2] whose adherence to the rebellious stance of the Ceddo or, more recently, the noble but impoverished Guelwaar, was intended to provide today's youth with the backbone necessary to stand up and be counted. Sembene is, as Jane Gallop has dubbed Lacan, the quintessential prick.[3] That is, he is the "subject who is supposed to know," who tells the audience what it needs to hear, and who restores virility to the depleted organs of regeneration.

Why "prick"? Gallop dubbed Lacan a "prick" since his stance of psycho-provocateur, combined with an arrogant attitude toward women, seemed to have been deliberately chosen to provoke challenges to the received attitudes of deference to the authority of the analyst, "le sujet supposé savoir." Now it is Sembene who has abandoned his initial clichéd vision of the griot as exploiter provided in *Borom Sarret* (1962) and has fallen into the griot's trap of thinking himself a mouthpiece, of being the one who can define and then speak for all those diminished beings who have long been the butt of his humor, as well as for the weak or oppressed in need of being conscientized: the semi-évolués ("semi-civilized"), the neocolonized, the women, the masses, and most recently, the children.

Sembene has been established as the father of African cinema, the griot of modern Africa, the voice of the people, but there is little left in his most recent Faat Kine (2000) of the comic but sympathetic Ibrahima Dieng of Mandabi (1968), whose eructations have been replaced by the displacements of the trickster's erections into signs and assertions of truth. Sembene has always assumed the power of ideological, and especially Marxist, class-based truth to sway his audience; assumed the rightness of the savoir implied in the position of the author, the director; assumed with the narrative position of the camera the very role of spokesman, "griot"—a role eschewed by Trinh T. Minh-ha and, in general, feminist film critics and filmmakers for whom "speaking for" has always been understood as the conventional role of the phallocentrist.[4] The struggle between the classical ideologues of the 1960s and the feminists of the 1990s could not be more clearly demarcated in this gap between the male director of Faat Kine and female director of Reassemblage (1982).

The griot represents the failure of ideology's role in the transformation of Africa from colonialism to independence. If Sembene has been the voice of that failure, it is time we now left behind the project begun with Le Docker noir (1956), nostalgic though we might be for its stirrings of feeling and sentiments of justice, and face the realities of Sembene's role today, that is, the role of El Hadj Abdou Kader Beye, not as the reformed capitalist, the restored militant, or the revitalized symbol of an emasculated Senegal, but as the failed trickster.[5] Only as such might it be possible to return once again to Sembene's work with the hope of turning a questionable order into ordure.

But to arrive at a place in which ordure, or abjection, might function so as to disrupt without necessarily leading to the restitution of order—to pass beyond the conventional patterns erected into logocentric structures—we must first explore the structuralist understanding of the trickster's role as established by Pelton. For Pelton, who works from a Levi-Straussian model grounded thoroughly in binary oppositions, the most fundamental opposition is nature/culture. The trickster represents, for him, the guardian of the space between the two, the border figure between inner and outer, the "limen." Pelton cites Eliade, Van Gennep, and Turner in evoking the liminal period created in "shamanic and initiatory transformations" (1980, 33) in numerous rituals, including especially those that permit the initiation "communitas" to be formed. Although the space and time of the initiation community would appear to be antithetical to that of the normal social order, its function is precisely to establish that order:

This communitas . . . reveals the hidden depths of social order, its true center. Thus the movement outside, where life is lived "betwixt and between," is in fact a movement inside, a movement disclosing the inner cohesion of society even as it makes available to society those forces of contradiction and anomaly which ordinarily seem to lie outside its scope. (34)

This is the "recreative power" of the liminal state of which the trickster is the agent and symbol. Pelton cites Victor Turner, who states, "One dies *into* nature to be reborn *from* it" (35). To clarify the meaning of this role, Pelton analyzes the stories about Ananse[6] that demonstrate his disrespect for the powers of the gods and for their sacredness itself: his breaking or inverting the social rules governing incest. Ananse has intercourse with his daughter-in-law or mother-in-law, ultimately, not so as to defy order, but to reestablish a "new ordering" of the limits of the sacred and the social.[7] Inevitably his ordering will turn on the domestication of nature—of the earth, of the creative forces of life, and most of all, "the force that males persist in seeing as the vastest, most threatening, most essential irruption of nature into culture—woman herself" (40). Woman here is a metonymy for female sexuality, and it is the lines delineated by that sexuality and transformed by the operations of the phallus that determine the orderings of society—creating "the lines of force that bind society together." Implicit in the notion of society, of center and periphery, of nature and culture, is the logocentric principle or ordering, that is, the principle that requires presence for meaning to be established. And as that logos is built upon the conventions of the heterosexual binary, it is phallocentric.

"Phallocentrism" has come to stand for many things: male-centeredness; masculinism; sexism; heterosexism; the association of authority with male power; and, eventually, less popularly, when theorized, that set of values conventionally based on the dominance of the first term in the binary male/female.[8] For Lacan, the term *phallus* varies in its meaning depending on whether it is the imaginary or the symbolic phallus. For our purposes, the simplest sets of usages involve the association of the term with the object of desire, to begin with, and secondarily, after the effects of the threat of castration are experienced, the association of the term with the signifier of signifiers—the object and mechanism on which the act of signification depends. What is of interest to us is the centrality of the phallus in the processes of the subject entering into language use, the phallus being the object of desire for which each signifier becomes, in a sense, a substitute, a displaced object. Not irrelevant to this discussion is the "perversion" of this process whereby the effects of castration are denied by the displacement of the phallus onto a less threatening object: a fetish. Before examining *Xala* as the fetishist's dream, we need to establish one more aspect of the trickster's role, that of the mediation based on his phallus: the trickster as phallus, the trickster as linguist. For this we turn to Legba.

Pelton first presents Legba, the Fon trickster god, as Mawu's mouthpiece. He knows all the languages of Mawu-Lisa, the High Goddess of the Fon; he speaks in place of his brothers, who are each given a realm of creation over which to rule; he mediates between the others and Mawu, between the sacred and the human, and ultimately, between those on the outside of a threshold and those on the inside. For Pelton this is where the Fon understanding of reality leads them—not to anomy, but to order, to a centered structure: "Legba's mediation discloses the underlying connection between the transcendent center of reality and the human matrix of life, the family" (1980, 73). The nature of that connection may be figured as sexual, as in a copulative joining in which the tongue of language is expressed with the sexual organs. This marks the very language used to describe speech itself—a language characterized by such terms as "copula," "intimate" and even "limen," understood as a sort of hymen. The ruler of this linguistic space, the one who is also ruler of the crossroads, penetrates both inner and outer spaces without occupying them; turns the hymen from a barrier into a threshold that permits intercourse between two spaces. As a result, Legba becomes the guardian of the entrances to the household, just as he is the guardian of the word:

> Legba is the divine linguist—the master of their unique dialectic, the copula in each sentence, and thus the embodiment of every limen. If the threshold has become his special place, and if he is intimately associated with the crossroads and the market, it is because he is preeminently a being of the boundaries. He has sexual relations with any woman he chooses because those boundaries—physical, social, religious, and even metaphysical—dissolve and reform in his presence. . . . [The Fon] realize that he cannot live inside their houses or reign over their kingdom; his power to open passages and shut them will serve human life, and not debauch it, provided that he not be allowed to assume control over its center. (88)
>   As both initiate and initiator, Legba puts the power of sex at the disposal of the human community. With drums and phallic dance, he ritualizes sex. That is, he takes it out of the arcane and dreadful realm of the potential and fixes it firmly in the center of social life by the use of symbolic gestures, actions, and music. By making sex ritually public, he makes it socially creative. Thus Legba's dance is repeated each time that novices are initiated into the cult of Mawu. (92)

As with Ananse, the conjuncture of a metaphysics of the center and phallocentrism is made clear: "The ritual domesticates the power of female sexuality even as it sets free the power of male sexuality. Sex no longer threatens to introduce chaos into human order because it has become true intercourse" (92). Legba's foolish insistence on sexuality, his public displays and acts turn into a principle of life and society: "[H]e is allowed to penetrate every woman so that order can be continually enlarged. Furthermore . . . , in becoming the personal guardian of each man and woman, Legba penetrates human consciousness itself. He reveals that most hidden and dangerous limen of all—the one inside each person. His ubiquity is synonymous with human life because he is identified with the inmost processes of that life" (92).

The play of the phallus becomes the trickster's dance: the play of the signifier along the endless chain of signification; the play of the displaced desire onto the object that signifies that desire; the play of repression and supplement refigured as the ordering process whereby culture supplants nature. Mawu-Lisa chooses her daughter or son for her cult, to become *vodunsi*, "wives of the deity," their transformation to be consecrated by Legba. In this ritual Legba, the embodied penis, enters the dance through the body of a young girl, dressing her in a purple raffia skirt and a purple straw hat. Herskovits described her role as she danced to the drums:

> When she reached the drummer, she put her hand under the fringe of raffia about her waist . . . , and brought out a wooden phallus. . . . This was apparently attached in such a way that it would remain in the horizontal position of the erect male organ, and as she danced . . . toward a large tree where many women were sitting watching the ceremony, . . . they ran from her shrieking with laughter; and they were made the butt of many jokes by the spectators. (qtd. in Pelton 1980, 101)

This is the dance of the phallus unveiled. For Lacan, the uncovering of the phallus only engenders another masking of its presence. What is striking here is the extent to which this is thematized, the extent to which the act of revealing the hidden organ engages the entire community in its act, both extending the limen to include the entire community and delineating the trickster as the figure of that liminality: "The capturing of the initiates by Mawu-Lisa is equivalent to a sexual possession, yet that possession is not complete until Legba possesses the whole people on behalf of the deity. [. . . Legba's] penis becomes a moving limen through which Mawu-Lisa passes into both initiates and society, the initiates pass from outside to inside, and 'outside' itself becomes 'inside'" (102).

The sign of the limen is the penis: Legba's role is both to enable the passage from inside to outside, and more, to be the instrument of passage, the hidden phallus that functions to establish the reign of a hidden center by revealing the unrevealed organ of its implementation:

> "It is Legba's penis which symbolizes, both ordinarily and most ceremoniously, the bond between the divine and the human worlds. He is a living copula, and his phallus symbolizes his being, the limen marking the real distinction between outside and inside, the wild and the ordered, even as it ensures safe passage between them." (108–109)

What Pelton misses, in his careful elaboration of the Fon schematic design of limen, inside and outside, is the function played by the center at every turn, with every binary pair binding up the act of interpretation into the opposition of nature and culture, and reducing the play to a purposeful teleology. His love of the complexity and apparent ambiguity of the figure of the trickster comes to an end with the vision of the spiritual, sacred, or metaphysical center on which his vision of life rests. This drives the interpretative act, leading him into the familiar pattern described by Derrida as a metaphysics of presence:

> There are thus two interpretations of interpretation, of structure, of sign, of play. The one seeks to decipher, dreams of deciphering a truth or an origin which escapes play and the order of the sign, and which lives the necessity of interpretation as an exile. The other, which is no longer turned toward the origin, affirms play and tries to pass beyond man and humanism, the name of man being the name of that being who, through the history of metaphysics or of ontotheology . . . has dreams of full presence, the reassuring foundation, the origin and the end of play. (1978, 292)

Like Pelton, as we shall see, Sembene's play is subordinated, always, to the first of these acts of interpretation, one whose dependency on the grounding of a center and whose alienation are subordinated to an ordered epistemology.

* * *

What are we to make of El Hadj's *xala* (impotence)? At first blush we understand it to symbolize the failures of Senegalese society to realize the dream of independence. This is made painfully clear with the opening shots signifying the passage from colonialism to independent African rule. The passage was compromised at the outset, as we can see in the scene in which the silent Frenchmen in business suits buy off the newly established members of the Chamber of Commerce, a thinly disguised attack on the government under Senghor. As El Hadj announces his marriage at the same opening scene in which the African businessmen occupy the council's chambers, the parallelism between the state of affairs in the newly independent country and his own marital state of affairs is established. His *xala* signals the impotency of the neocolonial state.

In the scenes at his two households and at the wedding, the film quickly establishes the extent to which the impotency has extended its reach throughout most of the society, whose members are corrupted by materialist values and dependency upon European culture. The work of resistance is located in the few who attempt to adhere to more authentic values, be they Wolof or peasant. If the function of the trickster is to enable the passage between worlds, there would seem to be little space for him to occupy in this film, centered as it is on its certainties.

The safest place for the Western critic to occupy in reviewing this celebrated African classic would be to retreat into the space created by Sembene's truths; that is, to identify explicitly the ways in which the corrupted materialism corresponds to Marxist notions of commodity fetishism developed under capitalism and how the third wife, rendered speechless and objectified before the lens of the camera, figures the fetishism that accompanies the male gaze.[9] All this is to leave aside the relationship between Sembene and El Hadj, a relationship seemingly denied by the filmmaker's apparent distance from the negative character he created. Put differently, all this is to leave untouched the role of the phallus as it appears in the film. The resurrection of this film from the ashes of yesterday's ideological certainties, however, depends on pulling El Hadj's phallus out from beneath the surfaces, an action Sembene himself does not shy away from doing as literally as possible.[10] As the film's critics have often looked toward the condition of El Hadj's three wives, performing a political feminist critique, they have overlooked the possibilities of a liminality that the film desperately attempts to deny, all the while asserting its vital force. El Hadj is a failed trickster, but first we must see where he has hidden his phallus.

The most striking scene of liminal dislocation in the film occurs when El Hadj is riding an elevator on his way to see his "cuz," a banking official from whom El Hadj is to request a loan. El Hadj has just left the President's office, where he has been complaining about his convocation to a special meeting of the Chamber of Commerce—a meeting called to discuss the problems occasioned by El Hadj's bank overdrafts. Up to this point, El Hadj has tried everything to rid himself of his *xala,* and finally, with the help of his chauffeur Modu's village marabout, Serigne Mada, he has succeeded. However, he has paid Serigne Mada with a check that will bounce, ignoring the warning that he was given, "What one hand does, another can undo." In a sense, El Hadj is riding the triumphant edge of a curve, since he has managed to rid himself of the *xala* and now can devote himself to his business affairs. On the other hand, though the *xala* is gone, he discovers that his new wife Ngone is not available since she has her period, and now that he has spent his money on his third wedding and on the marabouts, his shop is empty. His major customer, Ahmed Fall, a Moor, has come to the shop looking for supplies, and when El Hadj attempts to hit him up for a loan, he refuses. "We Moors are traders, not moneylenders," he tells El Hadj, while a policeman brings the President's convocation to El Hadj. Simultaneously, the camera alerts us to the return of the beggars whom El Hadj has had ejected from the city, and the refrain of the beggar's playing is heard all the more insistently. The moment that El Hadj has been so desperately working for, the return of his manhood, corresponds to the moment in which are set in motion all these markers of his failure. Every scene that follows his departure from Serigne Mada marks his decline, without his knowing it.

Thus, we are prepared for what follows his departure from the President's office, his descent down the elevator, and the questionable reception at the bank. He expects the President to be calling the bank on his behalf, and as he departs the office, the President is on the phone to the bank. As he arrives, the *sous-directeur* is still speaking with the President and has been alerted to El Hadj's impending visit. Either the President has lost his power to control the banker, just as we later learn at the Chamber meeting that all the members of the Chamber are being denied loans because of El Hadj, or they have conspired to eject El Hadj from their group, and the scene at the bank would then be more or less a set-up that allows the President to pass the buck. In any event, it is clear by the time El Hadj leaves the bank that he will be denied his loan, and his downfall at the subsequent Chamber meeting is felt by the film's spectator as inevitable.

Following this construction, we can interpret the scene in the elevator as the moment of El Hadj's fall: the President has dropped him, and although he doesn't know it, although he thinks his *xala* is cured, although he now believes the President will insure that he will obtain his loan, just the opposite is taking place on the phone. He is falling, without knowing it, as the message passes from the President to the banker. That moment of falling, like the passage from erection to flaccidity, is presented in the form of a misrecognition:[11] thinking his phallus has made him a man again, made him whole, made him strong and erect, he constructs himself as an *homme d'affaires,* a man of business, with portfolio, business project, suit and tie, and smiling confidence. He tells his "cuz" at the bank to leave the air conditioning on. Indeed, he cannot sleep without it. He is "modern." Yet this "modernity" is taken by some as the very sign of his in-betweenness, not his arrival at the terminus of the passage to an identity. For

Xala, Ousmane Sembene (Senegal).
Courtesy of New Yorker Films.

the Bayden, his new bride's aunt, his impotency is due to this very aspiration to be a *toubab*, a White-Black man who is "neither fish nor fowl." For her, his in-betweenness explains his impotency, gains him no credit or authority. She leaves him with Ngone, a woman that "would give any man an erection," and returns to find the sheets as she had left them.

Like the trickster, El Hadj passes in and out of all the chambers of home and the world: from one wife to another, from Dakar's center to the wealthy neighborhoods to the distant village, speaking Wolof and French. If he is a businessman, he is so in the disguise of the trickster whose passage in and out of these spaces, these tongues, these situations is predicated on the assumption that he can outfox the opponent, and in so doing make passage fertile. Now he is caught in the moving space between the President's office and the street below.

The descent in the elevator takes a full seventeen seconds, an enormous expenditure of cinematic time at a crucial moment in the film. In retrospect, it is clear that it is a synecdoche of El Hadj's fall, although the irony of his unawareness is not yet fully apparent. His entrance into the elevator is seen through a mirror on the wall of the elevator, and the shot is set up so that we see half of his torso and head from the rear, reflected in the mirror, while simultaneously we see directly the front of his left shoulder in front of the mirror. He stands thus doubly split, like Bhabha's mimic man:[12] a partial being, bits and pieces of the man, divided against himself at the moment he thinks himself cured, whole. Sembene's portrayal of the fall, ticked off floor by floor, framed by the scene of the President calling and, on the other end, the banker receiving the message of denial, is intended to mark the trajectory of the narrative and to underscore the irony of the African protagonist thinking he can make himself whole through manipulating the corrupt practices of Senegal's new capitalist regime.

But Sembene would have this portrayal of El Hadj present the dislocation of the African man as an image that is itself undivided in its vision of the truth. The camera shot tricks the ideology, as the trick mirror shot conveys, more than a fall in fortunes, a fall in the constructedness of identity. We see a view of El Hadj that he could not see himself were he to look in the mirror, and it is more than the camera sees of him from the front. The mirror view is partial, giving us the only view of his head—mostly the back and partially the side—along with floors as he descends (see illustration). The effect of the juxtaposition of the mirrored image and the real is to create a pure double, with a line between them—the line formed by the edge of the mirror. This doubled image, belonging not entirely to either the space of reflected or of mimetic reality, captures as best it can the liminal space of the trickster whose real visage does not belong to either realm but in between the two. It is no coincidence that El Hadj thinks he has cadged the President, as he did the marabout, and will shortly do to the banker, and that at that moment the phone message is transmitting the message that will out-trick him.

He cannot talk his way out of this situation. To understand his failure we have to return to another of the trickster's functions, his role as the translator, and specifically the one who translates what is hidden or uncomprehended, effecting the communication between those who cannot understand each other. The key to the model, to begin with, will be the act of revealing the hidden, and then, secondly, that of transforming and translating the meaning of what is hidden—Legba's true role as the linguist.

The nature of the phallus in Lacanian analysis is that it is always veiled, that even in the act of unveiling it, it remains all the more hidden by virtue of its apparent visibility. What is veiled and then revealed in *Xala* shifts from the sexual to the hidden history of expropriation, the real history that lies buried in the consciousness of the oppressed and that is expressed only at the end in their act of spitting on El Hadj.

El Hadj's *xala* is hidden. He is unaware that he is afflicted. He laughs and assures the President and Minister that his two wives were virgins, and that so is his third, and that he needs no aphrodisiac or magical substances to achieve satisfaction with Ngone. Like the other members of the Chamber of Commerce, he believes that he is in on all the real secrets: he has opened his briefcase, and the secret of French bribery is exposed to all the members and to the camera. He believes himself safe in his financial dealings, his secret, illegal sale of the rice subsidy. Whatever the secrets of his personal history, his business affairs, his physical condition, he believes that he is possessed of whatever knowledge and power he needs. That is why he so confidently turns the Bayden down when she requests him to sit on the mortar and change into a caftan; why he laughs at the offers to insure his sexual potency. He begins by having turned the

trick on every other opponent, including the most powerful of all, the colonialists, and has no reason to suspect that he is now in another person's grip.

The passage from hidden to open requires the movement from inner to outer
space. El Hadj is presented as easily making that movement, at least until the
revelation of his *xala*. He joins the ranks of the few who can enter into the prestigious Chamber of Commerce, and once inside, he joins those who are within
the inner circle of those needing to be bribed. Similarly, he passes from the
street, through the garden and corridors of the house, to the inner sanctuary of
the bedroom where the intimate act validating his manhood is to be performed.
The outward appearance of the fetish, as Mulvey points out, is both a symptom
and a disguise that calls attention to the act of putting on the disguise. Similarly
the revelation of the secrets of the inner chamber of both financial and sexual
commerce presents to the camera's eye, to the audience, the inner workings and
symptomology of neocolonialism, the hypocrisy of the leadership's nationalist
and socialist rhetoric—and alternatively, the vacuity of the masculinist boasts
of that leadership. The symptom, corruption, lies exposed and explained through
the revelatory recordings of the camera's eye and ear that capture its own ob-
sessive character; the disguised phallus remains all the more hidden as the new
symptom, the *xala* itself, makes its appearance.

Much of the motion after the wedding scene involves traveling to the village
from the city and back. Again, there is an outer life that is carried on in Dakar
and an inner mystery that drives the symptom of failure and that is to be discovered in the village. The removal of the *déchets humains* (human rubbish),
the beggars and handicapped, from the streets of Dakar to the more distant barren regions surrounding the city is due to El Hadj's complaints. Similarly, all he
needs to do to arrive at the proper village is to get into his Mercedes and have
his chauffeur take him there. El Hadj cures the city of its *déchets* and his body
of the appearance of a *xala*. Its hidden sources remain unchanged; the beggars
return, his *xala* will return. The trickster successfully negotiates the passage; El
Hadj likewise thinks he has made the run from village poverty to city wealth
without having to pay the price. He has taken a third wife, the sign of his wealth,
and joined the Chamber of Commerce, his sign of power. Yet the secrets return,
like the repressed, to attach themselves to yet another fetish. The *xala* will always
affect his penis, although he remains mystified as to its origins, to his true enemy.

Between the scene with Serigne Mada, who has removed El Hadj's *xala*, and
El Hadj's fall from power and wealth with the expulsion from the Chamber of
Commerce and the reinstatement of his *xala*, El Hadj meets with Ahmed Fall
and seeks to obtain a loan from him. In their exchange we learn the secret of
their shared corruption: El Hadj has sold him, under the table, his quota of rice
from the National Food Board, rice intended to feed those villagers starving
from the drought; and with this money, he has taken his third wife (money for
an expensive house, wedding, and a car as wedding gift). With the help of the
subtle, sly, conniving "Narr," El Hadj has transformed the gift of food and life.[13]

The sequence of shots that follows provides external echoes of the inner

Xala, Ousmane Sembene (Senegal).
Courtesy of New Yorker Films.

moral fall exposed in this scene. And they set up the final return of the repressed secret history, for after El Hadj has been stripped of his second and third wives, his business, his Mercedes, his place in the Chamber of Commerce, and finally, again, his manhood, there is little work left for the *xala* to perform, little truth left for it to signify except for the revelation of its own working. Sembene marks the passage to this last stage by a sequence of three shots—three images that link power to the phallic economy. In the first shot, El Hadj has just lost his shop and car and has had his *xala* restored by Serigne Mada. He is walking down the street with Modu, dejected and depleted, while the camera fixes on the wooden stool in Modu's hand. The stool had earlier served for the chauffeur as he awaited his master: it stands in complete opposition to the expensive machine he drove and to the luxurious furniture and trappings of the second and third wives' houses. The camera then draws back, revealing in the distance the rising form of the *Grande Mosquée* of Dakar, standing erect between the two men. However, this moment is another transition, another passage from apparent defeat to latent rebirth. Gorgui, the principal beggar, has told Modu that he can cure El Hadj if he will obey him, and as El Hadj and Modu are walking off, the mosque between them, the head of Gorgui's walking stick appears against the sky, round, firm, and though in the image of a head, definitely phallic in form and position (see image). The last secret stands ready to be revealed.

Sembene is about to take us as far as he can. The motive of history drives the currents of our lives, and that motive is neither sacred nor formed by individual volition: it is class interest. El Hadj's crimes were crimes of the family: he betrayed his half-brother Gorgui, stole the clan's inheritance, condemned his family to death or devastation, and established the pattern of crimes that were to be repeated again when a villager observing a car accident was robbed by a Mr. Thieli,[14] the very man who replaced El Hadj on the Chamber of Commerce. If capitalist theft will ultimately turn against the thief, then history itself, and its passage through time, will function like the workings of the trickster. The origins of the theft remain bound in the hidden history of the family, where greed for private ownership made its first appearance, only to be turned quickly to the family secret, the ghost in the closet.

"What I've become is your fault," says the beggar Gorgui. What all the dispossessed have become is the fault of all the wealthy men whose train of honking cars is seen at the film's beginning as they are headed to the parodic scenes at the wedding. Starting with a thief's *arriviste* celebration at the beginning, the film ends with his comeuppance, the beggars' revenge, the return of abjection.

El Hadj is exposed to the spittle as his sordid history is unfolded before the eyes and ears of his family, of the camera—of an audience intended to understand that this private truth has a public meaning. And that meaning, beyond the film's dogmatic agenda, must be sought in the last quality of the trickster, the transformative powers of his acts of translation, the final arena of El Hadj's failure.

"*Xala*" is, after all, a Wolof word. The subtitle of the English version renders it "the curse," a comic mistranslation of something much closer to impotency. How we translate "*xala*" might depend on the audience we wish to address (one French translation gives it as "impuissance temporaire," without any indication of a curse or spell). Translation involves the great passage of meaning and power, which explains why Hampaté Bâ represented Wangrin, the eponymous trickster hero of Bâ's great bio-novel, as powerful and wealthy because of his ability to exploit his position as official translator. Being a translator not only puts one in close proximity to power, but it allows the translator to supplant the power of the authority by feigning subordination while still controlling the communication. The lines of power that seem to pass through the translator are only apparently direct: translation is yet another form of displacement, of exposing so as to better conceal, and, by concealing, continuing the work of power.

This is why El Hadj gets so upset when his daughter Rama refuses to respond to him in French. He has had his *xala* removed; he has returned to his seat of power as CEO of his business; he has opened a bottle of imported French water, Evian, and offered this, his favorite drink, to his daughter, as he will offer her money. He assures her he will return to Adja and take care of her needs as well. He is as important as he can make himself, and it all depends upon his expressing himself in the French idiom. For Sembene's audience, he represents the failures of assimilation—a mockery of the Senghorian ideal at a time when Senghor was stressing the importance of French in Senegalese education. Although he still speaks Wolof when need be, it is his less prestigious self that emerges at such times—the villager, not the *patron*. The parody of the *évolué* ("civilized") is what we see and hear—the maladroit figure of the man in the suit, sweating on the cart, being taken to Modu's village, out of sorts with his own origins.

Sembene is a great advocate of originary thinking: from *Ceddo* to *Emitai* to *Guelwaar*, we are repeatedly told that there is an African base that underlies all the superficial differences imposed on the Senegalese and that we can return to that base if only we shed the foreign influences brought by the Narrs, the toubabs, and, most recently, the IMF and World Bank and their foreign donors. In the case of El Hadj, who slaps his daughter down when she challenges the right of Senegalese men to be polygamists, he claims that they fought the colonialists and threw them out so that they could maintain their traditional rights, polygamy included: "La polygamie c'est notre patrimoine religieux" (Polygamy is our religious patrimony). Yet the rights of the wives to their *moomé*—their allotted period of time to have their husbands with them—are ignored by these same patriots. Sembene sees no contradiction in espousing an untraditional feminist agenda along with a nativist program, as is implicit in his hostility to foreign cultural assimilation, the most nefarious effect of neocolonialism.

He is confident that he can negotiate feminism and cultural nationalism on the basis of the people's rights. The negotiation is between two truths, two centers: the truth of the Wolof, best conveyed in the glamorized resistances of the Ceddo; and the beggars and peasants combined into the truth of the proletariat —two grand narratives of liberation, pan-Africanism, and Marxism. At times this places Sembene in an awkward position vis-à-vis his audience: women who don't always or necessarily feel as deprived or oppressed as they are made to appear in his films; Muslims who don't feel themselves to have been the dupes of foreign proselytizers or to be drugged by dreams of pie in the sky so as to cope with earthly miseries. Yet Sembene does not perform the role of the mouthpiece as a function of public opinion: he is the interpreter *for* the people; closer to Guelwaar lecturing the audience at the stadium in Thiès; closer to Wangrin, who decides what the message will be that he is interpreting, not simply content to parrot another's line.

This is why the scene at El Hadj's convocation is so interesting. He has already fallen, as we have seen in the scene in the elevator. He doesn't know whether he will receive the bank loan, but being put off for a few days by the banker is probably enough of a clue. He had thought the President was still supporting him, but no doubt he was able to figure out that if he hadn't received the loan after the intervention of the President, he probably did not still have his support and that the convocation was to be what he feared, a lynching. There is nothing about El Hadj Abdou Kader Beye from the beginning of the film that would lead us to think he could speak either of the two central truths so dear to Sembene, nothing except his own seemingly self-serving references to his role in the struggle for independence. And even there, little in Senegalese history would suggest that one of the early comprador businessmen would have known anything about the truths of resistance.

So it is all the more surprising that both truths come to be spoken at the convocation. Accused of corruption and malfeasance, of endangering the positions of the other members of the Chamber, El Hadj defends himself by accusing all the others of having done the same things. More importantly, he accuses them, and himself, of being miserable middlemen, *minables commissionnaires*—and worse, tools of the colonialists who are stronger than ever. The full indictment is rehearsed in the novel version: "We are nothing better than crabs in a basket. We want the ex-occupier's place? We have it. This Chamber is the proof. Yet what change is there in general or in particular? The colonialist is stronger, more powerful than ever before, hidden inside us, here in this very place" (1976, 93).

This is the point at which "truth" displays its trickster function. Like Wangrin, El Hadj plays the chords of the truth when it serves his interest to do so, and the truth he claims, the trickster's truth, is that the authentic being of the African ruling class has been compromised from the outset. The battle with Senghor's Francophile and pro-Western policies and views is only the surface of the struggle Sembene engages here: it is his belief that this is the struggle for the soul of his people, for their African identity. That is why El Hadj's demand that he be allowed to speak in Wolof, and the ironic refusal he receives, marks the second, crucial pole of Sembene's truth claims: a Senegalese truth, a Wolof truth, in fact, cannot be articulated in the foreign dress of the Other, much less the language of the colonizers. "Chacun de nous est un salaud" (Each one of us is a bastard), he proclaims lamely in French (an irony highlighted in the film and lost in the novel that was written, after all, in French), bringing into the open the sentiments cultivated by the narrator, the invisible camera, throughout the entire film: El Hadj transforms himself into the mouthpiece for the director's camera and his silent, implied presence.

The presence of truth's central vision need only be fully exposed for the interpreter's role of spokesman to be completed. That is the function of the final scene: El Hadj is to be transformed into his true self; his bourgeois, corrupt clothes are to be discarded; and the beneficial reinsertion into the community to be effected. For the West, spit conveys scorn and denigration; for the marabout, in tale after tale, saliva is the concrete means by which the parole and baraka (here, "blessing") of the holy man is to be transferred to the petitioner.

From the beginning of *Xala* we have been informed what to believe about the wealthy ruling class and about the selling of women in Senegalese society. We are told, more explicitly in the novel, what functions the different people have: the term *Bayden*, for example, is translated, parenthetically, as "the bride's aunt and her father's sister"; her position as double widow is patiently explained ("traditionalists held that she must have her fill of deaths: a third victim. So no man would marry her for fear of being this victim"). And, the narrator continues, the social interpreter par excellence: "This is a society in which very few women overcome this kind of reputation" (35). At times this kind of information is placed awkwardly into the mouths of the characters. Adja tells her daughter, "Without a man's help a woman has to fall back on prostitution to live and bring up her children. This is the way our country wants it. It is the lot of all our women" (38–39). This is the thinly disguised voice of the implied author. The conventional distance between the audience and the author is re-duced in the film with less overt moments of translation. But the implied au-thor's interpretation functions, like the inner truths, to enlighten and motivate the viewers. The trickster then, turned truth-sayer, plays the images before the eyes of the audience to win them over; and if the act of self-exposure will better conceal this goal, then it will be deployed as well. This is what happens when Kebe, El Hadj's greatest antagonist on the Chamber of Commerce, uses the term "trickery" to describe El Hadj's former actions as militant:

> El Hadj thinks he is still living in colonial times. Those days when he harangued the crowds with his trickery are over, well and truly over. We are independent now. We are the ones who govern. You collaborate with the regime that's in power. So stop all this empty, stupid talk about foreign control. (92)

In exposing El Hadj as a trickster, Kebe's accusation of empty talk has to be turned against himself, as the trickster's discourse is one that always hides in the act of disclosure.

At every point at which we try to fix the truth of the accusation, Sembene's own role returns, as in this scene, to a moment in which we can expect an ar-ticulation of the truth. At first it was with Sembene assuming the role of the griot; then that of the trickster, as one whose interpretations of neocolonial tricks enable us to pass from ignorance to consciousness. In the end, he just as profitably might have been called the *seer-katt*, or seer. We are informed that this is what *seer-katt* means in the novel, when El Hadj thinks he is consult-ing with a traditional healer: "I am not a *facc-katt*—a healer—but a *seer-katt*. My job is to 'see'" (54). In all cases, like Legba, the porter of phallic tricks, he is interpreter, mediator of truth. What remains unrevealed is the common appeal of griot, trickster, *seer-katt* to a difference grounded in the assumption that the truth can be known and spoken for those who are deceived. This is the dif-ference Derrida deconstructs in his analysis of Levi-Strauss's notion of the engineer—the constructor of systems—and the *bricoleur*, the one who fashions things out of the materials at hand.[15] If the engineer is different from the *bri-coleur* in the same way that the narrator differs from the trickster, then we can conclude that just as the trickster plays on the registers of a hidden phallus, so does the narrator, unbeknownst to himself, fall victim to the very play he thought to deploy for his own purposes.

The phallus that appears at the end of *Xala* is that of the "authentic African man"—it is, in fact, authenticity itself, the original history, underneath whose subsequent clothing lies the original center. When Legba pulls out that wooden phallus and the women run off screaming with laughter, it is because there is nothing funnier than a disguised phallus that pretends, or purports, to reveal its workings, especially when it is done in the service of the trickster's concu-piscence.

Let us consider the figure of El Hadj Abdou Kader Beye in the final end, standing in the center of the room, unclothed and covered with spittle, frozen in the last frames while the sounds of the spitting continue—the complete im-

Xala, Ousmane Sembene (Senegal).
Courtesy of New Yorker Films.

age of abjection, or ordure (see image). We understand that this is supposed to
be the true ritual of restoration of manhood, and presumably of integrity, of
the reestablishment of community and even family ties. He is no longer the
prick, the object of the camera's scorn, but he is now the figure of passage, the
trickster who has made himself into the sign of the limen, the wooden phallus.
As he stands thus all the more revealed, our eyes are turned all the more from
the unseen presence of the camera to the disgusting sight and sounds that compound his image. The unseen phallus of the center, its lens aimed at the targeted, disguised wooden phallus, elicits our repulsion, as Legba's wooden phallus did the laughter and screams. But we can choose to join this image with that
of El Hadj doubled in the elevator so as to trick the trickster's trope,[16] and thus
return the workings of phallocentrism against itself.

Notes

1. This analysis is based primarily on the film version of *Xala*. Sembene also produced a version as a novel, indicated by the date of publication that follows the reference
to the text.

2. This is the label for Sembene Ousmane used by Françoise Pfaff in her authoritative study, *The Cinema of Ousmane Sembène*, in 1984. Sembene himself has commonly
employed it in designating the role of the African filmmaker.

3. Gallop's amusing discussion of Lacan the prick occurs in her study *The Daughter's Seduction: Feminism and Psychoanalysis*: "Lacan's practice, in so far as it is traversed

by resistances to metaphysical discourse and by irruptions against Oedipal paternalism, is only accessible in an earthier, less categorical discourse, attuned to the register of aggression and desire. Not simply a philosopher, but, artfully, a performer, he is no mere father figure out to purvey the truth of his authority; he also comes out seeking his pleasure in a relation that the phallocentric universe does not circumscribe. To designate Lacan at his most stimulating and forceful is to call him something more than just phallocentric. He is also phallo-eccentric. Or, in more pointed language, he is a prick" (1982, 36).

4. Trinh T. Minh-ha has inserted this concern into the voice over of her film *Reassemblage* (1982) with the refrain "I do not intend to speak about, just speak nearby." Jay Ruby picks up on this theme with his chapter "Speaking for, Speaking about, Speaking with" in his study of film and anthropology *Picturing Culture* (2000). The "shift in authority" with which he is concerned involves "the possibility of perceiving the world from the viewpoint of people who lead lives that are different from those traditionally in control of the means of imaging the world" (196). I am extending that concern in both a feminist direction (Sembene in control of imaging the women's concerns) and an epistemological direction (the director in control of the knowledge needed to conscientize an audience). In this respect, I am suggesting that Sembene's need to bring an audience lucidity or consciousness is in contradiction with such architects of Third Cinema as Solanas and Getino (1971), or García Espinosa (1971), for whom Third Cinema or an "imperfect" cinema should engage the audience in the process of analysis rather than provide the audience with answers to social problems.

5. The use of the term "failed trickster" refers to a particular trope based on the figure whose ostensibly disruptive behavior is interpreted by Pelton as serving the larger project of restoring order. In the larger sense, it is the role of the subversive figure whose ideological role is ultimately to provide meaning and unity to the apparent incoherence and conflict that threatens the social order. This role is phallocentric, and the burden of this chapter is to show how phallocentrism marks what I am terming the "failed trickster." For that reason, I am interpreting the role of El Hadj Abdou Kader Baye as that of the failed trickster, a role that serves as a marker for Sembene's own project in speaking for the failures of African society in the era of postcolonialism.

6. In turning to Pelton's various West African trickster figures, I am *not* attempting to establish the basis for an ethnographic reading of Sembene's use of the figure, *not* suggesting anything like a direct correspondence between the Akan Ananse, the Fon Legba, the Yoruba Eshu, or the Wolof Leuk. It is rather the broader, semi-allegorical turning of a figure, like that of a trope, that provides the structural model of the figure with which I hope to deconstruct the structuralist's reading of the film, and, more broadly, Sembene's own ideological structurations of the film as well.

7. Pelton makes this point further in his analysis of various Ananse tales, suggesting that it is only through disruption that Ananse can advance the cause of order: "[Ananse] renews by the power of antistructure. His relentless willfulness is not some archaic version of laissez-faire, but a passionate entry into the rawness of precultural relationships to reclaim and restore their potencies, to make them available to new patterns of order" (1980, 50–51).

8. Elizabeth Grosz's definition strikes me as useful: "The representation of *two* sexes by a single, masculine or sexually neutral model" (1989, 25).

9. Cf. Laura Mulvey, "*Xala,* Ousmane Sembene 1976: The Carapace That Failed" (1991). Mulvey's disclaimer comes at the beginning: "The critical perspective of this article cannot include the 'nuances of folk culture,' or, indeed, other important aspects of African culture and history" (rpt. 517). However, there is a certain disingenuousness

in her statement in that the essay turns on an interpretation of the role of the fetish in history and in the film, part of which involves the notion that the meaning of the fetish depends on the history that explains why the fetish was created as such in the first place. That is, one creates a fetish object for historical reasons, be they socially or individually historicized. Mulvey has no trouble looking for that history both in Senegal's colonial and neocolonial ties to France and in the role El Hadj plays in that world. Her essay is a model of clarity in the exposition of the role of the fetish in the film, but she accepts the history assumed by the narrator unproblematically. In the end, Mulvey approvingly cites Teshome Gabriel's interpretation in which the allegorical meaning of the ending, where the beggars spit on El Hadj, signifies the rebirth of African manhood, now made "whole through community" (rpt. 533). Mulvey thus accepts the trickster's function, that of agent of transformation, as successfully negotiated. Derrida's critique of Levi-Strauss, that the center, the presence, implied in structuralist theory erects a phallologocentric order, goes unanswered (see Derrida, "Structure, Sign, and Play in the Discourse of the Human Sciences," in *Writing and Difference*, 1978).

10. For instance, when Serigne Mada restores El Hadj's virility, he twitches and squirms as if his erection were pressing outward toward the camera.

11. This is Lacan's term for that moment in the mirror stage in which the child takes the "imago," the reflected, ideal image of itself to be the foundation for his or her ego or identity.

12. Bhabha (1994) gives a perfect description of this position of mimicry occupied by El Hadj. The "*ambivalence* of mimicry," he writes, "does not merely 'rupture' the discourse [of the civilizing mission], but becomes transformed into an uncertainty which fixes the colonial subject as a 'partial' presence" (1994, 86).

13. This is classic trickster behavior. "Narr" is a pejorative term for a Mauritanian. However, the stereotyped portrayal of the Mauritanian, visible earlier in *Mandabi*, serves Sembene's comic and pedagogical interests. It too depends upon a shared, secret knowledge: the kind that is grounded in notions of authentic identities and originary thought. For the audience, it cements the outer vision of the corruption of the wealthy as built upon the exploiting and destruction of the poor masses.

14. The name means scavenger bird.

15. Cf. the passage in which Derrida exposes the same workings of presence and center in the *bricoleur* or mythmaker as in the engineer: "As soon as we cease to believe in such an engineer and in a discourse which breaks with the received historical discourse, and as soon as we admit that every finite discourse is bound by a certain *bricolage* and that the engineer and the scientist are also species of *bricoleurs*, then the very idea of *bricolage* is menaced and the difference in which it took on its meaning breaks down" (1978, 285).

16. I am grateful to Lamonda Horton-Stallings for this felicitous phrase, which she employs in her dissertation on the role of the female trickster figure in African-American literature and film.

Works Cited

Bâ, Hampaté. 1973. *L'Etrange Destin de Wangrin*. Paris: 10/18.
Bhabha, Homi. 1994. *The Location of Culture*. London: Routledge.
Derrida, Jacques. 1978. *Writing and Difference*. Trans. Alan Bass. Chicago: University of Chicago Press.

Gallop, Jane. 1982. *The Daughter's Seduction: Feminism and Psychoanalysis.* Ithaca: Cornell University Press.

García Espinosa, Julio. 1971. "For an Imperfect Cinema." *Afterimage* 3: 54–67.

Grosz, Elizabeth. 1989. *Sexual Subversions.* Sydney, Australia: Allen and Unwin.

Horton-Stallings, Lamonda. 2002. "A Revision on the Narrative of the Trickster Trope in Black Culture for Alternative Readings of Gender and Sexuality." Diss. Michigan State University.

Mulvey, Laura. 1991. "*Xala,* Ousmane Sembene 1976: The Carapace That Failed," *Third Text* 16–17: 19–37. Reprinted in *Colonial Discourse and Post-Colonial Theory,* ed. Patrick Williams and Laura Chrisman, 517–34. New York: Columbia University Press, 1994.

Pelton, Robert. 1980. *The Trickster in West Africa: A Study in Mythic Irony and Sacred Delight.* Berkeley: University of California Press.

Pfaff, Françoise. 1984. *The Cinema of Ousmane Sembène.* Westport, Conn.: Greenwood.

Ruby, Jack. 2000. *Picturing Culture: Explorations of Film and Anthropology.* Chicago: University of Chicago Press.

Sembene, Ousmane. 1976. *Xala.* Trans. Clive Wake. Westport, Conn.: Lawrence Hill. Film version, 1974. Directed by Ousmane Sembene. Produced by Filmi Domireew and Société Nationale de Cinéma du Sénégal.

Solanas, Fernando, and Octavio Getino. 1971. "Towards a Third Cinema." *Afterimage* 3: 16–35.

Trinh T. Minh-ha, dir. 1982. *Reassemblage.* Distributor: Women Make Movies.

8   Manu Dibango and *Ceddo*'s Transatlantic Soundscape

Brenda F. Berrian

Ceddo is the first and so far the only collaboration by the Senegalese filmmaker Ousmane Sembene and the Cameroonian composer Manu Dibango. In 1976, after listening to Dibango's newly released record *Baobab Sunset*, which was based on an evening with Léopold Sédar Senghor, then president of Senegal, Sembene was convinced that Dibango was the right person to compose the music for his film-in-progress. He traveled to Abidjan, Ivory Coast, where Dibango was based, with the intent to convince a very reluctant Dibango to join the project. Dibango felt he would be out of his element since he considered Sembene to be a man of the savanna and himself a man of the forest. However, in spite of his objections and unfamiliarity with the Senegalese terrain and traditional music, Dibango finally accepted Sembene's invitation and challenge (Dibango, personal interview).

At the time of Sembene's arrival in Abidjan, Dibango was busy working as the director of the Orchestre de la Radio-Télévision Ivoirienne (ORTI). Leader of a band of fifteen musicians and singers from a variety of African countries, Dibango was content with writing, arranging, and hearing his own compositions.[1] At the same time, he had founded *Afro-Music,* a monthly magazine that gave priority to African, jazz, and popular music. With these commitments, it was understandable that he had to be coaxed by Sembene to take on the *Ceddo* project, even though he later composed music for other African films. Among these are: *L'Herbe sauvage* (Weeds, 1977) and *Bal poussière* (*Dancing in the Dust,* 1988) by Henri Duparc (Guinea/Ivory Coast); *Kimboo* (1989), an animated film by Gilles Gay (France); and *Roues libres* (Freewheeling, 2000) by Sidiki Bakaba (Ivory Coast).

The Sembene-Dibango partnership was hardly a smooth one. Although Dibango was enthusiastic about the *Ceddo* film script, he and Sembene often disagreed on the rhythms and instrumentation. Eventually they were able to reach a compromise. One of Dibango's problems was that he had to compose the film score while Sembene was still making the film. Sometimes, as soon as he had finished composing cues of 22 or 44 seconds, Sembene would ask him to cut them to either 20 or 40 seconds. Finally, Sembene arrived in Abidjan with an old recording of traditional Senegalese music, the piece on which Dibango based the theme music of *Ceddo,* but with his own vision. "Composing the music," said Dibango, "was one of the most difficult jobs in my career, but it caused me to know more about myself and what I was capable of doing" (personal interview).

From the opening credits of *Ceddo* to the final ones, Dibango's nondiegetic music is heard, but most of the criticism of the film has been concerned with its themes, filmic representation of history and popular memory, visual images, and technological composition. Instead of using the term "soundtrack," which is often and mistakenly used to refer only to film music, Robynn J. Stilwell's term "soundscape" has been adopted for this chapter. Soundscape refers to images, speeches, sound effects, and music. The four parts are virtually inseparable during the viewing of a film, for they illustrate the interdependence of music and filmic representation. Yet critics often attempt to discuss the different parts in isolation. As a departure, I will discuss the interdependence and interactions between music and the film narrative in which it participates.

Theme Music and Leitmotif

The opening scene of *Ceddo* substantiates that Senegalese women are the backbone of everyday society. For almost five minutes no words are uttered while the viewer sees, bobbing in the river, a calabash that a half-naked woman picks up to pour water over her body. This scene is followed by one of a woman pounding maize and two women raising the roof of a granary. Then the camera shows the arrival of two men who are shackled together and being led by a rope into the village. Slave trade is obviously an accepted routine because none of the villagers pays any attention to the shackled men. The next scene is of a French trader who exchanges European cloth for three women's agricultural products. The four-minute repetition of the theme music during the five minutes of nonverbal communication is underscored by the balafon and xylophone in different variations. Its minor mode alerts the viewer that something is about to happen. This is confirmed when the cries of seven women are heard, saying that Princess Dior Yacine, the king's oldest daughter, has been kidnapped.

The women's cries are punctuated by the sound of their running feet and loud wailing. Strangely enough, despite the bad news about the princess, the imam and his disciples do not disrupt their prayers to Allah. Their inaction establishes that the village is not unified, for the men are not affected by the news.

Ceddo (1976), a fictionalized film based on a composite of historical facts, centers on this kidnapping by a Ceddo rebel. The "Ceddo," as explained by Sembene, is "un homme de refus" (a man who says no) and a "guerrier" (warrior) (Hennebelle and Ruelle 1979, 125). The Ceddos were individuals who defended their African identity and rebelled against Muslim expansion in Senegal. *Ceddo* is the story of resistance to three hostile foreign influences (Islam, Catholicism, and the trade of guns and alcohol for men and women to be sold as slaves) at some indefinite time, probably between the seventeenth and eighteenth centuries or thereafter. By going back into the past, the film extols the indigenous values that were current before the invasion of Islam and European Christianity. However, the film's scope, as noted by Françoise Pfaff, "goes beyond the time period with the insertion of a nineteenth-century African mask, that of a twentieth-century umbrella, and an unexpected flash forward to a huge African Catholic mass of recent years" (1984, 166).

In an unidentified Senegalese village (constructed solely for the film near Mbour), the ambitious imam, an apostle of Islam, asserts his power and determination to convert King Demba Wari Tioub and all the villagers. The king is the first to be converted to Islam and, by his authority, urges the court, his family, and loyal servants to do likewise. However, the Ceddos and some male members of the king's family resist Islamic law because the king's oldest child would not be able to inherit his title or land. This is especially true of the Ceddo rebel, who pledges to release the princess only when the king restores the traditional order. For those who continue to resist the imam's authority, death or forced exile is their sentence. When the king dies mysteriously from snakebite, the imam pronounces himself the successor to the throne, orders a jihad against all non-Muslims, has the Ceddo rebel killed, and sends two disciples to rescue the princess, whom he intends to marry. Confident in his power, the imam does not stop the recently freed Princess Dior Yacine from walking toward him and shooting him at the end of the film.

"Often, there is no main character in my films," Sembene once said. "They are group stories. At a given time, at a given hour, each character plays a little role, and the sum of these roles make up the physiognomy of the group" (Niang and Gadjigo 1995, 176). In light of this statement, *Ceddo* is overwhelmingly male-centered. With the exception of three scenes during which the princess speaks, male voices dominate the film's two hours. On the other hand, the filmic narrative turns and moves around the princess's abduction, and the theme music in a minor mode is linked to the decisions made by the men with regard to the princess. When Prince Biram, the king's son, and Saxewar, the princess's fiancé, separately go to rescue the princess, variations of the theme music are played to alert the viewer that something ominous is going to occur. Unfortunately, both men will be killed by the Ceddo.

Reinforcing the rituals of social etiquette, the theme music is inserted at the beginning of two scenes that comprise conversations between the princess and her kidnapper. Fully aware of the princess's royal status, the Ceddo uses Fara, his griot who plays a *xalam* (a stringed instrument), as an intermediary to convey his messages to the princess. His instruction is: "Fara, tell her that she's being held to put an end to the subjugation that we endure." This is in reference to the king's decision that all of his subjects should convert to Islam. The haughty princess's reply is: "Fara Tine, tell him that only man can do what he has done, and that if men differ, so do women." While employing a courtly and ceremonial form of address to establish the social distance between herself and the Ceddo, the princess alerts the viewer that she is a fighter. In addition, such formalities of speech maintain the class and caste hierarchy of the society, and this form of address adheres to the Wolof concept of *jottali* (the passing on of ritual speech).

The traditional Senegalese social and cultural practice of *jottali* permeates the film. The lengthy series of debate scenes staged in an open field by the king to decide on how to handle the kidnapping of his daughter definitely point out the importance of *jottali*. The eight debate sequences are shot in a circular enclosure with the king seated in the middle among his court nobles. To his left are the imam and his disciples; to his right are the Catholic priest and French trader. Directly in front of the king are the speakers (at a distance), with the Ceddos further away in the back along the circle's border. Maintaining an aristocratic presence, the king remains silent for the majority of the time unless he suddenly raises a question or abruptly issues an order. In the meantime, as the montage continues, more and more attention is shifted away from the king to the imam, whose verbal statements begin to dominate. In addition, without consciously realizing it, the debaters gradually shift their attention away from the king to the imam, especially when the imam declares that the Koran mandates patrilineal rather than matrilineal inheritance.

The debates that involve the king, aristocratic cousins, a Ceddo elder, a warrior, and the imam reveal a fragmentation of interests on the linkages between political power, religion, and matrilineal succession. Threats are exchanged, and appeals are made to the king. Most importantly, the dialogues are to and for the entire village. The men's debates are also broken up with the intervention of Jaraaf, a court noble who functions as the king's griot, whose comments are spoken in a flowery language. Jaraaf introduces the speakers, comments on their words, and takes sides with a rhetorical flourish. Gifted as an orator and as a repository of social memory, Jaraaf proudly mediates the public speeches of the royal family while sharing center stage with them. However, time is excruciatingly slow during this lengthy sequence as the camera shifts its focus from the king and his followers to the imam and his disciples or the Catholic priest and his one convert. Yet the sandy, flat land is always there as the backdrop and a reminder that the film is about an agrarian society with a large number of characters, crowd scenes, and individual and collective narratives. To bring an end to this sequence, the drums are played again after the king reiterates his support of the imam and Islam and decides that his son, Biram, will confront the Ceddo rebel.

During the entire scene the only music heard is the drumming by the town crier to call the meeting and to herald the king's arrival. All activities are to come to a standstill; if not, as reported by the town crier: "Those who refuse will be punished. Their possessions seized." The drum is also played as the Catholic priest quietly looks on while the Ceddos arrive with bundles of wood on their heads. Drumming also punctuates Jaraaf's announcement: "Bring your bodies. The king and his court will arrive." The clever theme music with the balafon, xylophone, and kora is then associated with Biram's attempt to liberate his sister. Unsuccessful, he loses his life when he is hit in the chest by an arrow thrown by the Ceddo.

When Biram's body is returned to the village, Saxewar leaves to confront the Ceddo. This time the theme music enters in a slightly different mode, with a synthesizer to match the scene that will unfold. After shooting the first shot,

Saxewar assumes that he has killed the Ceddo. He picks up the rope that the Ceddo had placed on the ground to contain the princess and proclaims: "Dior, the scoundrel is dead." Unconvinced, the princess wants to see and step over the Ceddo-kidnapper's body before escaping. When she and Saxewar approach, the Ceddo leaves his hiding place, throws sand in Saxewar's eyes and plunges an arrow into his body. To heighten the emotional impact of the moment, the theme music accentuates the violent act and dissolves when the Ceddo re-positions the rope on the ground to delineate the sociopolitical and religious barriers between him and the princess.

In this scene and earlier ones that make up the long debate sequence, the first notes of the balafon often serve as a leitmotif. Not every version of the leitmotif uses the same pattern of orchestration, however. The changing circumstances are duplicated in the music with staggered, independent entrances into the cross-rhythmic pattern. The leitmotif is broken up to alert the viewer whenever there is to be a conflict among the characters or an act of violence. One exception is the scene where the princess takes a reflective bath in the sea while being watched by the Ceddo and Fara.

By shifting accents and emphasizing other rhythms, Dibango's music reminds the viewer that African music is not separate from its communal and cultural settings. Rooted in a historical context, the music, coordinated with the action, reveals the nature of community life. While Sembene points out the ambivalences and difficulties involved in the making of a film about postcolonial Senegal, the struggles around Islam are highlighted by Dibango's multiple rhythms and leitmotif.

Diola Choral Music

Well aware that the written version of Senegalese history has either been distorted or ignored, Sembene is committed to filling in the gaps and pointing out the contradictions and the confusion that arose around the ideological battles for and against imported religions. History is consequently an interplay of collective groups and forces. Even though the individual decisions of the imam are emphasized, they still affect the collective unit—the entire village. For example, when the imam forbids drinking and the worship of fetishes and orders the converts to pray five times a day, the silence in the village is broken only by the younger generation, with a cry from a baby. This cry symbolizes that the imam's domination will probably be contested by the youth (Princess Dior Yacine).

The baby's cry also leads the viewer to the priest, whose voice is never heard. The priest observes Prince Madior, the king's nephew, looking at his church. After the priest walks towards Prince Madior, he stands still and raises his head to the heavens. Startling the viewer is a flash-forward sequence that centers on the priest's dream of a Christian Senegal when the priest's upward gaze focuses on the interior of a cathedral dome painted with black angels. Attached to the dream is an energetic tune sung in Diola by the Chorale St. Joseph de Cluny of

Dakar. The tune, in a major mode with a fast tempo, has an optimistic feeling. The call-and-response singing, accompanied by a variety of drums and other percussion, is punctuated by several repetitions of "Alleluia."

There is also an outdoor, twentieth-century Senegalese Catholic mass, with spliced *cinéma-vérité* footage of a Catholic communion with nuns and other priests in attendance, interspersed with Prince Madior presiding as a bishop over the priest's funeral. In the next scene the priest, who represents the West, is seen clad in his chasuble to say mass standing under a canopy and being a witness at his own funeral. Among the mourners are the nonbelievers and the imam, who has converted to Catholicism.

The break in the film's straightforward narrative with a flash-forward dream sequence is directed at the twentieth-century viewer who knows that the present-day Senegalese population is 80 percent Muslim (Sembene qtd. in Ni Chréacháin 1992, 241–42). The insertion of Diola music from the Casamance region illustrates that Catholic services in African countries are being Africanized and are becoming more sensitive to cultural differences among its diverse membership. The Diola-style music is embellished with polyphonic textures and percussion, recalling that the Diola resisted French colonial rule until 1942 (Gadjigo et al. 1993, 40) as illustrated in Sembene's *Emitai* (1971). The music also holds together the cinematic succession of images that comprise the flash-forward dream sequence. Therefore, the choice of Diola music suggests that the Wolof and Diola peoples, cultures, and languages are not in conflict. Instead, they are closely intertwined.

African-American Gospel

The theme of slavery is a constant presence throughout *Ceddo*, and some of its historical consequences are emphasized with the insertion of a recorded African-American gospel song from the twentieth century. The diegetic music coincides with the slavery scenes and serves as a base of continuity to support the visual images. Dibango had been exposed to a variety of musical styles and techniques (including religious music) since his childhood in Douala, Cameroon. His philosophy is that he must explore many angles in life. Such an exploration is transferred to his music, for, as he once stated, "Curiosity can be limited by your environment, or you can expand it to take things from outside: a bigger curiosity for a bigger world" (1991, 7). That is how he composed his Grammy-winning hit, "Soul Makossa," in 1972 out of an amalgam of his loves: "traditional Cameroonian makossa rhythm with a little African American soul thrown in" (1994, 82). Thus, the appropriateness of matching an African-American gospel song with three specific sequences in *Ceddo*—the feeding of slaves, the branding of slaves with a hot iron, and the destruction of the Ceddos' property while their heads are shaven—reinforce the violent depersonalization and the total annihilation of the slaves' and Ceddos' prior identities.

The mass conversion sequence—where the Ceddos assume Muslim identities, have their heads shaven, and are forced to replace their Ceddo names with

Arab-derived names—illustrates Dibango's musical diversity. The insertion of Arthur Simm's gospel song "I'll Make It Home Some Day" within the soundscape is overheard over the images of the mass conversion. The song is both sad and wistful. The sadness is attributed to the loss of the villagers' birth names and their right to worship as they wish. The sadness also reminds one of the voyage the slaves underwent during their passage to the New World. It also relates to the fact that the Ceddos and non-Ceddos are shackled and branded in the presence of the king, the villagers, the priest, and the imam, but nobody comes forward to save them. Slavery was condoned because the king, the other nobles, and the imam had the attitude that they were invincible. Whenever there was a war, the defeated ethnic group was enslaved by the conquerors. As depicted in *Ceddo,* the slave trade was based on money and profit, and the gospel song represents a breaking off from the village in the direction of the Diaspora.

The slaves' wistfulness is contained in the gospel's English lyrics, "I'm not going to testify / I know freedom will be mine / I'm going to push my luck / I'll make it home one day," in counterpoint with the terrible images of houses being set afire and the murders of the priest and the French trader. The unseen journey of the shackled slaves is marked for the viewer by the sound of the African-American gospel song from the future. In spite of the Ceddos' temporal and spatial restriction to the village, their departure from Gorée Island includes a series of historical and physical journeys from Senegal to the African Diaspora. The silent visual presences of the Catholic priest, the slaves, and the French trader are thereby consequences of journeys external to the African continent. Yet the slaves never stopped believing they would be able to return to their land(s) of birth.

Snatches of "I'll Make It Home Some Day" accentuate the filmic narrative to cede to the spectacle of slaves being exchanged for gunpowder and rifles. An organ is played and "Amen" is voiced while men and women are branded. The "Amen" confirms a complicity between the Catholic Church and commercialism through the selling of human bodies. When the organ music fades away, it is replaced by the sound of a woman's piercing scream. The French trader has placed a hot iron with the emblem of a fleur-de-lis on her leg.

In an interview, Dibango wondered if there would have been any gospel music if Gorée Island hadn't existed. Recognizing the commonalities of African and African Diasporic experiences in gospel music, he commented: "When I hear a certain type of American music from the South, it sounds like the Ku Klux Klan. And when I hear gospel, I see African Americans and the chains" (personal interview). In other words, for Dibango, remnants of slavery still exist among African Americans deep down in the rural South of the United States.

The Jazz Sequence

In *Ceddo,* Dibango also blends in the jazz idiom. That is why his music has been called American in France, European in Africa, and African in the United States. He refuses to be labeled and proclaims that he belongs to a "race of musicians." In fact, Dibango once said that jazz gives him a kind of freedom and a fresh scope for the imagination:

> Jazz is the invention of a link between one continent and another even if the story behind is a terrible one. But the most beautiful flower can grow on a dunghill. . . . The dunghill is slavery and all its works. The flower is jazz, the fruit of what came from the West, on the one hand, and from Africa on the other. ("Interview with Manu Dibango," 5)

When the converts' names are changed to Arab-sounding ones, jazz is played, resembling Ornette Coleman's avant-garde style. The jazzy melody—accompanied by two piano solos with low notes, cymbals, a balafon, a bass drum, a bass, and a saxophone—is repeated when Princess Dior returns to the village. The hybrid piano music contains a melodic configuration common to blues and jazz. The esoteric and the sociological gaze are mingled along with the music and the princess's gestures and body movement. While the camera remains fixed on Princess Dior's face and body as she walks directly to the imam among the converts and Ceddos, the musical pitch rises as soon as she grabs a rifle from one of the imam's guards.

The princess's unexpected but drastic action resembles a piece of improvisational jazz wherein high and low accents startle the viewer. To protect her, the Ceddos immobilize the rest of the imam's guards by throwing themselves in front of them and placing the barrels of the rifles into their mouths. This demonstrates their willingness to sacrifice their lives for her. In a series of long and medium-long shots, the viewer follows the princess step by step when she pulls the trigger and shoots the imam in his genitals. The final scene is a half-shot, freeze frame, close-up of the princess as she walks unflinchingly among the imam's disciples, the new converts, and the Ceddos to look directly at the viewer. The princess's slow walk matches the repeats, returns, and closing figures of the two jazz piano solos. Simultaneously, the princess's action and the jazzy music break down the constraints and barriers created by the imam.

The princess's shooting of the imam in his genitals is a symbolic castration. Considering the secondary position of women under Islam, Princess Dior Yacine's calculated action upsets the patriarchal order. The complexity of the princess's character, as noted by Pfaff, is "a political symbol of bravery and courage," and her action makes up for "the weaknesses of her father and the men he used to rule" (1984, 175). The princess's fatal shot temporarily puts a halt to the psychological and physical conversion of reluctant villagers to Islam; she also inhales and exhales the strength that had evaporated from the male villagers. The deaths of the king and other family members have left a void in the traditional order of succession, so the princess assumes the throne by eradicating the imam, who had rendered the male villagers and the Ceddos impotent. To reinforce this notion, Nwachukwu Frank Ukadike remarks that *Ceddo* is "an iconoclastic film, devastatingly antireligious, focusing mainly on the Islamic impact and particularly questioning the subjugation entrenched in its ideology and the acceptance of this ideology by Africans to the extent of rendering traditional culture impotent" (1994, 183).

By killing the domineering and destructive imam, the princess liberates the villagers from their oppressor. She additionally eliminates the evil that caused the imam's disciples and the Muslim converts to behave like zombies. They might have been passive, but the princess rekindles the spirit of resistance and aligns herself with the Ceddos who had wanted to terminate the imam's rule. "When the princess kills the imam," Sembene explained, "it has great symbolic significance for modern Senegal. The action is contrary to the present idea and the role that women now hold. And this is the only reason the film has been banned in Senegal" (qtd. in Gupta, Johnson, and Allen 1978, 27).

The reshaping of Senegalese history and rewriting of Islam by Sembene in *Ceddo* created a controversy. Under President Senghor's leadership, the Senegalese government banned the showing and distribution of *Ceddo* for eight years. This decision to silence Sembene was unusual because the Senegalese government and Domirev, Sembene's production company, were the co-sponsors of *Ceddo* with a bank credit of 20 million CFA francs. Ironically, as noted by Paulin S. Vieyra: "It was the first film to benefit from this formula. Sembène's personality was no doubt connected with the operation" (qtd. in Downing 1987, 37). The official reason was based on a linguistic problem. President Senghor stipulated that Sembene had to respect the newly decreed Wolof standard of spelling the title of *Ceddo* with a single "d." For artistic reasons Sembene refused to comply; he also knew that the real reason for the film's censorship was the government's deference to the powerful leaders of the Muslim brotherhoods.

Despite its banning in Senegal, *Ceddo* was released outside the country and selected for the *quinzaine des réalisateurs* (directors' fortnight of films) at the Cannes Film Festival in May 1977. Seven years later, on July 4, 1984, *Ceddo* was shown for the first time before a packed audience in Dakar.

Just as the filmic narrative leaps across the centuries, Dibango's music within the soundscape functions as a transitional narrative device, easing in as quietly as possible and functioning as a griot. The music starts either at the top of a scene or within a scene, based on the details of the particular sequence. The sound effects and music counterpoint the image, causing the viewer to be gripped by a range of emotions: surprise, encouragement, sadness, and hope. This makes it impossible to be a passive viewer of Sembene's films. For example, the Catholic priest's flash-forward dream sequence and that of Princess Dior when she offers a gourd of fresh water to welcome the Ceddo as he comes home from a hunt cause the viewer to asks questions. Viewers especially wonder if they ought to interpret the princess's kneeling before the Ceddo as a signal that she is ready to join him to depose the imam. So the two flash-forward scenes surprise the viewer, but they add something new, giving the story a surrealistic quality.

To extend the surrealism, the recorded gospel and Diola music as well as the

African-oriented jazz (located in six sequences) jar viewers' senses of sound and sight, and place them inside the narrative. Dibango uses music from several sources as an assemblage. The musical collage replaces the function of a single coherent orchestral arrangement that is usually associated with a Western mainstream film. Dibango called upon a French Caribbean pianist from the Gibson Brothers (a French Caribbean band based in Paris) to play three-fourths of the piano music, with himself playing one sequence. To explain his decision, Dibango stated: "The music represents the foreigners who arrived with another kind of solidarity.... The imam and the Catholic priest did not come to Africa by themselves; they arrived with the Qu'ran, the Bible, the rifle, the guitar and the piano" (personal interview).

Projecting into the future, Sembene points to a path of change with the portrayal of the princess as a resistance heroine. Making the princess proactive results in an homage to the contributions African women have made to the liberation struggle. Figuratively, the fictional heroine joins predecessors who brought victory to their countries: Queen Nzinga of Angola, Dona Beatrice of the Congo, and Queen Amina of Nigeria. Thus, the scene of crossed gazes of the imam and the princess enables the princess to confront her environment in relationship to the indigenous inheritance before the invasion by Islam. The dialectical gaze, shared by the viewer, encompasses gender, ethnicity, and class while positioning the viewer to sense that something ominous is going to occur. At the same time, the viewer's temporal gaze is linked to that of the princess as she incorporates everybody in sight—the Ceddos, the nobles, the women and children, and the Muslim converts. With one glance, the princess unites royalty and the masses. The gaze shared by Princess Dior and the Ceddos provides the venue for her to recognize the injustice of the Ceddos' situation. Her power is contained in her social status, and her capture serves "as a narrative device to expose Sembene's central thesis concerning the loss of cultural identity and roots" (Petty 1996, 79).

The film's denunciation of passive resistance invents a new historical intervention by breaking the silence about the unspoken and exposing the concealed into the open. The Wolof proverb, "Kou wathie sa toundeu, toundeu boo feke mou tasse" (When one abandons one's own hillock, any hillock that one climbs thereafter will collapse), encapsulates the notion that the abandonment of one's culture and traditions equals destruction. Thus, it is appropriate to recall the tragedies that befall the unidentified village: the deaths of the king, the Ceddo rebel, the non-Muslims, Biram, Saxewar, and the imam. To restore order, the princess has to provide the indigenous foundation and serve as her father's successor. Since jazz is built on a reputation of breaking new ground, the finale follows the three-step process of silence, action, and music. Nobody spoke during the entire time that the princess dismounted the horse and killed the imam. She did what they most likely lacked the courage to do. In many ways the music is mingled with the atmosphere and the princess's action. This impression is strongly reinforced by the sounds of two pianos. Bit by bit, the viewer comes to feel that the music, rather than stereotypically evoking gloom because of the imam's death, is in fact upbeat and calls forth a note of optimism. To show an alliance with the princess, the jazz-style music, as noted by Philip Rosen, "re-shapes even such themes from the past into a twentieth-century mode. This alone is a signal of historiography in the process of being written for current purposes" (1991, 161).

The performance of different kinds of music underlines the idea of the film's time frame and projection into the twentieth century. Appearing in nine sequences in the filmic narrative, the mostly nondiegetic theme music comes the closest to a Western underscore with its minimally repeated rhythms to provide some kind of unification. Evident in the film's soundscape are Sembene's beliefs that "to get along together in harmony is the sole purpose of culture" and that "we can absorb other cultures, use them, adapt ourselves without any loss" (qtd. in Gadjigo et al. 1993, 75, 96). As a result, the soundscape embraces the two men's Pan-African vision of making a film for the whole world, not for only one ethnic group. Within this context, speech, sound effects, and music are blended, intermittent, and switched on and off throughout *Ceddo*. All three enter directly into the "plot" of the film, adding another dimension to the visual images. The three also fill in the soundscape with pauses in conversations that include the amplified sounds of bleating goats, the clicking of prayer beads, the repetition of "Allah," the pouring of water, the cries of a baby or of birds, the crackling of fire, the buzzing of flies, and the hoofbeats of horses.

In contradistinction, music in Sembene's earlier films—*Borom Sarret* (1963), *Mandabi* (1968), *Emitai* (1971), and *Xala* (1974)—is used as an accessory rather than as an integral element. In *Borom Sarret*, for instance, to delineate architectural and social differences, the Wolof guitar music that is heard in the African neighborhood is replaced by an orchestra playing Mozart as the cart man passes from the outskirts of Dakar into the French quarter. For *Mandabi* and *Xala*, Sembene collaborated with Samba Diabare Sam to compose Wolof songs as a part of the filmic narrative structure to speak out against social injustice. The music in *Xala* is especially heard during the dance scene that precedes El Hadji Abdoukader Beye's marriage to his third wife. And in *Emitai*, the Senegalese soldiers ironically sing "Maréchal nous voilà" (Marshall, Here We Are), a song in which some French people expressed their support to Maréchal Pétain during World War II.

In *Ceddo*, music allows Sembene to express an idea that is not voiced aloud. Whereas the verbose Jaraaf speaks for the king and the silent Fara retains the Ceddo's memory, the jazzy griot-like music that accompanies the princess becomes "a storytelling element capable of providing information by itself" and "carries the significance of the visual image" (Pfaff 1984, 68). This occurs when Princess Dior Yacine undergoes a rapid change upon hearing the sad news about her father's death. Although she speaks not one word, her thoughts dwell in her silence. Her silent thoughts also lead her to murder the imam, an action that no man in the village dared to do. Thus, the interruption of the princess's silence with jazzy music alerts the viewer to pay close attention to the princess and enhances the dramatic tension by stimulating an emotional response from the viewer.

In his role as the news-bearing griot–film director, Sembene recreates the structures of power relations in the Wolof state, recovering oral traditions and memory. Filmed entirely in a Wolof frequently couched in old, courtly proverbs that most present-day urban Senegalese do not understand, *Ceddo* exposes, chronicles, and delves into the struggles between indigenous religious values and those of Catholicism and Islam. The film is also a repetition of history, foreshadowing what has transpired with the 1979 Shiite Islamic revolution in Iran and the 2001 fall of the Taliban in Afghanistan.

Tied to *Ceddo*'s thematic diversification is Dibango's musical score that conveys feelings and touches the viewer's emotions.[2] The music accentuates and intensifies the action of the film. Going full circle, *Ceddo* begins with snippets of traditional Senegalese music and ends with African-oriented jazz. The rhythms Dibango used to achieve an integration of music and community demonstrate the reality that exists within the Senegalese village. To explain further, Dibango remarked:

> The people wanted to be themselves. They didn't want to be washed away by the foreign invasions of Christianity and Islam. . . . *Ceddo* is an allegory, and I attempted to transform the visual image, the emotion and writing in *une couleur sonore* [a sonorous color]. . . . When working with a filmmaker, I am at his service. I try to interpret in my own way what he has given me as a story in sound and resonances. . . . *Ceddo* is a sociopolitical film; it took a lot of courage for Sembene to make it. (personal interview)

The complex interweaving of contrasting rhythms from across Africa and its Diaspora supports and articulates Sembene's position on communal relationships. Dibango's musical score and arrangements demonstrate that neither he nor Sembene were looking for a music connected with dance.[3] Emphasis is placed on silence, noises, and repetitive, slow, insistent rhythms not limited to Africa. The collaboration between Sembene and Dibango on *Ceddo*'s transatlantic soundscape certainly helped to erase some misconceptions about the penetration of foreign religions (Islam and Christianity) and the selling or bartering of objectified Africans for profit in Senegal. Most of all, their artistic collaboration is a metaphorical reinterpretation of Islam, Christianity, and slavery in West African history.

Notes

1. See Dibango, *Three Kilos of Coffee* (1994, 97).
2. The original film score arranged by Dibango can be listened to independently on the vinyl recording entitled *Ceddo,* consisting of seven songs and slightly over thirty-seven minutes long (Fiesta LP 362 002).
3. See Gregor 1978, 37. During this interview, Sembene stated that he and Dibango were looking for music "which would not, in any traditional sense, make the film more attractive" and that Dibango used bottles to make xylophonic sounds. He further stated: "Africans have got used to the idea that African films always have to have traditional

music. But we're trying to provide through the music a route to a world problematic, a sense of the world."

Works Cited

Dibango, Manu. 1977. *Ceddo*. Fiesta LP 362 002.
———. 1991. "Music in Motion." Preface in *Africa O-Ye*, by Graeme Evans, 7–8. London: Guiness.
———. 1994. *Three Kilos of Coffee*. Trans. Danielle Rouell. Chicago: University of Chicago Press.
———. Personal interview. 25 October 2000. My translation.
Downing, John D. H., ed. 1987. *Film & Politics in the Third World*. New York: Praeger.
Gadjigo, Samba, et al., eds. 1993. *Ousmane Sembene: Dialogues with Critics and Writers*. Amherst: University of Massachusetts Press.
Gregor, Ulrich. 1978. "Interview with Ousmane Sembene." *Framework* 7–8: 35–37.
Gupta, Udayan, Deborah Johnson, and Nick Allen. 1978. "Seven Days Interview: Sembene." *Seven Days*, 10 March, 26–27.
Hennebelle, Guy, and Catherine Ruelle. 1979. "Interview No. 39: Sembène Ousmane." *L'Afrique littéraire et artistique* 49: 111–26.
"Interview with Manu Dibango." 1991. *UNESCO Courier* (March): 4–7.
Ni Chréacháin, Fírinne. 1992. "If I Were a Woman, I'd Never Marry an African." *African Affairs* 91.363: 241–47.
Niang, Sada, and Samba Gadjigo. 1995. "Purity Has Become a Thing of the Past: An Interview with Ousmane Sembene." *Research in African Literatures*. Special issue on African cinema. 26.3: 174–78.
Petty, Sheila. 1996. "Towards a Changing Africa: Women's Roles in the Films of Ousmane Sembene." In *A Call to Action: The Films of Ousmane Sembene*, ed. Sheila Petty, 67–86. Westport, Conn.: Greenwood.
Pfaff, Françoise. 1984. *The Cinema of Ousmane Sembene*. Westport, Conn.: Greenwood.
Rosen, Philip. 1991. "Making a Nation in Sembene's *Ceddo*." *Quarterly Review of Film and Video* 13.1–3: 147–72.
Stilwell, Robynn J. 2001. "Sound and Empathy: Subjectivity, Gender and the Cinematic Soundscape." In *Film Music: Critical Approaches*, ed. K. J. Donnelly, 167–87. New York: Continuum International, 2001.
Ukadike, Nwachukwu Frank. 1994. *Black African Cinema*. Los Angeles: University of California Press.

Part Three: *Original and Burgeoning Cinematic Practices*

9   The Other Voices of Documentary: *Allah Tantou* and *Afrique, je te plumerai*

N. Frank Ukadike

In reviewing the history of cinema and documentary film practice, one finds a pattern of deliberate mockery of Africans and their historical traditions and cultures by Western filmmakers. This pattern upholds an insistence on using visual images for the purpose of so-called scientific documentation. In fact, critics have observed that most documentary films, specifically ethnographic and anthropological films, are mere spectacles constructed to titillate Western viewers. At best, they serve as fragments of reality, depending on the nature of the real or what one conceives of as the real.[1]

This chapter examines new African documentary practices and the strategies used in the construction of cinematic "reality" of Africa in the context of two films: *Allah Tantou* (God's Will, 1991) by David Achkar (Guinea); and *Afrique, je te plumerai* (Africa, I Will Fleece You, 1992) by Jean-Marie Teno (Cameroon). These films are considered in relation to their theoretical contexts so as to redefine the relationship between the dominant (Western) and oppositional (pan-Africanist) cinematic representations of Africa. A critical issue at stake is whether the new African documentaries can be wholly comprehended without fathoming the radically divergent ways in which the pan-Africanist imagery positions the subject, the viewer, and the filmmaker to promote spectator participation. In addition to stressing the documentaries' manifestations as social art, I will consider their inventive approaches to issues of formal structuration, experimental modalities, and modes of address.

African documentary seeks to interrogate the African experience; the documentary frame presents what might be seen as a transparent window on history, culture, and other issues of resistance. The social issues, cultural values, and politics of the African world are portrayed with both sensitivity and realism. It is this connection between the documentary and the real circumstances depicted, between the filmmaker and the subject/audiences, that is the most distinctive characteristic of this genre. I will argue that the passion for truth stems from the penchant for historical accuracy and communicability, hence the impact of "the belief that what is seen (and heard) is the essence of what is, and of what is knowable about what is" (Burton 1990, 77), which forms the basis for African historical truth.

Toward the History: Toward the Criticism

Bill Nichols's observation regarding the dichotomous relationship between fiction and documentary film is germane to our discourse. He notes that "if narratives invite our engagement with the construction of a story, set in an imaginary world, documentary invites our engagement with the construction of an argument, directed toward the historical world" (1991, 118). The hegemony of the colonizer relative to the colonized peoples has, in conjunction with the history of oppression, institutionalized social differentiation and inequality. This imbalance has also promoted the assumption that colonial histories offer a privileged perspective from which to analyze both worlds. Countering this assumption implies the demystification of colonial histories, exposing their method of reification, objectification, and representation of the "Other." Hence, the quest for African cinematic reality (the image) in film has produced a genre of social documentary meant to combat the false image presented by traditional cinema. In attempting to confront the distortion, the perspectives of "alternative" cinema specify an ideological mission that functions as a specific mandate in reexamining hegemonic power relations.

Stating that "narrativity emerges as a fundamental condition that binds together all three representational practices—history, documentary, and the fiction film," Philip Rosen argues that "meaning arises through a process of sequentation which is constitutive of historical discourse" (qtd. in Renov 1993a, 2). This latter concern, as Rosen rightly points out, has been an integral component that documentary theory and practice have embraced since the time of John Grierson, founder of the British documentary movement. But the truth is that documentary films about Africa have also privileged fiction at the expense of authentic history in exactly the same way that the history and theory addressing the genre most often ignore the willful destruction of the relationship that non-Western subjects enjoyed in early documentary experiments.[2] These flaws result from an inability to comprehend the complex relationship between history and culture, which requires patience and integrity to circumnavigate. As we shall show, it is from this perspective that we locate the mission of African cinema, specifically the documentary genre.

The development of cinema in Africa is directly connected to both historical circumstances and movements in film practices. There is a relationship between history/politics in society and history/politics in the text, which may culminate in the decolonization of the screen and the repositioning of the cinema as the site for what critics are calling political contestation. A concerted effort to crystallize national struggles and identities may be an indication of a society that is moving to regain its belief in itself. This belief had been shattered by the "[un]humanitarian uses of the cinema,"[3] entrenched in the standard narrative and visual structure of the dominant tradition, which the "alternative" reinventing representations of Africa now seek to reverse.

Western methods applied to the construction of African film images constitute what might be termed spurious art, antithetical to the longings of a genial art that indigenous cultural productions predicate. *Afrique* and *Allah Tantou* contrast sharply with many films, both documentary and fiction, that have made Africa their focal point. For example, in the two popular films used in American classrooms, *Reassemblage* (1982) by Trinh T. Minh-ha and *Unsere Afrikareise* (1961–66) by Peter Kubelka, the African lives proffered make a mockery of human intelligence. In *Reassemblage*, for instance, which obfuscates African subjectivity, the all-knowing voice of God in the film is that of an itinerant docent—a Peace Corps volunteer, the filmmaker herself. Similarly, *Unsere Afrikareise*, heralded by Constance Penley and Andrew Ross (1985) for its "innovative" editing technique, and by Michael Renov for "shar[ing] with mainstream documentary a commitment to the representation of the historical real" (1993b, 34), deliberately disregards African sensibility. Here an African is used as a stand to hold the White man's rifle as it blasts its salvo right next to his ear to hit a lion. Moreover, the Austrians in the film, who constantly ridicule the Africans, exhibit themselves as racists and poachers, their manners no less animalistic than the giraffes they slaughter mercilessly in their Kenyan safari. The filmmaker's bias is epitomized in a shot where the long neck of one of the giraffes is contrasted with the elongated necklaces adorning an African woman. Yet this blatant racist and sexist image is not even mentioned by the critics who admire the film for its cinematic inventiveness.

Most attacks on such works focus on the abuse of authorial power, an abuse that in turn invalidates claims to documentary authenticity. Elements of authenticity can be found in segments of any film, but this does not mean that the segment carries the full weight of the entire film. The question is, should the audience or critics capitalize on the importance of a film's particular stylistic tendency at the expense of the elements that have vitiated the reality that the film ought to be exposing? History has proved this to be true if we remember the virulent impact of D. W. Griffith's *Birth of a Nation* (1915), Luis Buñuel's sardonic *Land Without Bread* (1932), Jean Rouch's *The Mad Masters* (1953), or Terry Bishop's *Daybreak in Udi* (1949)—all of which were vehemently protested or criticized because of their racism but nonetheless classified as "masterpieces" and classics.

How does one know that certain aspects of history and culture have been misrepresented, and why does the audience see the images presented differently from the perspectives of the filmmaker? I have argued elsewhere that it might be theoretically correct to polemicize authorial interventions with intriguing theories, as some artists have done when they try to help the consumer understand their "complex" approaches to visual representation.[4] However, in the visual and performing arts, one would have to agree that the image speaks louder than, say, the voice-over in any documentary film or the polemical treatise that explains or miseducates the audience. (It is ironic that frequently the theories deriving from most films also create mental confusion for readers.)

For the critical observer, issues concerning selectivity (choice of shots/image), and intrusion (method of selecting) play important roles in deciphering any work of art. In the case of film, this observation applies to the use of camera, composition, and the way the footage has been assembled to convey meaning. Since film has always been an ideological project, it cannot be politically neutral. Its ideological subjectivity also prepares the curious observer to think about how methodology influences what is presented on the screen (the cinematic sign) and what was out there in the open (the referent).

While many African fiction films are structured as fictional narratives, they exhibit a documentary/fictional synthesis. Stylistically, we find here reminiscences of treatment that recalls Latin American documentary film practice. For example, such early films as *Afrique-sur-Seine* (Africa on the Seine, 1955) by Paulin Soumanou Vieyra (Benin/Senegal); *La Noire de...* (*Black Girl,* 1966) and *Mandabi* (1968) by Ousmane Sembene (Senegal); *Last Grave at Dimbaza* (1974) by Nana Mahomo (South Africa); and *Harvest: 3,000 Years* (1976) by Haile Gerima (Ethiopia) are inundated with a documentary mode of address. The juxtaposition of fiction and documentary images embeds the diegesis in oral tradition and heightens the emotional impact. Like their Latin American counterparts, African filmmakers believe in the political use of film and see less entertainment value in films than Hollywood does. If anything connects African and Hollywood films, it is that African cinema is directly related to the results of earlier movements in film practices and historical circumstances.

The rise of the realistic and formalistic tendencies—neorealism, docudrama, and Marxist dialectics—expedited the dissolution of the line between fiction and reality, between documentary and ethnographic film practice, and, I may add, stressed the anomalies of representation—the North and South dichotomy. From this perspective I have argued that although African films exhibit hybrid convention—those originating from Hollywood, Russian Socialist dialectics, Italian neorealism, and avant-garde traditions—no single stylistic criterion predominates. Therefore, any critical component applied to the evaluation of this film practice must also consider how these syncretic "master codes" are disarticulated by the cultural codes embedded in the oral tradition (Ukadike 1993).

From the very beginning of filmmaking, some of the above distinctions already began to emerge to address the visual polarities and characteristics of Lumière's *Workers Leaving the Factory* (1895) and Méliès's *A Trip to the Moon* (1902). While Lumière's film was believed to have captured an unmediated event, Méliès extended the potential of the cinematic apparatus beyond the capture of "physical reality" (Kracauer 1960) to encompass a rearrangement of filmed events. This counterhegemonic impulse has greatly influenced filmmaking ever since.

In the African sector, in oral art, film production, and other cultural productions, an event can be rearranged without necessarily distorting the meaning as connected with the historical, social, and political realities. This intervention is appreciated for radiating the fictional impulse in the process of enhancing the creative and didactic value of the intended message. On this level, film watching becomes synonymous with history lessons; it is instilled with culturally specific codes and awareness, rendering this tradition unabashedly political. This is why, depending on the circumstances that have influenced a film's production, audience acceptability is a given. Hence, the polemical discourse around documentary veracity would also take a new approach. What is generally discernible as a documentary in dominant analysis assumes another name, a filmed essay in documentary dialect, a topic that will recur in the subsequent sections of this chapter.

Historical Specificity: Documentary Conscience

Films from the Francophone zone popularized African fiction film and the didactic trend, and although documentary segments interspersed most narratives, the documentary never manifested itself as a common genre. It is in the Anglophone and Lusophone regions that documentary film continues to thrive —unfortunately, at the expense of fiction film. However, documentary film practice had different agendas in these regions. The practice of the Anglophone region was modeled after the British colonial pattern of instructional filmmaking—documenting the activities of the ruling oligarch, praise-singing even when there was no genuine development to boast of. The practice of the Lusophone region was much more focused—film was accorded the status of weapon of liberation in the war against Portugal. Pedro Pimenta, assistant director of the Mozambique Film Institute (Instituto Nacional de Cinema, or INC) felicitously remarked that it is necessary to change the dominant image to "produce a new thing, the product of a new ideology" (Taylor 1983, 30). This production of a "new thing" came to mean as much for Angola, Guinea-Bissau, and Mozambique as socialist film ideology meant for Russia—in this case leading to the acquisition of a documentary film practice engendered in Africanist/Socialist ideology.

As an emancipatory project, African cinema has always concerned itself with wide-ranging issues—from decolonization of history and liberation, to Africa's resistance against oppression. During the first decade of African film practice, this concern specifically manifested itself in anticolonialist projects. After independence, however, when African elites proved to be even more perfidious than the colonial administrators they replaced, cinema placed all contemporary issues on its agenda. As Harold W. Weaver has pointed out, there developed "a cinema of contestation between the filmmakers and the political leadership" (1982, 85). Some of the films that were extremely critical of the establishment were censored, and some filmmakers embarked on social criticism only after the political leadership was driven out of office or eliminated through natural causes. One such instance was *Allah Tantou,* which was made in Guinea. Both this film and *Afrique* are remarkable for the manner in which they address larger issues of continental dimensions.

Two elemental analyses can be set in motion: the first is contextual and concerns the forces bearing on the production of films—the social institutions and production practices that construct media images of Africa; the second entails personal/ideological manifestations as a synthesis of the collective struggle against oppression. Four principal characteristics in documentary film practice define this agenda:

1. Authority: a metadiscourse referring to the validity of the subject's treatment, or even the legitimacy of the filmmaker, and his/her knowledge and relation to the issues being portrayed;

2. Transparency: embodying the processes of introspection, as in "looking in" (hence subverting the original meaning of the term, "transparency"—that which appears to be mere recording), and presenting issues as transparent windows on the world, raising and increasing public awareness;

3. Immediacy: the reflection of "nowness," the subject's or viewer's relationship to the present, which may involve the invocation of past events to explain the present situation, or even the use of present events to amplify past events in order to make them more immediate;

4. Authenticity: almost synonymous with reality, an expression of the filmmaker's truthfulness in presenting the real, questioning societal norms, and increasing public awareness of issues and dichotomies.[5]

Allah Tantou and *Afrique* have used their structures to transform these filmic attributes to further cinematic scrutiny of the African issues depicted, which, in turn, forcefully informs and moves the audience. In their respective ways, each film uses creative modes of address and conventions of traditional documentary cinema, but each is recontextualized to offer a means of challenging the nature of representation. This can be seen, for example, when footage originally broadcast to promote colonialist or neocolonialist propaganda is given a new meaning. The films are reconfigured as *turn-around* images, refurbished as veritable critiques of colonialist/repressive ideologies. Before we analyze these documentaries in more detail, however, it is pertinent to consider some critical assumptions of the documentary film practice since they are bound to influence my approach, particularly in relation to my understanding of how certain conventions may have been appropriated or subverted.

Bill Nichols (1991) points out that in documentary film practice, of the "dominant organizational patterns around which most texts are structured," four modes of production stand out: "expository," "observational," "interactive," and "reflexive." He notes that in this paradigm, the expository text speaks to the viewer "directly, with titles or voices" that are meant to convey progressive thoughts "about the historical world." The voice-over narration, dubbed "voice-of-God" or "talking heads," presents objectively persuasive arguments. The observational mode is more directly connected with "direct cinema" or *cinéma vérité* and "stresses the nonintervention of the filmmaker," who relinquishes control of the image to the unobtrusive camera. In the interactive mode, the coalition of monologue and dialogue predominate in the narrative, and thereby "textual authority shifts toward the social actors recruited," thus, "putting the actors into direct encounter with the filmmaker," involving participation, conversation, or interrogation. Lastly, the reflexive mode of representation positions the viewer to experience the method or process of representation and actively

Allah Tantou (1991) by David Achkar (Guinea). Photo courtesy of California Newsreel.

stimulates awareness of both the cinematic form and the issues inherent in the text.[6]

The modes of representation described above also apply to African documentary film practice. What is most interesting in Nichols's theory, however, is his contention that reflexivity "need not be purely formal; it can also be pointedly political." As he states: "[W]hat works at a given moment and what counts as a realistic representation of the historical world is not a simple matter of progress toward a final form of truth, but of struggles for power and authority within the history arenas itself" (1991, 33).

In this respect, the structures of *Allah Tantou* and *Afrique* reveal a deliberate application of mixed modes of address, with filmmakers opting for a combination of two or more of the above characteristics in one film. "Since few documentaries are pure examples of their form," observes Burton, a mixed or multiple mode of address "is the category in which most documentaries will fall —those from an oppositional tradition that encompass experimentation, innovation, and marginality all the more abundantly" (1990, 5). This statement also alludes to the interrogation of cinematic codes and dominant cinematic practices. In oppositional structures, experimentation with technique conforms with the search for new organizing principles in the construction of a new image.

Afrique, je te plumerai
(Africa, I Will Fleece You,
1992) by Jean-Marie Teno
(Cameroon).
Photo courtesy of
California Newsreel.

When the filmic criteria work, they strengthen the rapport between the film-maker and the spectator—a rapport, as cultural producers and critics in the developing world have argued, that could not be realized with the cinematic codes originating from formal structures.

Both documentaries pointedly present themselves as prototypes of African investigation-in-progress (Burton's term). By using cinematography, sound, and commentaries to scrutinize present history and issues, they not only contribute to the resuscitations of popular memory but also construct an active audience as witnesses of that history. The unconventional structures of *Allah Tantou* and *Afrique* stem from the juxtaposition of documentary with fictional images, and from narrative discontinuity. In the dominant tradition of African cinema, the fictional and the documentary coexist to illuminate and expand the borders of reality. Similarly, in the documentaries discussed here, documentary reality is infused with fictional images to achieve the same goal. But what would seem on the surface to be a mélange of film styles (documentary, experimental, and narrative; montage editing, lighting, alternation of silence and sound) becomes a cohesive film that expresses significant, deep-rooted issues.

Although the method of representation is imaginative, the subject matter is real. As historical reenactment, these two films are also very reflexive. In each case, the film begins with a voice-of-God type of narration; however, the images quickly take control, transforming it to a kind of voice-of-the-people presentation. Much of the dialogue and monologue is premeditated; and the background and dramatic sequences, staged. Yet in both films the dialogue, monologue, and off-screen voice-over deal with real issues. *Allah Tantou* exposes the lies propagated in the official account of the death of Marof Achkar, father of the filmmaker, and the suppression of individual freedoms by Guinea's tyrannical regime. Similarly, *Afrique* reveals the colonialist and neocolonialist methods of exploitation and subjugation. At times the artistry renders some of the mesmerizing sequences of torture too ethereal or attractive for the viewer, but it is this enchantment that also compels the viewer to examine, confront, and contemplate the real images behind the illusion.

The viewer sees the actor in *Allah Tantou* playing David's father, the chiaroscuro effect of the lighting throwing him almost offscreen to haunt the viewer. However, the impact lies, not in the lighting itself, but rather in the darkness of the torture cell, which signifies a dark moment in history. For the viewer ingrained in Western realist aesthetics, it is the dissonance of this thought in relation to the artistry of the lighting effect in the background that forces him or her to reflect on its artificiality. In pondering its effect, it is not unreasonable to be skeptical about the impact of art in such a fictional/historical reenactment, but it is the fusion of reality (the fact that Achkar languished and died in jail) and fiction (the reenactment and artistic magnification of the mood in his cell) that compels the viewer to concentrate on the message and the details of the argument. Robert Stam has argued that "reflexive works break with art as enchantment and call attention to their own factitiousness as textual constructs" (1992, 1). Here in *Allah Tantou,* it is the mental anguish illuminated with artistic devices, not the beauty of the sequence, that enables the viewer to share the experience of the tortured victim.

Allah Tantou is an autobiographical film that uses personal reflections to examine a dark chapter in Guinea's history. It is also the first African film to address human rights abuses in the African continent outside of South Africa.[7] In the study of documentary theory and practice, critics have noted that the "autobiographical documentary consists of evidentiary sound/image constructions" (Lane 1993, 21) that focus on "oneself or one's family, and the subject of the film and filmmaker often begins with a level of trust and intimacy never achieved or even attempted in other films" (Katz and Katz 1988, 120, qtd. in Lane 1993, 21).

In *Allah Tantou,* David Achkar mobilizes a search for his father in the "Guinean past, his father's search for himself inside prison, and Africa's search for a new beginning amid the disillusionment of the post-independence era."[8] Thematically, this is a unique film in that it sheds light on important aspects of African history that would otherwise not be told. For example, the image of Sekou Touré, as we know him in the West, is that of first president of Guinea and undaunted pan-Africanist. But inside his empire stood the gigantic and infamous Camp Boiro Prison, where political detainees languished and wasted away without trial. As the film shows, no official explanation is provided for those who died.

Because Achkar had been charged with treason and jailed, his family was obliged to flee into exile, and it was not until after President Touré died that Achkar's family was told that their relative had long since been executed. Ironically, he who championed his country's crusade against apartheid at the time he was Guinea's ambassador to the United Nations would suffer exactly the kind of maltreatment against which he had spoken. The filmmaker constructs audio and visual images of his father's state of mind, his anguish, his personal criticism, and self-evaluation, and his spiritual transformation from Islam to Christianity. This ordeal is meticulously expressed because of David's own personal involvement and because of the recovery of his father's secret "memoir," which was written in jail and which aided in the story's reconstruction. The "memoir," an archival gold mine—horrifying and introspective as the account undoubtedly is—has the impact of an historical document of significant value. And if indeed, according to Nichols, "documentary offers access to a shared, historical construct," it is accurate to say that "instead of a world," *Allah Tantou* gives us "access to the world" (Nichols 1991, 109).

If *Allah Tantou* is a historical film that addresses, by implication, the appalling human rights record in Africa, *Afrique* is an intensive study of one nation's history, that of Cameroon. However, *Afrique* offers a continent-wide critique of colonialism, especially cultural colonialism, and openly calls on Africans to reclaim what is theirs. According to Angelo Fiombo and his colleagues, "Africa today is linked to the past by a close cause/effect bond: from colonial violence to the single political party, from repression to intolerance." It is from this perspective, they go on to note, that *Afrique* verifies this claim with cinematic pyrotechnics: "In a skillful mélange of contemporary images, fiction, important period documents and precious reconstruction, the director ventures in the corridors, often forbidden, of the memory of his country, with a will to reaffirm that 'right to speak' which has been denied too long" (1992, 29).

Reminiscent of *The Hour of the Furnaces* (Argentina, 1968) by Fernando Solanas and Octavio Getino, *Afrique* employs multiple conventions, mixing elements of caustic satire, comedy, music, straightforward didacticism, and neorealistic camera work. The film does not simply ask Africans to wake up to the challenges ahead; it indicts tyranny through a critique of colonial decadence made comprehensible from colonial and neocolonial histories.

Teno, the filmmaker, had originally intended to make a film about African publishing. After witnessing the brutal suppression of public demonstrations in Cameroon, however, he decided "to examine language as either a tool of liberation or of domination." He went on to state that "in confiscating language, in reducing language to codes accessible only to the minority, it becomes easier to silence and exploit the people" (qtd. in *Library* 1993, 4). Before the film's title appears on screen, a teaser provides the viewer with a brief synopsis of the entire movie. It is early morning, and an intimidating voice-over ("Yaoundé, you inspire shame—Cruel city, city of official lies") introduces the viewer to the

168 *N. Frank Ukadike*

routine life in this boisterous capital. A hand-held camera maneuvers jerkily through the crowd. We are told that the situation is similar in various big cities and that one death has already occurred. A scene from archival footage takes us back to the 1960 independence celebration, where we witness people dancing with joy at their freedom. The first president, Ahmadou Ahidjo, acknowledges the crowd's greetings. He dies, and Paul Biya takes over, eventually imposing ironfisted control, with repressive crackdowns and concomitant upheavals. This segment summarizes the history of Cameroon.

Afrique inundates the viewer with a barrage of images. They are not collages of images in the usual sense, but historical documents and political manifestoes. This strategy is a calculated way of presenting complex histories. The film is carefully researched, emanating as it does from the filmmaker's understanding of the colonial history before his birth, extending into his present life, and made more incisive from his hybrid stance—his status as an exile living in Paris. Teno creates a metacinema that draws from the archival propaganda newsreel images of the colonial media. This cinema, constituting an unintentional critique of its own history, is evolved by powerful images compelling the viewer to understand the media's impact on African consciousness; it shows how that consciousness was eroded over the years, paving the way for the creation of more young *évolués*.[9] Too often Western news media—including films and documentaries—have failed to probe African problems; rather, they report them in a prejudiced and biased manner. Says Teno: "I wanted to trace cause and effect between the intolerable present and the colonial violence of yesterday to understand how a country could fail to succeed as a state which was once composed of well-structured, traditional societies" (*Library* 1993, 4).

Many scenes in the film foreground these concerns. They can be examined from the privileged position of the oral tradition and works written in the early Cameroonian alphabet,[10] from the official Cameroonian information network, from foreign print media, and from television.

In another sequence, *Afrique* focuses on the dearth of African-authored books in Yaoundé when a young lady reporter discovers that there are only a handful of books written by Africans in the French Cultural Center, the British Council, and the Goethe Institute libraries. Even audiovisual and children's book sections contained holdings relating only to Europe. Despite the establishment of sophisticated printing presses, thirty years after independence Cameroon and other African countries still import books from Europe. Although the film did not examine this important issue after the economic developments of the past eight years or so when African economies began to be mortgaged to the IMF and World Bank, new forms of slavery and economic subjugation have emerged. Indeed, it is increasingly difficult to manufacture books in Africa due to IMF-imposed "Structural Adjustment Programs" and currency devaluations.

If lack of books written from the African perspective is one area that continues to promote Western hegemony, the influence of electronic media is even more devastating. *Afrique* identifies this problem. Just as the filmmaker recalls his youth reading Western comics and being told in school and at home to study hard so as to become White, so too television continues at an alarming rate to become the arbiter of cultural change. Consider the scene where the director of Cameroon National Television asks the producer of *Afrique* how much he will pay to have his film shown on television. The producer brags that "*Dallas* and films [*sic*] like *Dynasty, Chateauvallon, Derrick,* and *Mademoiselle,* are offered to us free, and the people love it."[11]

In both films we find a constant shift in the voice of authority, as the form of narration turns to what we might term a filmed essay in documentary dialect. The many kinds of presentation within the films, such as dramatic narrative, allegorical monologue, and film-within-a-film, diversify the authoritative voice. These forms are also evocative of multiple voices, as in Africa's oral tradition, which appropriates many forms of representation in its abundant use of culturally established iconographical codes of explication. Since the inception of African cinema, oral tradition has formed the basis of its cultural and aesthetic grounding. It is interesting that the structure of both films, particularly that of *Allah Tantou,* is indebted to this traditional technique of disseminating knowledge. In returning to the actual impact of oral tradition, we find that oral art can bear upon the method of narration, including repetition of dialogue and images, satire and dramatization; the primary result is to externalize the text, validating the voices of authority by neutralizing their hierarchy.

Afrique and *Allah Tantou* position African filmmakers and audiences in a world dominated by injustice, and they offer a vehement and sardonic critique of the oppressive mechanisms of power. Both use a variety of cinematic approaches to examine history, the self, and the collective in that history, as do many African fiction films. *Allah Tantou* is especially concerned with the family and with the filmmaker's position in it. Although it does not seem to involve the collective, the state apparatus that tore Achkar's family apart has national and international implications. For example, by juxtaposing newsreels of recognizable Third World liberation leaders—Castro, Kenyatta, Lumumba, and Nasser—with Achkar's prison experience, the film resonates with memories of "testimony of existence and struggle," in Teshome Gabriel's terms (1989, 64). In this way one is also forced to think about all those other people who have died fighting for just causes, "those unrecorded and unremembered millions of Africans" who have disappeared (*Library* 1993, 9).

By contrast, *Afrique* takes a different approach in its questioning of history and the positioning of the self in that history. Unlike *Allah Tantou,* it confronts the collective head-on. The film emphasizes historical and contemporary European hegemony and cultural domination in Cameroon, particularly in print and electronic media, and urges Africans to "reclaim their culture as well as their political and economic institutions in order to achieve true independence from Europe and the West" (Clark 1993, 1158). That is a positively conclusive statement directed toward achieving a specific goal. The title *Allah Tantou* means "God's Will"—a denomination as speculative and restrictive as the events it depicts. For some critics, this is why the film "refuses to construct an authoritative narrative space/time" (*Library* 1993, 8). The director is careful not to alienate his audience. In fact, it is the clever juxtaposition of "fragments of contrasting, sometimes contradictory, texts into a resonant collage of home movies, newsreels, a forced confession, a prison journal . . . and his own dramatization of his father's prison experience" (8) that maximizes the cumulative impact.

In essence, the strategies employed by both films prove that every documentary is equally a product of its period. The biases of the time, the place, and the concerns of individual filmmakers all work to dismantle the myths of objective or subjective documentation. The legacy of these multi-accentuated works of art provides for new ways of exploring the African experience.

Notes

This chapter is reprinted from *iris* 18 (1995): 81–94.

1. See, for example, Rayfield 1984.

2. The French pathologist-turned-anthropologist Félix-Louis Regnault (the first practitioner of ethnographic filmmaking) had good intentions for the use of cinema for cross-cultural study of movement. His earlier experiments dating back to 1895, the same year the moving image was first projected to paying audiences, involved studies of Africans that he contrasted with images of peoples from other great civilizations such as Egypt, India, and Greece. Shortly thereafter, subsequent foreign filmmakers turned Africa into exotic décor. See Brigard 1975.

3. This statement originates from Paul Rotha's contention that "Hollywood did little to further the humanitarian uses of cinema" (cited in Nichols 1991, 108).

4. Vertov's theory in relation to his socialist cinematic practices is a clear example, but theoretical tendencies such as this are gaining prominence among avant-garde filmmakers, who sometimes use theory to give meaning to what otherwise would have been meaningless images except for the aesthetic orientations.

5. Although the four characteristics mentioned are pivotal to the dominant film and media practices, their application to this chapter is influenced by Koberna Mercer's reformulations of the terms. I also acknowledge the views of students in my Cultural Issues in Cinema classes about these concepts and their applications to the discourse of the Black British Cinema.

6. See Nichols 1991, chapter 2, "Documentary Modes of Representation," 32ff.

7. *End of the Dialogue* (1969) and *Last Grave at Dimbaza* (1974) are well-known films made by Nana Mahomo about apartheid.

8. As described in the catalogue *Library of African Cinema 1993–1994* (1993, 8).

9. Before independence and during the early years after independence, the assimilated class consisted of the few educated elite. This number is now rapidly growing: more and more Africans seeking better lives outside of the continent are leaving in droves, creating a more assimilated class of people. Even those in their respective classes find they cannot hide from the onslaught of foreign influences: radio, TV, billboard advertising, and textiles (T-shirts, etc.) are Western oriented.

10. One scene shows that before colonialist intervention there already existed an indigenous system of writing—the Sho-mon alphabet developed in 1885 by Sultan Ngoya. It was taught in schools until 1914 when French imperialists outlawed it and introduced their own.

11. After the Gulf War, CNN extended its services to China, India, and Africa, among other countries. In Nigeria, for example, rich people who can afford cable TV do

not waste their time tuning in to the poorly produced Nigerian Television Authority (NTA) programs. CNN and BBC provide the news, and MTV provides the entertainment—to the detriment of the children. In hotels and restaurants, MTV, which most people equate with decadence, plays twenty-four hours a day.

Works Cited

Brigard, Emilie de. 1975. "The History of Ethnographic Film." In *Principles of Visual Anthropology,* ed. Paul Hockings. The Hague: Mouton.

Burton, Julianne. 1990. *The Social Documentary in Latin America.* Pittsburgh: University of Pittsburgh Press.

Clark, Andrew F. 1993. "*Lumumba: Death of a Prophet* and *Afrique, je te plumerai.*" *American Historical Review* (October): 1156–58.

Fiombo, Angelo, et al. 1992. "*Afrique, je te plumerai.*" *Ecrans d'Afrique* 2: 29.

Gabriel, Teshome. 1989. "Third Cinema as Guardian of Popular Memory: Towards a Third Aesthetic." In *Questions of Third Cinema,* ed. Jim Pines and Paul Willeman, 53–64. London: BFI.

Katz, John Stuart, and Judith Milstein Katz. 1988. "Ethics and the Perception of Ethics in Autobiographical Film." In *Image Ethics: The Moral Rights of Subjects in Photographs, Film and Television,* ed. Larry Gross, John Katz, and Jay Ruby, 119–34. New York: Oxford University Press.

Kracauer, Siegfried. 1960. *Theory of Film: The Redemption of Physical Reality.* New York: Oxford University Press.

Lane, Jim. 1993. "Notes on Theory and the Autobiographical Documentary Film in America." *Wide Angle* 15.3: 21–36.

Library of African Cinema 1993–1994. 1993. San Francisco: California Newsreel.

Mercer, Koberna. 1988. "Diaspora Culture and the Dialogic Imagination." In *Black Frames: Critical Perspectives on Black Independent Cinema,* ed. Mbye B. Cham and Claire Andrade-Watkins, 50–61. Cambridge: MIT.

Nichols, Bill. 1991. *Representing Reality.* Bloomington: Indiana University Press.

Penley, Constance, and Andrew Ross. 1985. "Interview with Trinh T. Minh-ha." *Camera Obscura* 13–14: 86–111.

Rayfield, J. R. 1984. "The Use of Film in Teaching About Africa." *Film Library Quarterly* 17.2, 17.3 and 17.4: 34–52.

Renov, Michael. 1993a. "Introduction: The Truth about Non-Fiction." In *Theorizing Documentary,* ed. Michael Renov, 1–11. New York: Routledge.

———. 1993b. "Toward the Poetics of Documentary." In *Theorizing Documentary,* 12–36. New York: Routledge.

Stam, Robert. 1992. *Reflexivity in Film and Literature: From Don Quixote to Jean-Luc Godard.* New York: Columbia University Press.

Taylor, Clyde. 1983. "Film Reborn in Mozambique." *Jump Cut* 28: 30–31.

Ukadike, N. Frank. 1993. "African Films: A Retrospective and a Vision for the Future." *Critical Arts* 7.1–2: 43–60.

Weaver, Harold W. 1982. "The Politics of African Cinema." In *Black Cinema Aesthetics,* ed. Gladstone L. Yearwood, 80–95. Athens: Ohio University Center for Afro-American Studies.

10 Booming Videoeconomy: The Case of Nigeria

Françoise Balogun

Video films, long considered second-rate products of the film industry, have now gained recognition not only from audiences but also from critics, organizers of film festivals, and filmmakers themselves. The phenomenon of video film is due partly to technological progress and partly to economic factors. Nigeria was one of the first countries to develop abundant video film production. In this chapter, based principally on personal experience, I want to give an account of the "birth" and development of video production in Nigeria and consider selected video films.

At the end of the 1970s in Lagos, it was a "must" to have a videocassette player at home. Violence and insecurity, particularly at night, dissuaded cinema-going, and people preferred to be entertained in the relative safety of their homes. However, this was an urban phenomenon confined to the rich. Thus, while the network of cinema houses was progressively disintegrating due to lack of maintenance, equipment, and local or imported films, video viewing was flowering all over the cities in the privacy of posh sitting rooms. Mfon, Akintunde, and Selbar associate this craze with a "growing elitist attitude towards cinema. The average Nigerian elite hates to rub shoulders with those he considers as society's dregs. It is offensive to him to be classified together with every Tom, Dick and Harry who can pay the price of a ticket to watch a film in the cinema hall" (1994, 20). Whatever the validity of this societal aspect of the development of video, it is true that, because of the cost of viewing equipment, only the well-off could afford it. Moreover, considering the numerous power failures that plagued (and still plague) Nigeria, it was necessary to have a backup generator to fully enjoy electronic devices.

At this stage, what were these privileged people watching? Twenty-five years ago in Nigerian cities, there were no shops for the sale or rental of videocassettes, so they were watching imported tapes acquired during trips abroad and pirated copies bought locally from street hawkers. Piracy is a major problem for the film industry (as well as for book and clothing industries). It was not uncommon in Nigeria at that time to find pirated copies of films just released or about to be released, as was the case with Richard Attenborough's *Gandhi* (1982), a copy of which could be bought on the streets of Lagos even before the film was released in Europe! According to Mfon, Akintunde, and Selbar, "in some markets, the video sales and rental business consist of up to 80% pirated products" (1994,

21). Although the effective implementation of a copyright law is a serious issue that needs to be addressed, my present concern is the video business and its development.

The same people who could afford to buy cassette players and tapes also enjoyed having family events and ceremonies taped. A few companies were making a brisk business videotaping wedding ceremonies, funerals, graduations, and the like. The products were "raw" footage without much editing, and sound and lighting tended to be poor. However, customers proudly showed their friends and relatives these tapes in which they were usually prominently featured.

In the meantime, Nigerian cinematography, which had developed very slowly, mainly through the Film Unit—a legacy of colonial days—and was still in its infancy, was given a major boost with the appearance of independent filmmakers and the "birth" of Yoruba films. The first film in that language, *Ajani-Ogun* (1975) by Ola Balogun, enjoyed tremendous success with Nigerian film audiences, both Yoruba and non-Yoruba, and initiated a series of films which involved the major traveling theater companies.

These theater companies quickly understood the benefits of the development of Yoruba films, and Ade Afolayan (director of the Ade Love Theatre Company), who had the lead role in *Ajani-Ogun,* promptly embarked on the production of his first film, *Ija Ominira* (Fight for Freedom, 1977), with Ola Balogun as director because he had no knowledge of filmmaking himself. Hubert Ogunde and Moses Olaiya Adejumo (stage name, "Baba Sala") embarked on similar enterprises with Balogun. Though the three productions met with commercial success, the producers–theater group leaders found making films too expensive, especially given the competition over who would produce the longest film and the one with the most stunning special effects. They had second thoughts about the way of making films and were of the opinion that expenses could be reduced if they became film directors themselves. And so they did.

This development took place at a moment when the economy of the country plummeted under devaluation and structural adjustment. It became impossible to transfer money abroad for film processing, special effects, and postproduction expenses. However, the craze for Yoruba films had just begun. Nigerian audiences were eager to hear a familiar language, watch popular actors, and be thrilled by the magic which was, and still is, a required ingredient in Nigerian and many other African films. There was great demand for local images and for stories reflecting local problems such as corruption, polygamy, modernity versus tradition, anachronistic and/or overly-controlling religious beliefs, and tyranny. Under these circumstances, the use of video gave an obvious advantage.

Thus, while at the end of the 1970s and beginning of the 1980s there was an ascendant movement toward the development of quality Nigerian films, with 35mm shootings and the involvement of foreign directors of photography such as José Medeiros (Brazil) and of technicians who trained Nigerians, in the following decade, Nigeria practically stopped producing films on celluloid. There was a sharp increase in the production of video films and a decline in technical quality due to the obvious lack of formal training and professional know-how.

The quick switch in the mode of film production was dictated by several factors, in summary:

- demand for local images
- deterioration of existent cinema halls
- inadequate distribution services
- involvement of leaders of traveling theater companies in filmmaking and their will to capture this industry and turn a profit
- deterioration of the Nigerian economy
- development of home video

Compared to the three or four full-length feature films produced yearly at the beginning of the 1970s, recent statistics show a boom in the production of video films. The Nigerian Film Censorship Board provides the following figures for the years 1995 to 1998: 858 video films previewed, including 244 in English; 473 in Yoruba; 62 in Igbo (one of Nigeria's major languages, along with Yoruba and Hausa); and 6 in Pidgin (Nigerian English). Jean-Christophe Servant (2001) notes that according to the same Board, 1,080 video films have been commercialized since 1997. This is impressive, especially if we consider the broad distribution of copies, which can reach hundreds of thousands of viewers.

Eder Lizio writes in a 2002 article entitled "Nigeria Video plein la vue" that there are 15,000 videoclubs in the country. He adds that according to the Independent Television Producers Association of Nigeria, for each video film about 15,000 cassettes are produced for distribution and sold at 2,300 CFA Francs (about US $3.50) or rented at 200 CFA francs (US $0.30).

The importance of video production in Nigeria cannot be assessed only in terms of numbers, however. Video production is a reaction to a demand and a situation. A strong need for images reflecting identity was responsible for the development of video production as the only possible way of producing images in the economic context of Nigeria. It came to a point where the same images that satisfied the popular audience also satisfied the elite in Nigeria, though the videos were criticized by outsiders, mainly for their lack of quality.

Other triggers for the development of video films were the potential market in Nigeria, with over 110 million inhabitants, and the number of video players in the country, which increased over the course of the 1980s. The celluloid film production and distribution crisis gave way to a new mode of market-oriented production.

Nigerian video film production, though severely criticized, is an authentic expression of Nigerian identities, and technical shortcomings do not mask the inventiveness of storyteller-scriptwriters. This is also totally independent production, since Nigeria, in contrast to Francophone Africa, where the film industry was subsidized by France, principally through the Ministry of Cooperation, never received any help from the former colonial masters or any foreign source, at least in film production. In fact, video production was developed in its initial phase mainly by people who were not trained in filmmaking and who saw this form of activity as a shortcut around distribution problems. While the few trained Nigerian filmmakers who were working independently hesitated switching to video production because of a loss in quality, the almost spontaneous generation of video producers had no special feelings about it, their only aim being "business"—recouping their money as quickly as possible and turning a profit. So they made films on the most commonly available format, VHS, without concern for quality. Films were shot at very low cost—as little as US $5,000 each—and distributed on VHS.

Ola Balogun made a short documentary on this subject at the beginning of the '90s for Canal+ (France), which shows part of the shooting of a Yoruba film on video. What is amazing is that everybody seems to be acting, including the technicians. The filmmaker, a Mr. Adebajo, says he is a teacher by training, but he developed an interest in the arts and decided to go into the video business because "it's the best way one can reach people." He explains that the VHS format is the cheapest means to produce images that can reach a market with a chance for profit. In addition to the low-cost format, there is another condition for the success of the enterprise: the producer must control distribution and protect against piracy, and the best protection is beating the cost of pirated copies. Mr. Adebajo says he is the sole producer and distributor of his films, though he sometimes associates with the owner of a barber salon who acts as coproducer, when he sponsors the film, and as distributor, when he sells or rents cassettes to his barber shop customers!

As Ola Balogun has remarked, by marketing films directly to audiences on tape, video producers bypass the obstacles created by the weakness of the available cinema theater outlets. Tapes are shown in comfortable drawing rooms-turned-video rooms for a small audience charged just a few *naira* each, and of course there is no ticket office for such viewings.

The video phenomenon is, in my view, comparable to what happened in the field of literature: although Nigerian writers such as Wole Soyinka, J. P. Clark, and Chinua Achebe became famous in literary circles in Nigeria and abroad, they were not widely read in their own country, where the literate masses preferred what came to be called "Onitsha literature," sold at prices and in a format that made it available and appealing. The success of Yoruba films like *Ajani-Ogun, Aiye* (The World, 1979), *Orun Mooru* (Hell is Hot! 1982), and *Aropin Tenia* (We Always Have Surprises, 1982) stands in sharp contrast to the lack of audience for 35mm films such as *Black Goddess* (1978) and *Cry Freedom* (1981) by Ola Balogun; or *Bullfrog in the Sun* (1971), an adaptation of Achebe's novel; and *Kongi's Harvest* (1970), from a play by Wole Soyinka with Soyinka in the lead role of Kongi, both produced by Francis Oladele. Likewise, the tremendous output of indigenous video movie production, coupled with the abandonment of celluloid films, speaks for itself.

For a long time, African films were largely dependent on overseas financial assistance, which led to a cinematography geared to Western art houses that was not necessarily well-received by African popular audiences. Video is an economic response to a craving for images to which a popular audience can relate. The proliferation of video films that satisfy the tastes of African viewers is

Cry Freedom (1981) by Ola Balogun (Nigeria).
Poster courtesy of Françoise Balogun.

healthy, in a sense, because it counterbalances the production of "art films" more or less imposed by outsiders. Video production, in fact, contributes to the production of popular films, which constitute a necessary base in each cinematography on which more refined and sophisticated films can be elaborated. Could Satyajit Ray have directed *The Music Room* (1958) or *Charoulata* (1964) in the absence of any mass production in India? Could *Derzu Uzala* (1975) and *Ran* (Chaos, 1985) by Japanese director Akira Kurosawa have existed if there had been no popular cinema in Japan? The question could be repeated for Egypt, France, and the United States. All films will not be great works of art, but I contend that allowance should be made for productions of good technical quality with appeal to the masses, a cultural medium out of which masterpieces may emerge.

Nigerian video films produced for a quick turnover are meant for the domestic audience or the Nigerian Diaspora and are not, so far, easily available outside the Nigerian market and community. A film such as *Ajànàkù*, which is of poor technical quality and presents loopholes in its continuity, is of little interest outside the Yoruba community. Written and produced by Charles Olumo Agbako, who became famous in Yoruba traveling theater for his portrayals of villains and witch doctors, *Ajànàkù* tells the story of rivalry in the polygamist family of King Adelanwa, with action in the traditional setting of a village. The direction by Monsuru Obadina is unimaginative and very close to what is done in traditional theater. The scenes, mainly outdoors, are shot in a very static way: typically, characters come out of a hut and set themselves against a background of traditional hand-woven material and mats before speaking.

However, years of practice and the emergence of digital technology have contributed to rising standards of home video in Nigeria. *Twins of the Rain Forest* (2000) is a short film directed by Odion P. Agbott, screenplay by Albert Egbe, with Tunde Kelani as director of photography and two London-trained actors, Olu Jacobs and Joke Silva. It tells an interesting story of twins, who in some ethnic groups must be sacrificed but here are saved, thanks to the eldest son in the family. The film is narrated and photographed quite creatively. Albert Egbe is a seasoned scriptwriter with a long television career who now heads a video production training company. After a short period of study in England, Tunde Kelani worked as second assistant cameraman on some of Balogun's productions. He was rapidly promoted to the rank of chief operator with the development of Yoruba video films, and after twenty years in the industry of image production, he is now an experienced technician and film director. He owns Mainframe Production Company, which produced, among other video films, *Ayo ni mo fe* (I Love Ayo 1 & 2, 1995) in Yoruba with English subtitles; *Ti Oluwa ni ile* (God Owns All Lands, 1997), marketed by Alasco Video Films Production Ltd.; and recently, *Thunderbolt* (2001), a Yoruba-style Romeo and Juliet with a happy ending!

Ayo ni mo fe was adapted from a Thema Award–winning narration written by well-known Yoruba playwright Wale Ogunyemi. It is the story of a woman, Jumoke, who is raped during an attack of insanity; and the film is "a commentary on our societal attitude to mental illness," as director/producer Tunde Kelani announces on the jacket of the videocassette. The complex intrigue involves Jumoke's family; Chief Tomobi, on an elusive quest for offspring; and Ayo, who falls into destitution and becomes a gang leader. There are sequences, especially in part 2, that offer commentary on issues of interest to a mass audience. For instance, when Jumoke's son is discharged from the hospital where he has been treated for diphtheria, the doctor remarks on the necessity of good drinking water. Later, there is a scene on the definition of rape, and Chief Tomobi consults his lawyer in a bid to be recognized as the biological father of Jumoke's child. Apart from numerous other developments, at times incredible, that appeal to the public, such scenes give some sort of guidance on health or behavioral problems.

Ti Oluwa ni ile, also directed by Tunde Kelani, develops a story of corruption around the sale of a piece of land, a very popular theme in a country where corruption infects all classes of society, from the road mechanic in search of excessive profit to top government officials (former presidents Babangida and Abacha will go down in history as notorious figures of corruption).

Nemesis (1996), in English, produced by Diamond Motion Picture in conjunction with FAD Productions, is also typical of Nigerian video production. It is the story of a woman who rescues a man after he has been attacked. Later, she offers him hospitality and gives him all she has, including her love. She gets pregnant with his child only to discover that her best friend is having an affair with him. The ending is Oedipal.

In the Line of Duty, directed by Izu Ojukwu, screenplay by Chuks Obiora and Chidi Ifekwem and produced by Ephriam Arinze, is an action film, a story of counterfeit currency in which the chief of police and the governor of the Central Bank are involved. "Ruthlessness is the rule, money is the game," says the jacket. Indeed! It is a fast-moving film with car and boat chases. Although the framing shows occasional flaws, there is a clear effort to create an atmosphere of suspense through sound and lighting (for example, in the opening scene). This film is representative of the huge Ibo video production—mostly in English—from the Eastern Nigerian people known for their business talents.

Another example of Ibo production is *Glamour Girls* (1994), directed by Chika Onakwafor, screenplay by Kenneth Nnebue, and produced by Nek Video Links, Ltd. The action is set in a big city, and the main characters are glamorously dressed young women in luxurious flats, who live off old, wealthy men and who, in the end, have enough money to "buy" themselves young husbands. It is a story of blackmail with numerous twists and turns.

Finally, I thoroughly enjoyed the Ibo film *August Meeting* (released in the 1990s), especially since when I lived in Nigeria I observed how women prepare for social occasions. The film, written and produced by Prince Emeka Ani, demonstrates that women will go to any length to try to outdo their rivals and friends, sometimes with the encouragement of their husbands. Money is the nerve of the war to look their best and steal the show, but they also resort to witchcraft—a necessary ingredient in Nigerian films. The two candidates for the presidency of the annual August Meeting are glamorous in their lace wrappers and silky red scarves as well as uncontrolled in their lust for power. Noticeably, the director of photography is a woman (Ngozi Nkebakwu), and she beautifully captures the women's gestures and body language.

In my search for documentation on Nigerian video production, I came across a small leaflet about a woman who associated faith and the film business in the 1990s with apparent success: Mrs. Helen E. Ukpabio, identified as pastor of the Liberty Gospel Church and "Evangelist Chief Executive" of Liberty Films, a video film production company. Titles of films advertised are as follows:

Power to Bind: "There are spiritual beings and powers which are constantly troubling the world... causing untold hardships... Does man have any strength on his own to oppose these destructive powers?" So reads the advertising blurb.
Magic Money: Probably a story of money "doublers," people who double money through magic.
End of the Wicked: On witchcraft.
Holy Crime: "Mozumba has come and he claims that he is God and Savior of mankind. . . . "
Wasted Years.
Married to a Witch.
The Price: A pastor is seduced by an attractive, silly girl and has to pay for his sin.

I had the opportunity to view *The Price* and found the development of the story quite interesting and the acting good. Richard Mofe-Bamijo, playing the part of the pastor, was trained in the drama department of a Nigerian university. He became known through his work at the PEC Theatre, the first Nigerian repertory theater created by poet/writer J. P. Clark at the beginning of the 1980s. The production of Christian videos in Nigeria has been analyzed by Obododimma Oha (2000).

The main interest of Nigerian video film production, in my opinion, is that it is yet another proof of the ability of Africans to respond to specific situations and produce something totally original and adapted to local conditions, as has been demonstrated in other fields of production. For example, it is now established that Subsaharan African iron metallurgy was most certainly an indigenous invention dating back to 3000 B.C. and that it developed in original ways that are of interest to anthropologists, archaeologists, and scientists.

Video film production in Nigeria is significant and/or original in several respects: quantity; themes referring mainly to Nigerian societal issues; mode of production and distribution (in this respect it is noticeable that each cassette presents advertisements of other video films on the jacket and at the beginning of the tape); financing: films as a consumer good to be produced fast and at the lowest possible cost, for a quick turnover. Let us wait and see... Out of the effervescence of current production, works of art may emerge that will raise Nigerian cinematography to the rank of universal art.

Works Cited

Lizio, Eder. 2002. "Nigeria Video plein la vue." *L'Autre Afrique* 13.
Mfon, John, Stephen Akintunde, and Julna Selbar. 1994. "Cinema—Cracks on the Mirror —Suffers from 'Videomiasis,' Society Hunch and Lack of Personnel." *Film & Video* 2.1: 20–23.

Oha, Obododimma. 2000. "The Rhetoric of Nigerian Christian Videos." In *Nigerian Video Films*, rev. and exp., ed. Jonathan Haynes. Athens, Ohio: Ohio University Center for International Studies. First ed., Jos: Nigerian Film Corporation, 1997.

———. 2000. "Yoruba Christian Video." *Cahiers d'études africaines* 165: 121–39.

Servant, Jean-Christophe. 2001. "Boom de la video domestique au Nigeria." *Le Monde Diplomatique* (February): 6.

Part Four: *Inside/Outside:*
Expatriate Filmmakers

11 Africa through a Woman's Eyes: Safi Faye's Cinema

Beti Ellerson

Although Safi Faye is no longer the only woman African film director, she was a pioneer in the 1970s and still figures among the most significant representatives of African cinema. This analysis of her work is presented in four sections: (1) an overview of the tendencies, evolution, and development of Safi Faye's cinema and thoughts over the years, which will contextualize her most recent filmmaking and her experiences during the process; (2) my interview with her at the 1997 Pan-African Festival of Cinema and Television of Ouagadougou (FESPACO); (3) a transcription of a public discussion after the screening of Faye's film *Mossane* at FESPACO 1997; and (4) a timeline of her filmmaking career.[1]

A Pioneer Filmmaker

By considering the history of African women in film production, we can better appreciate Safi Faye's place as a pioneer. Moreover, it is not by chance that the person recognized as the "father" of African cinema—Ousmane Sembene—is also Senegalese. The time span between the emergence of these two firsts is relatively short: Sembene made his first film in 1963, while Faye's debut film was released in 1972. However, the interval between the birth of African cinema and the visible presence of African women playing key roles has been much longer.

Ousmane Sembene released *La Noire de...(Black Girl)*, the first feature film by a West African filmmaker, in 1966, the year that Safi Faye was initiated into the world of international culture as an official guide during the First World Festival of Black Arts in Dakar, Senegal. There she began her connections with people and places that led her to her career path. She also became aware of the importance of the preservation of African history and culture, a theme that was omnipresent at the festival and became a leitmotif in her work. She describes that event as an expression of national energy and recalls her desire to meet the intellectuals and researchers who had gathered there (Cissé and Fall 1996, 6). Her encounter with French ethnologist and filmmaker Jean Rouch at the festival was important, since it allowed her to travel to France a year later as an actor in his 1968 film *Petit à Petit* (Little by Little). She returned to her position as primary school teacher of French in Senegal after the film was completed.

Later, as an experienced filmmaker, Faye looked retrospectively at Rouch's

Safi Faye in *Sisters of the Screen* (2002) by Beti Ellerson (United States).
Courtesy of Beti Ellerson.

film and admitted that she did not like it at all, viewing it as too unwieldy and
unstructured, naïve and somewhat silly. Even as she found the film amusing, she
did not especially like this display of entertainment and found it rather foolish
to make a film with no real plot or ending (Haffner 1982a, 64). While Faye did
not explain why she found the film silly, I would suggest that she simply outgrew
it, and in retrospect found her character to be superficial and perhaps completely in opposition to her experiences as an African woman in Paris. Other
African viewers who critiqued the film during a ciné-club screening and Q&A
in 1979 in Kinshasa agreed with her sense of its superficiality (Haffner 1982b,
88). Jean Rouch even admitted, after being pressed by film critic Guy Hennebelle, that the film presented a folkloric impression of Africans (M. Martin
1982, 92). A loosely-structured film about Africans who encounter Paris for the
first time, *Petit à Petit* has been viewed as controversial because of its ambiguous
interpretation of Africans and is considered one of Rouch's least successful
works (Serceau 1982, 159).

Rouch is often described as Faye's mentor because of similar elements in
their work—anthropology and documentary-style filmmaking. However, Faye
herself is unsure to what extent he influenced her evolution into filmmaking
and her study of ethnology. While film critics and historians have drawn these
conclusions, she views her decisions as more intuitive. Not knowing exactly
what area of study to pursue, and realizing that she did not know Africa very
well, Faye opted for ethnology in order to better understand the continent. One

significant component of the ethnography curriculum at the Sorbonne in Paris was the use of the camera as an instrument for field research. Faye discovered that the camera was an important tool for comprehending what she observed:

> During that time there were many abstract things in the course of events that could not be explained, such as African ceremonies. One observes them but cannot actually explain them. I thought perhaps that in analyzing these elements, I might find the foundation of these things. I decided that the best solution was to do film. (Cissé and Fall 1996, 6)

Faye also became aware of the importance of film as a means of communication with the predominantly oral people of her country. She realized that even though they did not read literature and books, the 70 percent of the population that was nonliterate knew how to read images (Amarger 1998).

Faye learned how to use the camera during her studies in ethnology and began to study filmmaking at the Louis Lumière Film School in Paris in 1972. At the end of that year she completed her first film, *La Passante* (The Woman Passerby). While this student film is not generally included in the analysis of her body of work as a filmmaker,[2] she defines it as an "intimist" work. She recalls that she initially filmed for her own pleasure, but later her filmmaking interest evolved around her research (Traoré 1979, 28).

It is noteworthy that Faye's first work is a short fiction film inspired by the theme of beauty and fantasy, a theme that recurred in full glory some twenty years later in her film *Mossane*. She describes *La Passante* as influenced by French poet Charles Baudelaire's poem "A une Passante." In an interview, Faye said of her film:

> [It is] the story of a beautiful African woman who arrives in Paris. Dreamlike, she notices that everyone watches her, admires her. Among her admirers she chooses a White man and allows him to dream, then a Black man who dreams as well. They watch her walk down the street. In fact, they are dreaming. That is not at all my reality; Baudelaire inspired me. (Cissé and Fall 1996, 6)

It is significant that in her film, Faye acts as the main character and uses Paris as the setting. In a very individual way, the film echoes her own experiences as a woman "divided between two cultures—French and Senegalese," yet defining herself as not "a Westernized or liberated woman" (Rémy 1996, 34). Faye's poetic sensibility, viewed early in her filmmaking with *La Passante*, evolved into an important element of her cinematic *écriture*. Beyond the film's poetic incantation, Faye attempted to deal with cultural diversity expressed in a woman's encounter with two men from different cultures, particularly in the way they experience food (Bouzet 1991). With the European man, she dines at a restaurant. With the African man, she prepares a meal at home. They both live out their fantasies with her according to their cultural habits related to eating and cuisine. Food is explored as a medium of culture, a theme Faye also investigated later in the documentary *Ambassades nourricières* (Culinary Embassies, 1984).[3]

From the start of her filmmaking career in France, Faye's visibility as an African woman was immediate. She recalls that it was relatively easy for her to enter into the profession. Since she was the only African woman making films, a lot of attention was given to her and her work. In contrast, she finds that women now have a much more difficult time entering the domain of filmmaking (see interview following).

While Faye is a proponent of women's rights, she does not use the term "feminist" to describe herself or her work but rather sees herself as affirming women's rights and opportunities (Cissé and Fall 1996, 7). She looks for the African specificities regarding women and their experiences, noting that many Western feminist issues are unrelated to African realities. While stating that "phallocracy is universal," she emphasizes that there are women in African societies who want to change their situations (Faye 1984, 8). She remarks on external misconceptions about African women:

> It is always difficult for Europeans to see Africa, and its women, without taking sides and without bringing European notions of civilization. Today, we do a lot toward the emancipation of women. It is a subject of many of the films on our continent, but women are not as dependent, submissive or deprived of rights as one thinks. If I consider the situation where I live, in the country, in the Serer region, and the responsibilities that the women take on, for their families and the household, I see women as active partners—courageous and liberated—in relation to their husbands. In the city, on the other hand, women's dependence, financially speaking, appears to me to be much greater. (Eichenberger 1976, 2)

Faye rejects Western feminist filmmaking, which has often privileged only women's lives, and emphasizes the very different experiences of African women and what she views as the more important issues regarding the agricultural sector and its ability to sustain itself. It is much more effective to present women in the context of their experiences and society. Faye does, however, call attention to the empowering aspect of a matriarchal society, where women are raised to be independent and self-sufficient (Faye 1984, 4). She attempts to evoke the contrasting aspects in women's lives, for example, with the character Mossane, whom she describes as "living between rebellion and effacement." Likewise, her film *Selbé et tant d'autres* (Selbé and So Many Others, 1981) describes village women left behind after men have migrated to cities in search of work. Selbé works hard to raise her children but finds herself alone in this endeavor, despite the fact that she has a husband, and she comes to understand her power when she relies only on her own strength.

Though modest in her acknowledgment of her role as "pioneer," Faye recognizes that other women respect her accomplishments. When asked about her role as a "woman filmmaker," she does not make a distinction between "Safi as a man or Safi as a woman"—to her, they are one (Cissé and Fall 1996, 7). She emphasizes the similar problems that African men and women encounter as filmmakers; however, she also notes that it has been especially difficult to attract women to filmmaking:

I think it is important that there are women filmmakers, and it is a pity that film work is so hard and that many African women don't get involved in it. Women should have an important role to play in African cinema, given their sensitivity and their truthfulness. There is also the reluctance to tackle such a hard and unstable job that doesn't offer much financial security. (*Ouaga*, 1989)

The tenacity and conviction necessary to survive in a profession such as filmmaking may also mean a level of tension in a relationship with a male partner. This is especially the case when the woman is self-sufficient and economically autonomous, as Faye remarks:

I think it is very difficult when you are an intellectual, to find a man who accepts these things. They become jealous, the relationship is destroyed. But sometimes I say to myself—if you are born free, buying your own clothes, bringing your own money to get your own food, then if you are not with a man, you have more time to think about your own work. And that is very important. What a woman like me needs is only affection, nothing else. If it is possible, okay; if it is not possible, I prefer to get affection from my child rather than staying without work because a man wants to destroy me. I am not afraid of anything. (Vasudev 1985, 3)

Even when her films have not focused on women's issues, they reflect a perceptible woman's sensibility. There may not be a clear distinction between how Faye as a woman makes films compared to how men do so, but *Mossane* projects a female subjectivity in the way the female characters are assigned agency. Moreover, it shows a very distinctive interpretation of female sensuality and specific emphasis on the female protagonist. For both, Faye draws from her personal experiences: she reflects her own sexual education during adolescence and her motherly adoration for her daughter. Faye has declared, in fact, that she made *Mossane* for herself and her daughter in order to show a certain reality within African society (Rémy 1996, 34). The close bond with her daughter exemplifies the importance of motherhood in her identity. Locating herself within the simultaneous identities of mother, filmmaker, and anthropologist, she illustrates their interconnectedness and the impossibility of indulging in only one role. She sometimes incorporates her daughter into her work, as in the film *Trois ans cinq mois* (Three Years, Five Months, 1983), which portrays her daughter as an infant. Faye's fourteenth film and her daughter at fourteen years of age were two seemingly disparate elements that Faye linked together and celebrated by choosing the subject of *Mossane*. She noticed her daughter was at a magical age when she turned fourteen, a specific moment in life where the transformation was distinctive and visible (see interview below).

Faye's interest in anthropology and the visualization on film of experiences in her native village has continued throughout her career. While her earlier films privileged the documentary style in order to foreground social, political, and economic realities of the village, *Mossane* is a completely fictionalized saga of the eponymous protagonist who is the "most beautiful girl in the world." Woven into the story of a fourteen-year-old girl and the myriad experiences she faces at that age is the Serer myth that every two hundred years a girl is condemned by her beauty to a tragic destiny. Mossane is so stunning that her beauty haunts even the Pangool, the ancestral spirits of the Serer. In the end, through the arms of Mamanguedj, she is returned to the seashore where the ancestors live, the only place where she may be protected.

Critics have associated much of Faye's work with reality-based documentary so that some resist her contention that her first fiction film, *Mossane,* is not an ethnological account of actual events in her society but rather a story that came entirely from her imagination. Even the impressive rituals and ceremonies in *Mossane* were her invention (Barlet 1997, 11). This was particularly striking during a press conference at the 15th FESPACO in 1997, when Faye was invited to discuss *Mossane* with the public and a panel of various members of the press. Faye is not very keen on giving interviews about her films because she feels that after the film has been made, it belongs to the public. At the same time, she believes that she should not have to defend her work. During the discussion, several European members of the audience insisted on an anthropological explanation for portions of the film, but Faye insisted that it was a fictional account not based on actual events, and a debate ensued. That Faye wanted to present a mythical figure based on her own imagination became a point of tension and was ultimately rejected by those who viewed her work as based on anthropological research even if fictionalized (see press conference transcription below).

This exchange suggests that in the minds of some viewers, Africa remains a continent that can be fully explained through anthropological studies that have undergirded European-based research on Africa, as if an African filmmaker/storyteller were prohibited from exercising the artistic authority to create from her own imaginary. For instance, one European speaker insisted that the arranged marriage scenario in the film was based on Faye's account of what actually exists in Senegal, whereas Faye maintained that it was drawn, not from her experiences, but from her imagination.

In another instance, in a published dialogue, the French interviewer asked why Faye portrayed filial sensuality toward Mossane by her brother, since this is not an actuality in African societies (Rémy 1996, 34). Faye emphasized that the events of the story were strictly a product of her imagination, and she was suggesting that the fascination inspired by Mossane's breathtaking beauty could torment even her own brother, just as the entire village had been hypnotized by it.

Refusing to focus only on traditional aspects of African cultures, Faye attempts to go beyond the superficial tradition/modernity dichotomy that many Western viewers perceive in any portrayal of resistance to beliefs and customs. She does not offer a moral to the story but rather shows that tradition and modernity are undifferentiated in the reality of today's Africa. For Faye, Mossane is an adolescent like any other: adolescence is a time of confusion, and resistance to the wishes of parents prevails (Barlet 1997, 10). Faye would view *Mossane* as a universal story within the specificities of an African culture and interpreted from an African perspective.

Such tensions and debates that center on labels of "documentary" versus "fiction" and "reality" versus "fantasy" appear to be the basis for Faye's refusal to make these delineations. As a filmmaker, she views life as a story—unlike Western filmmakers, who try to tell a story (*Playback* 1981, 7). Faye considers her works documents, oral reportage (A. Martin 1979, 18). Thus, her films are records, texts, or correspondence, especially in the dialogic sense of an exchange between interlocutors—the visual text, the "interpreters" in the story, and the viewer.

Faye does not distinguish between fiction and documentary or see linear progression in her work from documentary to fiction or in terms of thematic evolution over time. One element, however, has been constant throughout her career—representing the realities of Africa. Based on research of her native village, Faye highlights the economic upheaval caused by the imposition of groundnut monoculture and gives voice to inhabitants as they recount their stories in *Kaddu Beykat* (Peasant Letter, 1975). In *Fad'jal* (Come and Work, 1979), Faye recalls Amadou Hampaté Ba's well-known phrase: "When an old person dies in Africa, it is as if a library has burned down," as she portrays the richness of African oral tradition and the importance to future generations that people learn and pass on their history. And while *Mossane* was largely created from Faye's imagination, it draws from Serer mythology.[4]

Mossane is a fiction film in the sense that the scenes do not correspond to actual events, although specific situations presented in the film, such as arranged marriages, have historical or contemporary referents. *Kaddu Beykat* and *Fad'jal*, while documentary in style, have fictionalized aspects in that there are reenactments or certain events created for the film. Listening to her explanation of *Kaddu Beykat*, we can better appreciate how Faye interprets her work:

> Certain sequences in the film . . . were a *mise en scène*. So what is it that one calls fiction? The scene . . . was set up especially for the film. . . . Is that what one calls fiction, or is it reality that one calls fiction? For me all these words—fiction, documentary, ethnology—have no sense. All I know is I base what I do in reality, be it for a reconstitution or for a film. . . . And that's what I call the punctuation in my film: the life of a village, the problems of life and death, economic and social problems. . . . At the end of my films people wonder if there is a *mise en scène* or not. I think I have chosen this way, [mixing] what is [with] what is done especially for the film. (A. Martin 1979, 18)

This clarification underscores critical specificities of Faye's work and also responds to interpretations that attempt to categorize her films according to a fiction/documentary dichotomy. Her style is described as "realistic yet poetical, anthropological yet with a fierce social concern" (*Playback* 1981, 7). Faye uses her camera to discover African life (Traoré 1979, 28). She and her camera are observers. The camera becomes part of the discussion as if it were a participant in the conversation (Maupin 1976, 78). Her approach to filmmaking privileges the voices, experiences, and perspectives of the actors/participants, who, for example, made suggestions during the shooting of *Kaddu Beykat* that were then incorporated in the scenario. Problems were solved as a team, and when sequences were changed, they were made spontaneously on the set. In Faye's search for an African filmmaking practice, she rejects certain cinematic conventions regarding camera position, shot, or duration: "When I am in the village with my grandparents, I stay in my place and I listen to them talk. The camera remains fixed" (Maupin 1976, 78).

Just as Faye opposes the documentary/fiction dichotomy, she also questions the notion of ethnology as a field of study that most often involves Westerners going to so-called Third World societies in search of information. Asserting that there is no translation for *ethnology* in African languages, she describes her studies and research as a way to better understand her own society, country, and continent (1984, 7). Faye finds it frustrating that she had to go to Europe in order to learn how to study her own culture (Vasudev 1985, 2). In the end, she met the challenge of using European-acquired research tools to understand the realities of African societies and to dispel the myths and misconceptions that have been perpetuated about Africa, ironically, by the same Europe to which she was obliged to go for an education.

Faye continues her first profession as teacher and takes up the baton as griot, carrying on the oral tradition by recording the voice and memory of her people in film. Paradoxically, her initial interest in studying anthropology grew from her desire to understand Africa, about which she knew little as a graduate of the French colonial education system in Senegal. Returning to her Serer community as researcher, she was amazed to find that the oral historians of her village could trace back seventeen generations to tell their history, and she wanted to give homage to them (Vasudev 1985, 2). Faye debunks the misunderstandings and falsifications of African history by giving a voice to those who have recorded this history in their memories for generations (Schissel 1980, 7). Referring to the community participants in *Kaddu Beykat,* she describes rural farmers as the "greatest economists and sociologists" (Vasudev 1985, 2). They do not read or write, in contrast to those who interpret from an intellectually detached perspective, yet they know about the local economy and are able to interpret and understand the pragmatic realities of farming. This point is brilliantly made by one of the interlocutors who asks: "If groundnuts weaken the soil, what good are they?" And the implied response is: "To pay taxes."

Faye thinks that Africans presently live in a period of neocolonialism in which Western film monopolies dominate distribution, which means that African audiences have little control over which films they can see (Vasudev 1985, 2). While colonial education previously prevented Africans from learning their own history, foreign film industries now make it difficult for Africans to see their own images. For this reason Faye was pleased at the warm reception of her films by the very people to whom she gave a voice to narrate their experiences. When she showed her films to the community, viewers often said that it was "the first time they had seen on film something with which they could identify" (*Playback* 1981, 7). Using films as a tool for teaching and learning, Faye's goal is to teach future generations of Africans about their origins. Commuting between Paris, where she resides, and Senegal, where she was born, she has evinced a passion for her continent and its people throughout her career as teacher, anthropologist, and filmmaker: "I do what I can for my Africa, to tell how beautiful Africa is, and show that the people will not disappear, even if we are forgotten" (*Mossane* promotional brochure, 1996).

Safi Faye Interview with Beti Ellerson at FESPACO, February 1997, Ouagadougou, Burkina Faso

The many interviews with Safi Faye by film critics and historians over the years have generally been spontaneous conversations with her at screenings of her films, as was the following.

Safi, you hold the title of "Dean of African Women Filmmakers." What do you think of this title that has been bestowed upon you?

I don't mind having it. Fate had it that I was the first woman to make films; I accept the role as such. However, it leaves me neither hot nor cold.

Do you feel in some way a model for the women who follow you?

Yes, the women who follow show a great deal of consideration for me. They respect me because I try to do my work as a filmmaker by giving my best, which, I suppose, commands respect. But also, the Senegalese people feel the same way. They call me the "National Safi." However, those are not the things that I am concerned about or even think about.

What was it like during the time when you began in the 1970s?

I did not come to the cinema by chance. I studied ethnology at the Sorbonne. We had access to cinematographic equipment once a week and had to learn how to use it. I realized that in order to be more efficient, I should go to film school. That's why I went to L'Ecole Louis Lumière, one of the best film schools in France, in Paris. I learned like everyone else—I was the only African woman there—how to handle a camera, and I became familiar with how to use the cinematographic equipment.

At the end of the first year, I made a little film [*La Passante*]. It was mainly to put myself to the test, for me to know whether I had learned cinematography well or not. That is how I came to learn filmmaking; it was very easy during those years. I made the film in 1972. Right away, everybody began to talk: "There is an African woman who is making films." It was easy for people to hear about me because I was the first to appear on the scene. It was by chance and by choice that I made this little film, a little film, rather intimist, that I made for myself. Afterwards, out of curiosity, people began to ask about the film.

Your film Mossane *is very striking and very touching. It treats the themes of beauty, virtue, and sensuality. In many ways, the film language is very different from your other films in the manner in which you tell the story. Could you talk about the themes of* Mossane *and its evolution? What inspired you towards the idea of* Mossane?

All my other films were half-fiction, half-documentary. Since I worked with the rural population, it was not possible to arrange the community and its people to fit within the story line of my films. Only in *Mossane* was I able to adapt the community and the people to the story that I had imagined.

I don't know how a film is born. It's an idea that comes and then I begin to work on it. I had been working on *Mossane* since 1982, while I was cooking, getting dressed, taking a bath, and everywhere I went. During that time, I made small films that were commissioned, which allowed me to earn a living. I don't know how *Mossane* was born. All that I know is that I have a daughter, my only child, whom I cherish. And perhaps because of these feelings, I wanted to cherish Mossane and make her the most beautiful, the purest, and most virtuous.

The beauty in the film is expressed not only as it relates to the girl Mossane, but also it is portrayed in the images, in the cinematography, and there is an intense beauty in the story-telling. It was mythical. Is it a mythology of your daughter or a metaphor for women, for Senegal, for the Serer people of the village of Mbissel, where the film was shot?

In the film, Mossane is thirteen and a half years old. When you have a fourteen-year-old daughter, her changes are visible to you; each photo is different from the others, yet the girl is always the same. There are transformations that a mother perceives in her daughter at that age. This is what I wanted to sculpt. I wanted to recreate a beauty that exists only at this age. Afterwards, she would be too old; before, she was too young. Before, she did not respond, and after the age of fourteen, she complains "Mama, I don't want this, I don't want that."

I used the occasion to glorify this girl, to make, as you stated, a myth. It's also a tragedy. I don't know how to explain it. I tried to take my imagination as far as it could go with this girl that I also loved, whom everyone in the village loved, whom I hope the audience will also love.

Magou Seck, the girl who plays the heroine, is very striking. She plays the role of Mossane in a very sensitive yet intense way. How did you find her?

It was inevitable. It was written for her. Before shooting the film, we announced the casting call throughout Senegal. All the Senegalese girls of that age, and even some who were older, responded. With the crew in place, I invited them to try out and took photographs at the same time. Each time one of the girls performed and I photographed her, I said, "No, she is not the one I envisioned; she is not the one I imagined. She is not the girl for whom this story was written." And in the end, we were all discouraged because, in fact, everyone who had read what I had written felt that none of these was the right girl.

Then suddenly my daughter, who was there with me, said, "Mama, you know I have a friend down the street...," and then she lifted her eyes and looked out the window and we saw the girl carrying a bowl of coal that her mother had sent her to fetch. My daughter went to get her, and when she came in, we immediately took a photograph, and there she was. To think that here she lived right on my same street while all of Senegal responded to the call! Fate had sent her.

As a film viewer, I felt a lot of sensuality in the film, a sensuality in the images, a sensuality in the movements and gestures, and above all, a sensuality from the women. This was felt in the women's bodies, the affection between women, whether it was Mossane and her mother, or Mossane and her friend, Dibor. Is this a sensuality as you lived it?

Yes, it was like that. I more or less experienced that with my childhood girlfriends in Senegal, and I wanted to tell it as such. This film that I have made is, for me, a song to women. The things that I find so beautiful, the things that I have lived, that I have experienced or that I have been told. And then, I made these images according to my vision.

I was struck by the explicit and daring portrayal of women and sexuality in the film. In the love-making scene in particular, Dibor played an active and assertive role, and this sexual knowledge was also conveyed to Mossane. Was this also portrayed as you lived it?

Yes, my sexual education was like that. We always had an older girlfriend who was married before us, and she explained to the others what went on. One does not go into marriage naïve and unaware. No! You know, but without having actually experienced it.

What do you have to say to the women filmmakers who follow you?

I have nothing to say in particular. I am afraid to acknowledge that I have seen their films so as not to have to say what I think of them. All that I know is that, for me, cinema is a passion and you must satisfy that passion. You must go all the way to the point of elation. Having a child, too, has given me great satisfaction, working in anthropology from time to time, also. I feel no matter who you are, without that passion, you will not succeed in making a credible film. Which means to make the audience sit in the same place for one hour and forty minutes without moving. But you can accomplish this better after a few years. I cannot say that at the beginning I would have been able to make a film like *Mossane,* but with time, with perseverance, with tenacity, you can get a great deal of fulfillment. So, doing cinema gives some self-satisfaction.

During the press conference after a screening of Mossane, *I was very frustrated by the direction of the questions. I felt some level of aggressiveness from certain journalists and certain audience members. Did you sense this as well?* (See the transcript of the discussion in the next section).

No, I don't think they were aggressive. I think they wanted to know more about anthropology because they know that I am an anthropologist. Questions about marriage, customs, tradition, I refuse to answer. They can read a book or come to the university when I lecture. I did not come here to give a course on African society. I made a story, and that is all there is to it! I am not going to answer those kinds of questions because Mossane already answered them in the film. She said, "If I were not compelled to stop my studies, I would wait for the man I love." She had to abandon her studies because she was put into the situation of a forced marriage.

When the responses are like they are in the film, I feel that I am wasting my time having to explain them. Because I am someone who speaks very sparingly, I say only what needs to be said. If I had not stopped it, the conversation would have continued in the direction of: "excision, it exists; forced marriage it exists." I say, "No!" I refuse to answer these questions. I made a film; I give it to the public; and I hope they will like it.

You have made fourteen films during the many years since you entered the world of cinema. Do you think that Mossane *is in some ways a climactic point of your work during these past twenty-five years?*

Mossane is the result of a lot of work, but it was work that I did with much joy. I began to write the first sentence in 1982. I had *Mossane* in my head as I cooked. I had *Mossane* in my head while I helped my daughter with her schoolwork. *Mossane* was always with me. You must hold the ideas of your film like this, I think. You must possess your film in this way in order to achieve the results that I have now. There is no respite. There is no peace as long as the film is not finished.

Now, you are at peace?

No, I am not yet at peace. The copy of the film that you saw here is the same one that was at Cannes in 1996. There is only one copy. There are debts to be paid. I have all the laboratory work to do. Because a copy exists does not mean that a film is complete. I will return to Paris to have the inter-positives made. I think that by May 1997 I will be able to free myself totally of this film. As long as I am not free of it, I can do nothing else.

Press Conference Held after
the Press Screening of *Mossane*
during FESPACO 1997

Panel Member #1: Safi Faye, this is the first time that you have participated in FESPACO. What was your reaction to the warm reception of your film at FESPACO?

I think there are many film viewers who were touched by the film, perhaps because I am a woman, an African woman who makes films. Secondly, because I never attend festivals, and perhaps there was a curiosity to see my work. Even during the festival I am locked up in my room. I am afraid of crowds.

Panel Member #1: A great deal of time passed from the beginning of the production until the film was finally finished. How was the problem finally resolved?

The production of *Mossane* started in 1990, and the entire film was shot at that time. The primary reason that I did not bring the main actor with me here to FESPACO 1997 is because she is now twenty years old. There were problems with the handling of the finances by the French producer. Since the financing involved an international coproduction which included Germany, England, France, and Senegal, which really invested a lot in the film, it had to be clarified who was who, and who did what before I could continue. The film was tied up in the legal system from 1990 to 1995. Then, when I was finally given the rights, I began to edit it. Now, six years after the initial shooting, it is ready, it is credible.

Panel Member #2: In 1996, at Cannes, the film was not very visible, and the press did not say much about it. How was the film received at Cannes?

No, it received a good reception throughout. There was a strong Senegalese delegation; the ambassador was also present. Though everyone knew that I had shot the film in 1990, no one actually knew its status during the time up to its completion. Everyone was waiting to see this film, to see if it was still worthwhile. The fact that it was selected for the special category "Un Certain Regard" at Cannes was an affirmation of its value.

Panel Member #1: There has been criticism that beyond festivals, African films have not reached the African population. Have you thought about the life of the film beyond festivals?

As I stated earlier, the film has several coproducers. It was released in Switzerland beginning in September 1996 and is still being picked up presently. In terms of distribution in Africa, Ousmane Sembene is arranging for the release in April 1997. There is already an investment in the distribution, notably in Germany, England, Switzerland, and in Africa.

Panel Member #2: The beauty of this young woman is the focal point of the film. Are you saying that her beauty is something that fosters jealousy?

No, I wanted to mythicize a thirteen-year-old girl. She has her purity, her beauty, her virtue. Those are the things that exist at that age of adolescence. It is what I observed as a mother. It is what I observed in my daughter who was the same age.

Audience Member #1: I just finished seeing your film and was very touched by it. I would like to know if you think that the tradition of forced marriage is still present, and if your film opens other horizons for African women. And, do you really see a difference?

I am not affected by this traditional practice, and neither is my daughter. In my film, I did not place this situation in the present. I structured this situation in the past, a past that could have involved my mother, my grandmother, but it did not affect us. I fictionalized this experience for the film; I don't know exactly why I touched on this problem of forced marriage because I was never confronted with it. However, it permitted me to know that it existed. The only thing that I can attest to is that my mother was married at age fourteen, and this situation is possible.

Audience Member #2: Is it still practiced today?

Not in my generation or the generation of my daughter.

Audience Member #2: But in general?

It existed; it existed in African history.

Audience Member #2: And it no longer exists?

No, not in my society, at least.

Audience Member #3: So you are saying the problem has been resolved?

No, I never said that. I said in my society—there are many societies, Africa is very diverse —I did not say that it didn't or it doesn't continue to exist. I said that in my society it no longer exists. My treating these images of forced marriage does not mean that I experienced it. It was an idea. I don't understand the point of these questions. My film is telling a story about something that I raised as an issue! It could have existed, just as it could very well not have existed. It is difficult to say that it only exists in Africa.

Audience Member #3: But there are areas in Africa where it exists . . .

But I am not trying to say that it does not exist. I am simply trying to say that my imagination explored an experience that was lived in the past, and it is this marriage that I wanted to relate, this forced marriage that does not affect me but could have, as I stated at the beginning, affected the generation of my mother or of my grandmother.

Audience Member #3: I am asking you to situate its importance in the social and political context of today . . .

I would prefer for someone who deals with this situation to respond to your question. Since *I* choose the man that *I* love; so!

Panel Member #3: Safi Faye, you have a formidable character. You have the reputation of being a serious and forceful woman . . .

I am happy to be alive. I am happy within my family. I am happy in general. I have my temperament. I must say that I detest these kinds of debates. You do your work, you show it to the public, and they appreciate it or they don't. I am not here to defend my choices in making the film. I imagined many things; I made a film about them. Now, I offer it to the public, and it is up to the public to say what they think.

Panel Member #4: And I think that in this debate people are saying what they think.

I am not here to defend my work. I did what I loved. I love what I did. I am not here to describe African society. I am an anthropologist; I have done enough not to have to come here and explain African societies. I simply imagined that the most beautiful girl in the world would be fourteen years old, would be African, and that everyone would fall in love with her, and she would leave because she does not belong to this world. I have this simple story. And within this story inhabits the community where she grows up.

Panel Member #4: Madame Safi Faye, you must not take this debate as an interrogation; it is an exchange between you and the public . . .

It is a clarification that I am giving!

Audience Member #4: I would like to know if there is a social and political interest in your subject choice. You say that you have not experienced forced marriage yourself. There must be an engagement in one's art. I think that we do not make films just to make films. One must look at society in relationship to its needs. One must bring certain answers to issues that are raised in Africa. Though the debate is interesting, you appear to be dodging the questions. Don't you think it would be interesting to stay and discuss your film with us?

I am not saying that I am fleeing from a debate. I am simply saying that when you have done your film, you do not have to give further explanations. The product is there, it exists, and to take it apart piece-by-piece is beyond my domain. As I said before, no one has ever seen me here before because I am afraid of crowds. Yes, you asked me to come, but I am not here to defend myself.

Timeline: Safi Faye's Career in Cinema

1970   Begins studies in ethnology at the Sorbonne in Paris.
1972   Begins studies in filmmaking at the Louis Lumière Film School, Paris.
       Completes student film, *La Passante* (The Woman Passerby). 10 min.
       Begins filming *Kaddu Beykat* (Peasant Letter).
1973   Completes collective film, *Revanche* (Revenge). 15 min.
1975   Release of film, *Kaddu Beykat*. 95 min.
       Receives award at the Festival International du Film de l'Ensemble Francophone
       (FIFEF), Geneva, Switzerland.
1976   *Kaddu Beykat* receives the Georges Sadoul Prize, France.
       Special award, 5th Pan-African Film Festival of Ouagadougou (FESPACO),
       Burkina Faso. International Film Critics Award, Berlin Film Festival, Germany.
1979   Release of film, *Fad'jal* (Come and Work). 108 min.
       Selected for "Un Certain Regard," Cannes Film Festival, France.
       Release of film, *Goob na ñu* (The Harvest Is In). 30 min.
       Studies video production in Berlin, Germany.
       Begins film, *Trois ans cinq mois* (Three Years, Five Months).
1980   Completes film, *Man Sa Yay* (Me, Your Mother). ZDF Production, Germany.
       60 min.
       Fad'jal receives award at Carthage Film Festival, Tunisia.
1981   Release of film, *Les Ames au soleil* (Souls Under the Sun) commissioned by the
       United Nations. 27 min.
       Release of film, *Selbé et tant d'autres* (Selbé and So Many Others). "As Women
       See It" Series, UNICEF and Faust Films Production. 30 min.
1983   Completes film, *Trois ans cinq mois*. Daad Production, Germany. 30 min.
       Selbé et tant d'autres wins Special Prize, Leipzig Film Festival, Germany, and
       Vancouver Film Festival, Canada.
1984   Completes film, *Ambassades nourricières* (Culinary Embassies). "Regards sur la
       France" Series, FR3 Television, France. 58 min.
1985   Completes film, *Racines noires* (Black Roots) for Télé-Europ and FR3 Televi-
       sion, France. 11 min.
       Completes film, *Elsie Haas, femme peintre et cinéaste d'Haiti* (Elsie Haas,
       Woman Painter and Filmmaker from Haiti), FR3 Television, France. 8 min.
1989   Completes film, *Tesito*, commissioned by the Comité Catholique contre la Faim
       et pour le Développement (CCFD). 27 min.
1990   Completes the shooting of *Mossane*.
1990–1995   Legal proceedings for film rights to *Mossane*.
1996   Release of *Mossane*. 105 min.
       Selected for "Un Certain Regard," Cannes Film Festival, France.
1997   *Mossane* selected for Cannes Junior, Cannes Film Festival, France.
1998   Safi Faye Retrospective and Gala, International Women's Film Festival, Créteil,
       France.

Notes

1. Interview and press conference proceedings are transcripts from my videotapes of the events. My translations from the French throughout.

2. Mark A. Reid (1995), however, focuses specifically on *La Passante,* arguing that it represents a dialogic mode of womanist filmmaking.

3. Here she focuses on the cuisine of diverse immigrant populations in France. In *Man Sa Yay* (Me, Your Mother), a film that she made before *Ambassades nourricières,* Faye also examines the theme of immigration and adaptation in the host country, and like *Kaddu Beykat* (Peasant Letter), the epistolary form provides the thread of the story: a son reads a letter from his mother that begins, "It's me, your mother."

4. These three films are more often focused on largely because they have attained international recognition. However, Nwachukwu Frank Ukadike (1996) examines *Selbé* as an example of African feminist-oriented films.

Works Cited

Amarger, Michel. 1998. "Interview with Safi Faye." Brochure, International Women's Film Festival at Créteil [France], 95.

Barlet, Olivier. 1997. "Interview with Safi Faye." *Africultures* 2: 8–11.

Bouzet, Ange-Dominique. 1991. "Safi Faye, cinéaste à l'africaine." *Libération,* 15 May, 44.

Cissé, Alassane, and Madior Fall. 1996. "Un film en Afrique, c'est la galère." *Sud Week-end* [Dakar, Senegal], 12 October, 6–7.

Eichenberger, P. 1976. "Une Africaine derrière la caméra." *Unir Cinéma,* 1–2. Reprinted from *ZOOM, revue de l'Office Catholique du Cinéma de Suisse Allemande* [Switzerland].

Faye, Safi. 1984. Interview with Pantelis Karakasis. Paris. July. Typescript.

Haffner, Pierre. 1982a. "Interview with Safi Faye." *CinémAction* 17: 63–64.

———. 1982b. *"Petit à Petit* en question." *CinémAction* 17: 79–91.

Martin, Angela. 1979. "Interview with Safi Faye." *Framework* 11: 17–19.

Martin, Marcel. 1982. "Jean Rouch et la mémoire africaine." *CinémAction* 17: 92–96.

Maupin, Françoise. 1976. Interview with Safi Faye. *La Revue du cinéma: Image et son* (February): 76–80.

Ouaga: African Cinema Now! 1989. Directed by Kwate Nee Owoo and Kwesi Owusu. Ghana: Efiri Tete Films.

Playback: A U.N. Family Bulletin on Audio-Visual Matters. 1981. Radio and Visual Series #3. New York: United Nations.

Reid, Mark A. 1995. "Dialogic Modes of Representing Africa(s): Womanist Film." In *Cinemas of the Black Diaspora: Diversity, Dependence and Oppositionality,* ed. Michael T. Martin, 56–69. Detroit: Wayne State University Press.

Rémy, Catherine. 1996. "Interview with Safi Faye." *Amina* [Paris] 315: 21, 34.

Schissel, Howard. 1980. "Africa on Film: The First Feminine View." *Guardian,* 9 July, 7.

Serceau, Daniel. 1982. "Interview with Pierre Braunberger." *CinémAction* 17: 158–60.

Traoré, Moussa. 1979. "Interview with Safi Faye." *Bingo* [Paris] 319: 28–29.

Ukadike, Nwachukwu Frank. 1996. "Reclaiming Images of Women in Film from Africa and the Black Diaspora." In *African Experiences of Cinema,* ed. Imruh Bakari and Mbye Cham, 194–208. London: British Film Institute.

Vasudev, Aruna. 1985. "Interview with Safi Faye." *Festival News, Tenth International Film Festival of India* [New Delhi] 15 January, 1–3.

12 From Africa to the Americas: Interviews with Haile Gerima (1976–2001)
Françoise Pfaff

The following excerpts from interviews I conducted with Haile Gerima in Washington, D.C., over a twenty-five-year period serve as background for a recent discussion with him. These interviews focus on Gerima the man, and Gerima the independent filmmaker, whose highly personal works offer great thematic diversity and stylistic inventiveness. His films explore past and present topics relevant to Africa and the African Diaspora and stress the importance of historical memory in shaping one's life and identity. Gerima's cinematography reflects his experiences in Ethiopia, where he was born in 1946, and the United States, where he has lived since 1967.

Gerima was a member of the Ethiopian lower middle class and claims his development as a filmmaker was strongly influenced by his father, a priest in the Ethiopian Orthodox church, teacher, and playwright, and his mother, a school teacher: "I was primarily influenced by my father, who was a dramatist. He wrote plays against the Italian invasion before I was even conceived. So, the theater tradition of my country plays a major role in my storytelling skills" (11 May 1983).

In Ethiopia, Gerima was very receptive to Western culture and Hollywood movies: "After I came to America, I discovered I was disrespecting my country and my culture. I worshipped Western society—not its technology, but I liked its movies. I was influenced on the cultural level" (16 April 1976).

Gerima was first trained as an actor in Addis Ababa and studied for a brief period at the Goodman School of Drama in Chicago, where he learned to act in works by Western playwrights that had no relevance to the Black experience. He subsequently decided to become a filmmaker: "I found that I had to control what I would do. As an actor I didn't have much power. I was looking for a medium that would make me control what I'd say. I also chose cinema because it reaches more people and has the fastest style. Images are the simplest way to communicate, especially with African audiences" (16 April 1976).

Enrolling in the UCLA film school helped mold Gerima's political consciousness and define his vision of cinema:

In the 1960s, there was social upheaval in the United States. During that period, I was part of a group of Third World students at UCLA who fought to bring to the

Haile Gerima (Ethiopia) directing *Sankofa* (1993) in Ghana.
Photo courtesy of Mypheduh Films.

school Third World films from Africa and Latin America. We saw films by Sanjinés,
Solanas, Gutiérrez Alea, Solás, and Sembene, such as *Blood of the Condor, The Hour
of the Furnaces, Memories of Underdevelopment, Lucia, Borom Sarret, Black Girl*, etc.
I learned about Brazilian Cinema Novo. In *Mandabi*, Sembene's characters expressed themselves in their African language. This was a revolution! These films
gave me pride and confidence in my own culture and taught me that I did not necessarily have to follow Western conventions to make films. (11 May 1983)

Gerima describes his Fanonian steps from Hollywood imagery and consum-
erism to Third World filmmaking:

I have known Hollywood cinema since my childhood, and by the time I went to
California, it did not impress me anymore. I had totally outgrown it. I grew up
through three stages: First I wanted to be like motion picture characters, but this
made me very shallow and limited. My second stage was a stage of rejection. I
would hate anything the West stood for, but it took so much out of me that it took
away all my creativity. My third stage came when I became more rational and tried
to take the good things of the West, such as the tools and the technology, and
choose the positive achievements of the Western world. This selective process went
along with a deeper understanding and appreciation of Third World cinema. My
anger disappeared, and I recovered my identity. African and Latin American cinemas brought peace to me because they were stressing issues with which I could, as
an Ethiopian, thoroughly identify. (15 April 1977)

Gerima recognizes the influence of Western films:

I admire some films because of their form and others because their content has had an impact on me. I like Buñuel's *Los olvidados* because I could easily identify with its Mexican characters, and I also like De Sica's *The Bicycle Thief.* These are the two Western films that really influenced me. I have seen many others, but they didn't bring anything to me. They only would pacify me, which is what most escapist movies do. (15 April 1977)

Gerima chose the difficult path of independent filmmaking to ensure artistic and ideological freedom and has encountered countless hardships in the production and distribution of his works. This led him to create his own film company, Mypheduh Films. A meticulous and skilled craftsman, he has, over the years, mastered the art of compensating for the lack of financial means with technical ingenuity. Gerima writes and directs his films and often shoots them as well:

You don't have to fit the criteria and the definitions of Hollywood. A film can be 15 minutes, 20 minutes, or 10 hours long. People should consider their economical realities as predominant factors. It is important not to pretend. We should only make a color film when we really want to do it and we are able to do it. You should invest what you have, even 30 or 40 dollars, and you should get your film to the people. You should not be desperate to make a film every year but make a film when you can and when you have something to say! (16 April 1976)

The award-winning director firmly believes in the pragmatic and didactic role of cinema. Whenever possible, he likes to discuss his films with audiences. For him, the primary function of a motion picture is to express ideas and generate discussions:

Film is like a flashlight. You light different areas. I don't want to appeal to audiences through blood and killing. We are galvanized for *Shaft.* I don't think Blacks should treat white people only in terms of meanness. We should be more civilized —which we are, I believe. We should bring our civilization to the screen. Our subject matter is not touched yet, and that's what we should illustrate. We should not adopt racism in reverse. We only show the Black stud, not the Black civilized man. We should bring a new humanity to society, not perpetuate what was done before. (16 April 1976)

Gerima's dozen films and his career, which spans some thirty-five years, concretize and expand such early thoughts. His first work, a 13-minute, super 8, color film school project entitled *Hourglass* (1971), made on a $500 budget, tells the story of a black university basketball player raised in a white foster home: "The film is about his whole struggle of trying to go back to his origins. He lived through the turmoil of the civil rights movement and slowly manages to find himself as a black man" (14 November 1985).

Dedicated to Angela Davis, his next fiction film, *Child of Resistance* (1972) portrays an African-American woman in jail and the shaping of her political awareness. *Bush Mama* (1976) illustrates the plight and abuses suffered by a black welfare mother who kills the white policeman who attempted to rape her daughter. His fourth film and the first one set in Ethiopia is *Harvest: 3,000 Years*

(1976), which makes use of docudrama techniques and dream sequences to relate the exploitation of a peasant family by a feudal landlord. As can be seen, the filmmaker sides with the disenfranchised and insists on people's capacity to transform themselves and react against their oppressive environment.

Commissioned by the Wilmington Defense Fund, *Wilmington 10, USA 10,000* (1976) is a documentary on the ten civil right activists convicted for allegedly burning down a store in Wilmington, North Carolina. In Gerima's words, the film "explores human beings rather than facts. It goes beyond the case of the Wilmington 10 and shows people struggling to seek justice. *Wilmington 10, USA 10,000* was made to open people's eyes and to make people realize that human rights are violated every day in the United States" (29 September 1978).

Ashes and Embers (1981) recounts the psychological alienation and difficult return of an African-American Vietnam War veteran to his family and community. Asked whether the protagonist was in some ways autobiographical, Gerima answered: "I identify with Ned Charles. I think there is a certain aspect of my personality in him, but it is a fictional character that amalgamates many individuals. It exemplifies the black man on the planet" (11 May 1983).

Gerima's *After Winter: Sterling Brown* (the title derives from one of Brown's poems), released in 1985, was conceived and shot as a four-year project with his Howard University students. This film illustrates the life and thoughts of the African-American writer who taught for several decades at Howard. When asked how he became interested in the subject, Gerima replied:

> Initially, I wanted to illustrate the "Around the Fire" concept. The idea was to primarily go around Washington, D.C., and later around the United States, and then to Africa, to begin recording certain elderly people on film. This would be done in an "Around the Fire" way: they would be the central fire and young people would be surrounding them for information. Like in the African oral tradition, they would be listening to the elders recounting and sharing their experiences and wisdom. (14 November 1985)

Gerima's latest films include *Sankofa* (1993), shot in Jamaica and Ghana, in which a glamorous contemporary African-American model is possessed by spirits in Africa. This takes her on a journey to the past where she experiences abuses as a house slave on a sugar plantation. His most recent motion picture is *Adwa: An African Victory* (1999), a collage of present-day interviews and archival materials that celebrate the victory of Ethiopians over the Italians at the 1896 Battle of Adwa.

The following dialogue between Haile Gerima (HG) and the author (FP) took place at Howard University, Washington D.C., on January 30, 2002.

FP: Haile, you have been in the United States for more than thirty-five years, more time than you have spent in Ethiopia. Should you be defined as an African or an African-American filmmaker?

HG: I would say an African filmmaker. I could never be an African American because the cultural shaping of my childhood took place in Ethiopia. Yes, I have harvested a whole lot of other cultural ideas in America, especially in the

African-American community. I can hear jazz and understand it better now than when I first came, I can understand African-American literature better than when I first came, but I don't think my accent and my temperament are African American.

FP: *Although you do illustrate a lot of African-American topics in your films...*

HG: Yes, I do. It's a community that has been a base for my exile, it is a community that has embraced and encouraged me. In fact, without the African-American community's support, there is no way I could have made any kind of film, including *Harvest: 3,000 Years*. Most of the films I made came about due to the fundamental and unconditional support I received from the African-American community. If I have any postproduction office, or if I have a camera, it is because of the African Americans who went to see *Bush Mama*, who paid to see *Ashes and Embers*, and who allowed me to show my film *Sankofa* extensively and successfully. That is where my economic base is. My economic strength is the African-American community.

FP: *What are your goals as a filmmaker today? I know you probably answered this question some twenty years ago when I interviewed you, but I am curious to know what your goals are right now in 2002? Why do you still make films when being an independent filmmaker is so hard?*

HG: Initially, it is a declaration of my right to speak, to tell a story. I believe that the struggle in the world is determined decisively on the basis of who controls the story narrative. I am now more aware of my purpose in making films than, let's say, twenty or thirty years ago. Africans on the continent and in the Diaspora have one thing in common: their narrative is appropriated. So to me, the right to express one's own story is the battleground. It is really a continuation of my initial and, at times, blind emotion, however naïve and imperfect. I am more rational about it now, but my present position is just an extension of the objectives I had from the jump, which then was social change, the fact that the films I made had to participate in the transformation of society. Now I have become more realistic that films are nothing without the power of distribution, and I have become more realistic about the economic aspects of cinema. I thought you made a film and that automatically people saw it, that automatically cinema and people joined together to do something about any kind of injustice that was denounced in the film. My wife Shirikiana and I thought, for example, when we organized the 1987 Ouagadougou conference, that we could forge some kind of relationship between Africans on the continent and in the Diaspora and that resources, energy, and know-how could be shared. That part of our idea has not taken root. Cinema has become more complicated, funds have disappeared, and benevolent people are tired. So I have become more realistic, but not to a point where I would give up my initial idea.

FP: *Film is a very costly endeavor. Do you think of using digital video cameras or do you wish to remain faithful to the 7th Art on a big screen?*

HG: I surface everywhere. Now, for example, I have been in Ethiopia for part of *Adwa,* and I am desperately filming the old people, men and women who fought during the Italian war. I don't want them to die while I am looking for funds and the right camera. Black people shouldn't have this luxury of orthodox attachment to film. Of course, film is artistically the most sophisticated medium, and you can say so much with the way you deploy the colors or the way you deploy exposure. To me, recording, not letting the people die unrecorded, is the newest struggle, and I would use anything to do so, I would even use sound tape. I recorded my own father on tape. We have to record and tell our story using any weapon that we are able to get.

FP: *Because it seems that video is more of a guerilla weapon than film.*

HG: It is powerful. Video is good, digital is good. The problem then is really in distribution. It does not matter what equipment you use to make your films; distribution becomes the bottleneck in the end. Who determines what is to be seen and where, and who benefits from the economic fallout of your work. What's chilling to both African and African-American filmmakers is the fact that they do not immediately benefit from the very films they make. One of the biggest problems in the case of African-American directors like Charles Burnett or in the case of African filmmakers was the fact that there were no distributors for our films, no distributors as passionate as us. There were no business people who wanted to take the business. So you find a filmmaker killing himself or herself being a hustler, selling his or her own work. And again and again, the very fact of hustling as a business person has often killed the creative side of filmmakers.

FP: *At some point in time you were a disciple of the early independent African-American filmmaker Oscar Micheaux because he was creating his own audiences and marketing his products. But now you are saying that if filmmakers are too much involved in the business side of cinema they lose their creativity...*

HG: I am a prime example of this. I distribute my own work. At one point I took even a lot of my friends' films to distribute. Then I realized that I did not have the capital. I am not Bank of America's grandson to amass the funds to distribute their films, so I have given up distributing a lot of films. Initially, our whole idea, with Shirikiana, was that since distribution was critical, we couldn't afford just to be filmmakers. Now I am still continuing that, and the most successful example of my venture is *Sankofa.* But I am tired, literally exhausted after *Sankofa* showed in some thirty cities. We proved to the system that Black films were valid economically, but the next day there was no bank that could trust us to further extend funds to us. If we were White people, this film would be a credible departing point to empower our own future. So, even today, one of our biggest struggles is distribution.

FP: *Are you saying the color white is a collateral?*

HG: Oh it is, a trust fund I call it, actually! It's a trust fund you need to have to go to the banks. Automatically, there is a silent racial consent to say: "There is value in whiteness, and then in blackness, there is disaster and possible bankruptcy." Bankruptcy is the silent subtitle on our foreheads for our visions and ideas, and race contaminates people.

FP: *In the Spring 2000 edition of a newsletter published by the Indiana University Department of Afro-American Studies, Audrey McCluskey calls you a "cultural warrior." What do you think of such a definition?*

HG: Well, people will call you all kinds of names, and I will take it as a compliment. The problem is when you make a movie every twenty years, has your cultural warrior instigated an environment for a better cultural struggle? Are there more filmmakers? Are there more distribution outlets? Is the community aware of our dreams and our visions? How much are Black capitalists and the so-called Black intelligentsia aware of our struggle, and what role do they play in further fertilizing the idea? If this does not happen, you remain a label. Oftentimes, it is a hungry community that names me all kinds of names, because one thing we all have in common is this cultural hunger. Often people will give me a complimentary name because I touch a little bit of our hunger in my films. I call it a testimony of hunger.

FP: *Couldn't the term "cultural warrior" be associated with the word "Mypheduh," the very name of your film company, which refers to a shield?*

HG: "Mypheduh" is a Geez word, and it means "sacred shield." Culture is really a sacred shield, and you can't compromise culture.

FP: *So the word is not necessarily linked to weapons and wars...*

HG: It does deal with war. I believe cultural war has been the longest war. Missionaries did not start war with guns; they started it with culture and education. And so to me, culture has always been half the battle. In the future, more and more, as Latin American filmmakers have said, human beings will not need to be shot—they'll be literally laser burnt culturally in the brain to be satellites and walking zombies of imperialist cultures.

FP: *You made a film called* Imperfect Journey, *which was backed by the BBC. Does this film title reflect the Latin American cinema theory of "Imperfect Cinema"? What is the film about? When was it made?*

HG: It was commissioned by the BBC; it is a documentary film. It was not called *Imperfect Journey* in reference to Latin American cinema. The title meant something incomplete. I made a film that was incomplete. Due to the political and cultural climate in which it was done, I made an "imperfect film." The journey was an imperfect journey, and the film is really about how young people's future is determined by a dysfunctional, underdeveloped African reality—a global reality but as it manifests itself in one country. The film shows kids who all have the burning desire to be educated and how their faith is turned into violence. What's in store for young people under a military junta? I was paying attention to a lot of young people and politically displaced Ethiopians through one journey all the way from Addis to Gondar, my birthplace. *Imperfect Journey* is a documentary which was made in 1993. It took them years to influence me to do it. I made sure they signed everything and that I had total freedom to edit the film and to shoot the film the way I wanted. It was not easy, but in the end it is my film. It represents my expression.

FP: Sankofa *is perhaps the best-known film that you have made in the U.S.A. In two sentences, how would you summarize its plot? How did you finance it? What does the title of the film exactly mean?*

HG: *Sankofa* is about the importance of remembering. Without the past, no one comprehends the present, nor can one forge the future. The title of the film refers to a symbol in Ghana which means that. The structure of *Sankofa* is also based on that concept of past and present and the importance of memory. The film is about most of us who deny the therapeutic aspect or the therapeutic power of history. *Sankofa*'s main character, Shola, was in denial of who she was and wanted to create a world without the past, but the past hijacked her, making her more spiritually centered.

FP: *You said somewhere that* Sankofa *was part of a healing process. Doesn't it make people angry to see what happened with slavery? To see how Blacks were whipped and abused? How can it be that people leave the movie theater "healed"?*

HG: I wish you were there, Françoise, outside the theater, asking people coming out. When we first premiered the movie, only Whites came out with anger and guilt; Blacks took *Sankofa* as a healing film. I did not use the term "healing" before the film was released. I used to say about the film: "resistance is liberating." Black people who premiered the film in Washington called it a "healing movie" for everybody, including White people. However Whites brought guilt into the chemistry and thought the film was made to blame them. The white man's burden is a psychological burden of guilt, and this does not make them peaceful audiences in the theater. But, by and large, Black people were talking about this film or at least publicizing it as a healing film. That's one reason a great deal of religious people were the signposts of distributions. For example, in Chicago, Jeremiah Wright announced the film, saying: "There is a movie called *Sankofa* coming, let's make sure we catch it when it comes." In Baltimore, Detroit, everywhere, Muslims, Catholics, and Protestants came to see *Sankofa*. Black people advertised it to their community as a healing movie. I learned that resistance was not only liberating but also healing.

FP: *Because it gives value to the resistant?*

HG: Yes. Fundamentally the autocratic, dictatorial dissemination of knowledge in history says: "Oh, not much was done to you. Actually, on your bootstraps go

Sankofa (1993) by Haile Gerima (Ethiopia).
Photo courtesy of Mypheduh Films.

forward, don't keep harping on it," etc. But when you look at other societies, their past is their trust fund. If their past was not a trust fund, then why do White Americans name their streets and their boulevards after their ancestors? Why have this many statues? Just in Washington alone, though I've traveled all over the South, why have the statues of those confederates, colonists, and the so-called founding fathers? Why have their statues, and then turn around and say to Black people: "There is no economic, spiritual, cultural mileage out of recognizing an experience of the past"? You find a lot of Black people shamed about the history of slavery. This came out in our discussions with audiences all the way to Los Angeles. In *Sankofa*, we see Black people fighting and resisting slavery. It legitimizes what I've always felt with my own human instinct: there must have been people who fought, and in fact, that's what cornered Lincoln; that's what cornered the progressive abolitionists to fight for change. But oftentimes in history, Black people are placed as passive spectators, incapable of forging a history out of their own circumstances. This negates a whole chapter about Black people. With *Sankofa*, Black people look at slavery as an energy, as a departing point toward self-transformation, collective transformation, communal upsurge in economic, spiritual, and social ways. All this came out during discussions with audiences. Even an eight-year-old kid said: "Thank you for showing me that my people at least fought back, at least fought back." And I said to him: "That should have been your breakfast information, not the genie box signs you have in front of your cereal box. Your parents should have had posters of chain-breaking, these should have been the posters of your childhood."

FP: *To empower children* . . .

HG: To say, "I too matter." Black kids, boys and girls, are turned into just passive spectators because in all media, White kids are actively making history. Black kids look like passive spectators. This is the legacy they get. And so, when they see somebody who looks like them do something, they say: "I too matter. I am capable of making history." So in the end, the cultural struggle is to make little Black kids, all over the world, realize they too matter, that the world is forged out of their participation and that they are capable of making history like that White kid.

FP: *Is that why you made* Adwa?

HG: Oh yes! *Sankofa* made me look carefully back to my own history. I read that Garvey and W. E. B. DuBois mentioned the Battle of Adwa. I said to myself: "Why did I admire Garibaldi, Robespierre, and Dante in high school? Why were they my heroes, when I had Emperor Menelik, who made this revolutionary history at the turn of the past century during the fiercest moment of colonization in Africa?" But in my case, my father was a playwright. So, I'm schizophrenic. I'm positioned with my father's cultural obsession and my own colonized mind. And that fight is extensively interesting, because here I am with my father doing plays about these glorious kings that I excerpt at the beginning of *Sankofa*, and also my heart is with John Wayne in movies where he is killing Indians. In the end, when I divorced one of them, the other became now my nurturing memory to remember. Yes, *Sankofa* led me to *Adwa*.

FP: Adwa *reconciled you with your own past?*

HG: Yes.

FP: *Contrary to what you usually do, you used professional actors in* Sankofa. *Alexandra Duah, who plays Nunu, for instance, is a Ghanaian actress. How did you decide to make that choice?*

HG: Actually, if you remember, I sometimes mix people. Even in *Harvest: 3000 Years,* you notice that the landlord is a professional actor. But I am always gravitating with nonactors. In *Sankofa,* it's the same thing. Some people are professionals, and some are community people. Oyafunmike Ogunlano, who interprets the role of Shola, came out of this Washington, D.C., community and is an actress. Hasinatu Camara, who plays Jumma, was just a teacher in this area. Shango is played by Mutabaruka, who is a poet and a singer. He was scared to act. So there's that tendency of raw material, raw people, because I believe, one, logistically, it is less work for me to do, than to get star-struck people. Two, you get original material to work from.

FP: Pondering over the questions I was going to ask you during this interview, I was wondering whether you also made Adwa *for your kids, so that they would be proud of their Ethiopian heritage?*

HG: No, no, no. I was reclaiming the things I abandoned for John Wayne, for the love of people like John Wayne and Elvis Presley and all these movies that have nothing to do in my life now. I was making that film in revenge of that.

FP: So it's mainly your own quest that generated Adwa?

HG: Oh, yes, but I'll tell you this: Having kids has sensitized me, has taught me not to be reckless. Making *Sankofa* was a very nurturing time for me, because my kids came in the editing room, making me continue to be human. When you feel powerless and lonely, you could be fascist. In your messages and in your actions, you could be violent. My children made me more tender; having kids made me more tender. That's all I can say. As I write scripts, as I go over scripts I wrote ten, fifteen years ago, I see the human dimension of my scripts because I have children. They have become the tenderizing factor of my work. I am about to do a film with the Germans. It's called *Teza,* which means "dew" in Amharic. It's about an Ethiopian intellectual returning home during the military dictatorship. In this case, my kids have played a role in the writing of the script.

FP: But, as you said concerning Adwa, *you don't use your films to reinforce their Ethiopian identity?*

HG: No. In fact, I really think more of their Pan-African identity. I want them to be aware of my obsession with Africa, defining who they are in the history they study. There's nothing I would not tell them about racism. I tell them that it is very important to be a soldier, to fight racism, because it hurts a lot of people even when you are the privileged section. I make sure they understand the racial conflict. I want them to understand racism and be able to identify it. I want them to analyze news seriously. I don't want them to hear official news and make up their mind. I always instigate research. So my kids are very critical. They don't even take *my* view. They argue with me, and if I make what seems to be a racist statement, they catch me right there. If they find me contradicting my beliefs, they catch me, and we argue for hours. Everybody who knows us says that we are very lucky in terms of our children. One of the things also is that we don't have television in our house. They watch films, selected films, films that we feel empower them, though they can also see some of these stupid films made for children. They look at them critically. They see certain films, and they look at the roles of Black people a lot. They come and tell me: "You should have seen the role this guy was playing." We go to my office and watch films. They ask me: "What is your next film?" I tell them I want to make a film like that. And they always think I'm not making the kind of films I should make and that they want to watch, and that is the commercial kind of film. I tell them that when they get tired of that, they will need my films. They have watched *Sankofa;* they've watched *Imperfect Journey.* I think they understand that I am from Ethiopia and that my culture is Ethiopian. They understand they were born here and that their mother is an African American. I'm Ethiopian. They surf between these two polarities.

FP: They surf?

HG: Yes. They speak my language because I have told them I feel more real in Amharic. English is my second language.

FP: Do they feel African American or Ethiopian?

HG: I think they feel African American, Pan-African. They also know they have an Ethiopian heritage. They speak the language. They know the dance, but they were born here. So I don't want to confuse and say: "You are Ethiopian." I always say: "You decide how you gravitate. Don't be pressured by what I want you to be," because that is like another psychological drama to lead the children into.

FP: Your home has really a strong educational component. Do your children go to public schools?

HG: Yes.

FP: But they get their cultural nurturing at home?

HG: Yes. Very strongly. We have debates and discussions. There are many things I don't explain, but there is nothing Shirikiana would not explain if they asked her. And so they have good signposts. They know that I am very committed to my beliefs; they know my struggles, and they know I am not only born in this world to raise them, but I am also here to make my movies. I let them know all the time that just because I am cooking for them, I am not a servant. I am the filmmaker father.

FP: So you cook now? I did not know...

HG: I do all the time, all the time.

FP: How old is your oldest son, Yohannes?

HG: He is eighteen now.

FP: And the last one? She's about four?

HG: She is going on five now.

FP: When I saw Adwa *at the Lincoln Theater on U Street in Washington, D.C., I saw a lot of Ethiopians attend the screening with their children, as if to teach them what Adwa was, who the Ethiopian Emperor Menelik was. You were reaching out to Ethiopians and building new audiences.*

HG: Oh yes, but also a lot of Rastas are the consumers of that film. *Adwa* sold out in Dallas. The film is going to be shown in San Diego. You're right, Ethiopians go to see this film, but it attracts also a lot of Caribbean and African-American audiences. In San Francisco, a significant percentage of the viewers was African-American audiences.

FP: Adwa has a voice over, which is your voice; it is a very dramatic voice. Don't you think it hampers a little bit the objectivity of the film? Do you want it to be an objective film?

HG: Oh, no. I would never make objective films.

FP: Contrary to some of your other films, you used a lot of special effects to recreate battlefields in Adwa. Wasn't it a bit frustrating to work with a limited budget, which excluded the use of horses and battle scenes?

HG: Well, you are right. I wish I had had the budget. If I had had more money, I would have liked to do a dramatized version of it instead of a documentary. But you can't wait until you get the funds to do that. It was very hard for me to edit that whole battle scene, to create the whole idea of a battle. I was in the editing room cutting three frames, four frames, to create that effect. It was very taxing.

FP: Now, let us tackle the economic aspect of both Sankofa and Adwa. What was the budget for Sankofa? What profit did you make?

HG: It took about a million dollars to make it, but there are also things we did not add, like human contributions; countries like Ghana and Burkina joined in the making of the film. We have now paid off every loan we incurred.

FP: And you grossed a million dollars?

HG: No, the film made three million, but we had to cover expenses. When we rented theaters, 50 percent of the money went to the theater owner, 50 percent to us.

FP: So the benefit might be only one million dollars?

HG: Yes, about. The benefit also comes from the video sales that continue to help us pay the mortgage of our building and store. We own our place out of *Sankofa,* and we used the postproduction facilities and camera generated by *Sankofa* to make *Adwa.*

FP: You sell videos and books at your Sankofa store.

HG: Yes, you see, when Blockbuster said "no" to us in terms of their having our videos in their outfits, we approached African-American bookstores, and we created our own outlets. We wholesale our films to a lot of African-American bookstores. We've sold videos of *Sankofa* to over 500 or 1,000 universities across the country. We have not yet added all the profits to know what business *Sankofa* has done.

FP: I understand you also organize lectures and conferences at your store?

HG: Conferences, discussions. For example, during the Black Arts Festival, our place was used for poetry reading and film showings. We have a lot of Pan-African ideas, people meeting for Pan-African causes. We have, for example, starting in the middle of February all the way to March, lectures on Maroons, and we are going to film the lectures as part of our "Maroons" project.

FP: *What is the "Maroons" project?*

HG: We are trying to make a ten-hour documentary entitled "The Maroons." And then I have a fiction script to come out of this. The documentary is the necessary journey to make in order to concretize the fictional part of the story.

FP: *Will this documentary be shown on television?*

HG: Hopefully, it will be shown by television stations in Europe and America.

FP: *Educational television stations?*

HG: Yes, educational television stations. We have an internet Web site, a school guide, and a radio show linked to the project. It's a very holistic, three-pronged proposal. But my ultimate interest is to do a sequel to *Sankofa*.

FP: *Do you have a business manager to oversee all these activities?*

HG: Well, you know, Shirikiana, the family, unpaid work, my sister, my brother.

FP: *Your wife, Shirikiana Aina, also works a lot with your company Mypheduh Films. And she is also a filmmaker. Did she participate in the making of* Sankofa?

HG: She was the film's coproducer. I worked as editor for her film *Through the Door of No Return*. She is always involved in my films, at least at the executive producer level. With "The Maroons" project, for example, she oversees things I cannot oversee while I'm teaching at Howard. She deals with distribution. Then, she has her own lectures and her own trips aside.

FP: *Does she still have a chance to make her own films?*

HG: Well, she has two, three films down in the oven that she is trying to get grants for. She is always writing for grants.

FP: *Since we are talking about money, what was the budget for* Adwa?

HG: *Adwa*'s cost is about $500,000. *Adwa* has not recovered it yet. We are waiting to see what happens in terms of the film's videotape sales.

FP: *In many of your films, although not in Adwa, you mix dream and reality. Why do you have that pattern in many of your works, when a lot of African-American and African filmmakers insist on making sociorealistic films?*

HG: There aren't human beings who do not have imagination and dreams, fantasies—and that makes them more human. I think that filmmakers who do not go there miss a great deal or lack imagination. When you see a very hard-working worker doing a routinely oppressive physical action, if you assume that his brain and his whole life are in that redundant work, you are missing what the complexity of human nature is all about. Our brain does go into different levels to make us cope with arduous, daily oppressive reality. Especially with oppressed people, one of the things they have universally identical is this extra way of existing, coping with life through imagination, through escape, through fantasy.

FP: You don't think that what could be interpreted as a Freudian escape into imagination, fantasy, etc., would hamper the political side of the film?

HG: In fact it intensifies it, because what is politics without the human face? What's the use of the politically correct message without it being a human story? Politics becomes potent when we know that human beings have this human side to them. Black people would have died in this country during slavery. They lived because they created a form of existence by going into another part of their brain where they created other realities to make them cope with their lives as slaves. To wake up in the morning and realize that you are an enslaved person makes you create pockets of an imaginary existence to cope with reality. Jazz, for example, is a cultural by-product of slavery. It is primarily an expression of resistance, a rebellion, a departure from standard, classical Western music. It is the most sophisticated cultural synthesis that came out of slavery. Jazz is music, and music is imagination. To negate imagination is to deny how Black people survived in the Caribbean, the United States, and Brazil.

FP: How do you generally prepare your films? Do you write detailed scripts? Do you draw your shots like Sergei Eisenstein? Do you improvise as Idrissa Ouedraogo has been known to do? As a former theater actor, do you rehearse scenes with your actors? How do you proceed?

HG: Well, the script is the map of my story. I work a lot on the script. I am one of the people who obsessively draft and redraft. I am now on the fifteenth draft of the new film I'm going to make. I'm drafting another script called *In the Eye of the Storm* about missionaries who came to Africa. I'm rewriting it all the time. Rewriting is very important to me because I grow every day; the script has to grow with me. When you read my scripts, you will really see where the camera is. I don't do drawings. I just separate the actions: the pressure points of the shots, where the joints are. I separate them by themselves as a line to say this is one action. And you can see if I say, "she's nodding," you can get the position of the camera. She's agreeing. Whatever the action I describe, it's there. It saves on time and budget. Preproduction is very important. With actors, rehearsing is very important for me. I don't want actors to do anything if they do not understand what I want to do. For *Sankofa* I rehearsed with the people in Washington and said to them: "Listen, you're going to be paratroopers to be dropped in Jamaica, and you're going to dissolve easily with the rest of the ordinary people in Jamaica. You are not actors, but you are part of the texture of the film."

And so you use a lot of techniques. It's not something new that I'm doing. Rehearsing is what most filmmakers universally practice.

FP: You said to me many years ago that Washington, D.C., was a stopover before returning to settle in Africa. Do you still intend to go back to Africa? If so, to what country?

HG: You wait until I make *Teza;* I think *Teza* will answer you. When I left UCLA, I was in a hurry. I didn't want to stay in that area, and I felt Howard University was closer to Africa, and then jump from here to finally Africa. But I think there is reality versus dreams, and those are shaped by reality. Where would I be if I didn't have five kids now? So my kids are priority in terms of where I am right now. I don't want to confuse them. I think dislocating children is dangerous. So I've become very careful about that. The other thing is the job at Howard. As an immigrant, that's where my job is. It has been a good base for me to make my films. And the other thing is the reality of Africa, and the fact that I would have a problem being at the mercy of governments. Personally, I would have been maybe in South Africa now because of certain resources and technological advantages and because some of my scripts are set in the southern part of Africa. But reality shapes you in the end.

FP: So reality has shaped your life and your decisions. You are not sure of ever settling in Africa?

HG: Well, I'm always, in my head, an Ethiopian citizen. I have my passport, and I always feel I am an Ethiopian.

FP: You're not an American citizen yet?

HG: Oh, that would be too drastically out of my character. I never wanted to be anything but Ethiopian. It's not advantageous, and it has no benefits, but spiritually I feel better.

FP: Yet if you went to live in an African country, it would be South Africa rather than Ethiopia?

HG: I really think the artist in Ethiopia is in bad shape, and I do not like the fact that the Ethiopian intelligentsia does not have any iota on culture and is limited to politics. They do not understand cultural benefits outside of tribal dances. It's the same thing in most parts of Africa.

FP: So you wouldn't be more efficient in Africa?

HG: I would just be paralyzed. Not that I'm having the best of time here, but at least teaching students reinvigorates me.

FP: Your films are on Black issues, would you one day consider making films about other issues, or do you feel you have a mission of reclaiming Black experiences and Black history?

HG: Well, it's not even a mission; it's automatic, something organic for me. I do not have a White story that I'm burning to do.

FP: *So, in the foreseeable future, you don't think so.*

HG: White people are everywhere in films. They have enough films and enough filmmakers. They don't need another wretched filmmaker making a film on them.

FP: *You told me once that you liked some of Buñuel's and De Sica's films. You also mentioned being influenced by African and Latin American filmmakers such as Hondo, Sembene, Solanas, etc. Have there been other influences since?*

HG: Well, now I prefer to speak in terms of films. I like the film *The Island* by Shindo, a Japanese filmmaker whose works are very inspirational.

FP: *What did you like about that Japanese film?*

HG: I saw myself as a little kid, where I grew up. It spoke to my story. I could see that film and remember my own footprints.

FP: *Are there other directors that you like?*

HG: I think Francis Ford Coppola is a very well-developed filmmaker. He is very skilled; his stories and scripts are very well worked out.

FP: *Which of his films do you have in mind in particular?*

HG: *The Godfather, The Conversation.* Most of his films are a challenge to himself. He evolves from film to film. He knows how to navigate and say something within the parameters of Hollywood.

FP: *His own personal views.*

HG: Yes. *Apocalypse Now* is a major film on the war in Vietnam. He uses the *Heart of Darkness* character to show that it is the United States that has gone astray. The Swedish director Lasse Hallstrom, who made *My Life As a Dog,* was a very interesting filmmaker before he came to America. I don't know what he is doing now, but *My Life As a Dog* is a very important film for anybody from any society.

FP: *And who, in the literary or political world, has really influenced you or helped shape your life?*

HG: Frantz Fanon is a key author whom I use in terms of character analysis or even teaching script writing. Who would not learn from Fanon and his whole examination of the psyche of oppressed people? I have eaten up his books. Amilcar Cabral and his whole argument on culture has been key to me. Che Guevara, his passion for excluded people, and the way he expresses that, has been a major influence. I also read a lot of writings by Fidel Castro, Mao Zedong, and Ho Chi Minh. I can't say I exemplify their views in my films, because I would be too pretentious...

FP: But many of your works do reflect Fanon's thoughts.

HG: I hope so, because I have benefited from his views in my teaching and in my own works. Angela Davis is also a very important part of my political views.

FP: Last question, I promise. What are you most proud of in your life?

HG: My continued imperfect struggle to be a husband, a father, and a film-maker.

Part Five: *International Connections:*
Influences and Confluences

13 The Russian Connection: Soviet Cinema and the Cinema of Francophone Africa
Josephine Woll

Preface *cum* Disclaimer

The cinema of Francophone Africa... the phrase itself suggests the close relationship between the art and industry of filmmaking in Subsaharan Africa —especially in Senegal, Mali, Mauritania, and Burkina Faso—and the country that for so long dominated the area politically and economically. Even after these states achieved independence in 1960, they retained close economic, linguistic, and educational ties with France. Would-be filmmakers most often trained in France, and although the official mechanisms established by the French Ministry of Cooperation, theoretically intended to support and encourage independent African film production, have consistently aroused controversy,[1] their centrality, especially in the first decade of development, is indisputable.

France's pragmatic and cultural hegemony overshadows another strand in the fabric of Francophone Africa's cinema. I refer to the Soviet thread. Many scholars mention the *fact* that several prominent filmmakers studied or trained in the USSR. But the linguistic and cultural orientations of these scholars— toward Africa and/or toward Western Europe—have limited their inquiry into the actual significance of that training as well as into the admittedly vexed question of influence.

Soviet and post-Soviet scholarly investigation of this relationship has, with a few salient exceptions, been similarly sparse.[2] As a Slavic specialist with a background in Soviet cinema and a growing interest in the films of Africa, I venture into these relatively uncharted waters with no clear goal but with an open mind. With neither pretense nor aim of inclusiveness, this chapter is meant to initiate a discussion of a complex and promising subject, first by providing some factual background, and then by advancing a few observations on the work of three Soviet-schooled filmmakers of different generations: Ousmane Sembene (Senegal), Souleymane Cissé (Mali), and Abderrahmane Sissako (Mauritania/Mali).

Background

In the 1960s and 1970s, the Soviet Union offered a certain amount of support to the states of Subsaharan Africa, as it did to Third World or emerging nations elsewhere. Such support primarily took the form of military and economic aid. It was intended:

> to disrupt the traditional economic and political ties of [Soviet] aid clients with the West; to promote the state sector to the detriment of private enterprise, and to encourage existing socialist predispositions in many of these countries toward more Soviet-oriented forms of economic and social organization; and more generally, to help create the social and material conditions and the cadres deemed essential prerequisites for the transition of developing countries to a "noncapitalist" path of economic development and, ultimately, to socialism.[3] (Kovner 1971, 72)

Industrial development took high priority. Cinema did not.

Nevertheless, the paper record attests to a certain level of interest in, and commitment to, cinematic progress in the newly independent African states on the part of the Soviet Union. Throughout the 1960s and 1970s, the monthly journal of the Soviet film industry, *Iskusstvo kino* (Cinema Art), regularly carried reportage pertaining to the conjunction of African film and the USSR. In September 1960, for instance, A. Tarelin noted the shipment of Soviet cameras and an accompanying crew of specialists to train local cameramen in Guinea. Most issues included a column, "Otovsiudu" (From Everywhere) later called "Cinerama," commenting on film activity world-wide. Though the preponderance of entries dealt with Eastern and Western Europe, and later with the United States, "Otovsiudu" heralded every festival devoted to African and Asian cinema, whether abroad or within the Soviet Union,[4] and greeted the work of new filmmakers. In May 1964, for example, a short piece on Senegal mentioned that Semben Usman [sic] "did a year's study at the Gorky Studio" before returning to Senegal to make his first documentary and his first feature film. A plot summary of *Borom Sarret* followed (120). A Soviet link was obviously desirable, but not essential: *Iskusstvo kino* announced the debut film of a young Senegalese documentarian, Abubakar [Ababacar] Samb, even though he had studied, not in Russia, but in France and Italy. Beginning in 1969, the Uzbek capital of Tashkent hosted a (usually) biannual festival of Asian and African films on which the journal regularly reported.

With specific reference to Francophone Africa, *Iskusstvo kino* reported on "a week of Soviet cinema" in Senegal (Sept. 1964) and on the arrival of Soviet film crews in Africa to shoot documentaries about the end of colonialism. It anticipated forthcoming films such as an Ivory Coast–French coproduction, "Black Prometheus" (Dec. 1962), and hailed the release of new films from Mali (Feb. 1963) and from what was still called Upper Volta (Burkina Faso) (Nov. 1969). Valerian Nesterov, reflecting on the third Tashkent festival and doubtless echoing what he heard from Sembene and others, outlined the distribution and financing problems facing African filmmakers (Feb. 1975).

Soviets recognized a number of parallels, indeed affinities, between the way their own cinema had emerged in the 1920s and later in the studios established in the Central Asian republics, and the cinema of newly-independent states in Francophone Africa. Although Russia's prerevolutionary cinema began as a capitalist, privately owned, profit-oriented industry, much as it did in the United States and Western Europe, the Bolshevik revolution and its aftermath radically altered how, why, and for whom films were made.[5] Financial profit still mattered, but it competed with other goals: educational, political, promotional. The new regime in post-tsarist Russia, like new leaders in postcolonial African nations, willingly allocated part of its budget to subsidizing cinema because it recognized how effective the medium could be as an instrument of propaganda; and most Soviet filmmakers in the 1920s, though they had individual and often compelling aesthetic agendas, readily supported the politics of revolution.

Moreover, the Soviet Union housed, at the time of its formation, a decidedly heterogeneous and disunited conglomerate of ethnicities and languages. The majority of its population could not read. Cinema, especilly silent cinema, could turn these facts to the advantage of the state; it could enlighten and persuade and promote particular ideological programs by means of image, with minimal text.

The "father" of African cinema, Ousmane Sembene, also recognized these affinities. He turned to film precisely because, upon his return to Africa from France in 1960, he understood that price and illiteracy limited the power of books to reach mass audiences. As early as 1962, he acknowledged film's potency as a political weapon, its ability to "make us discuss and progress," to raise awareness of "sociopolitical constraints that impede the harmonious development of the African nations" (Pfaff 1999, 1; 58).[6] Nor has his position in that respect essentially changed over the years. In an interview he gave to *Iskusstvo kino* in 1969, after *Mandabi* was screened in Moscow, he articulated much the same point: "For us cinema has first of all political significance: cinema has more followers than any church or political party. It can help decolonize Africa," but only when Africans "see their own reality" on screen. *Mandabi*, he continued, "expresses our desire to change the world we live in. The people must understand its problems. They see and must ponder a comedy that turns into a tragedy" (Chertok 1969, 31).[7] Seventeen years later, at Tashkent, Sembene declared his opposition to "art for art's sake": "Such work," he commented, "fails to grow out of a living soil and cannot, therefore, be fruitful" ("Tsentr pritiazheniia" 1986, 124).

Thematics

Of all the African filmmakers who studied in the Soviet Union, Ousmane Sembene received the most consistent attention in the Soviet press. After years as a trade union activist in Marseille, and after publishing the novel *Le docker noir* (*Black Docker*), Sembene first went to the USSR in 1957 to attend a writers' conference. A few years later he accepted an invitation to return for a year of intensive training under director Mark Donskoy at the Gorky Studio. Whereas Soviet-trained Cissé and Sissako went to the Soviet Union young and unknown (Cissé in his twenties, Sissako still in his teens), Sembene already enjoyed a certain amount of fame as an author. In part because of his age, artistic maturity,

Emitai (1971) by Ousmane Sembene (Senegal).
Photo courtesy of the British Film Institute.

and ideological commitment, in part because of his subsequent steady productivity and the quick international recognition accorded his films, Sembene became a regular presence in Soviet discussions of African cinema—far more than any of his colleagues, including the venerable Benin-born Senegalese director, producer, and film critic Paulin Vieyra.

Thus in 1965, *Iskusstvo kino* noted the prize Sembene garnered at the Tours Festival for his debut film. Several years later, when Sembene was shooting *Mandabi,* the journal described at some length its plot and themes. It then ran both an interview with Sembene and a review of the film. *Iskusstvo kino* routinely asked Sembene to comment on the Tashkent festival of Asian and African cinema; it announced each of his films as they appeared and usually reviewed them.[8] He brought *La Noire de...* (*Black Girl*) to the first Tashkent festival, *Mandabi* to the second, and showed *Emitai* at the Seventh International Film Festival in Moscow in 1971, where it won a Silver Medal.

Sembene knew no Russian when he studied filmmaking in the Soviet Union: his "lessons" passed through an interpreter. He had, however, an immediate point of contact with Mark Donskoy, an eminent director whose career began in the 1930s and who was one of the heads of the Gorky Studio when Sembene went to Moscow. Both loved the writing of Maxim Gorky (1868–1936). Donskoy had directed screen adaptations of Gorky's autobiography, filmed as a trilogy: *Detstvo* (*Childhood,* 1938), *V liudiakh* (*In the World,* 1939) and *Moi universitet* (*My University,* 1940). He had filmed Gorky's didactic revolutionary novel *Mat'* (*Mother*) in 1956 and his early novel *Foma Gordeev* (The Hero's Name) three years after that.

Sembene shared with Gorky the experience of living rough and working with his hands: he spent his teens as a mechanic, carpenter, and mason and became a longshoreman in France after leaving the French colonial army (Pfaff 1988, 237–38). Gorky had comparable experiences, albeit many decades earlier: with virtually no formal schooling, his "university" consisted of strenuous manual labor in tsarist Russia as well as contact with underground revolutionary circles. Sembene appreciated the way Gorky depicted and motivated the transition from tsarism to Soviet times (Pfaff 1999, 9; 62); whether writing about himself, his relatives, or imagined characters, Gorky consistently portrayed and explained the process of political enlightenment among the innocent and/or ignorant.

Donskoy's best work, which includes, certainly, the first two of the Gorky trilogy and *Foma Gordeev*, demonstrates a "humane optimism"[9] that links his films with those of Jean Renoir and Vittorio De Sica as well as a careful attentiveness to the importance of everyday life that invites comparisons with Flaherty (Agel 1962, 111). From the Gorky trilogy, for example, Donskoy retained those characters and episodes that helped the child form an understanding of the world, its joys and its injustices. Donskoy expresses in visual terms Gorky's compassion for the vulnerable and victimized of the world without stripping away their dignity or their love of life and of beauty. The battered wife retains her ability to sing, to dance, and to love; the boy who can't walk creates a menagerie of insects and animals around him and exults in the sky and air when his friends transport him to a field.

Donskoy and Sembene share an ability to dramatize the brutalizing effects of poverty without demonizing those who become brutal. For both, the past survives into the present—in the griots who populate Sembene's movies, and in the folklore and fairy tales transmitted by the old grandmother in Donskoy's *Childhood*. Both directors favor natural metaphors (changing light, river flow, etc.) to represent time; and both contrast the rhythms of outdoor life—street brawls and fairs in Nizhny Novgorod, market stalls and public trysts in Dakar—with the confinement of indoor spaces, whether the cramped living quarters of Russian poverty or Diouana's high rise Riviera cage in *La Noire de....* Writing of a film, *Fad'jal* (Come and Work, 1979), made by another Senegalese director, Safi Faye, Olivier Barlet observed that the camera concludes its long panning shots by coming "to rest, in the end, on human labour. Africa is now no longer a backdrop, but the site of human activity" (2000, 39). Much the same can be said of Sembene's work and of Donskoy's adaptation of Gorky, where the river, its banks, the fields, and hills contain, engender, and define the labor and lives of the inhabitants.

Donskoy and Sembene both conceived of the filmmaker as activist and of film as a political tool, an understanding they shared with the Italian neorealists; and the Soviet regime permitted liberal distribution of films by De Sica, Rossellini, and De Santis because they "dealt with social issues and depicted 'simple' working-class characters" (Woll 2000, 35). But although Italian neorealism significantly informed the work of Russian filmmakers in the 1950s, validating and giving brilliant artistic expression to cultural values that became prominent in the post-Stalin thaw, the Italians were themselves influenced, if not indeed formed as political artists, by the Soviet directors of the 1920s. Soviet critics, like Western ones, recognized De Sica's legacy in Sembene's gift for "authentic atmosphere" and his "sympathy for the common man" so patent in *Borom Sarret* (1963) and *La Noire de...* (Chertok 1969, 30). But they saw deeper roots. Reviewing *Mandabi*, the critic Miron Chernenko wrote: "African cinema was born in the 1960s, when cinematography's genetic code already contained the pathos of Russian revolutionary film art, and the poetic realism of the 1930s, and the humanism of neorealism, and the anarchic mood of the "nouvelle vague," and the classical graphic art of the Japanese" (1969, 142).

Certainly Sembene himself consciously chose to emulate the revolutionary directors in his thematics: "I profoundly believe," he said in 1970, "that each [film] must treat an important issue, must resolve it in some fashion or at least suggest a solution. That's how Eisenstein and Dovzhenko made their pictures, pictures I studied in the Soviet Union" (qtd. in "'Etot festival' nam neobkhodim," 1970).

As Pierre Haffner notes, Sembene's films created a foundation that allowed other directors to seek and find their own distinctive voices (2000, 31). By the time Souleymane Cissé entered the profession, African cinema had its own institutions, its own organizations: FEPACI (Fédération Panafricaine des Cinéastes) and the Ouagadougou Festival (FESPACO) were created in 1969. Cissé encountered the Soviet Union and Soviet cinema on different terms than Sembene, though he too studied with Donskoy. Unlike Sembene, who came to Moscow at the age of about forty after living in or visiting many countries and who crammed as much learning as he could into one year, Cissé—a film fan from childhood—lived in Moscow for nearly eight years in the 1960s. It was his first experience of life outside Mali, his first exposure to a predominantly White society, and he discovered that people of another race felt, reacted, thought much as he did.[10] Grants enabled him to study photography and film projection first, and then to enroll in the standard five-year course at VGIK, the State Institute of Cinematography and the Soviet Union's most prestigious film school. Cissé's intense focus on learning the trade and art of filmmaking precluded, he says, much interest in politics. Nevertheless, politics in the broadest sense of the word informs all of his films, even if colonialism per se is no longer a burning issue.

Like all students in the directing course at VGIK, Cissé had to submit a short film, his "diploma work," in order to graduate. His degree project, *L'Aspirant* (The Aspirant, 1968), incarnated in a young doctor and his father, a traditional healer, the tension between modern and traditional African methods of medicine. Back in Mali after his Moscow years, Cissé took a job with the State Information Service directing newsreels and documentaries before turning to feature films. His first film, *Les cinq jours d'une vie* (Five Days in a Life, 1972), presents traditional Koranic education as failing its pupils, Bambara young people. His second, *Den Muso* (The Young Girl, 1974), portrays via a mute young heroine what Cissé called "the plight of the countless child-mothers that one sees in most African countries today."[11] In *Baara* (Work, 1978), working-class consciousness develops among factory workers, especially a young porter hired to work at the plant by the engineer-manager. Trying to be fair to both workers and bosses, the manager ends up trapped and, finally, murdered. *Finyé* (*The Wind*, 1982) depicts student unrest, and *Yeelen* (*The Light*, 1987)—a prizewinner at Cannes and a recipient of the British Film Institute's award for most imaginative and innovative film of the year—indicts contemporary abuse of power in Mali via a mythic story of a son who flees from his murderous father across the Sahel. Cissé's most recent film, *Waati* (1995), views ethnic, national, and gender conflicts through the prism of a journey from the south of Africa to its northern lands.

Obviously Cissé, like Sembene, expresses through his movies a passionate engagement in the political and social contradictions of his society. Each of his films tackles an issue or dilemma growing out of West Africa's colonial past but contextualized in (usually) Mali's postcolonial present. Cissé chooses to focus on African exploitation of vulnerable Africans: Ténin, the heroine of *Den Muso*, whose father kicks her out of the family home after she has been raped and impregnated by one of his workers; the workers in *Baara*, exploited by the factory owner; the students in *Finyé*, victims of police unleashed by a military regime. Even in *Yeelen*, set in an undefined mythic past, Cissé stigmatizes "a political class which was prepared to do anything to defend its interests, and had no hesitation in sacrificing its own children" (Barlet 2000, 91–92).

Cissé rarely makes his point explicitly (an exception occurs in *Finyé*, when the gods tell a supplicant to "rely on" himself, to take the initiative), and he takes a less overtly didactic approach than Sembene. More often he works metaphorically. In *Den Muso*, for instance, Ténin—perhaps a metaphor for Africa itself—commits suicide by burning down the whole house: her victimization has consequences not only for herself. But like Sembene, Cissé hopes to "arouse the conscience of his audience," in the case of *Yeelen* to "cleanse the government of corruption and restore the ethical integrity of the ancestral Mali commonwealth" (MacRae 1995, 57).

Cissé studied at VGIK just as the first films of a remarkably gifted and well-trained generation of directors, writers, cinematographers, and editors were appearing (or, in some cases, not appearing due to censorship). The films came out of the newly flowering studios of Central Asia as well as the better-known ones in Russia, Ukraine, and Georgia.[12] The young men and women who made them—Andrei Tarkovsky, Andrei Mikhalkov-Konchalovsky, Sergei Paradzhanov, Kira Muratova, Larisa Shepitko, Otar Ioseliani, Tolomush Okeev—had grown up after Stalin's death, during years of relative cultural tolerance. They were Cissé's counterparts in the sense that they built on the accomplishments

Den Muso (The Young Girl, 1974) by Souleymane Cissé (Mali). Françoise Pfaff collection.

of the first thaw generation, men a decade or two older whose first movies came out in the mid-1950s (Chukhrai, Khutsiev, Riazanov) and who taught them, just as Cissé built on what Vieyra, Sembene, and others had done. And their work left an imprint on Cissé's, as it did later on Sissako's.

Like them, Cissé problematizes his national history and the legacies of that history in the present. To commemorate the fiftieth anniversary of the Bolshevik revolution, several young Soviet directors made films in which they examined and revised some of the core myths of Soviet revolutionary ideology. The Kirgiz director Tolomush Okeev, in a lovely film entitled *Nebo nashego detstva* (Sky of Our Childhood, 1967), genuflects to enshrined Soviet values of education and progress, yet records the collision between traditional nomadic life and Soviet modernity in highly ambiguous terms. The Russian engineers, who at Moscow's behest are blasting a highway through the steppe, understand very little about the indigenous culture, and their explosions despoil the natural landscape and its ecological balance. Cissé moves beyond the colonial interlude in two directions—into the older past (what he once called "the ancient depths of African culture"[13]), and into the anticipated future—in order to reconsider with similar ambivalence the patterns and the contradictions deriving from his country's complex history.[14]

The youngest of the three filmmakers discussed here, Abderrahmane Sissako, first went to the Soviet Union to study Russian in the provincial city of Rostov. He then proceeded to VGIK, where he studied from 1983 to 1991 in the studio run by director Marlen Khutsiev. Sissako's reasons for study in Moscow were mainly pragmatic: after graduating from high school in Mauritania, he "went off to the Soviet Union, like thousands of other African students. It was easier to go there than to France. I had a scholarship to study film" (Boukhari 2000).

He knew very little of literature and cinema, especially compared with his fellow students at VGIK (a high proportion of whom came from educated backgrounds), and perhaps out of his feeling of intellectual inadequacy, he abandoned the first two projects he began for his diploma film. Typically, students could expect to be expelled for such expensive "mistakes." Sissako credits Khutsiev for recognizing something in him that others failed to see and persuading the VGIK authorities to allow Sissako to remain.[15] In 1988 he fulfilled his graduation requirement with *Le Jeu* (The Game), a short film shot in Tadjikistan in a Central Asian desert not dissimilar, he says, from Mali's terrain. It is about a boy who plays soldier with his friends while his father, sent on a mission as a real soldier/spy, is caught and executed. In 1990 Sissako went back to Russia to film *Octobre* (1991), which he took to Cannes. Although he frequently returns to Mali (his birthplace) and to Mauritania, he edited *Rostov-Luanda* (1997) and *La Vie sur terre* (*Life on Earth*, 1998) in France, and he remains there, primarily for financial reasons: "It's very hard to work in our countries. . . . There's no money to be had, no local film industry, no film schools." Realistic as ever, Sissako concludes, "You can't have a ski champion in a country where there's no snow" (Boukhari 2000). Sissako's *Heremakono* (Waiting for Happiness, 2002), a Mauritania/France production, won a prize at Cannes 2002 and the top feature film award at FESPACO 2003.

By age and experience, then, Sissako is a generation younger than Cissé, two generations younger than Sembene. The Soviet Union no longer existed by the time he left Moscow. As a student, he watched films from all over the world as well as Soviet films from the 1970s and 1980s and the previous decades. He saw Soviet films that had previously been shelved or banned and that were released in a process that began in the spring of 1986, thanks to Gorbachev and glasnost.[16] He studied with teachers thirty years younger than the old guard that had trained his senior colleagues (Donskoy died in 1981; Sergey Gerasimov, also at Gorky Studio and also a teacher of Sembene's, in 1985). Political events inform his films—like the long Angolan war, in *Rostov-Luanda*—but as background. Instead, Sissako turns what Haffner calls his "lucid and generous" lens (2000, 40) on the intertwining of human relationships—African-African and African-European—and the social realities in which they exist. Thus, he explains that with *Octobre*, he wanted to "make a film about a mixed-race couple in Russia—a society which, without necessarily being racist, does not easily accept the Other" (Barlet 2000, 121).[17]

Aesthetics

Inevitably, just as the political concerns of these three filmmakers interacted with their Soviet experiences in differing ways, so too did their aesthetic concerns. Though one must be chary of ascribing influence, affinities are clear, and all three directors share certain stylistic preferences with Soviet filmmakers. Coming to their films with eyes educated in Soviet cinema, I see first of all a relationship with the silent classics of the 1920s. (It is not irrelevant that Donskoy, in filming Gorky's *Mother,* was in part responding to Pudovkin's 1925 version.) Like Pudovkin, Eisenstein, and Vertov, both Sembene and Cissé often prefer to use nonprofessionals as actors: for *Finyé,* for example, Cissé hired a sixteen-year-old lycée student he encountered on the street. Their characters sometimes remain nameless in order to enhance their function as socially and politically generalizable types. Pfaff identifies this form of characterization with traditional African storytelling. "Most of Sembène's characters," she writes, "are types reflecting collective ideas and attitudes. In oral African narratives these types respond to typical situations. . . . [Such is] the protagonist of *Borom Sarret,* who has no name and is remembered through his trade and the problems he is unable to overcome" (1993, 17). As Sheila Petty notes, each character "embodies a different strategy for dealing with the changing nature of Africa. . . . [E]ach type act[s] as an agent or represent[s] a point of view or choice of action and its subsequent consequences within the African reality" (1996b, 68). To my mind, however, this categorizing of characterization recalls Soviet cinema of the 1920s. Like Eisenstein in his early films, where Bolshevik, ship doctor, officer, and priest assume significance for their social *cum* political roles rather than for their private, individual motivations; like Pudovkin's explicit identification of protagonists in *Konets Sankta Peterburga* (*The End of St. Petersburg,* 1927) as "Village Boy," "Bolshevik," and so forth, Sembene and Cissé define their characters by their "function in the narrative and not by [their] psychology in the classic Western sense." They want to avoid—to subvert, Petty claims—the emotional involvement "typical of classical Hollywood narrative cinema, and provoke the audience intellectually to question the implications of embracing neocolonialism" (69).

Like Pudovkin, albeit with different goals, Sembene, Cissé, and Sissako all use journey as a narrative structure to "negotiate geopolitical space," whether the journey is external (to France, to Angola, to Russia) or internal, to the modern city or to the Muslim village (Rosen 1996, 30). One obvious difference results from circumstance as much as timing: with little dissent, the Soviet directors of the 1920s accepted prevailing ideological insistence on the absolute superiority of the city over the countryside. For Pudovkin's villagers to become politically conscious and capable of revolutionary activity, they had first to move to centers of industry, factory towns and cities where they learned to identify with their fellow industrial proletarians. In social comedies about contemporary life like Abram Room's 1927 *Tret'ia Meshchanskaia* (*Bed and Sofa*) and Boris Barnet's

Devushka s korobkoi (*Girl with the Hatbox*), the city is the locus of modernity, enlightenment, empowerment. Alone among Soviet directors of that era, in the 1929 *Zemlia* (*Earth*) Dovzhenko's love for the Russian countryside expressed itself in a lyricism that far outweighed his ideological conformity.

Sembene, on the other hand, and Cissé as well, present the city far more ambiguously. In *Mandabi* and in *Xala* (1974), as in Cissé's *Baara* and *Finyé,* an uneasy tension vibrates between city and country, between the traditional mores, manners, and values of village life and the modern, often mysterious ways of a newly urban population. One Soviet critic clearly understood the reasons why African filmmakers so often portrayed urbanization and its consequences: the destruction of patriarchal organization within the village community, intensifying social stratification among rural populations, the pull of city culture on younger generations. "As a result," Nesterov wrote, "a new relationship has emerged between urban and village populations. On the one hand, it results in a substantial growth in the urban working class; on the other, it causes the disappearance of certain popular rituals and traditions, some of which signify an age-old national culture." Still, he concluded accurately, if with a bow to Soviet political correctness, nostalgic motifs "do not dominate. . . . The progressive filmmakers of Africa are equally concerned with questions of the present and future, the problem of linking past and present" (1975, 141).

The early Soviet directors left their mark on the African directors' manipulation of cinema's basic aesthetic components—camera placement, *mise-en-scène,* shot duration, pacing. (Although Cissé expresses admiration for classic Soviet montage and admitted the possibility of influence, I don't see it myself.) Camera distance, for instance, serves Sembene and Cissé much as it did Pudovkin and Dovzhenko. In *The End of St. Petersburg,* Pudovkin's opening shots place two deliberate and slow-moving peasants, father and son, against endless, windmill-dotted plains; in *Earth,* Dovzhenko's peasants and cattle stand against limitless sky. Like them, Sembene and Cissé use long shots (long in duration as well as distance) to locate characters within their natural physical and social surroundings, "not by aestheticizing the world, but by slotting bodies directly into their environment."[18] The length of many scenes in *Yeelen,* for instance, or the *tirailleurs'* capture of two conscripts in *Emitai,* and the dirt path receding into the horizon, "emphasize the land as much as the action. . . . For the most part the camera refuses to close in and attend to individual reactions [of captors or captives]" (Rosen 1996, 46). Cissé relies on long shots—of kids taking drugs in *Den Muso,* of a crowd of students breathlessly waiting to hear the results of the *bac* exam in *Finyé,* of vast spaces in *Yeelen*—to underscore the observer's perspective. In his films and in Sissako's two documentaries, *Rostov-Luanda* and *La Vie sur terre,* even conversations appear at a distance, so that speakers remain in the frame against their normal backdrop instead of being shown in the shot/reverse-shot pattern more characteristic of Western cinematic tradition (Barlet 2000, 159–61).

Especially in his earlier films, Sembene uses *mise-en-scène* in ways strikingly similar to Pudovkin. As the Village Boy and his grandmother cross a St. Petersburg square, Pudovkin positions his camera to look down on them at a very sharp angle, from behind a statue that casts its intimidating shadow over these two "insignificant" figures. Accustomed to the open skies of their native northern landscape, they stand in an urban tenement courtyard and look up to see a tiny patch of sky crossed by a line of drying laundry. Just as the carter in *Borom Sarret,* cheated of his wages, trudges home in a daze, lost among streets full of modern administrative and residential buildings, so do the Village Boy and his grandmother gaze at symbols of might and power in the city, as much the inanimate bronzed generals on horseback as the living mounted policeman who inclines his head slightly but sits tall in the saddle as he deigns to give them directions.

For all three directors, slow pacing allows thought processes and rituals to unfold in real or nearly real time. (One critic notes of Sembene what applies equally to the others, that he never manipulates editing "to gain speed on events" [Pearson 1973, 46–47].) Perhaps they learned from Dovzhenko, who in *Earth* holds his camera for several minutes on the closed door of a peasant house, behind which a peasant of the older generation—Apanas, father of the slain hero Basil—undergoes a gradual transformation of consciousness.

Lengthy silences punctuate the films of all three filmmakers and capture in naturalistic fashion the complete absence of awkwardness that rural or village characters feel when no one speaks. In *Mandabi,* for instance, Ibrahima Dieng sits with his friends in relaxed tranquility that sharply contrasts with the jabbering office workers he must (and cannot effectively) deal with. Indeed, in all of Sembene's films, urban functionaries prattle meaninglessly; and in *Ceddo* (1976), the scheming court griot Jaraaf blathers incessantly while the ceddo griot remains silent. Just as the wordless intimacy of soldiers in Pudovkin's *The End of St. Petersburg* contrasts (via dramatic montage) with shouted phone conversations and the frenetic uproar of stockbrokers, so too the measured, pause-filled dialogue of villagers in *La Vie sur terre* contrasts with the radio disk jockey's steady stream of words and music. In all of Sissako's films, pauses form an integral part of verbal communication, with the capacity to listen as important as the ability to speak. Thus, Sissako leaves his camera trained on individuals as they silently hold the phone to their ears or as they face one another.

Beyond naturalism, silence functions as a dialectical medium. In silence dwells thought, eventually leading to action. When Apanas opens his door to the priest who wants to bury Basil "in the old way," according to church precepts, the priest's talk is self-serving and hollow, and it batters almost comically against Apanas's noble, meaning-laden silence. Eventually, he resolves to bury his son "in the new way," with Soviet songs instead of hymns and a Soviet airplane soaring overhead. In *The End of St. Petersburg,* the ignorant Village Boy confronts for the first time evidence of the absolute perfidy of the exploitive and deceitful factory manager. As he turns in his fingers the glittering coin given him by the manager for his (inadvertent) betrayal of a fellow villager, he wordlessly ponders the significance of what has just happened. His musing ultimately produces a change of consciousness and transforms him into a sentient political being ready for revolution. Cissé's heroine Ténin, as noted above, cannot speak at all; and the porter-turned-worker in *Baara,* whom Cissé considers the "central character" (Leahy 1988, 348), says little, in contrast to the strident chatter of the market woman or even the more measured speech of the engineer-manager. "Silence and even inarticulateness," writes Rosen, "can be both a mark of political oppression and a form of privileged refusal, a refusal of the privileges of language" (1996, 34).

In Sissako's *Octobre,* silence is freighted with the emotional and social pain of an atomized and lonely society. A Russian woman, Zhenya, and an African man, Idrissa, about to leave Russia after finishing his studies, have been lovers. She, carrying his child, considers what to do about the pregnancy. At Zhenya's flat the lovers hardly say a word, communicating in gesture and touch and by Idrissa's playing the piano. Nevertheless, nosy neighbors—each seeming to live in isolation—call the police to report "suspicious" noises. The two are no more loquacious with anyone else. Idrissa "speaks" to a young African woman without exchanging a word when he dances with her on a subway platform. Zhenya barely speaks to her doctor, her girlfriend, even her mother on the phone. Throughout the film what is most important goes unsaid. "The dialogue becomes thinner and thinner, because everything has already been said: the confusion and pain of our divided origins are expressed with the full force of sound and image" (Barlet 2000, 121).[19]

Soviet filmmakers in the 1960s and 1970s, Cissé and Sissako's peers and mentors, resisted tidy categories of genre and style. So do Cissé and Sissako. For Soviets and Africans alike, two cinematic trends manifestly overlap. One is documentarian, a preference for objectivity, evidence, dispassion, fact. The other is poetic or lyric, suggesting subjectivity, emotion, individual voice. Though the two seem contradictory, in fact they blend, serving to enhance the *verismo* and authenticity of these films.

Marlen Khutsiev, Sissako's section chief at VGIK, succeeded in capturing the *Zeitgeist* of his society in nearly all his films. His early films, *Vesna na Zarechnoi ulitse* (Spring on Zarechnaya Street, 1956) and *Dva Fedora* (Two Fyodors, 1958), responded to Soviet viewers' voracious desire to see their own experiences truthfully portrayed on screen; his later films, *Zastava Il'icha* (Ilyich's Gate, 1961[20]) and *Iul'skii dozhd'* (*July Rain,* 1967), reflected the growing alienation and anomie of Soviet citizens. Each of Khutsiev's films reconsidered certain Soviet conventions of thought and of image. *Spring on Zarechnaya Street,* for instance, revised the standard "re-education" theme—in which work, or a worker, can reform and improve everything, including human beings—by its complicated and against-the-grain protagonists, a young worker and a young teacher. In *Two Fyodors,* in which a soldier returns from World War II to a blighted landscape, Khutsiev suggests—most heretically, by Soviet standards of the day—that postwar life may have been more unsettling for returning veterans than the war experience itself.

The overlap of documentary and lyric so often found in Soviet films of the 1960s characterizes Khutsiev's films from that decade as well. He inserted documentary and quasi-documentary scenes into feature films, thereby underscoring the topicality and verisimilitude of the films. For *Ilyich's Gate*, Khutsiev organized a poetry reading at the Moscow Polytechnic Museum nearly identical to the many enormously popular readings that took place in 1961 and 1962. The sequence looks spontaneous as well as authentic, as "real" as the documentary footage of a May Day parade that forms the climax of the first half of the film. In *July Rain* Khutsiev used long shots to convey the estrangement and isolation of Soviet citizens from one another and from any sense of community. In these and other films, nonprofessionals appear alongside trained actors. For instance, Andrei Mikhalkov-Konchalovsky used only three professionals in his second film, *Istoriia Asi Kliachinoi, kotoraia liubila da ne vyshla zamuzh* (*The Story of Asya Kliachina, Who Loved but Didn't Marry,* 1966), and he incorporated the improvisations of villagers into the final script (Anninskii 1991, 212).

For Soviets and Africans alike, lyrical intonation derives from various sources: from soundtrack, from color, from the use of interior monologue or voice-over narration. One of the most gifted Soviet directors, Sergei Paradzhanov, released his first film in 1964; though its commercial distribution was limited, VGIK students certainly saw it. *Teni zabytykh predkov* (*Shadows of Forgotten Ancestors*) is a lushly colored folkloric tale, as rich in traditional music as in the landscape of the Carpathian mountains where it is set and in the clothing and traditions of the Huzul community of its characters. It surely left an imprint on Cissé's visual and aural imagination, visible in the spectacular beauty of *Yeelen*.

Andrei Tarkovsky made his film about Russia's greatest icon painter, *Andrei Rublev* (1966), in black-and-white, reserving color for its final images. Sissako, with the help of the extremely gifted cameraman Georgi Rerberg (who worked with Mikhalkov-Konchalovsky on his first two films, made in the mid-1960s), shot *Octobre* in black-and-white, splashing color into only one scene. Although financial considerations doubtless played a part in the decision to film in black-and-white, so did thematics: in *Octobre*, as in Sembene's *La Noire de...*, the visual composition exploits the obvious black-white dichotomy, providing the "formal and semantic basis of the film."[21] Color intrudes when Zhenya pricks her finger on a thorn from the roses Idrissa brings her. Drops of crimson blood trickle down her finger, disorienting the viewer. Sissako probably didn't consciously think of *Rublev,* but perhaps he learned to use color for both visual and thematic purposes from some of his Soviet teachers and colleagues.

Images dominate Sissako's films far more than words in the same way that they dominate in the films of Tarkovsky and of Tarkovsky's cinematic heir, Alexander Sokurov. (Sokurov, who studied at VGIK in the late 1970s, had difficulty winning official distribution for his movies, but the elite—including VGIK students—usually managed to see them.[22]) Sissako attributes the power that visual images hold for him to his childhood emigration from Mali to Mauritania, where Bambara, his mother-tongue, no longer served him as a medium of communication: "It is perhaps because of the rupture caused by my uprooting that I make films today."[23]

But although *Octobre* ends in separation, Sissako's films suggest that over-all, his Russian experience forged bonds—between him and other Africans, and between him and individual Russians. When he sets out on his journey through Angola in *Rostov-Luanda*, he phones his former teacher, Natalia Lvovna, for a photo of the fellow student with whom he first studied Russian seven-teen years earlier, Afonso Baribanga; they converse with warmth and affection. The language itself bespeaks attachment: Sissako speaks Russian not only to Natalia Lvovna but to Africans he meets during his trip. When he finally locates Baribanga, who now lives in Berlin, Baribanga's first (and last) word in the film is Russian: "*vozvrashchenie*" (return).

Russia provides background to Sissako's journey: Soviet policy brought to-gether Africans from many countries. So many Angolans went missing during the long years of war that Sissako's search, the search for a missing person, is nearly a commonplace. Finding Baribanga—the original goal—gives way to the journey itself, its primary illuminations not Baribanga himself but the discov-ery, en route, of Angola's diverse faces and peoples, their choice to remain in Angola or emigrate from it, the languages they speak.

Conclusion

Function, thematics, aesthetics: the three aspects of cinema where I sought a connection between Soviet cinema and the films of Sembene, Cissé and Sissako. Patently, for most African filmmakers, and certainly for the three discussed in this essay, cinema has and should have political *cum* educational significance beyond its entertainment potential—a core principle throughout seventy years of Soviet filmmaking and one that explains much of the aid of-fered by the Soviets to the embryonic African film industry.

Beyond that obvious congruity, thematic and aesthetic affinities take prece-dence over direct, demonstrable influences. Whether the "perception of space, notion of pacing and rhythm, and narrative tradition[s]" of these directors' films derive, as Gaston Kaboré suggests,[24] from African culture and history rather than from Soviet cinema may, in the end, depend on who is watching. Knowledge, like beauty, may well be in the eye of the beholder. What emerges with absolute clarity is the ongoing, endless and endlessly rewarding dialogue engaged in by artists of every country and culture—Senegalese, Malian, and So-viet included.

Notes

1. See, for instance, Petty's Introduction in *A Call to Action* (1996); Armes 1996; and Andrade-Watkins 1993.
2. Two of those exceptions are Chernenko 1969 and Nesterov 1975.
3. See Kovner 1971, 63, for figures on Soviet aid between 1954 and 1966.
4. See, for instance, reports in *Iskusstvo kino* on a four-day conference in Venice

(Feb. 1962); Igor' Vasil'kov's report on the cinema of Africa and Asia (Mar. 1962); reports on each festival of Asian and African films held in Tashkent (Feb. 1969, Sept. 1970, May 1974, May 1976, May 1986, and others); reports on the first Pan-African Film Festival held in Ouagadougou (June 1972); and subsequent Pan-African festivals (e.g., Sept. 1985).

5. See Youngblood 1999 for a history of Russian cinema in the decades before and after the revolution.

6. The first page number refers to the typescript in English, the second, to the published translation in Spanish.

7. Sembene ends the interview by explicitly comparing the process of reaching large, illiterate and multilingual audiences with what happened in Central Asia in the 1920s, except that the Soviet state "created all necessary conditions for the development of national culture," while African filmmakers must struggle against "those who tried for several centuries to force African nations to forget their history and their traditions" (Chertok 1969, 32).

8. *Iskusstvo kino* Apr. 1965, June 1968, Mar. 1969, July 1969, Sept. 1970, Jan. 1973, May 1974, etc.

9. André Devalles, "Chelovek, tvorchestvo kotorogo zvuchit gordo." Cited in "O tvorchestve Marka Donskogo" (About Mark Donskoy's Work), *Iskusstvo kino* (Dec. 1962): 108. Abridged translation from *Positif* (Paris), no information given.

10. In the 1980s Cissé spoke briefly of his Moscow experience during a panel discussion after a screening of *Finyé* on French television, "Cinéma sans visa."

11. Cited in Leahy 1988, 348.

12. See Woll 2000, 201–8.

13. Cited in Leahy 1988, 348.

14. Discussing the opening and final images of *Yeelen,* Manthia Diawara comments: "Past and Future are reunited; only we in the present must remember and search." Cited by Aufderheide 1992.

15. Personal interview, June 2001.

16. See Lawton 1992, 52–60 and 111–25.

17. Elsewhere, Sissako described the world of Black people in Russia as a contaminated "zone," its boundaries invisible but palpable, like the poisoned zone of Chernobyl or Tarkovsky's in the film *Stalker.* Inside the zone—the university and its environs—they are safe; outside, they become vulnerable. Cited in *Revue noire* 1993.

18. Serge Daney, "Cissé très bien, qu'on se le dise," *Libération* 9–10 May 1987, cited by Barlet 2000, 146.

19. Barlet goes on, less persuasively: "The film's *originality* lies, without doubt, in the fact that it opens up our imaginations to this inner world, this silence, in which the conscious images of the limits of a society collide with that other division of our wholeness which Freud revealed to us: the existence of an unconscious."

20. The title denotes a Moscow neighborhood. The film was released only in 1965, in a cut version under the title *Mne dvadtsat' let* (I Am Twenty). See Woll 2000, 142–50.

21. Lieve Spass, *Jump Cut 27* (1982), cited by Pfaff 1988, 248.

22. Cissé's *Yeelen* reminds me of Sokurov's first film, *Odinokii golos cheloveka* (A Man's Lonely Voice, 1978), with its slow motion, long takes, and poetic-epic view of history. On Sokurov's earlier work, see Lawton 1992, 132–37 and 226–29; on his recent work, including the static, visually stunning, nearly wordless *Mat' i syn* (*Mother and Son,* 1997), see Iampolski 1999.

23. Cited in *Revue noire,* 1993. My translation.

24. Cited by Petty 1996a, 6, from a video, *Regard sur le Cinéma Africain*, directed by Philippe Lavalette (1990).

Works Cited

Agel, Henri. 1962. "Liricheskoe proniknovenie v zhizn'" (Lyrical Penetration into Life). *Iskusstvo kino* (December): 111.

Andrade-Watkins, Claire. 1993. "Film Production in Francophone Africa 1961–1977: Ousmane Sembène—An Exception." In *Ousmane Sembène: Dialogues with Critics and Writers*, ed. Samba Gadjigo et al., 29–36. Amherst: University of Massachusetts Press.

Anninskii, Lev. 1991. *Shestidesiatniki i my* (People of the '60s and Us). Moscow: Kinotsentr.

Armes, Roy. 1996. "The Context of the African Filmmaker." In *A Call to Action*, ed. Sheila Petty, 11–26. Westport, Conn.: Praeger.

Aufderheide, Patricia. 1992. "Cross-Cultural Film Guide 1992." <http://www.library .american.edu/collects/media/aufderheide/yeelen.html>. Accessed 11 September 2003.

Barlet, Olivier. 2000. *African Cinemas: Decolonizing the Gaze*. Trans. Chris Turner. London: Zed.

Boukhari, Sophie. 2000. "Directors in Exile." Interview with Rithy Panh, Alejandra Rojo, and Abderrahmane Sissako. *UNESCO Courier*. <http://www.unesco.org/courier/ 2000_10/uk/doss28.htm>. Accessed 11 September 2003.

Chernenko, Miron. 1969. "Pochtovoi perevod" (The Money Order). *Iskusstvo kino* (March): 142–43.

Chertok, S. 1969. "Semben Usman." *Iskusstvo kino* (July): 30–32.

Cissé, Souleymane. "Cinéma sans visa." French television. 1980s.

"'Etot festival' nam neobkhodim" (We Need This Festival). 1970. *Iskusstvo kino* (September): 116.

Gadjigo, Samba, et al., eds. 1993. *Ousmane Sembène: Dialogues with Critics and Writers*. Amherst: University of Massachusetts Press.

Haffner, Pierre. 2000. "D'une fleur double et de quatre mille autres: Sur le développement du cinéma africain," *Afrique contemporaine* [Paris] 196: 27–35.

Iampolski, Mikhail. 1999. "Representation—Mimicry—Death: The Latest Films of Alexander Sokurov." In *Russia on Reels: The Russian Idea in Post-Soviet Cinema*, ed. Birgit Beumers, 127–43. London: IB Tauris.

Kovner, Milton. 1971. "Soviet Aid to Developing Countries." In *The Soviet Union under Brezhnevand Kosygin*, ed. John W. Strong, 61–74. New York: Van Nostrand Reinhold.

Lawton, Anna. 1992. *Kinoglasnost: Soviet Cinema in Our Time*. Cambridge, U.K.: Cambridge University Press.

Leahy, James. 1988. "Stories of the Past—Souleymane Cissé." *Monthly Film Bulletin* (BFI: London, November): 348.

MacRae, Suzanne H. 1995. "*Yeelen*: A Political Fable of the Komo Blacksmith/Sorcerers." *Research in African Literatures* 26.3: 57.

Nesterov, Valerian. 1975. "Èkran bor'by i nadezhd" (A Cinema of Struggle and Hope). *Iskusstvo kino* (February): 139–42.

"Otovsiudu." *Iskusstvo kino* May 1964: 120.

Pearson, Lyle. 1973. "Four Years of African Film." *Film Quarterly* 26:3: 42–47.

Petty, Sheila. 1996a. "Introduction." In *A Call to Action: The Films of Ousmane Sembène*, ed. Sheila Petty, 1–10. Westport, Conn.: Praeger.

———. 1996b. "Toward a Changing Africa: Women's Roles in the Films of Ousmane Sembène." In *A Call to Action*, 67–86. Westport, Conn.: Praeger.

Pfaff, Françoise. 1988. *Twenty-five Black African Filmmakers*. Westport, Conn.: Greenwood.

———. 1993. "The Uniqueness of Ousmane Sembène's Cinema." In *Ousmane Sembène: Dialogues with Critics and Writers*, ed. Samba Gadjigo et al., 14–21. Amherst: University of Massachusetts Press.

———. 1999. "Ousmane Sembène: The Man and His Work." Typescript. Published in translation as: "Ousmane Sembène: el clásico de los clásicos." *Nosferatu* 30 [Donostia/San Sebastián] (1999): 58–68.

Revue Noire. 1993. <http://www.revuenoire.com/francais/S08-1.html>. Accessed 11 September 2003.

Rosen, Philip. 1996. "Nation, Inter-nation and Narration in Ousmane Sembène's Films." In *A Call to Action*, ed. Sheila Petty, 27–55. Westport, Conn.: Praeger.

Tarelin, A. 1960. "Kino v Gvineiskoi respublike" (Cinema in the Republic of Guinea). *Iskusstvo kino* (September): 153–55.

"Tsentr pritiazheniia—navstrechu IX Tashkentskomu..." (Center of Attraction: Toward Tashkent's Ninth). 1986. *Iskusstvo kino* (May): 123–26.

Vasil'kov, Igor'. 1962. "Den' segodniashnii i den' zavtrashnii" (Today and Tomorrow). *Iskusstvo kino* (March).

Woll, Josephine. 2000. *Real Images: Soviet Cinema and the Thaw*. London: IB Tauris.

Youngblood, Denise J. 1992. *Movies for the Masses*. Cambridge: Cambridge University Press.

———. 1999. *The Magic Mirror: Moviemaking in Russia, 1908–1918*. Madison: University of Wisconsin Press.

14 African and Latin American Cinemas: Contexts and Contacts
María Roof

Background for Research

African and Latin American cineastes occasionally have acknowledged their awareness of films from the "other" continent, despite the limited international distribution of these films. For example, Haile Gerima (Ethiopia) speaks of the influence of Latin American films on his development, naming directors Sanjinés, Solanas, Gutiérrez Alea, and Solás and Brazilian Cinema Novo along with Senegal's Sembene (Interview, 1983). He also felt a deeper link: "I like Buñuel's *Los olvidados* because I could easily identify with its Mexican characters" (Interview, 1977). We know that Latin Americans had a chance to see Gerima's 1976 *Harvest: 3,000 Years* when it was screened in Cuba (Pfaff 1988, 142) and that his *Sankofa* (1993) was taken to Brazil (Ukadike 2002, 261). Cuban filmmaker Rigoberto López exclaimed regarding a "Black Roots" festival in Cuba: "Films from Africa and the Francophone Caribbean, for the first time with subtitles in Spanish! It's wonderful to be able to peer into our neighbors' window, find our historical relatives, and surrender to the telling of their tales" (R. López 1999).[1]

Mauritanian director Med Hondo recalls the influence on his development of Brazilian director Glauber Rocha, especially his *Black God, White Devil* (1964); of Cuban Manuel Octavio Gómez's *First Machete Charge* (1969); and of Fernando Solanas and Octavio Getino's *The Hour of the Furnaces* (1965-68), "not so much for their cinematographic technique, strictly speaking, but for what I would be tempted to call a foundational cinematic act: the bursting of the masses onto the screen, where they appropriate the word to denounce lies and hypocrisy, reveal social contradictions and explore new avenues" (qtd. in Signaté 1994, 24–25).

Documentary filmmaker Samba Félix N'Diaye (Senegal) recognizes Brazilian directors who "worked on the frontier between documentary and fiction" as important in his evolution (Garcia 2001, 90). N'Diaye (1991) also includes Cuba among the "great family of documentarists" and comments that "the Cuban Film Institute [ICAIC] influences and promotes the production of documentary films in almost all the countries of Latin America."

It is surprising, then, that so little scholarship has explored the historical connections between African and Latin American cinemas. With the exception of studies by Andrade-Watkins on Brazil and Lusophone Africa, Gabriel's theorization that includes both continents, suggestions by Ukadike and Willemen of certain commonalities in African and Latin American films, and Van Wert's comparison of Sembene and Glauber Rocha, there seems to be scant published research on linkages between cinemas of Latin America and Africa.[2] This chapter —the first attempt to examine the contexts for linkages and to document the ample contacts over the past forty years between these cinemas—charts new ground for further research.[3]

Common Contexts and Initial Contacts: Politics and Cinematography

The extraordinarily fervid period that began in the late 1950s and early 1960s gave Africa and Latin America a common context for beginning a dialogue: civil wars and armed struggle by national liberation movements, specifically those in Algeria, Angola, Cape Verde, Guinea-Bissau, Kenya, Mozambique, Namibia, South Africa, Cuba, and Vietnam; the Black Power movement in the United States; the Black Consciousness movement in various parts of the world; and violent police actions against protesting students in Paris, Mexico City, and Ohio (Kent State).

Groundbreaking studies led to a reconsideration of the relations between areas of the world and obstacles to change in "underdeveloped" nations.[4] Intellectuals and cultural workers in Africa, Latin America, and Asia recognized the commonality of their struggles and embraced the concept of unity among so-called "Third World" peoples fighting to free themselves from neocolonial, capitalist structures and relations. Cuba's involvement in the international historical moment was concretized in its contributions of military forces to African struggles, and it "redrew the political map" of the Southern Cone of Africa by sending some 300,000 Cubans into the fight (King 1990, 158). This solidarity in arms had implications also for Cuban cinema: documentary techniques learned after the 1959 triumph of the Revolution led by Fidel Castro were used to portray liberation struggles in Africa.[5]

The broad context for these actions and films was given in 1968:

> At the beginning of 1968 came the momentous Havana Cultural Congress on the theme of "The Intellectual and the Liberation Struggle of the Peoples of the Third World," which brought together about five hundred revolutionary and progressive artists and intellectuals from as many as seventy countries in a great act of affirmation. They were . . . Europeans, Asians, Africans, delegates from Vietnam, India, Mexico, Algeria and Laos. (Chanan 1985, 216)

Shortly thereafter, African filmmakers organized as the Fédération Panafricaine des Cinéastes—FEPACI (1970), which resonated with Latin American producers and directors who had begun hemispheric organizing attempts as early as 1958 (A. López 1997, 146ff.), though a continuing entity, the Comité de Cineastas de América Latina (CCAL), began only in 1974.

African film professionals assumed a leading role in organizing the important 1973 Third World Film-Makers Meeting in Algiers, which brought together North and Subsaharan Africans and Latin Americans to "discuss common problems and goals and to lay the groundwork for an organization of Third World film-makers" ("Resolutions" 1973, 463). Committees of mixed national and continental composition studied specific aspects of cinematic practice and allowed filmmakers to work together on common issues. Among the future bridge builders between Africa and Latin America at Algiers were Med Hondo (Mauritania), the great Cuban documentarist Santiago Alvarez, Flora Gomes (Guinea Bissau), Fernando Birri (Argentina), and the "Pioneer of African Cinema," Ousmane Sembene (Senegal).

Resolutions crafted at Algiers broadly structured collaborations between African and "New Latin American Cinema" over the next fifteen years. It was resolved that Third World cinema and filmmaking should fight against the cultural repercussions—acculturation and deculturation—wrought by imperialism and neocolonialism and concomitant with the incorporation of certain regions into a worldwide capitalist system that required their "underdevelopment" and "dependency," with a resulting distortion of local economies, impoverishment of the masses, creation of a comprador bourgeoisie, and social inequities. The culture of dominated peoples—language, arts, history, traditions, sciences, and social relations—had been destroyed or usurped for the imperialists' benefit, with the creation of pseudo-racial, community, and language differences and assignations of inferiority and superiority.

Algiers 1973 defined cinema as an instrument of class struggle, which historically had propagated capitalist and false ideological values, with a special preponderance of U.S. official and Hollywood versions, but which, by the same token, could also be a potent weapon of resistance in the hands of militant filmmakers. Films could dis-alienate and resensitize colonized peoples, including those marginalized within colonizing countries, by reflecting objective conditions and "swinging the balance of the power relationship in favor of using cinema in the interest of the masses" in order to eliminate (in Fanon's conception) colonized mentalities and to educate a public that would actively question the premises of cinematic as well as other informational and cultural media. National cinema infrastructures were of crucial necessity, but international solidarity was also important, requiring special support by already-independent national cinemas, now invited "to organize and develop the teaching of film techniques, to welcome the nationals of countries in which the training is not ensured." Filmmakers resolved to compile data to determine the best ways to improve film distribution and to promote governmental agreements in support of coproductions ("Resolutions" 1973).

The two-pronged African–Latin American basis in the 1973 Algiers Resolutions is indicated in the decision to filter all information on the implementation of these Resolutions through FEPACI and to establish a permanent secretariat of the Third World Film-makers Organization in Cuba.

Out of these contacts and struggles came new perceptions of cinema such as the Cuban suggestion of Imperfect Cinema, whose "core is the call that García Espinosa shares with other key polemicists of third world struggle, like Fanon and Freire, for cultural decolonisation" (Chanan 1985, 252). Didactic Cinema, Third Cinema, Third Aesthetics, and Militant Cinema all suggest a revision of concepts to rethink the potentialities of film, especially "the adoption of a historically analytic yet culturally specific mode of cinematic discourse," exemplified, according to one critic, in films by Africans, Brazilians, and others (Willemen 1989, 3–4; see also Gabriel 1982; Pines and Willemen 1989; Solanas and Getino 1973).

"The euphoric mood of the late 1960s is very apparent in the work of many of the filmmakers who, born mostly in the 1930s, began as feature film makers at this time" (Armes 1987, 89). Whether they came from Algeria, Argentina, Bolivia, Brazil, Chile, Cuba, Egypt, Mauritania, Senegal, Tunisia, or Turkey, they shared a belief in the political function of cinema (Armes 1987, 89–91).

Contacts: Film Training in Cuba, ICAIC

The Cuban Institute of Cinematographic Art and Industry, known by its Spanish acronym, ICAIC (Instituto Cubano de Arte e Industria Cinematográficos), was created just months after the victory of the Revolution and gave state funding for filmmaking, collaborated with the Cuban armed forces to make frontline documentaries on liberation struggles in Africa, and established the possibility of training African filmmakers in its facilities. Several of them gained prominence as directors.

Florentino "Flora" Gomes (Guinea-Bissau, born 1949) studied as a high school student in Cuba, then at the ICAIC (Ukadike 2002, 102), and has become an accomplished filmmaker. He made two short semidocumentaries, codirected with Sana Na N'hada, who also studied in Cuba: *Regresso de Cabral* (Return of Cabral, 1976) and *Anôs na oça luta* (We Dare to Fight, 1978). His feature fiction films have been quite successful. The first, *Mortu Nega* (The One Whom Death Refused, 1988), a story of guerrilla warfare and its aftermath, "was the first fiction film produced inside the country and the second Guinea-Bissau feature film ever made" (Ukadike 2002, 102). It was a prizewinner at the 1988 Venice Film Festival and competed at the 1989 Festival Panafricain du Cinéma de Ouagadougou (FESPACO). Gomes's second feature, *Udju azul di Yonta* (The Blue Eyes of Yonta, 1991), was selected for the 1992 Cannes Film Festival. It narrates the story of a beautiful young woman's silent love for a friend of her parents, a hero of the independence struggle, and of a young worker's love for her. The film was hailed by critics for its humor, vitality, beauty, freshness, and "masterful use of sentimental comedy," as well as for the "didactic effectiveness of a social imaginary that goes to the essential: economic problems, unemployment, evictions, and the hope of the young in Bissau, some twenty years after independence" (Garcia and Lenouvel 1992). Gomes considers this film a contrast to his *Mortu Nega*:

Udju azul di Yonta (The Blue Eyes of Yonta, 1991), Flora Gomes (Guinea-Bissau). Photo courtesy of California Newsreel.

> There is the Africa that cries and the Africa that laughs. . . . My first film, *Mortu Nega*, tried to show the march of the Guinean people toward liberty. . . . Today, though the memory of that time is still very present, Guineans have stopped wrapping their wounds and crying bitter tears. With the return of peace, they have tried to recover a culture, a way of living and of thinking that are their own. ("Un certain regard: *Les yeux bleus*" 1992)

Gomes's feature film *Po di Sangui* (Tree of Blood, 1996), concerning villagers who must leave their sacred forest, was screened at Cannes 1996 and has been shown at various international film festivals, where it has won several awards. "These films are remarkable for their creativity and sharp-witted reflections on history, culture, and society" (Ukadike 2002, 102). Gomes's latest film, *Nha fala* (My Voice, 2002), is a spirited musical that challenges African traditions.

The following exchanges in a 1993 interview with Gomes conducted by Ukadike are revealing:

NFU: How did your training in Cuba affect the way you look at cinema?

FG: From my point of view as a filmmaker, when one goes abroad to study, what one should learn is the technique. . . . It's true that the Cuban cinema is very advanced. It has a very descriptive technique, and this is where its strength lies, in its technique. . . . Once one acquires this technique, one has to blend it, mix it with one's own personality and way of looking at life, at the world. Cubans are Cuban, so their cinema is Cuban. When I return home, to Africa, to Guinea-Bissau or elsewhere, I have to find the views that correspond to our reality. . . .

NFU: While watching your films, one can see some influences traceable to Cuban dialectic revolutionary film practices. Are you a revolutionary filmmaker?

FG: I don't know if I'm really a revolutionary. *Revolutionary* is such a big word. I would rather say of myself that I am a "contester." In my films I try to bring up the most striking issues in our society. (Ukadike 2002, 102–3)

Gomes's codirector on the two early semidocumentaries, Sana Na N'Hada (Guinea-Bissau, born 1950), also studied at the ICAIC. His filmography includes other documentaries and the feature film *Xime* (1994), a story of love, traditional initiation rites, political intrigue, and colonial cruelty under Portuguese rule in 1963. *Xime* was the only film representing Subsaharan Africa in official competition at Cannes in 1994.[6]

Two Angolans studied in Cuba and were active in documentary production until the mid-1980s: Asdrubal Rebelo da Silva (Angola, born 1953), who studied TV directing in Cuba in 1977 and also worked there (Toffetti 1987, 160), and Carlos de Oliveira (Angola, born 1955) (*Les cinémas* 2000, 146, 398).

Film Training in Cuba: EICTV

In 1974, a few years after the FEPACI united African directors, the Committee of Latin American Cineastes (CCAL) was established. Eleven years later it created the Foundation of the New Latin American Cinema, presided over by Nobel Laureate Gabriel García Márquez. "Its most ambitious undertaking was the establishment of the Film and Television School . . . at San Antonio de los Baños near Havana" (Pick 1993, 32–33). The new school, inaugurated in December 1986, offered its first courses in January 1987. Officially named the Escuela Internacional de Cine y Televisión de San Antonio de los Baños (EICTV), it is often called the "International Film School of Three Worlds"—Africa, Asia, and Latin America. Argentine cineaste Fernando Birri was the moving force behind the creation of the school and its inclusion of Asian and African students, and was its first director.

Fidel Castro, in a speech at the closing ceremony of the 7th International Festival of New Latin American Cinema in 1985, reminisced on the initial process that would bring the school to reality:

> An idea came to us . . . to create a film school for Latin American and Caribbean students. This is, without a doubt, a good idea, but I think, also, that as long as the Africans have no similar possibility, the idea should be extended so that the school will also be for African students, or those from any other Third World country. (1986, 10)

Symptomatic of Castro's conceptualization of Africa as a unit is his semantic equivalence here of the African Continent with any "other country"! This embrace of Africa was not at all incidental, but was rather an act of solidarity and clearly aligned with the resolutions cited above from the Algiers meeting of 1973. African professionals were included in programmatic ways also: accepting an invitation to participate in the EICTV Advanced Studies Dialogues with established international filmmakers was Ousmane Sembene, cited in an initial group that included Nelson Pereira Dos Santos, Nikita Mikhalkov, and Francis Ford Coppola (Vázquez 1986).

By the end of 2002, EICTV claimed 308 graduates from 40 countries, in addition to 2,185 participants from 36 countries in its workshops ("Un poco de historia" 2003). Between 1986 and 1993 at least fifteen Africans from five countries graduated in the five areas of concentration: Directing, Sound, Editing, Photography, and Scriptwriting (Diago Pinillos 2002). Issoufou Tapsoba (Burkina Faso, born 1962) was in the first group of African students at the EICTV (1987–1990), graduating with a diploma in Directing, along with Domingos Sanca (Guinea-Bissau) in Photography, and José Passe (Mozambique) in Sound (Tapsoba, personal communication 2003; see more on Passe below).

Since graduation, Tapsoba has worked for Burkina Faso state television and has made a number of *telenovelas*[7] and documentaries, including the popular TV series *Les jeunes branchés* ("Hip" Youths, 2000) on the life of school dropouts who live on their own. Tapsoba has his own production company and is currently preparing a long film on juvenile delinquents and a TV series, "Les citoyens" (Citizens). He describes the 1992 EICTV graduates from Burkina Faso—Arsène Yembi Kafando in Photography and Habibou Barry Zoungrana in Editing—as well known in filmmaking (Tapsoba, personal communication 2003).

Guy-Désiré Yaméogo (Burkina Faso, born 1960) earned a EICTV diploma in Scriptwriting in 1992. In 1996, a critic observed:

> Yaméogo . . . belongs to the newest generation of professionals in the country
> to have benefited from training at the International Film & TV School of San
> Antonio, Cuba, which he attended . . . following a competition organized by the
> Pan-African Federation of Filmmakers (Fepaci) for the young people of the conti-
> nent. . . . In Cuba, instead of specializing in directing, he chose film and television
> scriptwriting, because, as he says, "I wanted to learn how to narrate better the sto-
> ries to be filmed and also because I greatly appreciated the lessons on the subject
> by one teacher in particular, the famous Colombian writer Gabriel García Már-
> quez." (C. T. 1996, 20)

Lest we assume that the Cuban school might be locked into teaching outmoded cinematic techniques and values, Yaméogo stated his plans to depart from the "classic style of African cinema which at times is judged as too didactic. . . . '[T]he evolution of our cinema requires, in my opinion, that today we further integrate the factor of the public by creating works that both arouse awareness and entertain'" (C. T. 1996, 20). Yaméogo's filmography includes both documentary and fiction. *Si longue que soit la nuit* (As Long as the Night Might Be, 1996), his well-received short fiction film on children in a soccer club and their indignation at parents who recklessly left their handicapped son in the care of an employee, won the "Prix Jeunesse" at the 13th Vues d'Afrique Film Festival in Montreal and was selected for a special program of independent cinemas at Cannes 1997.

A new fictional TV series, "Les voyeurs professionnels" (Professional Voyeurs), in preproduction in 1999, listed Yaméogo as the scriptwriter for the episode *De l'or dans le sable* (On Gold in the Sand), one of six in the series ("Les voyeurs professionnels" 1999). Yaméogo's *Le pacte* (The Pact, 2002), a short fiction film in competition at FESPACO 2003, tells the tale of a man who makes a pact with his village's fetishes to become rich but "finds it difficult to keep his promise of sacrificing two rams, a cock and then a human being every seven years" ("Première" 2003).

Mariano Bartolomeu (Angola, born 1967) studied filmmaking at Angolan television and worked at the National Film Archives of Angola and Luanda Radio and Television before enrolling at the EICTV, where he coincided for a couple of years with Guy-Désiré Yaméogo. He graduated in 1991 with a diploma in Directing ("Mariano Bartolomeu" 2003). In Havana, Bartolomeu made two films: *Caribeando* (Caribbeaning), a 1990 video on contemporary dance in Cuba, and *Un lugar limpio y bien iluminado* (A Clean and Well-lit Place), based on the story "The Killers" by Ernest Hemingway and produced by EICTV ("Un lugar limpio" 2003; Gallone 1993). After returning to Angola, Bartolomeu continued to make documentary and fiction films. Among them are *Quem Faz Correr Quim?* (Who Makes Quim Run? 1992), a short fiction film that mixes dream and reality and is "a metaphor for the drama lived by Angola for the last fifteen years" (*"Quem faz"* 1994); and *The Sun Still Shines* (1995), 30-minute video documentary on a village struggling to exist among the minefields left by the civil war in Angola, which was awarded a special prize, "Premio Fao Osiris," at the 1996 Milan Film Festival. *Eden,* Bartolomeu's first feature film, is in progress as of 2003.

Mozambicans José Passe and João Carlos Ribeiro studied at EICTV. Passe directed the documentary *Kuxukuvala* (1990) on the failure of former Portuguese colonists to adapt after independence, and the short fiction film *Solidão* (Solitude, 1991) on anticipated social changes on the eve of independence. Ribeiro (born 1963), earned a diploma in Directing at EICTV, works as director at Experimental Television of Mozambique, and is in charge of the film archives at the National Film Institute (*Les cinémas* 2000, 401–2). Perhaps thinking of Ribeiro, Pedro Pimenta, long associated with the National Film Institute in Mozambique and known as a producer of Mozambican films through Ebano Productions, remarked in 1992 that, paradoxically, many technicians still continue to get their training at the film school in Havana "for an industry that no longer exists" (Garcia and Helburg 1992, 11). Pimenta considers Ribeiro "a very talented young man" and has produced one of his films (1995, 26). Films by Ribeiro include a short fiction film, *Fogata* (Bonfire, 1992), and *Le regard des étoiles* (The Gaze of the Stars, 1997), the latter commissioned for the six-part South African series *Africa Dreaming* and produced by Pimenta. Like fellow EICTV graduate Guy Désiré Yaméogo, Ribeiro distances his work from the past and defines the function of cinema in 1996 as social, but in a different way from the militant cinema of the 1960s: "Cinema, fantastic by nature, should resume its role as a creator of dreams, to help restore the social cohesion that has been weakened" ("*Le regard des étoiles*" 1996).

In a 1992 interview Pimenta recognized the role of the EICTV in forming the new Mozambican cinema:[8]

> With regard to pure fiction, few films have been made, not for lack of ideas or projects, but for lack of funding. . . . The directors all studied at the School in Havana and returned to Mozambique with this new element, fiction, and the ability to write a script as it should be done. If we had to find an influence on Mozambican cinema, it is without a doubt Latin American, because the relations between Cuba and Mozambique have always been very strong. (Garcia and Helburg 1992, 11)

Philippe Akitoby and Sikiro Tidjani, from the Popular Republic of Benin, studied at EICTV in the 1980s. Pictured in a summary of the 1986 Havana Film Festival, one of them is quoted as saying: "This is a great opportunity, since we don't have our own cinema. I think that when we finish our studies, we will fight for the development of our cinema because we are sure that, as cineastes, we can bring new concepts" (Rivero 1987, 6).

An idea of the integrated film training available at EICTV can be garnered from a description of Cuban filmmaker Fernando Pérez, former war correspondent in Angola in 1976, who taught film history at the University of Havana and filmmaking at EICTV. Pérez "encourag[es] his students to experiment in order to develop their own individual styles. [He] draws upon the work of a variety of directors in his teaching, including Sergei Eisenstein, Orson Welles, and Steven Spielberg, and in doing so demonstrates that 'the popular' and 'the intellectual' need not be contradictory" (Borter 1997, 155).

EICTV has developed international agreements with educational entities and TV networks in Australia, Europe, and Latin America but currently has none with African countries ("Convenios" 2003; "Entidades" 2003). Francophone African students may be more attracted to programs in Paris, such as those at the Institut de Formation et d'Enseignement aux Métiers de l'Image et du Son (FEMIS), which in 1986 replaced the traditional mecca for African cineastes, the Institut des Hautes Etudes Cinématographiques (IDHEC). EICTV and FEMIS do have an exchange agreement.

Contacts: FEPACI at Havana Festival 1985

1985 was a key year for enhanced relations between Latin American and African cinemas, with increased mutual recognition, tributes, and contacts continuing over the next four years.[9] Patrick G. Ilboudo describes the "renaissance" of FEPACI at the Niamey Conference in 1983. In February 1985, new leadership was elected to revive FEPACI:

- Gaston Kaboré (Burkina Faso), General Secretary
- Rasmané Ouédraogo (Burkina Faso), Vice General Secretary
- Emmanuel Kalifa Sanon (Burkina Faso), Treasurer
- Naceur Ktari (Tunisia), General Secretary, North Region
- Jacques Béhanzin (Benin), General Secretary, West Region
- Jean-Michel Tchissoukou (Congo), General Secretary, Central Region
- Mengistu Yihum Belay (Ethiopia), provisionally representing the East Region
- Lionel Ngakane (South Africa), African National Congress, representing the South Region. (Ilboudo 1988, 151)

The reorganization of FEPACI coincided with the embrace of African film at the International Festival of New Latin American Cinema held annually in Havana. The entire new FEPACI leadership participated in 1985, in addition to the doyen of African cinema and scholarship, Paulin Soumanou Vieyra (Benin/ Senegal), as president of the Committee of African Cineastes, and filmmakers Moustapha Alassane (Niger) and Haile Gerima (Ethiopia). Also present were the directors of the Angolan and Mozambican Film Institutes, Arnaldo Moreira dos Santos and Samuel Matola, respectively; Chris Hesse, head of Ghana Film; and the directors of two major African film festivals: Rachid Ferchiou (Carthage) and Philippe Sawadogo (FESPACO).

A special "Meeting of African and Latin American Cineastes," December 9– 10, was an integral part of the Festival, with papers and discussions and broad coverage in the local press, which celebrated the African presence.[10] One promising result of this festival was the Joint Resolution by FEPACI and CCAL on cooperative organization and participation in festivals, film screenings, and the exchange of information; organization of film markets at festivals; coproductions and other collaborative arrangements; training of film professionals; and constitution of a Cinema Front for the Third World ("Declaración Conjunta" 1986). This Joint Resolution can be considered a more specific continuation of the principles of the Algiers Resolutions of 1973. Fidel Castro remarked, at the closing session of the 1985 Havana Film Festival, on the foundational ideas that had fostered the Latin American-African connection. In 1984 he and the CCAL had discussed:

> action on the need to establish links with cineastes from Africa and other areas of the Third World, because we are aware that they are living a situation that is the same, or worse, than ours in Latin America. . . . We talked about making Africa's reality, its social and cultural situation, known throughout Latin America. . . . [The cineastes] are even talking about a panorama of African cinema at next year's Festival. (Castro 1986, 8)

"The Largest Retrospective on African Cinema in the World," Havana 1986

The panorama of African cinema at the 1986 Havana Film Festival presented seventy-three films, thirty-nine of them fiction, from twenty countries.[11]

It "demonstrated the technical and artistic qualities in the nonpaternalistic representation of cinematographic production in all parts of the African continent" ("Inauguran la mayor retrospectiva" 1986). Gaston Kaboré considered the program a testimony to the struggle by the African people to achieve political, economic, and cultural freedom. He called for a cinema at the service of the masses (which at the time, would have resonated with his Latin American colleagues), and his essay "What African Cinema?" was published in *Cine Cubano* in 1987 ("¿Qué cine africano?").

FEPACI or the festival organizers may have selected these particular films because of the screening venue—a Latin American film festival—or because they were judged to offer an overview of African cinematic production at the time. In either case, it is correct to observe that the majority of the films reflect issues of class struggle and active resistance to situations of oppression. In this sense, they respond, as do many contemporaneous Latin American films, to similar historical circumstances.[12]

Cuban Vice Minister of Culture, filmmaker Julio García Espinosa, presided over roundtables on African cinema, where key filmmakers from the Continent—Gaston Kaboré, Férid Boughedir, Paulin Vieyra, Med Hondo, Emmanuel Sanon, Safi Faye, and the director of the Algerian Cinémathèque, Boudjama Kareche—spoke on the challenges of making movies and the hope engendered by the establishment of EICTV (Piñera 1986). Kaboré delivered an address at the opening ceremony of the Film School, where nine African students were entering the inaugural basic course ("Inauguran hoy" 1986).

Latin America Film at FESPACO 1987

FEPACI reciprocated at the 10th FESPACO in 1987, allowing an exchange of ideas and the viewing of many Latin American films, some of them never before shown in Africa. Several significant events occurred:

1. For the first time, Latin Americans were members of the jury—Cuban filmmaker Sergio Giral, representing ICAIC, and the Argentine Fernando Birri, director of EICTV. The official program includes a brief summation of Birri's career and lauds his "exemplary" struggle to create "a cinema that is realistic, national, popular and critical" (*FESPACO 1987*, 74).

2. In its "Retrospective on Latin American Cinema," FESPACO 1987 screened a number of films described in the official program as: "Cinema from a continent very close to Africa in its realities and aspirations to live free" (19). The films selected are classics in the New Latin American Film repertoire—from Brazil's Cinema Novo, Nelson Pereira dos Santos's *Vidas Secas* (Barren Lives, 1963), and Glauber Rocha's *Antônio das Mortes* (1969); from Cuba, Tomás Gutiérrez Alea's *Memorias del subdesarrollo* (*Memories of Underdevelopment*, 1968); exiled Chilean Patricio Guzmán's *La batalla de Chile (1973–79)* (*Battle for Chile [1973–79]*); and from Argentina, by Fernando Solanas and Octavio Getino, *La hora de los hornos* (*The Hour of the Furnaces*, 1965–68) (*FESPACO 1987*, 41–42). Daily programs distributed at FESPACO and the local newspaper *Sidwaya* also

gave screening places and times for Cuban films *Retrato de Teresa* (*Portrait of Teresa*, 1979) by Pastor Vega and *Una novia para David* (*A Girlfriend for David*, 1985) by Orlando Rojas.

3. Four Latin American productions appeared in FESPACO 1987's Film Festival for Children and Young People, including *Los bebitos de Bebito* (Little Baby's Little Babies) by Gerardo Chijona and a *Quinoscopio* by Juan Padrón, one of his award-winning animations of drawings by Argentine cartoonist Joaquín Lavado (called "Quino"), well-known for his creation of *Mafalda*. Paulin Soumanou Vieyra had been a member of the jury at the 1986 Havana Festival that selected *Quinoscopio* for a prize.

Latin American Film at FESPACO 1989

Again, two years later, FESPACO included Brazilian professor Lelia de Almeida Gonzalez on a jury, and an "Homage to Latin American Cinema" screened films from Argentina, Brazil, Cuba, Guadeloupe, and Haiti, including: *Los chicos de la guerra* (The Boys of War, 1984) by Bebe Kamín (Argentina); *Rancheador* (Slave Hunter, 1975) and *Maluala* (1979), Sergio Giral's classics on palenques—hidden villages of maroons who had escaped from slavery—and attempts to destroy them; *Un hombre de éxito* (A Successful Man, 1986) by Humberto Solás (Cuba); *Clandestinos* (Living Dangerously; also, Underground; 1987) by Fernando Pérez (Cuba); and *Haitian Corner* (1989) by Raoul Peck (*FESPACO 1989*).

Coproductions

With the exception of Cuban-African documentaries related to African liberation struggles and natural problems such as droughts,[13] collaborative projects between African and Latin American cineastes have been rare. Initial coproductions were conceived as models for the future, but instead they turned out to be exceptions.

A deusa negra *and* Cry Freedom

Nigerian director Ola Balogun filmed *A deusa negra* (Black Goddess, 1978) in Brazil and coproduced it with his production company, the Brazilian government's Embrafilme, and Brazilian Jece Valadão. His script and previous work had interested a Brazilian producer, and he was invited to make the film there. Balogun was the first Black to direct a film in Brazil, and despite certain tensions related to this and to funding shortfalls, he was able to carry the project to completion (F. Balogun, personal communication 2001).

The story line reverses the usual "return to Africa" that is part of the African-American experience: on his deathbed, a father asks his son to trace the family history in Brazil and gives him, as an aid in his quest, a statue of the goddess

Yemaya. The man travels to Brazil and learns that he is the reincarnation of an enslaved ancestor and that the woman who has assisted him in his journey is the woman the ancestor loved and who had been killed during an escape attempt from the plantation. He concludes that the purpose of his quest is to (re)unite with this woman. Some have considered this work partially autobiographical, since, on his mother's side, Balogun descends from Afro-Brazilians who returned to Nigeria after emancipation (Ilboudo 1988, 192). The film was critically acclaimed and won prizes at film festivals (Pfaff 1988, 21).

One interesting aspect of *A deusa negra* is its incorporation of Afro-Brazilian music in an African film. This echoes the "boomerang" of African rhythms and sounds back to the continent, like Cuban films that incorporate Hispanic African music. It recalls Miriam Makeba's humorous comment filmed by Juan Carlos Tabío during her tour of Cuba in 1973 that when she hears Cuban musicians playing, she can't tell whether they are African or Cuban (Chanan 1985, 265).

Collaboration with Brazilians for filming *A deusa negra* was such a positive experience for Balogun that he used a number of Brazilian technicians and actors from it in his next feature film, *Cry Freedom* (1981), on an "uprising in an African country, under colonial rule, leading to guerrilla warfare" (Balogun, qtd. in Pfaff 1988, 26), and in other films. He foresaw such joint efforts as an opportunity for Africa and Latin America to enhance their cinemas. He involved foreign directors of photography such as José Medeiros from Brazil in his films, promoted the use of Brazilian technicians in the training of Nigerians, and hoped that the model would be imitated (F. Balogun, personal communication 2001). With the exception of Mozambique, where the new National Film Institute used Brazilian directors to make its first films in the 1970s and to teach film production (Ukadike 1994, 239ff.), the example did not become a model for transcontinental collaboration. *Cry Freedom* received mixed critical reviews, was not commercially successful outside Nigeria, and eventually found itself upstaged by Attenborough's 1987 film of the same name. Balogun made two other feature films, then turned to documentaries.

Desebagato, le dernier salaire

The coproduction of the 1986 feature film *Desebagato, le dernier salaire* (Desebagato, The Last Pay) by Emmanuel Kalifa Sanon was widely hailed as the "first" Cuba–Burkina Faso coproduction, and it appears to be the only one.[14] Sanon was part of the FEPACI delegation at the 1985 Havana Film Festival, during which the plans must have been initiated.[15]

Coproduced by Faso Films and ICAIC, the film was "a product of the new policy of the Burkina Faso government to support cinema" and included actors of various nationalities (Hamalla 1987). Cuba contributed 35 percent of the budget, was wholly responsible for postproduction, and also provided technical support, with Cuban specialists in charge of photography, sound, and script.

The story had obvious appeal for Revolutionary Cuba, since it portrays the exploitation of African construction workers by multinational corporations

Desebagato, le dernier salaire (Desebagato, The Last Pay, 1986) by Emmanuel Kalifa Sanon (Burkina Faso).
Photo from Film Press Kit.

and the beginning of the workers movement. The protagonist is a young man who goes to Ouagadougou to find work in order to make enough money to buy a parcel of land and get married. He signs on as a worker at a construction site and lives a modest existence. He soon comes to realize, however, that between his meager living expenses and the money sent home to his family, his pay will never allow him to break free of poverty. He encounters a destitute unemployed worker who had been fired for his organizing activities at the construction site and also observes that his foreman lives a life of luxury that will always be beyond his reach. His growing consciousness of his condition and his inchoate efforts to bring about change mark him for dismissal. In Bambara, *desebagato* means someone who has reached his limits, physical or psychological, and can no longer cope (Ilboudo 1988, 370).

Desebagato won the City of Perugia (Italy) Prize awarded at the 1987 FESPACO by a jury composed of Italian film critics and previous recipients of the prize, filmmakers Mohamed Challouf, Férid Boughedir, Moustapha Diop, Gaston Kaboré, and Taïeb Louhichi. The coproduction aspect was a factor in the jury's decision: "For its technical mastery, its courageous engagement in service to the cause of the Oppressed, its poetic simplicity in the depiction of the city of Ouagadougou, and for the meritorious effort represented by its successful coproduction with a sister-country" ("FESPACO 1987: Prix de la Ville de Perugia").

Desebagato was successful at other film festivals but was not universally acclaimed by critics. Sanon has not made another feature film, though he worked on Idrissa Ouedraogo's *Yaaba* (1989) and the filming in Burkina Faso of part of the Canadian-French film *La Plante humaine* (The Human Plant, 1997) (*"Plante humaine"*). He is currently director of the film and video production company Productions Audiovisuelles (PRAUVIS) in Ouagadougou ("Burkina Faso" 2003).

Sporadic Contacts after 1989

FESPACO 1989 was, sadly, the last major exchange of films and cinematic ideas between Africa and Latin America. Pledges of mutual support and the opening of respective markets that so significantly marked the 1985–89 period thereafter fall into silence. Despite the expressed desire to expand markets, for example, by 1990 the international distribution company for ICAIC films advertised the festivals and markets in which it usually participated, and FESPACO is notably absent (Distribuidora 1990).

Some Latin Americans do participate in later FESPACO juries, and an occasional Latin American film is screened at FESPACO, usually in the Films from the Diaspora category, but there is no systematic attention. As a rare exception, Argentine director Pablo César's film *Aphrodite (Le jardin des parfums)* (Aphrodite, Garden of Perfumes), a coproduction with Mali, competed at FESPACO 1999, and the official program gives a long list of César's films (*FESPACO 1999*). He also was a jury member for shorts and documentaries at FESPACO 2001, which included a short docudrama on African descendants in Uruguay, *Candombe* (1993) by Rafael Deugenio (*FESPACO 2001*).

Similarly, the Havana Festival failed to include African films or jurors after 1989,[16] and there is no later involvement between Africa and Latin America that parallels the contacts between 1985 and 1989.[17] The Havana Festival continued its tradition of international screenings but reverted to an emphasis on Latin American, European, Soviet, and independent U.S. offerings.

One explanation for these changes is undoubtedly the economic crisis in certain areas of the developing world. The early 1990s saw the disintegration of the Soviet Union and of the socialist bloc, with devastating economic implications for Cuba's ability to support cinematic production in its own country, not just in coproductions, as well as the beginning of a "Special Period" of economic contraction in 1989. A significant factor in the discontinuance of African-Latin American cinematic solidarity after 1989 is undoubtedly the concomitant questioning of the viability of joint programs or Third World unity (and even the validity of the concept) after the profound historical readjustments of the 1990s. Both FESPACO and the Havana Film Festival seemed to refocus emphasis on their respective continental unity and integration.

The economic consequences of readjustments were immediately felt. By 2000, the incoming president of ICAIC could note that in 1971 cinema in Cuba had reached a record 110 million spectators, but by the 1990s "the lack of financing capability and the abrupt changes in Eastern Europe and the rest of the world practically paralyzed [ICAIC] and other cultural industries in Cuba" (González 2000, 11).[18] In lamenting the effective absence in 2000 of documentaries, one of the landmark genres in Revolutionary Cuba, a critic observes that during the "Special Period," the production of documentaries has been "alarmingly affected." The Film Studios at Cuban Television disappeared; the Cinema and Television Studios of the Revolutionary Armed Forces became TRIMAGEN; and "ICAIC has reduced to a minimum its production of documentaries. Between them, these three producers made some 80 documentaries per year, about half of them produced by ICAIC. That number has been reduced to less than a dozen" (Vega 2000, 31).

Similar economic problems are reported throughout Latin American film industries. Spanish television, TVE, abruptly ended in the early 1990s its previously generous support for coproductions with Latin America, including films to be shot in Africa on Cuban music. Brazil's giant national film production agency, Embrafilme, folded in 1992. A major downturn in Latin American film production was attributed in 2001 to several factors, some of which indicate the unresolved challenges of obstacles noted at Algiers in 1973: distribution problems, adverse markets, lack of government support, continual and expensive technological changes, and U.S. monopoly by big studios (Vives 2001).

In the context of "globalization"—or, we might say, "Americanization"—non-Hollywood film values have declined, and African and Latin American directors have assumed certain characteristics in order to make commercially successful films. This has allowed a statement such as the following, made in 1998 by a Western critic, that will sound surprising after our review of Cuban cinematic productions:

Cuban cinema has only recently been recognized, dating back to 1993, the year when *Fresa y chocolate* (Strawberry and Chocolate) was hailed and applauded throughout the world as no Cuban film had ever been before. Two years after having picked up several "Bears" at the Berlin International film Festival, *Fresa y chocolate* became the first film made on the island to obtain an Oscar nomination. (Casamayor 1998)

Interest in African cinema has continued in Latin America, but on a reduced scale compared to the 1980s. A blip of renewal occurred in 1995 when, for the first time, the Guadalajara (Mexico) Film Festival screened African films: "Never had that country, with such a rich cinematography, shown such a panoramic selection of films." The selection of films "depended on available copies" and included: *Samba Traoré* (1992) by Idrissa Ouedraogo (Burkina Faso); *Djeli* (1982) by Kramo-Lanciné Fadika (Ivory Coast); *Comédie exotique* (Exotic Comedy, 1984) by Kitia Touré (Ivory Coast); and *Le ballon d'or* (Golden Ball, 1993) by Cheik Doukouré (Guinea) ("Gros Plan: Mexique" 1995). This festival undoubtedly underscored aspects of Mexican demographics and culture that had been explored just a few years earlier in Rafael Rebollar's film on Afro-Mexicans in the Veracruz and Acapulco areas, *La tercera raíz* (The Third Root, 1992), produced by the Mexican Nacional Council on Culture and Art.

African films were part of the 7th French Film Festival in February 1999 in Havana, Camagüey, and Santiago de Cuba, in the "Black Roots" traveling exhibit. Cuba, since the 1960s, had defined itself as a mulatto nation. Especially in the eastern region of Cuba, in close proximity to Haiti and therefore with a large African-descended population since the 1800s, the Black Roots films must have given residents there a sense of their historical ancestry.

Brazil has made some attempt to connect to Lusophone Africa through film. The 2nd Film and Video Festival in Vitoria, Espirito Santo, Brazil (Nov. 20–26, 1995), with support from the Association for Communication and International Artistic Encounters, ACORIA (Paris), was organized around the theme of "African-Brazilian Encounters." African films included were: *Mopiopio* (1991) by Zeze Gamboa (Angola), Flora Gomes's *Mortu Nega* and *Udju azul di Yonta*, and *Alma ta fika* (The Soul Remains) by João Sodré (Cape Verde). Also shown was the multinational production on a Mozambican village defending itself against bandits, *Colheita do diablo* (Devil's Harvest, 1988) by Licinio Azevedo (Brazil) and Brigitte Bagnol (France) ("Festival Rencontres Afrique-Brésil" 1996). The September 1998 25th Jornada Internacional de Cinema da Bahia on Afro-Iberian-American cinema, held in Brazil, showcased new independent films and videos from Latin America, Spain, Portugal, and Africa ("Festival: XXV Jornada" 1998).

Post-1989 Coproductions

O Testamento do Senhor Napomuceno

The first Brazil–Cape Verde coproduction, *O Testamento do Senhor Napomuceno* (*Testamento*, 1997), with three other countries involved as well (Portugal, France, and Belgium) is based on a story by a Cape Verdean author about the life of a successful businessman who leaves his considerable inheritance to a daughter no one knew he had. Cape Verde diva Cesária Évora performs in the film, and one actor is Portuguese, but all the rest are Brazilian (Kennedy, personal communication 2002). Given the commercial success of the film, perhaps other coproductions will be planned.

Brazilian film historian João Carlos Rodrigues raises issues that could impinge on future productions:

> The Portuguese-speaking countries of Africa (Angola, Mozambique, Cape Verde, Guinea-Bissau, and São Tomé), which are of particular interest to Brazilians, have been unable to sustain film production, and their emerging cinematographies are still dominated by documentaries. There is little or no fiction film. In this genre, the highly regarded Angolan filmmaker (Ruy Guerra) is not Black, nor is the Cape Verde cineaste Francisco Manso, director of the interesting Brazil-Portugal coproduction, *O testamento do senhor Napomuceno* (1997). (Rodrigues 2001, 173)

Pablo César

Argentine Pablo César is the only Latin American cineaste who has directed feature film coproductions with Africa. His long filmography includes *Aphrodite (Le jardin des parfums)*, coproduced in 1998 by Producciones Miguel César in Argentina and the Centre National de Production Cinématographique in Mali—the first Argentine-Malian coproduction in history.

In an unusual twist to the Greek myth, Aphrodite is a young man who has children with the gods, yet "no one questions the sex of this being whom they have designated as Aphrodite" ("Films en avant-première: *Aphrodite*" 1999). The action is situated "in the heart of Black Africa, in the old villages, during an undefined period" and is performed by "Black actors from Mali and Argentina." The film, which uses a language invented for it,

> invites reflection on the conflict between apparently objective reality and virtual reality—the attitude of the gods toward sexuality, the existence of Aphrodite's children—and the significance of this figure of Aphrodite, who doesn't attempt to change the course of History. He is a real man and, at the same time, a desperate being. [The film] shows the universal character of certain myths and their perfect fit with cultures and countries that are totally different. ("Films en avant-première: *Aphrodite*")

Aphrodite completes a trilogy of films made in countries "which have made an impression on César. . . . After *Equinoxe (Le jardin des roses)*, a coproduction with Tunisia, [and] *Licorne (Le jardin des fruits)* in India, the Argentinean brings his cycle to an end in Mali" (Amarger 1998). Critical reception has not been entirely positive:

> *Aphrodite* perhaps brings more questions than meanings. Its images caress the black anatomies up to the point of blasphemy. By deviating [from] conventions and myths, Pablo César seems to project himself into Mali to expurgate his white

filmmaker's view. An unconscious challenge that marks the film's singularity and links the contours of a story that at times is hermetic. (Amarger 1998)

Licorne (Le jardin des fruits) (Unicorn, The Fruit Garden, 1996) was shown at the 1997 FESPACO.

César recognizes that his "discovery" of African and Asian films in Paris in 1986 was a turning point in his career, and he wished to film Africa's "fertile lands, full of ancient culture and uncontaminated by capitalist fundamentalism." He sought the help of Malian filmmaker Cheick Oumar Sissoko and found experienced Malian actors through the National Arts Institute in Bamako. He considers the film a counterbalance to the morbid images dominating screens around the world (César 1998).

In March 2001 Pablo César announced his new film, *Sang* (Blood), a South-South coproduction by Argentina, Sudan, and Madagascar, concerning a "voyage of initiation" of a Buddha-like figure between Buenos Aires, an island in the Indian Ocean and Sudan (César 2001). Filming was completed in 2002.

Contacts in Other Venues

Latin American television has been more successful than feature films in winning African markets, often to the detriment of domestic production, as noted in the complaint that African television cannot compete against imported series: "Brazilian telenovelas which began to be broadcast in 1986 are now very familiar to African TV audiences" ("La production de series par les TV africaines" 1995). Haynes notes that Latin American *telenovelas* (mainly Mexican and Brazilian) are a staple of Nigerian television and cites their influence on the development of melodrama as a video genre in Nigeria (2000, 22–29).

To the extent that Latin American films are shown in France, it is very likely that African filmmakers and students residing there have the opportunity to view them. The magazine *Cine Cubano*, for example, reports that between January and May 1990, Cuba presented at the Georges Pompidou Center the largest and most panoramic exhibition ever presented outside the country, with 80 films, from the first productions (1906) to the most recent feature films, documentaries, and animations ("Gaumont" 1991, 38).[19]

The possibility that African filmmakers in France can view Latin American films increases with the number of related organizations and festivals. Since 1999, the Brazilian cultural organization Jangada has sponsored films and an annual film festival. Jangada has also shown films as part of celebrations of Brazilian culture organized in cooperation with mayors of several of the *arrondissements* of Paris (Jangada 2003). A new movie theater, Cinéma Le Latina, was opened in September 1984 by the Latin Cultural Association for the purpose of increasing awareness of Latin American cinema and was lauded by *Granma* ("El Latina en París" 1984). It can manage up to four shows per day and cooperates with Jangada for special screenings. Analogous possibilities exist for African directors and students in other major centers for film study, with annual festivals such as Cinelatino in Germany, Cinema Novo in Belgium, and the London Latin American Film Festival.

African and Latin American participation in international film festivals—Amiens, Cannes, Locarno, Namur, San Sebastián—theoretically promotes contacts, since films from both continents are shown and the directors are often in attendance and form part of the juries. For example, African directors Dani Kouyaté, Mohamed Camara, Drissa Touré, and Moussa Sene Absa offered a roundtable at Amiens in 1995, where the Mexican film *Mujeres insumisas* (Untamed Women, 1995) by Alberto Isaac was in competition and won the Public's Award ("Amiens: Films du Sud Primés"). And at the 1999 Amiens Festival, Samba Félix N'Diaye (Senegal) and Gabriel Retes (Mexico) participated together on a jury that awarded prizes to two Latin American films ("Les Dossiers" 1999). But this type of contact is haphazard and pales in comparison to the sustained interactions of the 1980s.

Filming the Other/Ourselves

Latin American directors, especially in areas with a notable presence of African-descended people, have made documentaries and fiction films on Africans under slave conditions in the Americas and on the survival of African traditions in contemporary cultures. Some of the best-known features are Cuban films, such as Sergio Giral's trilogy on slavery and slave rebellion: *El otro Francisco* (*The Other Francisco*, 1973), *Rancheador* (Slave Hunter, 1974), and *Maluala* (1979); Tomás Gutiérrez Alea's *La última cena* (*The Last Supper*, 1976); and even Cuba's first musical comedy, *Patakín* (1984), by Manuel Octavio Gómez; and Brazilian productions such as Carlos Diegues's *Ganga Zumba* (1963) and *Quilombo* (1984) on the seventeenth-century maroon community of Palmares, and Walter Lima's *Chico Rey* (1985).

With the exception of Pablo César as described above, Latin Americans focusing on Africans in Africa have tended to use documentary rather than fiction film. Cuban filmmaker Rigoberto López, for example, made *Africa, círculo del infierno* (Africa, Circle in Hell, 1985), which won the 1986 UNICEF award. The documentary "gives witness to and reveals the true causes of the tragedy of hunger in Africa" (R. López, personal communication 2002). López filmed in areas of Ethiopia, Mali, Burkina Faso, and Tanzania, "forgotten areas, an ignored face of the world," and showed the drama caused by the international economic order and the advance of the desert, which threatens the very existence of certain African peoples. Rigoberto López studied the presence of Yoruba rites in contemporary Cuba in his *Mensajero de los dioses* (Messenger of the Gods, 1989), which shows a ceremony of offering to the two most important and popular *orishas*, Shango and Yemaya. López sought out the origins of Afro-Cuban *santería* among the Yorubas in Nigeria as part of a project on the history of Cuban music and its influence in the world, and he plans to return there for filming at a future date.

If film historians have noticed a certain reluctance by African directors to examine historical practices of slavery on the continent,[20] there seems to be some interest by Africans in tracing the consequences of that history in the Americas (see films mentioned by Mbye Cham in this volume). We already have noted the exploration of the self/other in the Brazilian-Nigerian coproduction by Ola Balogun, *A deusa negra*. N'Diagne Adechoubou (Benin) traveled to Cuba to film a documentary on a Cuban painter, *Manuel Mendive ou l'esprit pictural yoruba* (Manuel Mendive, or The Yoruba Pictorial Spirit, 1987).

Sidiki Bakaba, the Ivory Coast actor who starred in the Burkina Faso-Cuban coproduction *Desebagato*, traveled to Colombia to codirect, with Cameroonian Blaise Njeboya, a documentary on a maroon slave settlement, the Palenque de San Basilio, founded in the fifteenth century in Colombia by a prince from Equatorial Guinea (*Les cinémas* 2000, 56), *Los palenqueros, Cimarrons de Colombie* (The Palenqueros, Maroons of Colombia, 2000; titled "Five Centuries of Solitude" when shown at the 2002 Pan African Film and Arts Festival in Los Angeles). Given these examples and Haile Gerima's announced project on Maroons (see chapter 12, "From Africa to the Americas" in this volume), the focus on the African Diaspora in the Americas by African film directors is a promising topic for further research.

Africans and Latin Americans, Competitors for Funding

Competition for European funding may inhibit potential promotion of each other's cinema, although coproductions would not be penalized. Indeed, Pablo César's South-South coproductions have been rather successful in securing European funding. French government funds earmarked for film and television production in the South have been awarded to Latin American as well as to African countries ("Lauréats du Fonds Francophone" 2001). Likewise, African and Latin American film directors compete against each other for awards from the Hubert Bals Fund in Rotterdam ("Festivals" 2001, 30), German television ZDF's "One World" coproduction program ("ZDF: Propositions for Co-Productions" 1992), the Goteborg Film Festival, European Union, and French Foreign Affairs Ministry "Priority Support Zone" Fund. For Swiss funding, African, Asian, and Latin American filmmakers are also positioned as competitors, with no particular published quotas or attempt to distribute the funds equally among geographical regions ("La Fondation Montecinemaverità" 1995).

A very useful recent publication that may encourage coproductions by African and Latin American directors and producers is *Sous l'arbre à palabres II*, especially focused on the "South." This guide gives a wealth of data (with e-mail addresses, Web sites, and, often, titles of supported films) on possibilities for financing, production, and distribution (through both for-profit and nonprofit entities), as well as a review of legal questions and contact information for film festivals, schools, revues, film libraries, professional organizations, and Web sites, including hard-to-find information on funding sources and production companies in South America.

New Possibilities

The initial production and distribution challenges faced by cinemas in the developing world as described by FEPACI and the CCAL have become exacerbated rather than resolved over the years. For example, in Mexico most visual material for rental or purchase is from the United States; few Mexican films are listed in local sales catalogues; European and Latin American (and African) titles "are absent altogether unless distributed by U.S. company"; 62 percent of the films released in Mexico are from the United States, and the percentage will soon reach 80 percent. The possibility of the transmission of movies via satellite to the entire continent (and the world) onto large hi-fi video screens in medium-sized viewing rooms means film distribution will be cheaper for the United States (García Canclini 1997, 250–54). This represents another parallel to the situation in Africa, where screens are likewise flooded with non-African products, emanating mainly from the United States, Europe, India, and Taiwan.

Seasoned film critic, filmmaker, and observer of Subsaharan African cinema Férid Boughedir, president of the 17th FESPACO (2001) jury, clearly perceives the changes and appropriate responses to them:

> African film has become a head without a body, the poorest cinema on the planet, and it can disappear very quickly. . . . Video offers a chance, especially digital video, which will allow the best productions on video (distributed locally as video-cassettes) to be transferred onto 35mm film. . . . Tomorrow's African cinema will be made by people who have assimilated the language of music videos and advertisements and will invent a new way of filming and distributing in Africa. (qtd. in "Festivals" 2001, 28)

A newcomer to African cinema, Gabonese filmmaker Imunga Ivanga in 1999 considered television an "unexpected godsend" for filmmakers who can develop new video production practices and genres. He recognizes the contact between Africa and Latin America and uses the widespread familiarity with Brazilian *telenovelas* as a source of inspiration, yet a model to be avoided by Africa: "Should we, by imitation or under the pretext of the high costs of cinematic productions, replicate popular sitcoms like . . . the Brazilian soap opera *Rosa*? That would mean a lack of invention and creativity."

Cuba has a solution that could benefit film and TV production in Africa, Latin America, and elsewhere—the First International Non-Budget Film Festival (in Spanish, "Festival de Cine Pobre," Festival of Poor Cinema). Held April 21–25, 2003, in the eastern city of Gibara, Cuba, competition included some 118 films, mostly from Latin America, with others from Europe, Turkey, Greece, Iran, Lebanon, and New Zealand, but none from Africa. The "Non-Budget Film Manifesto" by well-known Cuban cineaste Humberto Solás, the festival director, suggests the continuing validity and resonance, thirty years later, of the 1973 Algiers resolutions. The event was designed to:

1. combat the danger of a "unique model of thought" imposed by "wealthy films";
2. legitimate "polyvalence in styles, legacies and purposes";
3. further the democratization of audiovisual production by encouraging film production by social groups without access to the industry;
4. support emerging national cinematographies;
5. break up monopolistic control of distribution;
6. fight against the alienation of publics from their own cultures;
7. provide an alternative to the "wanton display of violence that degrades audiences"; and
8. familiarize participants with the latest sound and image technology through and exhibit and hands-on workshops with state-of-the-art equipment. ("Festival International de Cine Pobre" 2001)

The Non-Budget Film Festival offers prizes for films and for unproduced scripts (in English, French, or Spanish) of feature films and shorts. This festival may indicate that contemporary video technology is beginning to catch up to contemporary dreams. Just as Gothic architecture found the physical means to concretize the desire to reach from earth toward the heavens, "technotronics" might be considered a solution-in-evolution to the demands of African, Latin American, and other "Third World" filmmakers.

Notes

My appreciation to Josephine Woll for her suggestions on improving an earlier version of this chapter and to Françoise Pfaff for allowing me access to her personal collection of film books and files. Special thanks also to Françoise Balogun and to Sylvie Pernotte. I especially appreciate repeated acts of kindness by filmmakers and critics whose personal communications provided information not elsewhere available. I am grateful that the collection editor has allowed the inclusion of details—lists of films screened at festivals, filmographies, citations for what appear to be mere facts, and so forth—with a view to providing ample, well-documented raw data for other researchers. The difficulty in locating and obtaining these data supports their inclusion.

1. My translations throughout, with thanks to Françoise Pfaff for help with French and to James Kennedy for assistance with the Portuguese and Cape Verdean creole.

2. The directors themselves have suggested parallels. Consider Tunisian director Nouri Bouzid's comments regarding the aesthetic of "respectfully lifting the veil on society": "This aesthetic somewhat recalls the aesthetic of hunger in the Brazilian Cinema Novo developed by Glauber Rocha. In fact, Glauber Rocha's *Terre em transe* [Land in Anguish] could have been an Arab film" (1996, 57).

3. This study excludes the Mozambican/Brazilian filmmaker Ruy Guerra, whose career is well documented.

4. See, among others: (1) Andre Gunder Frank's work on the capitalist center/metropolis development of underdevelopment in the periphery/satellites: *Capitalism and Underdevelopment in Latin America: Historical Studies of Chile and Brazil* (1967; 1969); (2) Frantz Fanon's *The Wretched of the Earth* (1961), between his *Black Skin,*

White Masks (1952), and *Toward the African Revolution: Political Writings* (1964); and (3) Walter Rodney's *How Europe Underdeveloped Africa* (1972; revised, 1981).

5. Among others: (1) José Massip's *Madina Boe* (1968) "on life in the liberated areas of Guinea-Bissau . . . and in the rearguard aid areas of the Republic of Guinea," which includes an interview with Amilcar Cabral, founder of the PAIGC independence movement (Myerson 1973, 184). "Massip brings to the screen a close identification with African culture which is one of the constant features of his work" (Chanan 1985, 191). (2) Santiago Alvarez's full-length chronicles of Fidel Castro's trips to Africa in 1972 and 1977. (3) Rigoberto López's documentary *Roja es la tierra* (Red is the Earth, 1984), on Cuba's internationalist troops in Angola fighting against South Africa.

6. Paulin Soumanou Vieyra, a meticulous early historian of film data, states that two filmmakers from Guinea-Bissau studied in Cuba: Mlle. Joséphine Lopez Crato and José Boloma (1975, 114 n.3, 388). However, he also notes among the Ivory Coast directors a Mme. Joséphine Lopez, television director, with studies in Paris (384). I have found no further information on them, but I note that the 1973 Algiers document lists as observer "Josephine, last name unknown," from Guinea-Bissau.

7. The Spanish term *telenovelas* is being used among Africans to identify the Latin American soap opera form that has become popular on African TV screens. It differs from ongoing series by its programmed end. A typical *telenovela* might have, for example, a hundred episodes.

8. Ukadike details the National Film Institute of Mozambique's early use of Brazilian directors to make its first films in the 1970s and to teach film production (*Black African Cinema* 1994, 239ff.).

9. Diawara states that Cuba and Ghana have run seasons of each other's films (1992, 118). Cuba's official newspaper, *Granma,* reported: (1) "the First Retrospective of New Latin American Cinema" in July 1984 in Luanda, Angola, with documentaries, fiction and animated films ("Luanda"); (2) a Cuban Film Week in Accra, Ghana, in July 1985 ("Accra"); and (3) a diplomatic protocol for 1986–88 between Cuba and the Ghana Film Industry Corporation for cinema cooperation: mutual film weeks, commercial showing of films, coproductions and Cuban technical support for Ghanaian cinematography ("Protocolo Cuba-Ghana en cine" 1995).

10. See especially the reports and photographs in *Cine Cubano* 115 (1986): (1) Castro's speech, "Nada es imposible" (Nothing Is Impossible) at the closing session of the Festival; (2) article on the "Presence of Africa," for the first time, at the Festival; (3) paper delivered at the Meeting by Cuban critic Isaac Ramírez on the history of African cinema, in which we might note that his dated references are a good indication of the paucity of scholarship available in Latin America on African cinema and where Ramírez points out the attractiveness of the large African market for Latin American cinema; (4) interview with Paulin Soumanou Vieyra, "Useful Cinema and the National Consciousness," introduced with this comment: "From the very beginning, Vieyra has said that the most important aspect of this Festival for him, and for all the Africans present, is the opportunity to explain what has been accomplished in that area of the world in the field of cinema, despite colonialism, hunger, Apartheid, isolation, illiteracy, and so many other factors ("Cine útil y conciencia nacional" 1986, 58); (5) photographs of many of the African delegates delivering speeches and participating in the meeting; (6) declaration by the FEPACI cineastes, close to Gaston Kaboré's presentation at the meeting, regarding intentions to unite African and Latin American cinemas, and similar to the Joint Resolution eventually adopted.

11. Included were: director Moustapha Alassane (Niger), *Le retour de l'aventurier*

(The Adventurer's Return, 1966), the animated *Bon voyage Sim* (Have A Good Trip, Sim, 1966), *FVVA: Femmes, villa, voiture, argent* (Wives, Villa, Car, Money, 1972), and *Toula ou le Génie des Eaux* (Toula, or the Water Spirit, 1973); Merzak Allouache (Algeria), *Omar Gatiano* (1976); Souheil Ben Barka (Morocco), *Alf Yad Wa Yad* (*One Thousand and One Hands*, 1972); Youssef Chahine (Egypt), *Iskandarya . . . leh?* (*Alexandria . . . Why?* 1978); Souleymane Cissé (Mali), *Finyé* (1982); Jean-Pierre Dikongue-Pipa (Cameroon), *Muna Moto* (The Other's Child, 1974); Désiré Ecaré (Ivory Coast), *Concerto pour un exil* (Concerto for an Exile, 1968); Kramo-Lanciné Fadika (Ivory Coast), *Djeli* (1981); Oumarou Ganda (Niger), *Cabascabo* (1968), *Saitane* (1972), and *Le Wazzou polygame* (The Polygamist's Morale, 1970); Chris Hesse (Ghana), five documentaries grouped as *Solidarity in the Struggle* (1961–1974); Med Hondo (Mauritania), *Soleil O* (O Sun, 1970), *West Indies: Les Nègres marrons de la liberté* (West Indies: Black Maroons of Freedom, 1979); Gaston Kaboré (Burkina Faso), *Wend Kuuni* (1982); Nacer Khemir (Tunisia), *El haimoun* (Searchers of the Desert, 1984); Mohamed Lakhdar-Hamina (Algeria), *Chronique des années de braise/Waqai sinin al jawr* (Chronicle of the Years of Embers, 1975); Nana Mahomo (South Africa), *Last Grave at Dimbaza* (1974); Djibril Diop Mambety (Senegal), *Contras' City* (1969), *Badou Boy* (1970), and *Touki-Bouki* (The Hyena's Journey, 1973); Idrissa Ouedraogo (Burkina Faso), *Les écuelles* (The Wooden Bowls, 1983) and *Issa, le tisserand* (Issa the Weaver, 1984); Sanou Kollo (Burkina Faso), *Paweogo* (1982); Ousmane Sembene (Senegal), *Mandabi* (1968) and *Xala* (1974); Jean-Michel Tchissoukou (Congo), *La chapelle* (The Chapel, 1979); Jean-Marie Teno (Cameroon), *Fievre Jaune-Taximan* (Yellow Fever Taximan, 1985); Brahim Tsaki (Algeria), *Hikayat Liqa* (History of an Encounter, 1983); Paul Zoumbara (Burkina Faso), *Jours de tourmente* (Days of Torment, 1983); and Férid Boughedir (Tunisia), *Camera d'Afrique* (African Caméra, 1983) with interviews of African filmmakers.

12. The database for all 24 Havana Film Festivals (1979–2002) at <www.habanafilmfestival.com> allows searches by countries, but African countries are not listed.

13. *Granma* cites a 1985 Cuba-Ethiopia coproduction by Miguel Fleitas and Menghistu Yihum Belay, *Hacia la vida* (Toward Life) ("Acaba de realizarse una coproducción cubano-etiope" 1985). In addition to the documentaries, the fictional war film *Caravana* was produced in 1990 by ICAIC, Granma Studios, and the National Film Laboratory of Angola (*Caravana* 1990, 70).

14. Among ICAIC coproductions for the decade 1980–89, Burkina Faso is the only African country listed (Evora 1991, 22).

15. Some circles connect, and in one of the photos included in the *Desebagato* publicity brochure, we see the interpreter for the Cuban producer is none other than Guy-Désiré Yaméogo, later selected by FEPACI to study at EICTV. *Desebagato* was not included in the Ivory Coast's 8-week TV testimony to Sidiki Bakaba, *Desebagato's* lead actor, which did, however, include Bakaba's *Les guérisseurs* (The Healers) and *Tanowe des lagunes* (Tanowe of the Lagoons) as well as films from France, Niger, Ivory Coast, and Senegal ("La télévision ivoirienne" 1999).

16. A partial exception in 1991 was the participation as juror by Sarah Maldoror, often included among African filmmakers, who is identified at the festival, however, in terms of her Caribbean origin—"Guadeloupe" ("Jurado" 1991).

17. Aufderheide (1991) gives a detailed and well-grounded analysis of the tensions at the 1987 and 1989 New Latin America Film Festival surrounding production difficulties, disaffection among younger directors, a "crisis in rhetoric," problems and restructuring at EICTV, and other issues.

18. In the overall analysis of the eventual decline in contacts that seemed so promising, we should note as one concrete factor the closely ensuing deaths of two participants in the 1985 and 1986 Havana exchanges: Paulin Soumanou Vieyra in 1987, and Jean-Michel Tchissoukou in 1988. Also, Burkina Faso President Thomas Sankara, a strong supporter of cinema, was assassinated in 1987.

19. *Granma* reports for the same event over 250 films, including 75 feature films (Pollo 1990).

20. See the 1998 "Dossier: Esclavage et images/Slavery and Images," with Michel Amarger's article, "African Filmmakers Exposed to the Amnesia of the Slave Trade."

Works Cited

"Acaba de realizarse una coproducción cubano-etiope." 1985. *Granma,* 13 December, 4.

"Accra." 1985. *Granma,* 25 July, 5.

Amarger, Michel. 1998. "*Aphrodite.*" *Ecrans d'Afrique* 7.24: 136.

"Amiens: Films du Sud Primés." 1996. *Le film africain* 23: 25.

Andrade-Watkins, Claire. 1995. "Portuguese African Cinema, 1969–1993." In *Cinemas of the Black Diaspora: Diversity, Dependence, and Oppositionality,* ed. Michael T. Martin, 181–203. Detroit: Wayne State University Press.

Armes, Roy. 1987. *Third World Film Making and the West.* Berkeley: University of California Press.

Aufderheide, Patricia. 1991. "Latin American Cinema and the Rhetoric of Cultural Nationalism: Controversies at Havana in 1987 and 1989." *Quarterly Review of Film & Video* 12.4: 61–76.

Balogun, Françoise. Personal communication. August 2001.

Borter, Beat. 1997. "Moving to Thought: The Inspired Reflective Cinema of Fernando Pérez." In *Through Other Worlds and Other Times: Critical Praxis and Latin American Cinema,* ed. Ann Marie Stock, 141–61. Minneapolis: University of Minnesota Press.

Bouzid, Nouri. 1996. "On Inspiration." In *African Experiences of Cinema,* ed. Imruh Bakari and Mbye Cham, 48–59. London: British Film Institute. Rev. of original in *Sources of Inspiration-Lecture 5.* Amsterdam: Sources, 1994.

"Burkina Faso Government Web site: Direction, Production, Distribution, Fournisseurs, Associations." <http://www.culture.gov.bf/M.C.A.T/monde_arts/monde_arts_cinema.htm>. Accessed 11 September 2003.

C. T. 1996. "Guy Désiré Yaméogo." *Ecrans d'Afrique* 6.16: 18–21.

"*Caravana* (Nuevo filme cubano-angolano)." 1990. *Cine Cubano* 130: 70–73.

Casamayor, Odette. 1998. "Tomás Gutiérrez Alea: Beyond *Strawberry and Chocolate.*" *Ecrans d'Afrique* 23: 84.

Castro, Fidel. 1986. "Nada es imposible." *Cine Cubano* 115: 2–10.

César, Pablo. 1998. "Témoignage: Un mythe grec, un pays africain." *Le film africain* 27: 12–13.

———. 2001. "*Sang:* entre Buenos Aires et le Nil." *Le film africain & Le film du Sud* 35–36: 96–97.

Chanan, Michael. 1985. *The Cuban Image: Cinema and Cultural Politics in Cuba.* London: British Film Institute; Bloomington: Indiana University Press.

"Cine útil y conciencia nacional." 1986. *Cine Cubano* 115: 58–60.

"Convenios entre la EICTV y otras Instituciones y Centros de Formación." <http://www.fncl.cult.cu/eictv/convenios.html>. Accessed 1 January 2003.

"Declaración Conjunta de los Cineastas de Africa y América Latina, 10 December 1985." 1986. *Cine Cubano* 115: 87–88.

Diago Pinillos, Regla. Personal communication, Trinidad & Tobago, October 2002, based on the cinema section of her unpublished doctoral thesis, "La tradición oral africana. Caracteres generales y expresiones particulares."

Diawara, Manthia. 1992. *African Cinema: Politics and Culture.* Bloomington: Indiana University Press.

Distribuidora Internacional de Películas ICAIC. Advertisement. 1990. *Cine Cubano* 131: 18.

"Dossier: Esclavage et images/Slavery and Images." 1998. *Ecrans d'Afrique* 23: 65–125.

"El Latina en París." 1984. *Granma,* 27 September, 4.

"Entidades Colaboradoras y Convenios." <http://www.fncl.cult.cu/eictv/entid.html>. Accessed 1 January 2003.

Evora, José Antonio. 1991. "Cielo a estribor: El largometraje de ficción cubano en la década del 80." *Cine Cubano* 133: 14–21.

Fanon, Frantz. 1952. *Peau noire, masques blancs.* Paris: du Seuil. *Black Skin, White Masks.* Trans. Charles Lam Markmann. New York: Grove, 1965.

———. 1961. *Les damnés de la terre.* Paris: Maspéro. *The Wretched of the Earth.* Trans. Constance Farrington. New York: Grove, 1965.

———. 1964. *Pour la révolution africaine, écrits politiques.* Paris: Maspéro. *Toward the African Revolution.* Trans. Haakin Chevalier. New York: Monthly Review, 1967.

FESPACO 1987. Ouagadougou: FESPACO, 1987. Official program.

"FESPACO 1987: Prix de la Ville de Perugia." *Unir Cinéma: Revue de Cinéma Africain* [Saint-Louis, Senegal] 135 (1987): 13.

FESPACO 1989. Ouagadougou: FESPACO, 1989. Official program.

FESPACO 1999. Ouagadougou: FESPACO, 1999. Official program.

FESPACO 2001. Ouagadougou: FESPACO, 2001. Official program.

"Festival: XXV Jornada." 1998. *Ecrans d'Afrique* 7.23: 139.

"Festival International de Cine Pobre." English version. <http://www.cubacine.cu/cinepobre/manifeng.html>. Accessed 1 January 2003.

"Festival Rencontres Afrique-Brésil." 1996. *Le film africain* 23: 27.

"Festivals." 2001. *Images Nord-Sud* 45–46: 28–30.

"Films en avant-première: *Aphrodite (Le jardin des parfums)* de Pablo César." 1999. *Le film africain* 29: 6.

Frank, Andre Gunder. 1969. *Capitalism and Underdevelopment in Latin America: Historical Studies of Chile and Brazil,* 2d ed. New York: Monthly Review.

Gabriel, Teshome H. 1982. *Third Cinema in the Third World: The Aesthetics of Liberation.* Ann Arbor: UMI Research.

Gallone, A. 1993. "Mariano Bartolomeu (réalisateur/director, Angola)." *Ecrans d'Afrique* 2.3: 42.

Garcia, Jean-Pierre. 2001. "Rencontre avec Samba Félix N'Diaye réalisateur (Sénégal)." *Le film africain & Le film du sud* 35–36: 89–92.

Garcia, Jean-Pierre, and Caroline Helburg. 1992. "Cinéma et télévision au Mozambique: Rencontre avec Pedro Pimenta." *Le film africain* 9: 11–12.

Garcia, Jean-Pierre, and Thierry Lenouvel. 1992. "*Les yeux bleus de Yonta* de Flora Gomes (Guinée Bissau)." *Le film africain* 7: 4.

García Canclini, Néstor. 1997. "Will There Be a Latin American Cinema in the Year 2000? Visual Culture in a Postnational Era." Trans. Adriana X. Tatum and Ann Marie Stock. In *Through Other Worlds and Other Times,* ed. Ann Marie Stock, 246–57. Minneapolis: University of Minnesota Press.

"Gaumont en la Habana." 1991. *Cine Cubano* 132: 32–38.

Gerima, Haile. 1977. Interview with Françoise Pfaff. 15 April. Typescript.

———. 1983. Interview with Françoise Pfaff. 11 May. Typescript.

González, Omar. 2000. "El tiempo es transparencia: Presentación como nuevo Presidente del Instituto Cubano del Arte e Industria Cinematográficos." *Cine Cubano* 148: 10–13.

"Gros Plan: Mexique." 1995. *Le film africain* 20 (May): 40.

Hamalla, C. 1987. "Bamako reçoit *Desebagato, le dernier salaire* en exclusivité mondiale." *L'Essor* [Bamako, Mali], 20 March, 4.

Haynes, Jonathan, ed. 2000. Introduction. In *Nigerian Video Films*, rev. ed., 1–35. Athens: Ohio University Center for International Studies.

Ilboudo, Patrick G. 1988. *Le FESPACO 1969–1989: Les cinéastes africains et leurs oeuvres*. Ouagadougou: La Mante.

"Inauguran hoy la Escuela International de Cine y TV en San Antonio de los Baños." 1986. *Granma*, 15 December, 1+.

"Inauguran la mayor retrospectiva." 1986. *Granma*, 8 December, 2.

Ivanga, Imunga. 1999. "C'est la télé qui 'gnage'." *Le film africain* 31: 23.

Jangada Web Site. <http://www.jangada.org/france>. Accessed 1 Jan. 2003.

"Jurado." 1991. *Granma*, 12 December, 3.

Kaboré, Gaston. 1987. "¿Qué cine africano?" *Cine Cubano* 117: 53–37.

Kennedy, James. Personal communication. 15 April 2002.

King, John. 1990. *Magical Reels: A History of Cinema in Latin America*. London: Verso.

"La Fondation Montecinemaverità." 1995. *Le film africain* 20: 26–27.

"La production de series par les TV africaines/ Serial Productions by African TVs." 1995. *Ecrans d'Afrique* 4.11: 51.

"La télévision ivoirienne rend hommage à Sidiki Bakaba." 1999. *Le film africain* 31: 23.

"Lauréats du Fonds Francophone de Production Audiovisuelle du Sud de l'Agence Inter-gouvernementale de la Francophonie (AIF)." 2001. *Le film africain & Film du Sud* 35–36: 48–49.

"*Le regard des étoiles* de Joao Ribeiro (Mozambique)." 1996. *Le film africain* 23: 15.

Les cinémas d'Afrique: Dictionnaire. 2000. Paris: Karthala.

"Les Dossiers de *Film africain:* Fonds d'Aide au développement du scénario, Festival d'Amiens." 1999. *Le film africain* 32: A-D.

"Les voyeurs professionnels: Série." 1999. *Le film africain* 31: 13.

López, Ana M. 1997. "An 'Other' History." In *The New Latin American Cinema. I. Theory, Practices and Transcontinental Articulations*, ed. Michael T. Martin, 135–56. Detroit: Wayne State University Press.

López, Rigoberto. 1999. "Palabras de Rigoberto López en la inauguración del Festival de Cine Francés." *Cine Cubano* 144: 23.

———. 2002. Personal communication.

"Luanda." 1984. *Granma*, 19 July, 4.

"Mariano Bartolomeu." <http://www.ecrans-nord-sud.com/ie/guide/real.cfm?idreal=129>. Accessed 1 January 2003.

Martin, Michael T., ed. 1995. *Cinemas of the Black Diaspora: Diversity, Dependence, and Oppositionality*. Detroit: Wayne State University Press.

Myerson, Michael, ed. 1973. *Memories of Underdevelopment: The Revolutionary Films of Cuba*. New York: Grossman.

N'Diaye, Samba Félix. 1991. "L'Afrique et le documentaire." *Le film africain* 3: 7.

Pfaff, Françoise. 1988. *Twenty-five Black African Filmmakers*. Westport, Conn.: Greenwood.

Pick, Zuzana M. 1993. *The New Latin American Cinema: A Continental Project.* Austin: University of Texas Press.

Pimenta, Pedro. 1995. "Situation du cinéma au Mozambique." Interview by Jean-Pierre and Amélie Garcia. *Le film africain* 18–19: 25–26.

Piñera, Toni. 1986. "Mesa redonda sobre el séptimo arte africano." *Granma,* 9 December, 6.

Pines, Jim, and Paul Willemen, eds. 1989. *Questions of Third Cinema.* London: British Film Institute.

"*Plante humaine.*" <http://www.nfb.ca/animation/aj/plante.html>. Accessed 1 January 2003.

Pollo, Roxana. 1990. "A Francia la mayor muestra de cine cubano en el exterior." *Granma,* 5 January, 5.

"Première of *Le Pacte,* a Film by Guy-Désiré Yaméogo." <http://www.fespaco.bf/premiere_ of_pacte.htm>. Accessed 1 January 2003.

"Protocolo Cuba-Ghana en cine." 1985. *Granma,* 9 December, 1.

"*Quem faz correr Quim?* de Mariano Bartolomeu (Angola)." 1994. *Le film africain* 17: 9.

Ramírez, Isaac. 1986. "El cine africano." *Cine Cubano* 115: 30–35.

"Resolutions of the Third World Film-makers Meeting, Algiers, December 5–14, 1973." 1973. New York: Cineaste. Pamphlet No. 1. Reprinted in *Cinemas of the Black Diaspora: Diversity, Dependence and Oppositionality,* ed. Michael T. Martin, 463–72. Detroit: Wayne State University Press, 1995.

Rivero, Angel. 1987. "En San Antonio de los Baños." *Cine Cubano* 118: 1–7.

Rodney, Walter. 1972. *How Europe Underdeveloped Africa.* London: Bogle-L'Ouverture; rev. ed., Washington, D.C.: Howard University Press, 1981.

Rodrigues, João Carlos. 2001. *O Negro Brasileiro e o Cinema.* Rio de Janeiro: Pallas.

Signaté, Ibrahima. 1994. *Med Hondo: un cinéaste rebelle.* Paris: Présence Africaine.

Solanas, Fernando E., and Octavio Getino. 1973. *Cine, cultura y descolonización.* Buenos Aires: Siglo XXI.

Sous l'arbre à palabres II: Guide pratique à l'usage des cinéastes africains et du Sud. 2001. Cottenchy: Caravane.

Stock, Ann Marie, ed. 1997. *Through Other Worlds and Other Times: Critical Praxis and Latin American Cinema."* Hispanic Issues 15. Minneapolis: University of Minnesota Press.

Tapsoba, Issoufou. Personal communication. 9 February 2003.

Toffetti, Sergio. 1987. *Il cinema dell'Africa Nera: 1963–1987.* Turin: Fabbri.

Ukadike, Nwachukwu Frank. 1994. *Black African Cinema.* Berkeley: University of California Press.

———. 2002. *Questioning African Cinema: Conversations with Filmmakers.* Minneapolis: University of Minnesota Press.

"Un certain regard: *Les yeux bleus de Yonta,* de Flora Gomes (Guinée-Bissau)." 1992. *Le film africain* 5–6: 2.

"Un lugar limpio y bien iluminado." <http://www.ecrans-nord-sud.com/ie/guide/fiche .cfm?idfilm=226>. Accessed 1 January 2003.

"Un poco de historia." <http:///www.fncl.cult.cu/eictv/eictv.html>. Accessed 1 January 2003.

Van Wert, William F. 1979. "Ideology in The Third World Cinema: A Study of Sembene Ousmane and Glauber Rocha." *Quarterly Review of Film Studies* 4.2: 207–26.

Vázquez, Omar. 1986. "Comenzará su curso regular el 5 de enero próximo, la Escuela Internacional de Cine y Televisión." *Granma,* 7 November, 1.

Vega, Belkis. 2000. "El documental ausente." *Cine Cubano* 150: 30–32.

Vieyra, Paulin Soumanou. 1975. *Le cinéma africain des origines à 1973*. Paris: Présence Africaine.

Vives, Camilo. 2001. "Apuntes sobre la Cinematografía Latinoamericana en el contexto actual: Incidencia de los Grandes Estudios." *Cine Cubano* 153: 1–3.

Willemen, Paul. 1989. "The Third Cinema Question: Notes and Reflections." In *Questions of Third Cinema,* ed. Jim Pines and Paul Willemen, 1–29. London: British Film Institute.

"ZDF: Propositions for Co-Productions." 1992. *Ecrans d'Afrique* 2: 123.

Part Six: *Sources and Resources*

15 Where to View, Rent, and Purchase African Feature Films: Africa, Europe, the United States, and Canada

Valerie J. Wheat

Over the last twenty years there has been an upsurge in the number and genres of African films produced and in the number of viewers who have seen them. Yet both in Africa and abroad, these films remain poorly distributed. In Africa, theater owners find U.S., Indian, and Taiwanese entertainment films more lucrative than continental and local productions, although this may change in the years to come with the emergence of a recent commercial vein of African films and videos with increased popular appeal. In Western countries, African films are not distributed to commercial movie theaters, and screenings are not generally advertised in the mainstream press.

Thus, a crucial question emerges: Where can African films be seen? The answer is oftentimes determined by economic issues. The usual theater outlets traditionally have not been open to showing a great number of African films, considering them not financially viable nor commercial enough to draw large audiences. As a result, African films are not frequently shown, or they are screened with limited publicity at nontraditional or alternative venues such as film festivals, museums, universities, libraries, and independent movie theaters specializing in foreign films. African films are also rarely shown on television, and the recent initiative by California Newsreel to present a series of three African films on public television during February 2003, the first national broadcast of African-produced films in the United States, should be commended and emulated. The challenge for those interested in African feature films is finding sources and viewing opportunities.

This chapter identifies where African feature films can be located by individuals who want to research African cinema, view more African films, or rent or purchase copies for their educational institution or community organization. It includes organizations and distribution outlets offering multiple African film titles. Information on individual filmmakers and private distribution companies for their works can be obtained from resources such as the FESPACO headquarters, the FEPACI office, or Cinémathèque Afrique (ADPF).

This listing focuses on major areas where African films can be located: Africa,

Europe, the United States, and Canada. Within each geographical area, selected resources include university research centers, libraries, museums, retail video stores, film distribution companies, and film festivals. Each resource citation includes a brief critical annotation, current address, telephone, fax, and Web site references. Information on the formats available (16mm, 35mm, video, DVD, SECAM, etc.) is given where known.

The Internet is an invaluable tool for up-to-date resource information. Using a good search engine such as google.com or yahoo.com and designating specific keywords such as "African cinema" provides a flood of data. This chapter ends with a selected list of Web sites as a starting point for further research.

The following compilation is an overview of principal resources that should serve as a useful guide for locating feature-length African films. In addition, local areas may have opportunities for viewing or obtaining films. Urban African immigrant communities often have stores with videos for rent or sale. For example, recently when walking through the "African section" in Brussels, I saw several shops advertising African films and many other products. The same is true in similar neighborhoods in other large cities. And finally, local and neighborhood newspapers often list alternative entertainment opportunities that fall below the radar screen of the major publications.

Africa

Alexandria International Film Festival takes place each September, showcasing films from Mediterranean countries.

Alexandria International Film Festival
9 Oraby Street
11111 Cairo
Egypt

Tel: 202-574-1112
Fax: 202-576-8727
E-mail: info@alexandriafilmfestival.com
Web site: www.alexandriafilmfestival.com

Apollo Film Festival is a recent film festival that showcases South African independent film and takes place in the historic Apollo Theatre.

Apollo Film Festival
P.O. Box 235
Victoria West, 7070
Northern Cape
South Africa

Tel: +27 053-621-1185
E-mail: apollotheatre@intekom.co.za
Web site: www.apollotheatre.co.za

Cairo International Film Festival has been in existence since 1976, initially launched by the Egyptian Association of Film Writers and Critics, and now a joint festival sponsored by the Ministry of Culture, the Association, and the Union of Artist's Syndicates.

Cairo International Film Festival
17 Kasr El Nil Street
Cairo
Egypt

Tel: 202-393-3962
Fax: 202-393-8979
E-mail: info@cairofilmfestival.com
Web site: www.cairofilmfestival.com

Cape Town International Film Festival is an annual film festival, usually held in November.

Cape Town International Film Festival
University of Cape Town
Private Bag, Rondebosch
Cape Town 7700
South Africa

Tel: 27 21-423-8257
Fax: 27 21-424-2355
E-mail: filmfest@hiddingh.uct.ac.za

Durban International Film Festival is a two-week festival presenting a diverse selection of 75–100 films, most of them first-time premiere screenings in Durban. Films from some 30 countries are represented, usually highlighting recent film productions of South African and African cinema. The festival is hosted by the University of Natal's Centre for Creative Arts and has been in existence more than twenty years.

Durban International Film Festival
Centre for Creative Arts
University of Natal
Durban, 4041
South Africa

Tel: +27 31 260-2506
Fax: +27 31 260-3074
Web site: www.und.ac.za/und/carts/ffestpage.html

Ecrans Noirs is a film distributor to movie theaters for the vast majority of Central African films. In existence since 1995, this organization also holds the film festival **Ecrans Noirs du Cinéma Africain et Francophone**, highlighting films from Cameroon, Gabon, and the Central African Republic.

Ecrans Noirs
BP 11 371
Yaoundé
Cameroon

Tel: 237-21 49 41
Fax: 237-21 49 42
E-mail: ta@iccnet.cm
Web site: www.africa1.com/ecrans.htm

Fédération Panafricaine des Cinéastes (FEPACI), created in 1970, is an Africa-wide organization devoted to the promotion and formation of African films, film festivals, and African directors. FEPACI used to publish the quarterly magazine *Ecrans d'Afrique* with the financial assistance of the Centro Orientamento Educativo (COE).

Fédération Panafricaine des Cinéastes
Ouagadougou 01 01
BP 2524
Burkina Faso

Tel: +226-31 02 58
Fax: +226-31 18 59

FESPACO (Festival Panafricain du Cinéma et de la télévision de Ouagadougou) is considered to be the premiere film festival in Africa, taking place every two years at springtime in Ouagadougou, Burkina Faso. It lasts one week and includes the major directors, scholars, reviewers, and critics of African film. Begun in 1969, this festival is the highlight of African cinema and will usually showcase more than 50 films during the week, mostly from the Francophone countries. The festival produces a daily newspaper, a quarterly newsletter, and an official catalogue with information on the films and activities of the festival, which is an excellent resource for distributors, resources, and contact information on filmmakers. During the festival, a film market includes distributors of African motion pictures.

FESPACO
01 BP 2505
Ouagadougou 01
Burkina Faso

Tel: +226-30 75 38
Fax: +226-31 25 09

E-mail: sg@fespaco.bf
Web site: www.fespaco.bf

Festival du Cinéma Africain de Khouribga has since 1977 presented an annual film festival, which includes film screenings, round tables, meetings, and debates as a means of promoting African cultures through the development of African cinema.

Festival du Cinéma Africain de Khouribga
Municipalité de la ville de Khouribga
Morocco

Tel: 212 3-49 34 04
Fax: 212 3-49 26 23
Web site: www.maghrebarts.ma/cinenews.020710.htm/

Festival of the Dhow Countries, formerly known as the **Zanzibar International Film Festival**, was established in the late 1990s to promote and develop film and other cultural industries and to spur the economic growth in the region. Today, this festival is East Africa's largest cultural event, with an extensive program of films, music, and the performing arts.

Zanzibar International Film Festival (ZIFF)
P.O. Box 3032
Zanzibar
Tanzania

Tel: +255 (4) 747 411499
Fax: +255 (4) 747 419955
E-mail: ziff@aziff.or.tz
Web site: www.ziff.or.tz

Film Africa Limited is a distribution company.

Film Africa Limited
P.O. Box 7151
30 Sobukwe Road
Accra
Ghana

Tel: 224 323 228 702
Fax: 223 320

Film Resource Unit (FRU) contains an impressive collection of African films to fulfill its mission for the distribution and development of African film. The FRU has several resources, including a collection of essays and articles on the history of African film, educational materials for workshops and courses, and a catalogue of feature films, shorts, and documentaries, searchable on the Web site.

Film Resource Unit (FRU)
P.O. Box 11065
1 President Street
2000 Johannesburg
Newtown
South Africa

Tel: 27 11-838-4280
Fax: 27 11-838-4281
Web site: http://www.fru.co.za/who/index.html

Johannesburg Film Festival is an annual film festival which takes place in April.

Johannesburg Film Festival
Festival Films Pty. Ltd.
8th Floor, Hallmark Towers
54 Siemert Road
P.O. Box 16427
Doornfontein 2028
Johannesburg
South Africa

Tel: +27 11-402-5477
Fax: +27 11-402-6646
E-mail: visionaf@mweb.co.za

Journées Cinématographiques de Carthage, created in 1966, is an international biennial cultural event with several goals, one of which is to promote African and Arab cinemas in terms of production and distribution. The festival includes competitions, retrospectives, workshops, seminars, conferences, and an international film market.

Journées Cinématographiques de Carthage
2, rue du Kenya
1002 Carthage
Tunisia

Tel: 216 1-287 776 or 862 668
Fax: 216 1-786 336
E-mail: culture.jcc@ati.tn
Web site: www.culture.tn/html/festivals/jcc.htm

Mayibuye Centre for History and Culture in South Africa at the University of the Western Cape comprises an archive, a museum, and space for exhibitions, films, music, theater, and other cultural activities.

Mayibuye Centre for History and Culture in South Africa
University of the Western Cape
PB X 17
7535 Bellville
South Africa

Tel: 21-959-2935
Fax: 21-951-3627

Mbolo.com is an online distributor of African films. In partnership with Amazon and FNAC, this Web site sells recent films by African directors in video and DVD.

Web site: http://www.mbolo.com/amazondvd.asp

Rencontres du Cinéma Africain de Niamey (RECAN) takes place annually in October.

Rencontres du Cinéma Africain de Niamey
CCFN
BP 11 413
Niamey
Niger

Tel: 227-73 48 34
Fax: 227-73 47 68
E-mail: recan@ccfn.ne
Web site: www.ccfn.ne

Rencontres Cinématographiques de Dakar (RECIDAK) has provided an annual opportunity since 1990 to showcase the cinema of Senegal and Africa. The festival includes a seminar and conversations with invited filmmakers.

RECIDAK
BP 10402
Dakar
Senegal

c/o Ministère de la Communication
58, Boulevard de la République
BP 4027
Dakar
Senegal

Tel: 221-821-1720
Fax: 221/ 821-4504
E-mail: recidk@metissacana.sn
Web site: www.metissacana.sn/recidak

South African Film Festival, jointly sponsored by the Film Resource Unit (FRU) and the *Weekly Mail* and *Guardian* newspapers, also includes a television and video market.

South African Film Festival
Film Resource Unit
P.O. Box 11065
Johannesburg
South Africa

Tel: +27 11-83 8 4280, 4281, 4282
Fax: 31 20-620-52

Southern African Film Festival is a biennial film, television, and video workshop, with a competition.

Southern African Film Festival
1st floor Pax House
89 Union Ave.
P.O. Box CY, 724 Cansenray
Harare
Zimbabwe

Tel: 263 4-79 11 56
Fax: 263 4-704 227
E-mail: saff@zimsurf.co.zw

Video Tiers Monde (Doornfontein) is a film distributor.

Video Tiers Monde (Doornfontein)
PB 16455
2028 Doornfontein
South Africa

Tel: 11-648-9550
Fax: 11-333-5353

Zimbabwe International Film Festival is an annual international festival held the first two weeks of September. Of note are the educational programs, the Film Forum, which brings in filmmakers from around the world to dialogue with the Zimbabwean film community, and the Festival Outreach Program, which screens selected films in high-density suburbs and in rural areas in an effort to raise the visual literacy and develop new audiences for African films.

Zimbabwe International Film Festival
P.O. Box A4
26 Cork Road
Avondale

Harare
Zimbabwe

Tel: 263-4-707 852
Fax: 263-4-795 898

Europe

Africa at the Pictures: A Festival Celebrating African Cinema is a one-week summer film festival held in London to promote the appreciation and distribution of African cinema in the United Kingdom. The festival includes screenings, lectures and opportunities for dialogue with invited filmmakers.

Africa at the Pictures
26 Shacklewell Lane
London E8 2EZ
England

Tel: 020 7690 0116
Fax: 020 7690 4333
Web site: www.africaatthepictures.co.uk

Africa in the Picture is a biennial festival on Africa and the Diaspora, featuring more than 80 films and many other events. Held in Amsterdam and other cities, the festival highlights recent films and invited filmmakers and includes a good selection of films from North Africa in an attempt to reach the North African population of the Netherlands.

Africa in the Picture
Stichting Notorious Film
P.O. Box 17456
1001 Amsterdam
The Netherlands

Tel: 31 20 625-2423
Fax: 31 20 620-5233
Web site: www.africainthepicture.nl/geschiedenis.html

Afrika Filmfestival presents recent African film to Belgian audiences.

Afrika Filmfestival
Leuvensebaan 323
2300 Turnhout
Belgium

Tel: 32 16-44 37 02
Fax: 32 2-245-85 83

E-mail: guido.huysmans@skynet.be
Web site: http://www.afrikafilmfestival.be

Bite the Mango Film Festival celebrates the work of Asian and Black filmmakers and provides an opportunity to see films rarely shown in the UK. It also provides a focus to explore issues in film production in the UK for Asian and Black filmmakers.

Bite the Mango Film Festival
National Museum of Photography, Film and Television
Pictureville, Bradford
West Yorkshire BD1 1NQ
England

Tel: 44 12-74 20 33 11
Fax: 44 12-74 77 02 17
E-mail: i.ajeeb@nmsi.ac.uk
Web site: www.bitethemango.org.uk

Black International Cinema is an annual Berlin film festival that showcases cinema and video, conferences, exhibitions, and shows concerning the Black Diaspora.

Black International Cinema
c/o Angela Kramer
Hohenfriedbergstrasse 14
D-10829 Berlin
Germany

Tel: 49 30-782-1621
Fax: 49 30-786-3466
Web site: www.black-international-cinema.com

British Film Institute (which includes the National Film and Television Archive) is the largest collection of film and television titles in Europe but holds only a small number of African films. These are available for viewing, rental, or sale. In contrast, the BFI National Library has a good collection of books on African cinema.

British Film Institute
Stephen Street Office/ BFI National Library
21 Stephen Street
London W1T 1LN
England

Tel: 44 (0) 20 7255 1444
E-mail: video.films@bfi.org.uk
Web site: www.bfi.org.uk/about/index.html

Centro Orientamento Educativo (COE) has six centers across Italy dedicated to maintaining an educational, community, and humanitarian dialogue on world issues. In Milan, the center specializes in Communication and Media, formerly producing the journal *Ecrans d'Afrique,* devoted to African cinema, sponsoring the annual Festival del Cinema Africano di Milano, and operating a movie theater (Cineteatro Sanlorenzo all Colonne), which shows African, Asian, and South American films. The COE has a list of films for purchase, available upon request.

Centro Orientamento Educativo
Via G. Lazzaroni 8
21024 Milano
Italy

Tel: 02-66712077, 6696258
Fax: 02-66714338
E-mail: coe@iol.it
Web site: www.coeweb.org

Cinéma du Réel—International Film Festival of Visual Anthropology and Social Documentation is an international festival and competition including more than 30 films from around the world.

Cinéma du Réel
Bpi—Centre Pompidou
25, rue du Renard
75197 Paris cedex 04
France

Tel: 33 1-44 78 44 21 or 44 78 45 26
Fax: 33 1-44 78 12 24
E-mail: cinereel@bpi.fr
Web site: www.bpi.fr/6/reel/indexe.html

Cinema Novo Festival has presented recent cinema from Africa, South America, and Asia since 1983, when it was first known as the Third World Film Festival. Its purpose is to provide alternative cultural expressions in order to enhance the understanding and appreciation of these cultures, and it screened more than 60 films in 2002. The festival includes other complementary activities such as exhibitions, concerts, lectures, debates, and workshops.

Cinema Novo Festival
Sint-jakobsstraat 36
8000 Bruges
Belgium

Tel: 32 50/ 31 30 71
Fax: 32 50/ 33 97 14

E-mail: info@cinemanovo.be
Web site: http://www.cinemanovo.be

Cinemafrica Film Festival, founded in 1987, is a biennial festival whose aim is to reflect the diversity and richness of African cultures through film. Cinemafrica shows African films that have not been previously distributed in Switzerland and is expanding the number of venues with each festival. In addition to film screenings, the program includes concerts, literary evenings, lectures, and meetings with African cinema professionals.

Cinémafrica Film Festival
Film Podium de la ville de Zurich
Postfach 8022
Zurich, Switzerland

Tel: 46 8-32 77 26
Fax: 46 8-33 17 06
E-mail: cinemafrica@hotmail.com
Web site: www.cinemafrica.a.se

Cinémas d'Afrique, also known as the Loudun Film Meeting, is a biennial film festival showcasing recent African films and offering filmmakers an opportunity to discuss their work with the general public and with students.

Cinémas d'Afrique
Cuzay
86120 Roiffe
Loudun
France

Tel: 33 49-8 77 79
Fax: 33 49-98 12 88

Cinémathèque Afrique, a department of the French Ministry of Foreign Affairs, makes more than 500 films available for viewing by appointment, or for educational uses at scholarly and cultural institutions in France and abroad, and at French cultural centers in most African countries. The collection of films includes shorts, documentaries, animated and feature films, produced from the 1960s up to the present day. An annual catalog, providing a brief description of each film, year of release, length and format is available upon request. Contact information for African filmmakers is available on the Web site.

Cinémathèque Afrique
Adpf Cinémathèque
6, rue Ferrus
75683 Paris cedex 14
France

Tel: 01 43 13 11 15
Fax: 01 43 13 11 16
E-mail: cinematheque@adpf.asso.fr
Web site: www.adpf.asso.fr

Ecrans Nord-Sud, founded in 1997 by a group of French cinema professionals, promotes and develops the diffusion of African cinema in France and Africa by means of a Web site, publications, exchanges, festivals, and a film library. It also maintains contact information on African filmmakers.

Ecrans Nord-Sud
11 place du Général Leclerc
92300 Levallois-Perret
France

Tel: 33 1-47 57 35 32
Fax: 33 1-47 57 52 18
E-mail: ecrans-nord-sud@wanadoo.fr
Web site: www.ecrans-nord-sud.com

F for Films is a distribution company.
15, rue de l'Ancienne Forge
27120 Fontaine-sous-Jouy
France

Tel: 33 2-32 26 25 39
Fax: 33 2-32 36 86 49
E-mail: seguy@f-for-film.com

Festival Black Movie, Cinémas des autres mondes, organized in 1991, is an annual film festival showcasing short and feature-length films from Asia, Africa, and Latin America to further the understanding of the "Other" through the power of the image.

Festival Black Movie
Cinémas des autre mondes
16, Rue Général-Dufour
CH-1204 Geneva
Switzerland

Tel: 41 22-320-8387
Fax: 41 22-320 8527
E-mail: info@blackmovie.ch
Web site: www.blackmovie.ch

Festival Cinémas d'Afrique presents, every other April, recent African films (features and shorts) during this celebration of cultural exchange between peoples. A professional workshop is also offered.

Festival Cinémas d'Afrique
44 Boulevard Henri Arnaud
49100 Angers
France

Tel: 33/ 41 20 08 22
Fax: 33/ 41 20 08 27
E-mail: cinemasdafrique@wanadoo.fr

Festival del Cinema Africano, in existence since 1991, screens approximately 100 films from Africa and the Diaspora. Sponsored by the Centro Orientamento Educativo, the film screenings are followed by debates and meetings with film-makers and other professionals. The festival includes a retrospective and round-table discussions.

Festival del Cinema Africano
COE
Via G. Lazarroni 8
20124 Milano
Italy

Tel: 02-66712077, 6696258
Fax: 02-66714338
E-mail: coe@iol.it
Web site: www.festivalcinemaafricano.org/index.php

Festival des Cinémas d'Afrique provides a selection of short and feature-length films from Africa, the Caribbean, and the Pacific.

Festival des Cinémas d'Afrique
Claudia Konde Vila
80, rue John Waterloo Wilson
1000 Bruxelles
Belgium

Tel: 32 2-286-9800
Fax: 32 2-286-9871

Festival des Films de Culture Noire, founded in 1993, is a celebration of Black cinema from Africa and the Diaspora, with roundtables, thematic debates, concerts, and exhibitions.

Festival des Films de Culture Noire
4, Villa Poissonnière
75018 Paris
France

Tel: 33 1-4251-8555
Fax: 33 1-4251-1885

Festival des Trois Continents is an annual festival that takes place the last week of November and presents films from Africa, Asia, Latin America, and Black America. Founded in 1979, the festival has presented more than one thousand films. Each year a retrospective is devoted to a specific filmmaker or country.

Festival des Trois Continents
19A Passage Pommeraye
BP 43302
44033 Nantes cedex 1
France

Tel: 33 2/ 40 69 74 14
Fax: 33 2/ 40 73 55 22
E-mail: festival@3continents.com
Web site: www.3continents.com

Festival du Jeune Cinéma d'Afrique et de Méditerranée

Rencontres Cinéma de Gindou, Le Bourg
46250 Gindou
France

Tel: 33 (0) 5-65 22 89 99 or 33 (0) 5-65 21 53 20
Fax: 33 (0) 5-65 22 88 89
E-mail: gindoucinema@wanadoo.fr
Web site: www.gindou.free.fr

Festival du Cinéma Africain, in existence since 1994, offers a week of African films and discussions with invited African filmmakers.

Festival du Cinéma Africain
Diaspora Productions-46
Bd. Charlemagne
1040 Bruxelles
Belgium

Tel: 32 2-23 05 858

Festival Images d'Ailleurs has presented cultural events since 1990 to promote an exchange of ideas and dialogues between the various communities of humanity. The annual film festival presents 50-70 films from Africa, Black America and the Caribbean and focuses each year on a specific theme, with roundtable discussions and exhibitions.

Festival Images d'Ailleurs
5 rue Mederic
75017 Paris
France

Tel: 33 1-47 63 74 00
Fax: 33 1-47 63 85 90
E-mail: images-d-ailleurs@wanadoo.fr
Web site: www.africultures.com/partenaires/images_dailleurs.htm

Festival Internacional de Cine de San Sebastián showcases an international array of films, frequently including African films.

Festival Internacional de Cine de San Sebastián
Plaza de Oquendo, s/n
Apartado de Correos 397
20080 Donostia / San Sebastián
Spain

Tel: 34 94-348-1212
Fax: 34 94-348-1218
e-mail: ssiff@sansebastianfestival.com
Web site: www.sansebastianfestival.com

Festival International de Films de Fribourg annually presents more than one hundred films from Asia, Africa, and Latin America. Originally created in 1980 as the Third World Film Festival, this festival has expanded to more than thirty cities and towns across Switzerland. The festival promotes the distribution of films by inviting distributors, cinema owners, and journalists. Each year the festival highlights the films of a selected filmmaker or country and publishes a detailed catalog.

Freiburger Internationales Filmfestival
Rue Nicolas de Praroman 2
Case postale 550
CH—1701 Fribourg
Switzerland

Tel: 41 26-347-4200
Fax: 41 26-347-4201
E-mail: info@fiff.ch
Web site: http://www.fiff.ch

Festival International du Film d'Amiens, now in its 24th year, has presented films from over 35 countries, specializing in Africa, the Caribbean and the South Pacific. Originally conceived as a means to show unknown cinema, the festival today presents a broader spectrum of world cinema. The festival usually includes a competition, a retrospective, and a film market.

Amiens International Film Festival
MCA
Place Léon Gontier
F-80000 Amiens
France

Tel: 33 3-22 71 35 70
Fax: 33 3-22 92 53 04
E-mail: contact@filmfestamiens.org
Web site: www.filmfestamiens.org

Festival International du Film Francophone de Namur distributes and promotes recent works by filmmakers from Francophone countries. Beginning in 1986 with 30 films screened, the festival today screens more than 150 films, publishes an official catalog, and includes competitions and awards.

ASBL Festival International du Film Francophone de Namur
175 rue des Brasseurs
B-5000 Namur
Belgium

Tel: 32 81-24 12 36
Fax: 32 81-22 43 84
E-mail: info@fiff.be
Web site: www.fiff.namur.be

Filmwelt Afrika, organized by the House of World Cultures, is an important biennial retrospective that takes place over several months and usually shows many of the films from the previous year's FESPACO.

Filmwelt Afrika
Haus der Kulturen der Welt
John-Foster Allee 10
D—10557
Berlin
Germany

Tel: 49 30 397-870
Fax: 49 30 394 8679
E-mail: film@hkw.de

FNAC is a media superstore headquartered in Paris, with outlets all over France selling books, videos, CDs, etc. FNAC has a searchable online catalog of African films and has also partnered with Mbolo.com to sell African cinema online.

Web site: www.fnac.com

Focus op het Zuiden is an annual film festival highlighting films from Africa, South America and Asia.

Focus op het Zuiden
2300 Turnhout
Belgium

Tel: 32 14-41 94 94
Fax: 32 14-42 08 21
E-mail: info@opendoek.be
Web site: www.opendoek.be

Forum des Images, in existence since 1988, is a space for exploring film that has Paris as a subject or in its landscape, including African films set in Paris. With a holding of more than 6,600 films from 1895 to the present, the Forum is open for interested researchers to view films and sponsors festivals, meetings, and other cinema events.

Forum des Images
Porte Saint-Eustache
Forum des Halles
75001 Paris
France

Tel: 33 1-44 76 62 00
Fax: 33 1-40 26 40 96
Web site: www.forumdesimages.net/qcq/qcq-pp.html

Giornate del Cinema Africano is an annual film festival showing recent African films from the Carthage and FESPACO festivals, and includes concerts and other activities to promote reflection on the relations between cinema and other expressions of African culture.

Giornate del Cinema Africano
Centro Sociale—Bia Bartolo 43/F
06100 Perugia
Italy

Tel: 39 75-57 28 905
Fax: 39 75-57 26 768

Images of Africa, is a cultural festival that takes place in Copenhagen and twenty other towns and that includes music, dance, theatre, and fashion as well as exhibitions, films, seminars, and activities for children. The film program includes feature films, shorts, and documentaries.

Images of Africa
Copenhagen International Theatre
Verstergade 5
DK 1456
Copenhagen
Denmark

Tel: 45 33-17 97 00
Fax: 45 33-17 97 01
E-mail: info@dccd.dk
Web site: www.utamaduni.dk/2000/27.htm

International Film Festival Rotterdam, a general film festival, usually includes a selection of African films.

International Film Festival Rotterdam
P.O. Box 21696
3001 AR Rotterdam
The Netherlands

Tel: 31 10-890-9090
Fax: 31 10-890-9091
E-mail: tiger@filmfestivalrotterdam.com
Web site: www.filmfestivalrotterdam.com/2003/en/index.html

Journées du Cinéma Francophone de Ferney-Voltaire is an annual film festival showcasing films from Francophone Africa. The program usually features a number of premieres as well as roundtable discussions and cultural evenings.

Journées du Cinéma Africain de Ferney-Voltaire
40 parc du Jura
01210 Ferney-Voltaire
France

Tel/Fax: 33 04 50 40 76 13
E-mail: Jca.ferney.voltaire@wanadoo.fr
Web site: www.jca-ferney-voltaire.org

La Médiathèque des Trois Mondes is a nonprofit French cultural organization whose goal is to gain wider recognition for African, Asian, and Latin American films. It has over 200 films for sale in various formats (16 mm, 35 mm, video, PAL, and/or SECAM). The Médiathèque produces a film catalogue with a listing of films divided by subject and geographic region. The African section contains more than 70 short and full-length feature films, animations, and documentaries. Contact information on African filmmakers is also available on the Web site.

La Médiathèque des Trois Mondes
63 bis rue du Cardinal Lemoine
75005 Paris
France

Tel: 33 (0)1 42 34 99 00
Fax: 33 (0)1 42 34 99 01
E-mail: groupe.3.mondes@wanadoo.fr
Web site: www.cine3mondes.fr

Racines Noires—Rencontres des Cinémas du Monde Noir

Racines Noires—Rencontres des Cinémas du Monde Noir
Bureau 1—10ᵉ étage
104 avenue Kennedy
75016 Paris
France

Tel: 33 1-44 30 83 13 or 45 86 58 29
Fax: 33 1-44 23 84 34
E-mail: catherine.ruelle@rfi.fr
Web site: www.africultures.com/partenaires/racines_noires.htm

Regards sur les Cinémas d'Afrique et du Sud is an annual film festival showing films from Africa, the Caribbean, Asia, the Pacific and Latin America.

Regards sur les Cinémas d'Afrique et du Sud
c/o Hevadis
353, rue du Général Leclerc
76230 Bois-Guillaume
Paris
France

Tel: 33 2-35 61 89 41
Fax: 33 2-35 61 31 24
E-mail: hevadis.films@wanadoo.fr
Web site: www.africazoom.net

U.S. and Canada

African Diaspora Film Festival, sponsored annually by Artmattan Productions since its inception in 1993, takes place in the fall in New York City. The festival is growing each year, with 35 films in 2000, more than 50 films in 2001, and more than 70 films in 2002. The festival celebrates the richness and diversity of the global Black experience, featuring shorts, features, and documentaries.

ADFF
535 Cathedral Parkway, Suite 14B
New York, New York 10025

Tel: 212-864-1760
E-mail: info@nadff.org
Web site: www.nyadff.org

African Film Festival, Inc. (AFF) is a nonprofit arts organization established in 1990 to promote and increase knowledge and understanding of African arts, literature, and culture; develop a non-African audience for African films; and expand distribution opportunities for African films in the United States. Established in 1993, it consists of a nine-day program of screenings and panel discussions. The films include both feature films and short works. While AFF functions primarily as a film and cultural events programmer, it also has a Video/Films Archive, which holds more than 200 African film titles produced since 1993 (VHS or 35mm). The Archives, which may be accessed via contextual links from the AFF homepage, has synopses, stills, and bios of featured directors in the African Film Festival, the Traveling Film Series, and Discussion Series.

AFF also sponsors the **Festival and Traveling Film Series,** which annually presents selections from the current African Film Festival in several U.S. cities. The homepage provides an up-to-date listing of featured cities for the calendar year.

African Film Festival, Inc.
154 West 18th Street, Suite 2A
New York, New York 10011

Tel: 212-352-1720
Fax: 212-807-9752
E-mail: nyaff@erols.com
Web site: http://www.africanfilmny.org

American Black Film Festival, formerly known as the Acapulco Black Film Festival, is an annual film festival founded in 1997 to provide exposure for the films of independent Black filmmakers to film buyers and the general public.

American Black Film Festival
c/o Film Life
100 Avenue of the Americas, 15th Floor
New York, New York 10013

Tel: 212-219-7267
Fax: 212-925-3426
E-mail: info@thefilmlife.com
Web site: www.abff.com

Annual Black Film Festival, The Newark Museum

Annual Black Film Festival
The Newark Museum
49 Washington Street
Newark, New Jersey 07102—3176

Tel: 973-596—6550 or 1-800-7MUSEUM (toll-free)

Artmattan Productions is a film distribution company that focuses on the experience of Black people in Africa, the Caribbean, North and South America, and Europe. It currently carries 35mm titles and is in the process of acquiring more films. A listing of films available is on their Web site, with ordering information for purchase or rental. A "Catalog of Films from Africa and the African Diaspora" is available by request from Artmattan Productions. Artmattan Productions also sponsors an annual "African Diaspora Film Festival" in the fall in New York City (see above).

Artmattan Productions
535 Cathedral Parkway, Suite 14B
New York, New York 10025

Tel: 212-864-1760
Fax: 212-316-6020
Web site: www.africanfilm.com

Blockbuster video stores, in addition to the many mainstream video selections, have a number of international films. Depending on the location of the store, there may be more videos catering to the demographics of the region. Blockbuster's Web site provides information on the African videos available, with a brief synopsis of each.

Web site: www.blockbuster.com

Boston University, African Studies Center maintains a video library to support the research and educational needs of educators locally, regionally, and nationally. Presently, the video collection consists of only a small number of feature films and folktales, but new materials are continually acquired. A listing of all videos is available on their Web site. There is a fee for borrowing videos.

Boston University
African Studies Center
Outreach Program
270 Bay State Road
Boston, Massachusetts 02215

Tel: 617-353-7303
Fax: 617-353-4975

E-mail: bbb@bu.edu
Web site: www.bu.edu/AFR/Outreach.html

California Newsreel, an independent media distributor in the United States specializing in film from Africa and the African Diaspora, maintains the **Library of African Cinema**, a diverse collection of feature films and documentaries mostly made by African producers and directors. The film collection currently consists of 62 films, available in VHS and/or 35 mm format. Recently, the Library has coproduced three titles, which are available for rental in their 2002 catalog. Titles are listed on their Web site, and a print catalog can be requested. Films are available for purchase or rental, and previews are available to educational institutions at no charge.

California Newsreel
Order Department
P.O. Box 2284
South Burlington, Vermont 05407

Tel: 1-877-811-7495 (Toll—free)
Fax: 802-846-1850
E-mail: contact@newsreel.org
Web site: www.newsreel.org

Facets Multi-Media, via Facets Rentals, has a limited number of African feature films from the major film-producing African countries available for rent to their members. Films are in VHS, 16mm and 35mm formats. Membership is open to all, with a descriptive catalog available online, searchable by film title or country of origin. Also, the "Facets Movie Lovers Video Guide" is available free by request.

Facets Multi-Media
Facets Rentals
1517 W. Fullerton Avenue
Chicago, Illinois 60614

Tel: 1-800-331-6197 (Purchase, toll-free) 1-800-532-2387 (Rent, toll-free)
Fax: 773-929-5437
E-mail: sales@facets.org
Web site: www.facets.org

Filmakers Library maintains a collection of titles for rental or sale to universities, schools, museums, businesses, and community groups. These are primarily documentary films and videos; however, there are a few African feature films. An index of films is included on the Web site, with synopses and prices of films. Complete ordering information is also available on the Web site.

Filmakers Library
124 East 40th Street
New York, New York 10016

Tel: 212-808-4980
Fax: 212-808-4983
E-mail: info@filmakers.com
Web site: www.filmakers.com

Griot Cinema at Erico Café is a series that showcases films from the African Diaspora every week, in a café setting with a light buffet included in the price of admission.

Erico Café
1334 U Street, NW
Washington, DC 20009

Tel: 202/ 518-9742
E-mail: info@ericocafe.com
Web site: www.ericocafe.com

Howard University, Media Center, located in the Undergraduate Library, has a significant collection of African films and videos which can be viewed only on site by Howard students, faculty and staff and by others with photo identification who schedule a viewing appointment.

Founders Library, Media Center
Howard University
500 Howard Place, NW
Washington, DC 20059

Tel: 202-806-5435
Web site: www.founders.howard.edu/Media_Center/default.htm.

Indiana University, African Studies Program offers faculty, staff, and students access to the numerous videos, slides, and teaching resources available at the program. All materials are listed in the Video and Resource Catalogs, which is on the Web site. Materials may be researched on site or borrowed for up to two weeks.

African Studies Program
Woodburn Hall 221
Bloomington, Indiana 47405

Tel: 812-855-6285
Fax: 812-855-6734
E-mail: afrist@indiana.edu
Web site: www.indiana.edu/~afrist/

Journées du Cinéma Africain et Créole is sponsored by Vues d'Afrique annually in the spring and includes a large selection of feature films, shorts, documentaries, and children's films. The festival also includes art exhibitions, concerts, and lectures.

Vues D'Afrique
67, rue Ste-Catherine Ouest, 5ᵉ étage
Montreal
Quebec H2X 1Z7
Canada

Tel: 514-284-3322
Fax: 514-845-0631
E-mail: info@vuesdafrique.org
Web site: www.vuesdafrique.org

Kino International maintains over 400 classic and contemporary world cinema titles, available in 35 mm, video, and some DVD. A free catalog is available upon request, and the Web site is searchable by country. Includes several African films.

Kino International Corporation
333 W. 39th Street, Ste. 503
New York, New York 10018

Tel: 212-629-6880 or 800-562-3330 (toll-free)
Fax: 212-714-0871
E-mail: contact@kino.com
Web site: www.kino.com/contact/mail.html

Library of Congress, Motion Picture & Television Reading Room provides access and information services to an international community of film and television professionals, archivists, scholars, and researchers. Since 1942 the Library has collected motion pictures, and today the collection includes African films. Only selected titles in special collections are searchable online.

Library of Congress
Motion Picture & Television Reading Room
James Madison Building, Rm. LM336
101 Independence Avenue, SE
Washington, DC 20540

Tel: 202-70-8572
Fax: 202-707-2371
Web site: www.loc.gov/rr/mopic

Martin Luther King Jr. Memorial Library, Audiovisual Division contains over 15,000 titles. Housed in the main building of the District of Columbia's public library, this collection includes VHS cassettes, audiobooks, 16 mm films, audio-cassettes, and phonograph albums. The collection includes African films.

Martin Luther King Jr. Memorial Library
Audiovisual Division
901 G Street, NW, Room 226
Washington, DC 20001

Tel: 202-727-0321
Web site: www.dclibrary.org/mlk/audiovisual/

Metropolitan Museum of Art has a film program that continuously brings in an international variety of films, including those from Africa.

Metropolitan Museum of Art
1000 Fifth Avenue
New York, New York 10028-7710

Tel: 212-535-7710
Fax: 212-659-2921
Web site: www.metmuseum.org

Museum of Modern Art maintains a Film Library, which includes more than 19,000 films. The collection is very strong in international films from all periods and genres and is housed in the Celeste Bartos Film Preservation Center. The Celeste Bartos Film Study Center is open by appointment only and has tempo-rarily relocated to MOMA QNS, in Long Island City, Queens, until the main building is reopened in 2005.

Museum of Modern Art
Celeste Bartos Film Study Center
New York

Tel: 212-708-9613
E-mail: info@moma.org
Web site: www.moma.org/collection.depts/film_media/index.html

Mypheduh Films, Inc. is a distributor of African and African-American films. Holding more than 20 titles, it offers special prices for retailers and educational organizations. Rentals are also available for public showings. The film rental catalog is online, with price quotations and booking information. Films are available in 16mm, 35mm, and VHS formats, depending on the film.

Mypheduh Films, Inc.
P.O. Box 10035
Washington, DC 20018-0035

Tel: 202-234-4755 or 1-800-524-3895 (toll-free)
Fax: 202-234-5735
E-mail: info@sankofa.com
Web site: www.sankofa.com

National Museum of African Art, one of the museums of the Smithsonian Institution, screens African films throughout the year, usually introduced by a film
scholar or critic. Films may accompany a current exhibit or theme, and the calendar is published well in advance.

National Museum of African Art
Smithsonian Institution
950 Independence Avenue, SW
Washington, DC 20560

Tel: 202-357-4600
Fax: 202-357-4879
Web site: www.si.edu/nmafa

New Yorker Films is a distributor of theatrical, non-theatrical and educational
independent films, videos and DVDs. Special rates are available for classroom
rentals and other educational purposes. A print catalog of their complete collection is produced annually. There are some 20 African films in the catalog.

New Yorker Films
16 West 61st Street
New York, New York 10023

Tel: 212-247-6110; 877-247-6200 (toll-free)
Fax: 212-307-7855
E-mail: info@newyorkerfilms.com
Web site: http://www.newyorkerfilms.com

Northwestern University, Melville J. Herskovits Library of African Studies
was founded in 1954 to support the research and curricular programs of the
Northwestern University Program of African Studies. Today it is the largest
separate library of the study of Africa in existence, holding over 245,000 vol-
umes. The video collection numbers approximately 400 feature-length films.
The Herskovits Library has a specialized staff who serve not only the University
community but regional, national, and international scholars as well.

Melville J. Herskovits
Library of African Studies
Northwestern University
1935 Sheridan Road
Evanston, Illinois 60208-2300

Tel: 847-467-3084
Fax: 847-467-1233
E-mail: africana@northwestern.edu
Web site: www.library.northwestern.edu/africana/afribroc.html

Pan African Film & Arts Festival, established in 1992, is an annual Los Angeles-based festival screening over 100 short, feature, and documentary films of the African Diaspora. In 2002 the festival also presented an abbreviated second festival in Atlanta as part of the National Black Arts Festival.

The Pan African Film Festival
P.O. Box 2418
Beverly Hills, California 90213

Tel: 323-295-1706
Fax: 323-295-1952
E-mail: info@paff.org
Web site: www.paff.org

Project Black Cinema is an annual international film festival committed to the presentation of cinema from Africa and the African Diaspora.

Project Black Cinema
Sarasota, Florida

Tel: 813-957-7944

SPIA Media Productions, Inc., in existence since 1998, is dedicated to the documentation, preservation, and dissemination of cultural productions from Africa, the Caribbean, and the United States, with a particular emphasis on Cape Verdean-American and Cape Verdean history, culture, and traditions.

SPIA Media Productions, Inc.
P.O. Box 230937
Astor Station
Boston, Massachusetts 02123-0937

Tel: 617-277-0278
Fax: 617-277-8278
E-mail: spiamedia@aol.com
Web site: spiamedia.com

Third World Newsreel (TWN) is an alternative media arts organization dedicated to the dissemination of independent film and video by and about people of color. Its collection includes over 380 titles, which are mostly short educational, documentary, or dramatic features.

Third World Newsreel
545 Eighth Avenue, 10th Floor
New York, New York 10018

Tel: 212-947-9277
Fax: 212-594-6417
E-mail: twn@twn.org
Web site: www.twn.org/index.html

Toronto International Film Festival (Section Planet Africa) is an annual festival in September screening international films; a permanent section is devoted to African film.

Toronto International Film Festival
2 Carlton Street, Suite 1600
Toronto, Ontario
Canada M5B IJ3

Tel: 1 416 967-7371
Fax: 1 416 967-9477
E-mail: tiff@cossette.com

Washington DC International Film Festival (Filmfest DC) is an annual film festival featuring more than 80 films and usually includes several African films.

Filmfest DC
P.O. Box 21396
Washington, DC 20009

Tel: 202-724-5613
Fax: 202-724-6578
E-mail: filmfestdc@aol.com
Web site: www.filmfestdc.org

Women Make Movies, the largest distributor of women's media in North America, is a nonprofit, feminist, media arts organization whose multicultural programs provide resources for both users and producers of media by women. The Film and Video Catalogue contains approximately 500 films and videotapes by and about women. Although the majority of the films dealing with Africa are short documentaries, there are a few feature films available.

Women Make Movies, Inc.
462 Broadway, Suite 500WS
New York, New York 10013

Tel: 212-925-0606
Fax: 212-925-2052

E-mail: info@wmm.com
Web site: www.wmm.com

University of California, Berkeley–Media Resource Center is the UC Berkeley Library's primary collection of materials in electronic non-print (audio and visual) formats. The MRC collection is intended to support the broad range of study and research interest at the university. The collection is searchable by an online catalog, with more than 50 African feature films under the subject heading "Movies by African Filmmakers." Although the collection is primarily for the research needs of UC students, faculty, and staff, one-time use of the Center by individuals not affiliated with the university may occasionally be granted if there is a valid research need.

University of California, Berkeley
Media Resource Center
Moffitt Library
Berkeley, California

Tel: 510-642-8197
Web site: www.lib.berkeley.edu/MRC/about.html

University of Florida, George A. Smathers Libraries, Africana Collection contains more than 50 video items about African films and filmmakers, which can be searched via the online catalog.

University of Florida
George A. Smathers Libraries
Africana Collection
P.O. Box 117001
Gainesville, Florida 32611-7001

Tel: 352-392-4919
Fax: 352-392-8118
E-mail: danrebo@ufl.edu
Web site: www.web.uflib.ufl.edu/cm/africana/filmvid.htm

University of Kansas, African & African-American Studies maintains a collection of over 75 videos and films. An annotated bibliography is located at the Web site listing. The films are features and documentaries. Materials can be checked out free of charge by faculty, and by special permission from the department chair for all other interested researchers.

African & African-American Studies
University of Kansas
1440 Jayhawk Boulevard, 9 Bailey Hall
Lawrence, Kansas 66045-7574

Tel: 785-864-3054
Web site: www.cc.ukans.edu/~afs/video.html

Selected Web Sites for General Information

Africa South of the Sahara provides information and links to web sites on festivals, organizations and distributors. Also has a section on "Films and Videos."

Web site: www-sul.stanford.edu/depts/ssrg/africa/film.html

Africultures offers information on African culture, with a section devoted to cinema, including film reviews and distribution information.

Web site: www.africultures.com/index.asp

H-AfrLitCine is a forum for discussion of African literature and cinema providing information and useful links.

Web site: http://h-net2msu.edu/~aflitweb/

Netribution Film Network is the homepage for filmmaking in the United Kingdom. This site provides film news, information on funding, and a section devoted to festivals that can be searched by name, country, month, or type.

Web site: www.netribution.co.uk/festivals/index.html

Suggestions for Further Reading

Armes, Roy. *Third World Film Making and the West*. Berkeley: University of California Press, 1987.

Bakari, Imruh, and Mbye Cham, eds. *African Experiences of Cinema*. London: British Film Institute, 1996.

Balseiro, Isabel, and Ntongela Masilela, eds. *To Change Reels: Film and Film Culture in South Africa*. Detroit: Wayne State University Press, 2003.

Barlet, Olivier. *African Cinemas: Decolonizing the Gaze*. Trans. Chris Turner. London: Zed, 2000.

Boughedir, Férid. *Le cinéma africain de A à Z*. Brussels: OCIC, 1987. *African Cinema from A to Z*. Trans. Dalice A. Woodford. Brussels: OCIC, 1992.

Diawara, Manthia. *African Cinema, Politics and Culture*. Bloomington: Indiana University Press, 1992.

Downing, John D. H., ed. *Film and Politics in the Third World*. New York: Praeger, 1986.

Eke, Maureen N., Kenneth W. Harrow and Emmanuel Yewah, eds. *African Images: Recent Studies and Text in Cinema*. Trenton, N.J.: Africa World Press, 2000.

Ellerson, Beti. *Sisters of the Screen: Women of Africa on Film, Video and Television*. Trenton, N.J.: Africa World Press, 2000.

Fédération Panafricaine des Cinéastes. *L'Afrique et le Centenaire du Cinéma*. Paris: Présence Africaine, 1995.

Gadjigo, Samba, et al., eds. *Ousmane Sembène: Dialogue with Critics and Writers*. Amherst: University of Massachusetts Press, 1993.

Gardies, André. *Cinéma d'Afrique noire francophone, l'espace-miroir*. Paris: L'Harmattan, 1989.

Givanni, June, ed. *Symbolic Narratives/African Cinema: Audiences, Theory and the Moving Image*. London: British Film Institute, 2001.

Gugler, Josef. *African Film: Re-Imagining a Continent*. Bloomington: Indiana University Press; Cape Town: David Philip; Oxford: James Currey, 2003.

Haffner, Pierre. *Essai sur les fondements du cinéma africain*. Abidjan: Les Nouvelles Editions Africaines, 1978.

Harrow, Kenneth, ed. *African Cinema: Post-Colonial and Feminist Readings*. Trenton, N.J.: Africa World Press, 1999.

———. *With Open Eyes: Women and African Cinema*. Amsterdam: Rodopi, 1997.

Haynes, Jonathan, ed. *Nigerian Video Films*. Athens: Ohio University Center for International Studies, 2000.

Larouche, Michel, ed. *Films d'Afrique*. Montreal: Guernica, 1991.

Le Festival Panafricain du Cinéma et de la Télévision de Ouagadougou et L'Association des Trois Mondes. *Les cinémas d'Afrique-Dictionnaire*. Paris: Karthala, 2000.

Malkmus, Lizbeth, and Roy Armes. *Arab and African Filmmaking*. London: Zed, 1991.

Martin, Michael T., ed. *Cinemas of the Black Diaspora: Diversity, Dependence, and Oppositionality*. Detroit: Wayne State University Press, 1994.

Monaco, James. *How to Read a Film*. New York: Oxford University Press, 1981.

Niang, Sada. *Djibril Diop Mambéty, un cinéaste à contre-courant.* Paris: L'Harmattan, 2002.

Niang, Sada, ed. *Littérature et cinéma en Afrique francophone-Ousmane Sembène et Assia Djebar.* Paris: L'Harmattan, 1996.

Petty, Sheila, ed. *A Call to Action: The Films of Ousmane Sembene.* Westport, Conn.: Praeger, 1996.

Pfaff, Françoise. *The Cinema of Ousmane Sembene, A Pioneer of African Film.* Westport, Conn.: Greenwood, 1984.

———. *Twenty-five Black African Filmmakers.* Westport, Conn.: Greenwood, 1988.

Pines, Jim, and Paul Willemen, eds. *Questions of Third Cinema.* London: British Film Institute, 1989.

Sherzer, Dina, ed. *Cinema, Colonialism, Postcolonialism: Perspectives from the French and Francophone Worlds.* Austin: University of Texas Press, 1996.

Signaté, Ibrahima. *Med Hondo-un cinéaste rebelle.* Paris: Présence Africaine, 1994.

Spaas, Lieve. *The Francophone Film: A Struggle for Identity.* Manchester: Manchester University Press, 2000.

Through African Eyes: Dialogues with the Directors. New York: African Film Festival, 2003.

Tomaselli, Keyan. *The Cinema of Apartheid, Race and Class in South African Film.* Brooklyn, N.Y.: Smyrna, 1988.

Ukadike, Nwachukwu Frank. *Black African Cinema.* Berkeley: University of California Press, 1995.

———. *Questioning African Cinema.* Minneapolis: University of Minnesota Press, 2002.

Vieyra, Paulin Soumanou. *Le Cinéma Africain.* Paris: Présence Africaine, 1975.

———. *Sembène Ousmane, Cinéaste.* Paris: Présence Africaine, 1972.

Wynchank, Anny. *DJIBRIL DIOP MAMBETY ou le voyage du voyant.* Ivry-Sur-Seine, France: Editions A3, 2003.

Special Issues of Journals

Black Film Review 6.3 (1991) and 7.1 (1991). Special issues on African cinema. Other issues contain articles on African and Caribbean cinemas.

CinémAction. "Cinémas noirs d'Afrique" 26 (1983). Jacques Binet, Férid Boughedir and Victor Bachy, eds.

CinémAction. "Sembène Ousmane" 34 (1985). Daniel Serceau, ed.

CinémAction. "Le Cinéma sud-africain est-il tombé sur la tête?" 39 (1986). Keyan Tomaselli, ed.

CinémAction. "Cinémas africains, une oasis dans le désert?" 106 (2003). Samuel Lelièvre, ed.

Ecrans d'Afrique, quarterly issues, 1992–1998.

iris. "New Discourses of African Cinema" 18 (1995). Frank Ukadike, ed.

L'Afrique littéraire et artistique. "Les cinémas africains en 1972" 20 (1972). Guy Hennebelle, ed.

L'Afrique littéraire et artistique. "Cinéastes d'Afrique noire" 49 (1978). Guy Hennebelle and Catherine Ruelle, eds.

Notre Librairie. "Cinémas d'Afrique" 149 (2002).

Research in African Literatures 26.3 (1995). Kenneth Harrow, ed. Special issue on African cinema.

Contributors

Françoise Balogun taught French for ten years at the Universities of Ife and Lagos and at the same time became involved in film production. When her husband, Ola Balogun, founded an independent film production company in 1974 in Nigeria, she joined as executive producer. They worked in film distribution in Nigeria, especially itinerant distribution. Balogun's book *Le cinéma au Nigeria* (1984) was also published in English (1987). She has translated into French two of Ekwensi's novels (*Jagua Nana* and *Burning Grass*), as well as *Kill Me Quick*, a novel by Meja Mwangi.

Brenda F. Berrian is Professor of Africana Studies, English, and Women's Studies at the University of Pittsburgh. She is also the book review editor of *MaComere*, the journal for the Association of Caribbean Women Writers and Scholars. Her most recent book is *Awakening Spaces: French Caribbean Popular Songs, Music and Culture* (2000).

Robert Cancel is Associate Professor of African and Comparative Literature at the University of California–San Diego. He is the author of *Allegorical Speculation in an Oral Society: The Tabwa Narrative Tradition* (1989), based on the field work he conducted on oral traditions in Zambia. He has written articles on Ousmane Sembene, Nadine Gordimer, Ngugi wa Thiong'o, and African vernacular writing.

Mbye Cham is Professor in the Department of African Studies at Howard University, Washington, D.C. In addition to numerous essays and chapters in books on African and Caribbean literature and film, he is the editor of *EX-ILES: Essays on Caribbean Cinema* (1992), and coeditor of *Blackframes: Critical Perspectives on Black Independent Cinema* (1988) and *African Experiences of Cinema* (1996).

Madeleine Cottenet-Hage is Professor Emerita of French at the University of Maryland. She has published articles on Francophone women writers in various journals and the first full study on the surrealist writer Gisèle Prassinos (1988). In 1995 she edited *Penser la Créolité* with Maryse Condé. She is also the coeditor, with Christiane Makward, of *Dictionnaire littéraire des femmes de langue française: De Marie de France à Marie Ndiaye* (1996). She has written articles on Francophone cinema, including "Decolonizing Images: *Soleil O* and the Cinema of Med Hondo" (in *Cinema, Colonialism, Postcolonialism,* ed. Dinah Sherzer, 1996).

Beti Ellerson teaches courses in visual culture in the Department of Art at Howard University. She was producer/host of *Reels of Colour,* a television series focusing on independent filmmaking by people of color, which aired in the Washington D.C. area. Her work on cinema of Africa and the Diaspora has been published in *Ecrans d'Afrique* and in a special issue on women and African cinema in *Matatu* (no. 19, 1997). She is the author of *Sisters of the Screen* (2000) and has produced a documentary film of the same name (2002).

Samba Gadjigo is Professor of Francophone African Literatures and Films at Mount Holyoke College. He has authored *Ecole blanche, Afrique noire: l'image de l'école coloniale dans le roman africain francophone* (1990). He is the guest editor of *Aminata Sow Fall's Literary Work* (special issue of *Contributions in Black Studies,* 1991) and coeditor of *Ousmane Sembene: Dialogue with Critics and Writers* (1993). His articles on African literatures and films have appeared in journals such as *Research in African Literatures, Présence africaine, Présence francophone,* and *African Studies Review.* Gadjigo is currently working on a biography of Ousmane Sembene.

Josef Gugler is Professor of Sociology and Director of the Center for Contemporary African Studies at the University of Connecticut. Research and teaching have taken him to the Democratic Republic of the Congo, Cuba, India, Kenya, Nigeria, Tanzania and Uganda. Much of his work has focused on urbanization in developing countries. More recently, he has begun to publish on African literature and film. Gugler is the editor of *The Urban Transformation of the Developing World* (1996) and *Cities in the Developing World: Issues, Theory, and Policy* (1997). His recent books are: *African Film: Re-Imagining a Continent* (Indiana University Press, David Philip and James Currey, 2003) and *World Cities Beyond the West* (2004). He has written many articles and encyclopedia entries.

Kenneth W. Harrow is Professor of English at Michigan State University. He is the author of *Threshold of Change in African Literature: The Emergence of a Tradition* (1994) and *Less Than One and Double* (2001). He has edited *Faces of Islam in African Literature* (1991), *The Marabout and the Muse: New Approaches to Islam in African Literature* (1996), and *African Cinema: Postcolonial and Feminist Readings* (1999). He is also the coeditor, with Maureen Eke and Emmanuel Yewah, of *African Images: Recent Studies in Cinema and Text* (2000) and has published numerous articles on African cinema.

Françoise Pfaff is Professor of French and Francophone Studies at Howard University, where she also teaches courses on literature and film from France, West Africa, and the Caribbean. She has authored *The Cinema of Ousmane Sembene, A Pioneer of African Film* (1984) and *Twenty-five Black African Filmmakers* (1988). Her book on the Guadeloupean writer Maryse Condé, *Entretiens avec Maryse Condé* (1993), appeared in an augmented English version as *Conversations with Maryse Condé* (1996). She has lectured extensively in the U.S. and abroad, curated a number of African film series, and published many scholarly articles.

María Roof teaches Latin American literature and culture at Howard University. She is author of several publications on Latin America and foreign language pedagogy, with a focus on writers from Chile, Panama, Nicaragua, and the Hispanophone and Francophone Caribbean. She has also published translations on international issues and literary criticism. She is currently preparing a bilingual edition of the poems of Vidaluz Meneses (Nicaragua) and a compilation of criticism on the works of Panamanian author Gloria Guardia.

N. Frank Ukadike is Associate Professor of Film in the Department of Communication and the Program in African and African Diaspora Studies at Tulane University. He has authored *Black African Cinema* (1994) and *Questioning African Cinema: Conversations with Filmmakers* (2002). He is the guest editor of a special issue of *iris* (no. 18,

1995) on African cinema. His articles on African video productions have appeared in several journals. Ukadike edited *Breaking Canons: Reformulating African Cinematic Discourse* (2003).

Valerie J. Wheat is the Branch Librarian at the Smithsonian Institution's Museum Reference Center, one of the largest sources of museological information in the U.S. She provides information and bibliographic services to museum professionals and researchers throughout the world. She is also active in the museum community and currently serves on the board of the American Association for State and Local History (AASLH) and the Museum Education Roundtable. Since July 1996, she has been writing the "Media Center" column for the *AASLH Dispatch* and last year wrote an article on "Halls of Fame" for the recently released *Encyclopedia of Appalachia.*

Josephine Woll is Professor of Russian at Howard University and Adjunct Professor at the Paul H. Nitze School for Advanced International Studies at Johns Hopkins University. She is the author of *Soviet Dissident Literature: A Critical Guide* (1983), *Invented Truth: Soviet Reality and the Imagination of Iurii Trifonov* (1991), and *Real Images: Soviet Cinema and the Thaw* (2000), and *The Cranes are Flying* (2003).

Index

Page numbers in italics refer to illustrations.

Dergue (Mengistu Haile Mariam regime), 54–55

Derrida, Jacques, 128, 138, 140–141*n*9, 141*n*15

Derzu Uzala (film), 178

Des Fusils pour Banta (film), 51

Desebagato, le dernier salaire (film), 253, *254*, 255, 261, 265*n*15

Deslauriers, Guy, 63

Detstvo (*Childhood*) (film), 226, 227

A deusa negra (*Black Goddess*) (film), 58, 59, 176, 252–253, 261

Devushka s korobkoi (*Girl with the Hatbox*) (film), 233

Diaspora, African, 58, 59, 61, 62, 149, 150, 154, 203, 207, 261, 295, 300. *See also* African Americans; slavery

Diatta, Tété, 40

Diawara, Manthia, 3, 6, 72, 76, 238*n*14, 264*n*9

Dibango, Manu: film score by, 9, 143–154

Diegues, Carlos, 260

Dikongue-Pipa, Jean-Pierre, 2, 265*n*11

Dinner with the Devil (film), 3

Diola language, choral music in, 147–148, 151–152

Diola people, 40–41, 50, 148

Diop, Boubacar Boris, 41, 43, 82*n*1

Diop, Cheikh Anta, 46*n*11, 66

Diop, Moustapha, 255

Diouf, Abdou, 41

Diouf, Mamadou, 41, 44

Djeli (film), 95, 257, 265*n*11

Le docker noir (*Black Docker*) (Sembene), 37, 125, 225

documentaries, 8, 9, 253, 258, 260, 301; on apartheid, 15–16, 19–23, 25–27, 52; autobiographical, 167; Cuban influence on, 241, 244, 245–246, 252; early subjects of, 162, 171; on !Kung people, 78, 79; modes of representation in, 164–166, 170; on Mozambique, 52; reality-based, 189, 190, 191; on video filmmaking, 176; vs. feature films, 70. *See also* films, African

Dôlé (film), 7

Dong, Pierre-Marie, 2

Donskoy, Mark, 225, 226–227, 228, 231, 232

Dosunmu, Sanya, 3

Douala (Cameroon), 90, 97, 101, 148

Doukouré, Cheik, 123*n*17; films by, 115, 117, 120, 257

Dovzhenko, Alexander, 228, 233, 234

Down Second Avenue (Mphahlele), 30*n*4

Downing, John, 72

Drabo, Adama, 98

A Drink in the Passage (film), 53

Drum Magazine, 16, 18, 29*n*4

A Dry White Season (film), 25

Duah, Alexandra, 62, 212

Dube, Micky Madoda, 53

DuBois, W. E. B., 212

Dunia (film), 97

Duparc, Henri, 7, 103, 109, 111, 113, 118, 122, 122*nn*5–6, 123*n*17, 143

Dva Fedora (*Two Fyodors*) (film), 235

Dylan, Bob, 26

Earth (film), 233, 234

Ecaré, Désiré, 2, 3, 121, 265*n*11

Echenberg, Myron, 72–73, 74

Ecrans d'Afrique (journal), 283

Les écuelles (film), 265*n*11

Eden (film project), 248

Egbe, Albert, 178

Egypt: filmmakers in, 244. *See also* Chahine, Youssef

EICTV (Escuela Internacional de Cine y Televisión), 246–249, 251, 265*nn*15,16

Eisenstein, Sergei, 91, 217, 228, 232, 249

Eliade, Mircea, 125

Ellerson, Beti: film by, *186*

Elsie Haas, femme peintre et cinéaste d'Haiti (film), 201

Embrafilme (Brazilian government film agency), 252, 256

Emitai (film), 33, 39–41, 43, 44, 50, 82*n*4, 93–94, 136, 148, 153, *226, 233*

The End of St. Petersburg (film), 232, 233–235

End of the Dialogue (film), 171*n*7

England: as colonial power, 64, 99, 163; Latin American films in, 260

Equinoxe (*Le jardin des roses*) (film), 258

Eshetu, Theo, 55

Eshu (Yoruba trickster), 140*n*6

Et la neige n'était plus (film), 3, 122*n*3

Ethiopia: coproductions with Cuba, 265*n*13; as cultural milieu, 218; film references to, 59, 205–206, 210, 212, 213, 260; filmmakers in, 8, 54–55 (*see also* Demissie, Yemane; Eshetu, Theo; Gerima, Haile; Mekuria, Salem)

L'Etoile noire (film), 101

L'Etrange destin de Wangrin (Hampaté Bâ), 135, 136, 137

L'Etranger venu d'Afrique (film), 123*n*9

Europe: and colonial spheres of interest, 64; film funding sources in, 261; and slave trade, 62. *See also names of countries*

Évora, Cesária, 257

Mbala, Roger Gnoan; Touré, Kitia; Trabi, Jacques); TV film showing in, 265n15

Trois ans cinq mois (film), 189, 201
The True Life of Domingo Xavier (Vieira), 52
Truth and Reconciliation Commission, 53, 54
Tsaki, Brahim, 265n11
Tumult (film), 54
Tunisia: coproductions with, 258; film funding from, 72; filmmakers in, 244, 255 (*see also* Boughedir, Férid; Bouzid, Nouri; Chikly, Chemama; Khemir, Nacer; Tlatli, Moufida); films about, 51
Turkey: filmmakers in, 244
Turner, Victor, 125, 126
Tutu, Desmond, 53
Twins of the Rain Forest (film), 178
Two Fyodors (film), 235

Ubuntu's Wounds (film), 53
Udju azul di Yonta (*The Blue Eyes of Yonta*) (film), 52, 244, 245, 257
Ugbomah, Eddie, 3
Ukadike, Nwachukwu Frank, 72, 150, 202n4, 242, 245, 264n8
Ukpabio, Helen E., 180
La última cena (*The Last Supper*) (film), 260
The Unfolding Sky (film), 67n1
United States of America: film distribution dominance by, 262, 273; and films on South Africa, 15–16, 19–21, 25, 77–78; and "historical" films, 8, 34–36; policies toward apartheid, 25–26; and racism, 20–21, 27; resources for African films in, 9, 293–303; social justice movements in, 26, 30n5, 203, 206, 242. *See also* African Americans; globalization
Unsere Afrikareise (documentary film), 161
Upper Volta. *See* Burkina Faso
Uriri, Prudence, 67n1
Uruguay, 255
Uys, Jamie: films by, 16, 76, 77, 78–81

Valadão, Jece, 252
Van Gennep, Arnold, 125
Van Lierop, Robert, 52
Van Wert, William F., 242
Van Zandt, Little Steven, 26–27
Vega, Pastor, 252
Vertov, Dziga, 171n4, 232
Vesna na Zarechnoi ulitse (*Spring on Zarechnaya Street*) (film), 235
VGIK (State Institute of Cinematography), 228, 229, 231, 235, 236
Vidas Secas (film), 251
video productions: archive of, 293; as cheaper alternative to film, 207–208; Cuban, 248;

distribution of, 262, 280, 294, 297, 301; festival showings of, 257, 262–263; library holdings of, 294, 295, 296, 299, 302; Nigerian, 6, 7, 9, 104, 173–180; popularity of, 273. *See also* music video productions
La vie est belle (film), 3, 7, 102, 103, 104
La vie sur terre (film), 231, 233, 234
Vieira, Luandino, 51, 52
Vietnam, 242
Vieyra, Paulin Soumanou, 10n1, 122n3, 151, 162, 226, 230, 250, 251, 252, 264nn6,10, 266n18
Visages de Femmes (*Faces of Women*) (film), 2
Vivre libre ou mourir (film), 67n2
Vliudiakh (*In the World*) (film), 226
Voulet, Paul, 65

Waati (film), 97, 229
Wade, Mansour Sora, 8
A Walk in the Night (LaGuma), 30n4
Wangrin. *See* L'Etrange destin de Wangrin (Bâ)
Waqai sinin al jawr (film), 51, 265n11
Wariko, le gros lot (film), 97, 104
Washington, Denzel, 36
The Way (film), 51
Le Wazzou polygame (film), 265n11
"We Are the World" (music video), 31n14
Weaver, Harold W., 163
Weill, Kurt, 15
Welles, Orson, 249
Wend Kuuni (film), 3, 4, 265n11
West Indies: Les Nègres marrons de la liberté (film), 33, 58, 63, 64, 265n11
Where Women Tread (film), 51
Willemen, Paul, 242
Wilmington 10, USA 10,000 (film), 60, 206
Wilson, Lindy, 53
Wolof language, 38, 135, 137, 145, 148, 151, 152, 153, 154, 204
women: in contemporary Africa, 182, 189, 199; as filmmakers (*see* Aina, Shirikiana; Boswall, Karen; Dash, Julie; Denis, Claire; Faye, Safi; Gaye, Dyana; Krim, Rachida; Krog, Antjie; Maldoror, Sarah; Mekuria, Salem; Nkebakwu, Ngozi; Roots, Ronelle; Sinclair, Ingrid; Tlatli, Moufida; Trinh T. Minh-ha; Uriri, Prudence; Wilson, Lindy); in interracial relationships, 113–114, 119, 231, 235; and Islam, 150, 151, 152; and national liberation movements, 152; in Nigerian video films, 178–179; traditional roles of, 112–113, 137, 144
Workers Leaving the Factory (film), 162